Christianity in Appalachia

Christianity in Appalachia

PROFILES IN REGIONAL PLURALISM

Edited by Bill J. Leonard

The University of Tennessee Press

Knoxville

Library of Congress Cataloging-in-Publication Data

Christianity in Appalachia : profiles in regional pluralism /
edited by Bill J. Leonard. — 1st ed.
      p. cm.
ISBN 1-57233-039-2 (cl.: alk. paper)
ISBN 1-57233-040-6 (pbk.: alk. paper)
1. Christianity—Appalachian Region. 2. Appalachian
Region—Religious life and customs. I. Leonard, Bill.
BR535 .C45 1999
277.4—ddc21   98-40115

To Helen Lewis
Teacher and prophet
In gratitude for her friendship, her insights,
and her life of advocacy for and with
Appalachian communities

Contents

Tables

Maps

Preface

The idea for this book began with the summer faculty of the Appalachian Ministries Educational Resource Center (AMERC) in Berea, Kentucky. Founded in 1985, AMERC offers seminarians the opportunity to study and experience aspects of Appalachian life, with particular attention to the practice of Christian ministry in the region.

AMERC is now the largest seminary consortium in the U.S., with over eighty-eight participating schools, including Duke, Harvard, and Yale divinity schools; Baptist Seminary—Richmond; Church of God (Cleveland) School of Theology; and Lutheran Southern, Princeton, Louisville Presbyterian, Wesley, and Asbury seminaries. Faculty or administrative representatives from each of the participating schools compose the organization's governing board. The summer program introduces students to elements of Appalachian social, religious, economic, and environmental life. The curriculum includes lectures and class discussion on the Appalachian social and religious contexts, along with studies in congregational application. Through the "experiential learning" component of the program, students are assigned to parish, family farm, or community development settings and make extended visits to various field locations. A small-group component creates the opportunity for "theological reflection" on the overall experience.

AMERC also brings together professors and lecturers who have significant personal and scholarly expertise in Appalachian studies. Mary Lee Daugherty, organizer, teacher, preacher, dreamer, founded the program, with the assistance of Helen Lewis. Lewis is a sociologist, community organizer, practitioner, and prophet; Myles Horton called her "the mother of Appalachian studies." Lewis brought students into her world, transporting them to Becky Simpson's Cranks Creek Survival Center; to Ivanhoe, Virginia, and its grassroots efforts in community development; and to the Highlander community, where Lewis now lives, perpetuating its tradition of empowerment for persons in Appalachia and throughout the world.

Most of the contributors to this volume have taught in some segment of the AMERC program during the last decade. As core faculty or visiting lecturers, they introduced students to the broad spectrum of Appalachian studies and religious networks, local, regional, and denominational. The AMERC exercise in crossdisciplinary teaching convinced us of the need for a one-volume work that would survey the broad spectrum of religious life in the Appalachian region. Perhaps the last work of this type was John Photiadis's *Religion in Appalachia: Theological, Social and Psychological Dimensions and Correlates* (1978). Although the book reflected the diversity of religious traditions in Appalachia, it was primarily sociological in orientation and emphases.

In developing plans for a new work on religion in Appalachia, we enlisted the help of writers with varied backgrounds in Appalachian studies. Chapters are written from the perspectives of historians, sociologists, folklorists, rhetoricians, academicians, parish ministers, denominational administrators, and community development specialists. The introduction and chapters 1–5 focus on general aspects of the Appalachian religious and cultural scene. Bill Leonard's introduction describes broad trends and polarities which inform religious discussion and interaction. In chapter 1, sociologist Barbara Ellen Smith surveys social, economic, and geographic realities which shape the Appalachian scene. Chapter 2, written by Bennett Poage, discusses religious implications of the family farm crisis in Appalachia. The third chapter, by Charles Lippy, details elements of popular religion and culture in the region. In chapter 4, Janet Welch explores ethical and religious issues that impact Appalachian religious communities. Ira Read's assessment of the contribution of church-related educational institutions in Appalachia constitutes chapter 5.

Chapters 6–10 center on specific elements of mountain religion. In chapter 6, Loyal Jones makes extensive use of interviews with Appalachian Christians to introduce the discussion of religion in the mountains. Deborah McCauley details the beliefs and practices of mountain Holiness folk in chapter 7. In chapter 8, Howard Dorgan describes the religious life of certain Baptist traditions in the mountains, including Primitive, Old Regular, Free Will, and United Baptist communities. Mary Lee Daugherty writes about her encounters with serpent-handlers in chapter 9, exploring the sacramental nature of their practices. In chapter 10, Gary Farley and Bill Leonard draw on their experiences with churches and pastors in Appalachia to examine the role of the preacher/minister. Chapter 11, written by James Sessions, describes the work of the Commission on Religion in Appalachia (CORA), a union of denominations and community groups.

Chapters 12–19 provide introductions to the history and activity of certain denominations, with particular attention to the Central Appalachian region. Chapter 12, written by Bill Leonard, reports on the Southern Baptist Convention, the largest denominational group in America and in Appalachia. Chapter 13, written jointly by Davis Yeuell and Marcia Myers, both Presbyterian elders, trace the work of that denomination. In chapter 14, Anthony Dunnavant discusses the Restorationist legacy, with particular attention to the Stone-Campbell-Christian churches. Chapter 15 details the history and practice of churches identified with the Wesleyan-Holiness heritage. The sixteenth chapter, written by Don Bowdle of Lee College, describes the theological and historical roots of the Church of God, Cleveland, Tennessee. In chapter 17, Catholic missioner Lou F. McNeil reflects on the legacy of Roman Catholic work in Appalachia. Chapter 18, written by Catholic activist Monica Kelly Appelby, offers insight into the experience of a group of Glenmary Sisters who confronted the region and the hierarchy of their own church. The final chapter, written by Samuel Hill, constitutes an epilogue to the work, linking Appalachian Christianity to elements of the broader southern regional and American contexts.

The book is indeed a survey, sketching general aspects of religious life in Appalachia. It profiles some, but certainly not all, of the religious groups and observances which exist in the region. Appropriate chapters on United Methodists, African American traditions, and mountain hymnody, though sought, were not available when this volume went to press. In fact, most of the religious communities described in this volume represent traditional expressions of Christian identity. They reflect elements of American evangelical, "mainline," and Pentecostal religion characteristic of certain communities of faith extant in Appalachia. Attention is not given to non-Christian movements—Jewish, Muslim, Buddhist, etc.—although the impact of those traditions within the region needs to be studied and might form part of another volume. Likewise, only limited attention is given to the urban religious scene in burgeoning population areas within the region. The attempt here is to describe various traditional Christian communions that exist in Appalachia and whose beliefs and practices have shaped and been shaped by the ethos of this section of the United States.

Mary Lee Daugherty, founder of the AMERC program, was an unfailing supporter of this endeavor. Her legendary gifts as fund-raiser enabled us to secure financial support for the enterprise. Grants from the Luce Foundation and the Louisville Institute for the Study of American Protestantism provided funding which enabled us to complete the project. We are particularly grateful to John Wesley Cook of Luce and James Lewis of the Louisville Institute for their help and encouragement in securing these grants.

Production of the manuscript involved the invaluable editorial assistance of Thelma Heywood and Jonathan Speegle of Samford University, Birmingham, Alabama, and Betsy Clement of the Wake Forest University Divinity School, Winston-Salem, North Carolina. Stephen Rhodes, Brian Cole, Valen Spears Poff, and other members of the AMERC staff also offered much-appreciated affirmation and support. We are grateful to all for their encouragement and commitment to this project.

Bill J. Leonard
The Divinity School
Wake Forest University

Introduction

The Faith and the Faiths

BILL J. LEONARD

Several years ago I was invited to lecture on Appalachian religion at a conference held at Jenny Wiley State Park, in the mountains of eastern Kentucky. The gathering included pastors and laity from churches situated in the Appalachian region, many of whom had worked in the area for years. All were Protestants, most affiliated with the Southern Baptist Convention. When I completed a presentation surveying past traditions and future trends, I asked if there were any questions. Immediately a seasoned pastor inquired, "Do you think we can ever go back to having two-week revivals again?"

"Doubtful," I replied, "especially since satellite dishes, cable television, and other 'worldly' distractions have come to stay." His question led me to recall the old story about the mountain boy who returned home from a Saturday visit to town and exclaimed: "Grandma, if you'll ever go to just one circus, you'll never go to prayer meeting again!" No longer can the church command community attention for protracted periods of time. In most congregations, the two-week revival is gone forever. Modernity, or "worldliness," as some would say, simply is too distracting.

That is not to say that religious life is dead or dying in Appalachian churches. It remains a powerful source of cultural and spiritual stability. Nonetheless, few will deny that major changes are under way throughout

American, southern, and Appalachian culture, changes which have significant implications for religion. Cultural transitions which began over a generation ago in the urban South—Atlanta, Charlotte, Birmingham—are fast descending upon the hills and hollows of Appalachia.

This book focuses on the nature of religion in the Central Appalachian region of the United States. Essays for this volume were prepared by scholars and specialists who explore diverse aspects of religious life evident in Appalachia. Such an effort is fraught with danger. Debates over the nature and meaning of the Appalachian region itself are unending, and each attempt immediately is subjected to scholarly challenge and critique. Any discussion of specific churches or denominations must not imply that these are definitive, normative, or even primary representatives of the religious ethos of the Appalachian region. Thus this work provides *selected* profiles of some of the best-known religious groups generally found in a specific segment of an extensive region of the United States. It is an effort to describe certain communities of faith, in order to highlight differences and similarities and enhance further investigation of yet other religious communions extant in the region.

Studying Religion in Appalachia: Varying Approaches

Appalachia itself is not one region, but many; it is not one culture but is composed of a multiplicity of cultural and social experiences, ideals, and subgroups. Likewise, the complex religious landscape of the region is difficult to chart. Even the most basic generalizations are easily contradicted. We begin with certain qualifications.

First, defining the Appalachian region and its culture is no easy task. As described by the Appalachian Regional Commission, "official" Appalachia includes some 397 counties in thirteen states. Through this definition, the region encompasses a portion of twelve states and all of West Virginia. Census statistics from July 1, 1985, list a population of 21,588,000 persons spread throughout the territory. This study gives primary attention to religious life within that segment of Appalachia known as the Southern Highlands, including an area composed of seven to nine states and stretching southward from Virginia to Alabama. This section of the country is a mosaic of small towns, rural communities, and expanding urban areas characterized by certain diverse, often overlapping religious, political, economic, and social concerns.

Second, one of the great debates among students of American studies concerns the divergent definitions of Appalachia as region, culture, "idea," and "problem."[1] While such discussions inform this study of religion in the region, writers do not enter into the broader argument over definitions, historiography, and interpretations relative to the question of "what is Appalachia?"[2]

Third, those who study Appalachian culture utilize varying approaches in investigating the region's religion. Some view religion within the broader context of culture, anthropology, sociology, musicology, or folklore. This approach is evident in sociologist John Photiadis's *Religion in Appalachia: Theological, Social, and Psychological Dimensions and Correlates* (1978), and in ethnomusicologist Jeff Todd Titon's *Powerhouse for God: Speech, Chant, and Song in an Appalachian Baptist Church* (1988). Others describe Appalachian religion primarily in terms of the multitude of denominations and denominationally identified congregations in the region. Elizabeth R. Hooker's work, *Religion in the Highlands* (1933), viewed by some as "the best single study of denominational activity in the region," provides a survey of denominational activity in Appalachia.[3] W. D. Weatherford's book, *Religion in the Appalachian Mountains*, published in 1955, also concentrated on the denominational nature of Appalachian churches. His investigations included those national denominations which moved into the region and those which, in one degree or another, were present early in the region's history. On the whole, standard denominational histories have given scant attention to the presence of specific traditions in Appalachia.

Yet another method is represented in a significant group of scholars concerned with the study of Appalachian mountain religion—those churches and individuals existing outside, or alongside, denominationally oriented congregations and reflecting a distinctly mountain religious ethos. Catherine Albanese describes these Appalachian churches, noting that, "by the twentieth century, . . . this intensely religious people would have the least need for official church structures of perhaps any people in the United States."[4] Appalachian specialist Deborah V. McCauley, a contributor to this volume, notes that this approach to mountain religion "constitutes an emerging discipline." It involves the study of a "native mountain church" which "does not belong to national, denominational organizational structures with a national purpose . . . and identity."[5] McCauley's own work, *Appalachian Mountain Religion: A History*, published in 1995, gives particular attention to the mountain Baptist and independent Holiness churches of the region. McCauley distinguishes between those Christian communions that exist inside and outside Appalachia, primarily American Protestant denominations, "and those church traditions that exist predominately—or almost exclusively—in the region and are very special to it."[6] Howard Dorgan's *Giving Glory to God in Appalachia: Worship Practices of*

Six Baptist Subdenominations (1987) investigates those mountain Baptist groups which continue to maintain their own unique ecclesiastical and communal lives. The student-generated interviews in *Foxfire 7* (1982) utilized denominational categories as a framework for an oral history of the beliefs and recollections of Appalachian Christians, many of whom testified to the unique impact of mountain religion on denominational identity. Each of these responses to Appalachian religion gives indication of the religious pluralism evident throughout the region. Studies by Deborah McCauley, Howard Dorgan, and Loyal Jones demonstrate efforts to differentiate the denomination-based churches in Appalachia and the mountain churches which represent a more independent, regionally related subgroup of religious communities.[7]

In light of these different approaches, this book gives attention to diverse religious expressions as evidence of the pluralism of multiple traditions (in this case, Christian groups) in the Appalachian region. It suggests that there is not a particular type of "Appalachian religion"; rather, religion in Appalachia has multiple expressions evident in a wide assortment of communions.

This introductory chapter is divided into three segments. The first surveys the relationship between religion and culture in Southern Appalachia, with particular attention to religious identity. The second part examines certain polarities which inform the way individuals and communities define "the faith." The third segment raises an array of questions concerning the state of religion in the Appalachian region, present and future.

Appalachia: Religion and Culture

The relationship between church and culture is an important topic for students of American religion. Many turn for definition to Clifford Geertz's now-classic work, *The Interpretation of Cultures,* and Geertz's idea that culture "denotes an historically transmitted pattern of meanings embodied in symbols, a system of inherited conceptions expressed in symbolic forms by means of which (persons) communicate, perpetuate, and develop their knowledge about and attitudes toward life."[8] Through culture, a particular people establish norms for behavior, values, meaning, and other aspects of common life. This belief that culture patterns are transmitted through symbols is especially important in the study of religion in Appalachia. For it is by means of common symbols that diverse regions and religions in the South were united. Through cultural symbols, southerners in general and Appalachians in particular developed a means of combining and interpreting the collective data of their existence.

Through certain common symbols, a society gives meaning to the actual empirical events of its history. Those symbols thus provide cultural identity and are perpetuated by the culture they help define. The American South has been one region where symbols have provided a major source of cultural unity and security. The issue of the relationship between Appalachia and the South frequently is debated among students of the region. Deborah McCauley is correct when she insists that it is "absolutely necessary to underscore . . . that mountain religious life and history should not be subsumed under 'southern religion' or 'religion in the South,' treated simply as one more variant of this broadly encompassing label."[9] Yet she also acknowledges that there "are certainly many significant similarities."[10]

Elements of the southern and Appalachian religious ethos intersect in several different ways. First, there is an intricate relationship between religious and cultural life. In discussing the antebellum South, Donald Mathews suggested that "religion and the American South are fused in our historical imagination in an indelible, but amorphous, way."[11] He also noted that, for southerners, religion provided adherents with "a sense of personal esteem and liberty."[12] Samuel Hill suggests that the "religion of the southern people and their culture have been linked by the tightest bonds. That culture, particularly in its moral aspects, could not have survived without a legitimating impetus provided by religion. . . . For the South to stand, its people had to be religious and its churches the purest anywhere."[13]

The elaborate relationship between church and culture led historian Martin E. Marty to conclude in 1976 that southern Protestantism represented one of the most "intact" religious subcultures in contemporary America. *Intactness* meant that a religious group exercised continuity with its past and provided a unifying sense of identity for its constituents in the present.[14] Marty insisted that southern Protestantism—particularly the Southern Baptist Convention—represented the "the Catholic church of the South."[15] Denominationally based Protestantism (especially certain forms of it) was a de facto religious establishment which set various agendas impacting all religious groups in the region. Within the cultural security of southernness was a theological and spiritual solidarity based on "the primacy of experience in religion."[16] Appalachian religious groups are heirs to many of those cultural and religious ideals. Religious life was, and to some extent remains, a primary source of identity for many southern and Appalachian people. It provided a place, a source, of security in the face of poverty, disease, and the many unpredictable elements of life. To an extent, the mountains themselves were a fortress which protected this unity of culture and religion for a surprisingly long time. Catherine Albanese writes that Appalachian religion "shared many ingredients from the general religiocultural synthesis of the nation, but it combined these ingredients in its own way and also added others."[17] In this sense, "religion in some measure becomes a function of the spatial location of people and the history of that spatial location *together*."

Second, Appalachia lends itself to the study of religion. Albanese believes that Southern Appalachia is particularly suited to a study of regional religion, because its "identity is marked and striking, shaped by its physical boundaries and relative isolation from the rest of the country."[18] Even in the nineteenth century, she explains, Americans outside the region were aware of various cultural expressions which distinguished Appalachian life from that in the rest of the country. Albanese contends that "Southern Appalachia also offers a chance to study religion with a strong traditional orientation in which both ordinary and extraordinary values are blended. It provides an explicit instance of how regionalism supplies an overarching frame within which religion and culture come together." And she concludes that "Southern Appalachia gives us a chance to study transition in regional religion. . . . In the case of twentieth-century Southern Appalachia, the changes are striking and sometimes dramatic. By standing out so distinctly from their background, the changes help us to see more accurately how history comes to grips with the geography of a specific place."[19]

Ultimately, the forces of pluralism and modernity which spread throughout American life were bound to find their way into Appalachian culture. Changes brought about by economics, education, civil rights legislation, mobility, family life, and secular culture have confronted evangelical Protestantism with new issues, challenging its religious hegemony in the region. The two-week revival is not the only thing the preachers have lost. As social and religious ties become increasingly frayed, both church and culture confront an expanding identity crisis.

Any effort to survey the religious situation in the area should begin with some awareness of the cultural and religious transitions occurring in Appalachia. It should also give attention to some of the basic religious symbols and belief systems which characterize religion in the region. Thus the second segment of this study focuses on the nature of evangelical religion in the southern and Appalachian settings.

Religion in Appalachian: Representative Typologies

Mary Lee Daugherty, director of the Appalachian Ministries Education Resource Center, based in Berea, Kentucky, describes basic "families" of Protestants evident in Appalachia.[20]

Mainline churches include Episcopal; United Methodist; Presbyterian; American Baptist, USA; Lutheran; Roman Catholic; the United Church of Christ; and the Christian Church (Disciples of Christ). They tend to be more denominationally oriented, with seminary-trained ministers and a worship that is more elaborate liturgically, seeking to reach persons through the nurturing sacramentalism of the church. They are apt to stress overt social action in response to political and cultural concerns.

Evangelical churches include various types of Baptists, Nazarenes, the Churches of Christ, Bible churches, and other independent, non-denominational, non-Pentecostal groups. These churches may or may not have seminary graduates as ministers. Many of their preachers are bi-vocational, supporting themselves primarily through secular employment and serving churches for little or no salary. Their worship tends to be less formal and reflects the influence of the revivalistic tradition with gospel hymns, Bible preaching, and altar calls. While some of these churches maintain denominational relationships, congregational autonomy is paramount. Individual conversion may involve both nurture and dramatic experience. Every person is encouraged to have a "personal experience" with Christ in order to receive salvation. Social concerns tend toward issues of personal morality, "traditional family values," and what has become certain "New Religious" political agendas. Fundamentalist theology is a powerful influence in these groups.

Pentecostal churches include the Church of God (Cleveland, Tennessee), the Assemblies of God, Fire-Baptized Holiness, and a variety of Pentecostal-oriented communions. Clergy are less likely to be college- or seminary-trained. Some congregations accept both men and women ministers. Along with conversion, they place a strong emphasis on the baptism of the Holy Spirit, as evidenced in speaking in tongues, healing, and other charismatic manifestations. Worship generally is spontaneous, with preaching, singing, and outbursts made "in the Spirit." Social concerns often relate more to personal than corporate morality. A strong sense of otherworldliness prevails. These groups call believers to holiness of life in response to the depravity of modern life.

Mountain churches, which Daugherty might list with evangelicals or Pentecostals, constitute a distinctive expression of religion in Appalachia. These churches are considered unique to the region. Their numbers include a variety of Baptists (United, Old Regular, Primitive, and Free Will), as well as numerous independent Holiness congregations. These communities of faith are not related to national denominational systems. Their services are characterized by the practice of certain traditional rituals, such as foot washing, outdoor baptisms, speaking in tongues, and Spirit-led preaching. Their ministers are bi-vocational and often have limited formal education. They are linked to the mountain culture in powerful ways, through grassroots constituency and kinship relations, as well as a pervasive piety and spirituality.[21]

Theological Polarities and Appalachian Religious Communities

While the attempt to categorize or cluster religious communities in Appalachia is beneficial, there is another way of mapping the religious phenomena found in the region. This approach is less concerned for the specific beliefs of individual faith communities than for certain broad, controlling ideas which characterize the theological and pragmatic identity of the churches, whatever their specific dogma. It is found in examining certain polarities around which belief systems, doctrines, and practices take shape. It asks: What is the faith behind the various faiths? These polarities reflect the unity and diversity, continuity and discontinuity, evident in various Christian groups in Appalachia. While most of these ideas are not unique to Appalachia, they nonetheless take peculiar shape in this specific cultural setting.

First, Appalachian churches struggle with the issue of authority. Authority is an essential element of the orthodoxy which most churches demand. By what authority does each group make its claims? As heirs of the Reformation, Appalachian Protestants long have insisted that Scripture alone is the rule of faith for the church and the individual. Yet they cannot always agree on the way in which Scripture is to be used. In the quest for authority, some claim to be People of the Book (Primitivism), while others claim to be People of the Spirit (Relevance). Still others want to have it both ways. These ideas are present throughout the churches of Appalachia. Faced with a pluralistic religious context, many groups claim to be the true and/or only church, because they are closest to the New Testament church in doctrine and practice. They are People of the Book, reconstructing the church directly from the Holy Scriptures. They define the church as a community which observes most precisely the practices of the earliest New Testament community. To be the church is to do what the early Christians did.

For example, Primitive, Old Regular, and other Baptist subdenominations insist that they are only a step away from the New Testament church, and that their doctrines, worship, and actions are simply reflections of those of the first Christian congregations. They eschew—as heretical at worst and inadequate at best—those denominations which promote "man-made" dogmas discerned to be outside the bounds of biblical Christianity.

Likewise, persons in the Churches of Christ, one segment of the Stone-Campbell (Restorationist) tradition, believe that they have restored the Christian church exactly as it was in the New Testament epoch. Through simple faith, immersion baptism "for the remission of sins," weekly communion, and no creed but Christ, they claim to have rescued the New Testament church from sectarian corruption.

The question of origins is extremely important to many Appalachian religionists. For instance, many Baptists in the region believe that they are heirs to certain gospel "landmarks" preserved by crypto-baptist congregations since the first century. This trail of blood and martyrs, largely outside of and in conflict with the Catholic Church and European religious establishments, can be traced all the way back to John the Baptist, who immersed Jesus in the River Jordan. This is a form of Baptist successionism ordered not through bishops but through local congregations of religious dissenters. Early Baptists in the region sang their theology unashamedly in hymns such as this:

> Not at the Jordan River, but in that flowing stream,
> stood John the Baptist preacher when he baptized Him.
> John was a Baptist preacher, when he baptized the Lamb,
> So Jesus was a Baptist, and thus the Baptists came.[22]

The so-called serpent-handlers carry biblical literalism to dangerous conclusions, asserting that their practices validate genuine Christianity. "If we don't do it [handle serpents]," one preacher says, "God will raise up a people that will do it."[23] If the serpent-handling passage in Mark 16 is not literal, these believers declare, then none of the Bible is trustworthy. Serpent-handler or not, many religious Appalachians view themselves as Bible-believing Christians, often contrasting themselves with other groups, who, by implication, are not.

Other Appalachians verify the truth of their doctrine and practice by its relevance—that is, by the activity of the Holy Spirit in the present age. They are People of the Spirit, guided by immediate inspiration, not by arcane "tradition." For them, the People of the Spirit are the true church, responding as boldly and uniquely to contemporary culture as the ancient Christians responded to theirs, building on valued traditions while discarding or adapting those which inhibit the Spirit's activity in the new age. Various religious groups in Central Appalachia reflect this idea, many responding directly to the poor and the broken; some also address those political and social structures which oppress and manipulate Appalachian people. In ordaining or otherwise encouraging women to serve as ministers, many congregations affirm the guidance of the Holy Spirit beyond the strictures of old traditionalism.

Pentecostals, on the other hand, claim to have it all. They claim primitivism aplenty, a conformity to the apostolic experience of Pentecost and the Book of Acts. Still, the Spirit which spoke at Pentecost speaks yet, through them. This dual alignment of Primitivism and Relevance, Book and Spirit, has made Pentecostalism a force to be reckoned with among the evangelical churches of the region. Non-Pentecostals often declare that the charismatic gifts ended with the apostolic age and therefore denounce the Spirit people as unbiblical. Pentecostals respond that they simply carry biblical inerrancy to its logical conclusion. Ray Dryman, a ninety-four-year-old Georgia Pentecostal, observed that, years ago, the Holiness doctrine "got up sort of a stir in this Pentecostal country, and I said, 'Fellers,' I said, 'they're right about it, they're preaching the Bible.'"[24] The events depicted in the Bible can yet be experienced in these "latter days," when Christ's return is imminent.

The idea of authority is an important issue in southern and Appalachian churches today. In diverse ways, both modernity and Pentecostalism have raised significant questions about the nature of authority for the church, the society, and the individual. Those who wish to know something of religion in the region must give serious attention to the debate over biblical inerrancy and Spirit baptism.

A second polarity evident in the religious life of Central Appalachia involves the idea of the church. Many Appalachian believers envisioned their churches to be pure churches, faithful to the New Testament norm and, unlike other churches, untainted by modernism, liberalism, and worldliness. The quest for purity compounds the tension between the church as People of God and the church as God's Only People. As People of God, they are called to cooperation and unity. As God's Only People, they often are given to diversity and division, competition and elitism.

Unity long has been elusive among the diverse churches of Appalachia. Sectarian tendencies made many groups hesitant to acknowledge that other churches and denominations also were part of the body of Christ. At the same time, some denomination-related churches looked askance at the beliefs and practices of traditional mountain churches. For years, cooperation and fellowship among churches, if it existed at all, most often was informal and localized. Churches sometimes found occasions for participation in various moral crusades in response to moral problems and social needs. Opposition to liquor sales, lotteries, abortion, and other moral issues led to some collaborative actions by the churches. Community revival meetings sometimes offered opportunities for joint evangelistic endeavors among churches. In the era of unpaid, traveling clergy (a phenomenon which continues in some traditions), Protestant churches in Central Appalachia shared worship whenever any preacher came to town.[25] More recently, community worship services have drawn churches together for common prayer and praise. Ecumenism has best been expressed informally, often selectively, throughout the region. Benevolence endeavors, food pantries, and clothes closets for those in need also give some evidence of unified ministry and witness as the whole people of God.

Such unity has been relatively limited, however. Some Appalachian religious communions continue to identify their particular group as God's Only People, in competition with others for orthodoxy and constituency. Many churches, seeking voluntary membership, competed by claiming to be the only true church, or at least the truest of the true. How better to secure constituents than to convince them that God has only one people, found in one particular communion? For many Appalachian religious groups, evangelism involves not only winning secular sinners to faith, but also proselytizing religious sinners away from false religion.

In the late nineteenth and early twentieth centuries, theological debates, formal and informal, abounded among almost all religious groups in the region. For years, Presbyterians debated Methodists over election and falling from grace. Presbyterians and Methodists united to challenge Baptists over infant baptism and adult immersion. Independent Baptists attacked Southern Baptists' allegiance to mission boards and denominationalism.[26] Restorationists ("Campbellites") debated everybody. Catholicism seemed a fertile mission field for many southern Protestants, who readily acknowledged that Catholics were "lost" and that often they were more difficult to convert since they had received "Romanist" indoctrination from childhood.

Today similar sentiments remain prevalent in the region though perhaps they are expressed more subtly. In many churches, the old doctrinal debates among denominations have shifted to internal confrontations over the nature of orthodoxy within a specific denomination itself. Inerrantist Methodists and Baptists, for example, now find greater theological compatibility with each other than with non-inerrantists within their own denominations. Pentecostals divide over trinitarian or "Jesus only" baptism—baptism in the name of Father, Son, and Holy Spirit, or solely in the name of Jesus. The idea of the church as God's Only People continues to characterize large segments of Appalachian Christianity. The boundaries simply have been readjusted.

A third polarity apparent in the Appalachian churches involves the idea of conversion. Many Appalachian Protestants are primarily con-

versionists in their theology of salvation. Eschewing distinctions between
the visible and invisible church, they insist that every individual must have
a personal experience with Jesus Christ in order to be saved from sin and
prepared for heaven. Thus the primary purpose of the church of Jesus
Christ is evangelism—telling the story of Jesus and snatching souls from
the burning.

This evangelical imperative involves a tension between conversion as
radical event and as nurturing experience. Heirs of the frontier revivalistic
tradition, most Appalachian evangelicals sound as if radical conversion is
the only acceptable way of entering into Christ's church. Preachers call for
immediate conversion, as persons follow the "plan of salvation" to trust
Christ and receive new life. Believers new and old testify to their own mor-
phology or process of conversion, detailing the transformation from a life
of sin to a new creation in Christ Jesus. Converts are urged to give witness
to their faith in order to bring all persons to "a saving knowledge of Jesus
Christ." The process of conversion in some Appalachian churches—Primitive Baptists and Old Regular Baptists are exceptions—has been shortened
considerably from the often laborious, agonizing process characteristic of
early Calvinism to the immediate event promoted by an Arminianized
mass revivalism.[27] Sinners are encouraged to pray a simple "sinner's prayer,"
by which grace is instantly secured and salvation assured.

At the same time, many Appalachian Christians also raise their
children in the nurturing atmosphere of the church, teaching them from
the earliest age that Jesus loves them and that they are welcome in the
community of faith. Thus numerous persons who grow up in church
testify that their conversion is less a dramatic turning from wickedness
and evil than a quiet acceptance of God's love. Many confess that they
never knew a time when they did not love God and believe in Jesus.
Others, particularly in the Pentecostal-Holiness tradition, suggest that
they did not understand the "full gospel" until they received the second
baptism of the Holy Spirit.

Likewise, Appalachian communions vary as to the normative age of
conversion and baptism. Howard Dorgan notes that missionary Baptists
(Southern and Independent Baptists) "go down in the water" around
"twelve to fifteen years of age." Old Regular Baptists, however, may defer
baptism until "in their forties or fifties."[28] Many Southern Baptist youth are
baptized during the elementary-school years, some even as preschoolers.

This latter practice often demands some rather fancy theological
footwork from those who insist on conversion as a radical spiritual and
moral crisis. Many Baptists, for example, rejected infant baptism but
worried that children might pass the "age of accountability," that mythic

time when the child becomes morally responsible and therefore deserving of damnation. Since no-one could be sure when that occurred, the imperative for baptizing children strengthened considerably. Often these children testified not to a dramatic conversion from sin, but to a willing response to the Christian nurture they had experienced in community of faith. When they encountered adolescence and adulthood and really sinned, many feared that their earlier conversion was invalid. Some repudiated their childhood experience for a newer, more dramatic experience of grace, one in which they "understood" what they were doing. Thus, conversionist churches often allow for nurture but require dramatic conversion as a means of securing full acceptance in the community of faith.

A fourth polarity in Appalachian churches involves the idea of the ministry, the nature of leadership in the church. There is an age-old tension between the priesthood of all believers and the authority of the ordained ministry. In one sense, many Appalachian churches are people's churches, founded upon a rabid egalitarianism in which all the saved are ministers, witnessing for Christ and carrying the Gospel to the world. Many mistrust denominational alignments as detrimental to the autonomy of the local congregation and the liberty of the individual believer. Many congregations exist unto themselves, denouncing hierarchies and institutional affiliations as unscriptural. Salvation thus becomes the great equalizer, by which social, economic, and spiritual elitism is abolished. Faith is not mediated by clergy or ecclesiastical institutions, but comes directly from God to the individual.

Whatever ordination may exist in the church is the result of a divine mandate—the call to preach—and not the approval of some ecclesiastical body. Authority comes from the Holy Spirit working in the life of the lone believer or the lay leaders of the entire congregation. As one Primitive Baptist preacher declared, "The preacher hasn't got any say-so at all in the Primitive Baptist church; it's the deacons that rule the church."[29] Tensions regarding the question of leadership often lead to schisms in congregations throughout the region.

At the same time, ministerial authority in Appalachian churches remains a powerful force to be reckoned with. Preachers, ordained or otherwise anointed, maintain an important position as mediators of the Word of God and leaders of the church. In many religious traditions in the region, the "call to preach" is the most exalted vocation in the world. Jeff Todd Titon recounts the testimony of one independent Baptist preacher: "I was saved a good while, brother, before God called me, and then when he did call me I tried every way in the world to get out of it."[30] A period of resistance frequently is a prerequisite before preachers submit to the will of God.

Fundamentalist churches, for example, place great emphasis on the authority of the pastor in the divine "chain of command," the sacred order of existence. The pastor is the "undershepherd" who is directly responsible to God for the souls of the faithful. In these churches, ministry and maleness are inseparable, again as part of the divine schema. The faithful are admonished, in the words of Scripture, to "touch not God's anointed" (Psalm 105:15). Likewise, the minister's place in the divine order is closely related to the place of the husband as head of the house, with women playing a subordinate role in both the family and the church.

In many Pentecostal churches, however, such distinctions are less arbitrary. The Spirit moves where it will and may fall on women as readily as men. Pentecostal women often are called to preach and serve as evangelists, sometimes even as pastors. Some Pentecostal churches regulate the way in which women function as ministers and preachers, however, defining their work differently from that of males.

Tensions between the people and the preachers occur with considerable regularity in Appalachian churches. Conflicts over ministerial authority create schisms in churches, which in turn spawn new churches. Sometimes the preachers depart, taking their supporters with them. Sometimes they remain, and a dissident group begins a new church. Likewise, self-proclaimed preachers appear throughout the region, founding their own churches and initiating their own ministries.

Denominationally based churches debate the effectiveness of a seminary-trained preacher over a non-seminary preacher. The increasing number of women pursuing vocation in pastoral ministry, even in Appalachia, promises to be a significant issue for the churches in the immediate future.

One final issue deserves attention. It involves the concept of religious ritual. On the surface, many Appalachian churches seem opposed to "ritualism" in their approach to worship and the sacramental. Their concern is for that spontaneity of the Spirit which eschews written prayers, sermon manuscripts, and "corpse cold liturgy." They denounce ritualism as unbiblical, detrimental to heart religion, and dangerously "Catholic" (no compliment intended). Ritualism is a sign of the decline of the church and of genuine faith.

In their suspicion of ritual, many churches so devalued traditional Christian sacraments as to leave them almost devoid of meaning. Many Baptist preachers, for example, assured their congregations that baptism and the Lord's Supper were *only* symbols, activities which Jesus had ordered and which the obedient New Testament church would obediently undertake. In many churches, baptism and communion were observances tacked onto the preaching service, carried out hurriedly and with little sense of the divine presence.

At the same time, Appalachian churches cultivated certain rituals which nurtured a sense of the sacramental. Numerous churches established simple but profound rituals evident in baptism, communion, foot washing, anointing with oil, Spirit baptism, and other events, thereby creating powerful sources of spiritual nurture and renewal. Many Appalachian congregations, like their counterparts elsewhere in the South, devised some powerful new rituals which provided the people with visual and symbolic expressions of personal and communal faith.

One of the best examples of such rituals is the invitation, or altar call. In various churches, worship services and revival meetings conclude with an invitation to conversion and Christian commitment. Persons are urged to "come forward" to accept Christ, join the church, or "surrender for full-time Christian service." In a sense, the invitation itself became a powerful sacrament, an outward and visible sign of an inward and spiritual grace. In fact, in many Appalachian congregations, the invitation paralleled or even replaced baptism as the primary sign of public confession of faith. Converts described their conversion in the language of the invitation: "when I came forward," "when I walked the aisle," "when I shook the preacher's hand." Some testified that conversion itself took place in the very movement from pew to aisle. Thus, the people who claimed to be nonritualistic, or nonsacramental, created and renewed their own symbols, sacraments, and signs, by which they acted out dramatic moments of faith. Students of Appalachian religion need to give continued attention to the role of rituals, old and new, in churches throughout the region.

Likewise, many so-called "liturgical" communions have sought to link their traditions with those of the mountains. Many Catholic Sisters note that their relationships with Appalachians began through simple prayer times and Bible reading, rather than with the elaborate observances surrounding the Mass.

These and other polarities, long present in Appalachian religious communions, serve to distinguish particular individuals and specific belief systems. They shape the theological and practical life of the churches, from rural to urban congregations.

Questions for the Future

Issues of history, theology, and practice raise numerous questions regarding the nature of religion in the Appalachian region. What is the relationship between religious traditions and cultural transitions relative to the farming or the mining economy? How do churches—mainline, evangelical, Pentecostal, mountain—function within the Appalachian environs? What is the nature of Christian ministry in the various churches? What is the impact of the broader secular and religious cultures on religion in the Appalachian region? Can religious groups retain distinctiveness and respond to changing situations in the church and the world?

These and other questions are explored throughout this volume. Chapters examine the nature of religious life in Central Appalachia, with attention to church and culture, mountain churches, denominations, beliefs, and practices. Each suggests that religion in Appalachia is a diverse and powerful force shaping individual and community life. It is also clear that religion, along with other aspects of the culture in the region, is in a time of significant transition, evident in local congregations as well as in broader denominational connections. Nonetheless, religious communities in the Appalachian region are alive and well, constituting important "signs of the times" for understanding the nature of faith and its place in American society in past, present, and future.

Notes

1. This debate is a key one in the Appalachian Studies field. Readers might consult such classic works as John C. Campbell, *The Southern Highlander and His Homeland* (1921; reprint, Lexington: Univ. Press of Kentucky, 1969); Horace Kephart, *Our Southern Highlanders* (1913; reprint, Knoxville: Univ. of Tennessee Press, 1990); Jack E. Weller, *Yesterday's People: Life in Contemporary Appalachia* (Lexington: Univ. Press of Kentucky, 1966); Harry M. Caudill, *Night Comes to the Cumberlands: A Biography of a Depressed Area* (Boston: Little, Brown, 1963); and David E. Whisnant, *All That Is Native and Fine: The Politics of Culture in an American Region* (Chapel Hill: Univ. of North Carolina Press, 1983). Historiographical surveys may be found in such works as Henry D. Shapiro, *Appalachia on Our Mind: The Southern Mountains and Mountaineers in the American Consciousness, 1870–1920* (Chapel Hill: Univ. of North Carolina Press, 1978); W. K. McNeil, ed., *Appalachian Images in Folk and Popular Culture* (Ann Arbor: UMI Research Press, 1989); and Mary Beth Pudup, Dwight B. Billings, and Altina L. Waller, eds., *Appalachia in the Making: The Mountain South in the Nineteenth Century* (Chapel Hill: Univ. of North Carolina Press, 1995). These are but a few of the works suggesting various approaches to Appalachian studies.
2. This approach is informed by Deborah Vansau McCauley, *Appalachian Mountain Religion: A History* (Urbana: Univ. of Illinois Press, 1995), 1–4.

3. Shapiro, *Appalachia on Our Mind,* 42; and Elizabeth R. Hooker, *Religion in the Highlands: Native Churches and Missionary Enterprises in the Southern Appalachian Area* (New York: Polygraphic Co. of America, 1933).

4. Catherine Albanese, *America: Religion and Religions* (Belmont, Calif.: Wadsworth Publishing Co., 1981), 229. Albanese uses Appalachia as an example of regional religion.

5. Deborah Vansau McCauley to Bill J. Leonard, Sept. 1990. Transcript in author's possession.

6. McCauley, *Appalachian Mountain Religion,* 1.

7. In addition to the work of McCauley and Dorgan, see Loyal Jones, "Old-Time Baptists and Mainline Christianity," in *An Appalachian Symposium,* ed. J. W. Williamson, 120–30 (Boone, N.C.: Appalachian State Univ. Press, 1977).

8. Clifford Geertz, *The Interpretation of Cultures* (New York: Basic Books, 1973), 89.

9. McCauley, *Appalachian Mountain Religion,* 7; see also Samuel S. Hill, "Christianity in Appalachia: The Virtue of Hope," chap. 19, this volume.

10. McCauley, *Appalachian Mountain Religion,* 7.

11. Donald Mathews, *Religion in the Old South* (Chicago: Univ. of Chicago Press, 1977), xiii.

12. Ibid., xv.

13. Samuel S. Hill Jr., *Religion and the Solid South* (Nashville, Tenn.: Abingdon, 1972), 34.

14. Martin E. Marty, "The Protestant Experience and Perspectives," in *American Religious Values and the Future of America,* ed. Rodger Van Allen (Philadelphia: Fortress Press, 1978), 40.

15. Ibid., 46.

16. Ibid., 47.

17. Albanese, *America: Religion and Religions,* 221–22.

18. Ibid., 222.

19. Ibid., 223.

20. Mary Lee Daugherty, "A Typology of Three Streams of Religious Traditions in the Appalachian Region" (typescript, 1989, copy at Appalachian Ministries Educational Resource Center, Berea, Ky.). I have added a fourth category, "mountain churches."

21. David Kimbrough, *Taking Up Serpents: Snake-Handlers of Eastern Kentucky* (Chapel Hill: Univ. of North Carolina Press, 1995). This book gives extensive attention to Appalachian stem-family relationships.

22. William Warren Sweet, *Religion in the Development of American Culture* (New York: Charles Scribners' Sons, 1952), 158.

23. Eleanor Dickinson and Barbara Benziger, *Revival!* (New York: Harper and Row, 1974), 128.

24. Paul Gillespie, ed., *Foxfire 7* (Garden City, N.Y.: Anchor/Doubleday, 1982), 200.

25. Ibid., 180.

26. Ibid., 37–38, 82.

27. Many Calvinists were evangelical in their efforts to convert persons, believing that God had chosen to awaken the elect by means of the preaching of the gospel. They preached as if all could be saved, knowing that it would be efficacious for the elect while ultimately having no influence on reprobates. The "hyper-Calvinist" groups— Primitives and Old Regulars, for example—rejected evangelistic methods, believing that God would save the elect on God's own terms. All human efforts at converting the lost represented a futile "works-righteousness." Arminians, however, accepted the teaching of the Dutch reformer, Jacob Arminius, who put greater emphasis on the participation of human free will in the salvific process. McCauley, *Appalachian Mountain Religion*, 170–78, discusses distinctions in conversion experiences among certain mountain communions.

28. Howard Dorgan, *Giving Glory to God in Appalachia* (Knoxville: Univ. of Tennessee Press, 1987), 27.

29. Gillespie, *Foxfire 7*, 65.

30. Jeff Todd Titon, *Powerhouse for God* (Austin: Univ. of Texas Press, 1988), 318.

Chapter 1

Legends of the Fall: Contesting Economic History

BARBARA ELLEN SMITH

Eden

In 1913, my thirty-four-year-old grandfather moved his family to the peak of Big Ridge, an irregular mountain that twists back and forth across the unmarked border of southern West Virginia and Virginia. Hoping to escape what he viewed as the corrupting influences of the iron-ore industry, which were spreading to his home in Rich Patch at the head of Blue Spring Run, Charles C. Smith was among a long list of settlers who sought refuge on the higher ground of the Allegheny Mountains. One of the first permanent residents of Big Ridge, John Lewis, escaped conscription during the Civil War by hiding out in the mountain's forested recesses. He soon was joined by an African American family named Peters, who were escaping from slavery. By the time my grandparents arrived, on the brink of World War I, Big Ridge was beginning to thrive, as settlers sought cheap land and refuge from the industrialization of southwestern Virginia. They built a sawmill, grist mill, and school. The latter doubled as the mountain's first church, a Primitive Baptist fellowship.

My grandparents initially moved with their five children into a log cabin on four hundred rocky acres of soaring mountaintop; they lived there for two years while building a farmhouse out of chestnut lumber sawn from fallen trees that once had towered over their land. The first item moved into the new house was the family Bible, carried by my grandfather and placed on a prominent shelf in the center of their home. His four-year-old son, my father, followed behind with the coffee pot.[1]

Many scholars, novelists, preachers, and family historians of Appalachia depict a preindustrial Eden of the mountains. As Ron Eller says, opening his seminal study of industrialization in the region, *Miners, Millhands, and Mountaineers,* "Few areas of the United States in the late nineteenth century more closely exemplified Thomas Jefferson's vision of a democratic society than did the agricultural communities of the southern Appalachians."[2] On the eve of industrialization, land ownership was widespread, the distribution of resources relatively equal, and class distinctions slight. Most mountaineers lived on family-owned farms, tending crops and range animals primarily for their own consumption. The natural plenitude permitted and reinforced independence—especially from merchants, large landowners, bankers, and other elites—as a cultural value and an economic mode. Neighborly cooperation, however, was necessary, especially during harvests and other occasions when family labor did not suffice. Sanctioning this egalitarian cooperation as a theological imperative was the church, which in many communities was the hub of extrafamilial social life.

In the same era when my grandparents and others of their generation were moving deeper and higher into the mountains, this pious, homespun depiction of Appalachian people had become popularized. During the late nineteenth and early twentieth centuries, proponents of settlement schools and domestic missionary efforts, for example, came into the mountains to work with the simple folk of the preindustrial image.[3] Advocates of the American folk revival traded (literally) on depictions of grannies in sunbonnets who produced quilts and apple butter the old-fashioned way.[4] Railroad magnates and mineral speculators deployed similar images to legitimize the transfer of much of the last locally owned mountain land into their more worldly, cultured, and enterprising hands.[5] The historiography implicit in all these images placed rural Appalachian people in a cultural museum, among other icons of the American pioneer past; it suggested that the lives of even twentieth-century mountaineers differed little from those of the original European settlers in the early eighteenth century.[6]

To this day, portraits of mountain people as direct links to a simpler, uncontaminated past, living in a timeless garden outside of history, remain a persistent theme in Appalachian historiography. In more recent years, especially during the 1960s and early 1970s, political activists utilized similar imagery to promote and legitimize their efforts to "save the land and people." A cultural "revival" swept the mountains: arts and crafts, music festivals, calendars, and T-shirts all celebrated (and constructed) an Appalachian heritage. As David Whisnant wryly commented, "A hundred years from now it will require a major feat of analysis to ascertain that traditional culture in the mountains before World War II is not represented by Ritchie dulcimer songs, Johnny Niles ballads, Richard Chase Jack tales, Churchill Weaver placemats."[7] Scholarly endeavors, such as Ron Eller's, periodized the depiction to the nineteenth century and used it to counter views of mountain people as degenerate and barbaric; rather, he argued, they were the quintessential Americans.[8]

Beginning in the late 1970s, however, as the momentum of social movements in Appalachia faltered and political retrenchment set in across the nation, Appalachian historiography took yet another turn. Although many activists had scorned the condescension of turn-of-the-century missionaries and the rapacious self-interest of industrialists, we had deployed much of the same quaint and uncomplicated imagery of "mountain people" to legitimize our own interventions. Henry Shapiro's *Appalachia on Our Mind* suggested that we all had endowed a fabrication called "Appalachia" with social meaning and coherence that encoded it as a "strange land and peculiar people"; the result was a sentimentalized fiction.[9] Scholars, activists, missionaries, journalists, cartoonists, devotees of *The Waltons*—we all had been led astray.

[I must pause here, for this deconstructionist line of argument has disquieting personal implications. When my grandparents settled on the peaks of Big Ridge, were they fashioning their lives out of the traditionalist imagery of Appalachia being purveyed at the time? Are my father's decidedly homespun stories of his boyhood on Big Ridge yet a further reconstruction, rendered even more romantic by age, contemporary anxieties, and the rosy lens of memory? What hierarchies of age and gender did his egalitarian self-portraits conceal? These are among the most important and obvious empirical questions, but I am drawn, too, to a more heuristic approach: Why have so many people located a rural paradise in the Appalachian past? What is to be learned from this persistent theme in the construction of history, or from the related pattern whereby individuals invent (or discover) meaning in stories of their own origins? I am not certain of answers to these questions, but I am inclined to agree with Alessandro Portelli, who asserts that the factual accuracy of historical events often is less significant than "errors, inventions, and myths [that] lead us through and beyond facts to their meaning."] [10]

In an influential 1982 essay, David Whisnant sounded the call for a "second-level" Appalachian history more attentive to irony, ambiguity, and contradiction—in short, to the messy complexities of lived human experience.[11] As the ebullience of the earlier era faded, replaced by grim concern for the severe regional economic decline and uncertainty about a politics effective to combat it, many scholars took up this challenge. A sober empiricism characterizes much of the most recent research. Although topics have ranged widely through the Appalachian past, no aspect has received more attention or discussion than preindustrial agriculture. County by county, cow by cow, researchers have been counting their way through agrarian Appalachia; not surprisingly, what they find challenges central features of the earlier historiography.

In its class structure, modes of production, and economic relationships with the rest of the nation and the world, agrarian Appalachia, they argue, was neither isolated nor unique. Remote portions of the mountains, such as Big Ridge, may have remained "pre"-industrial well into the twentieth century, but that does not necessarily mean that they were "pre"-capitalist. From the first days of European settlement, the majestic wilderness of the Appalachian frontier inexorably was being commodified as real estate and as an image used by the purveyors of Appalachian Americana. These scholars find evidence of great inequalities in land ownership; in some cases, they find early agriculture commercialized to a far greater extent than prior historiography had suggested.[12]

For example, Dwight Billings and Kathleen Blee's extensive research on Beech Creek, today a poor agricultural community in eastern Kentucky, documents that some of the earliest settlers in this area were wealthy white slaveholders and their black slaves. On the eve of the Civil War, an estimated 22 to 41 percent of farmer householders were landless tenants, cultivating acreage owned by others.[13] The average farm, including that of tenants, was large and productive compared with those in the North, but wealth overwhelmingly was concentrated in the hands of local slaveholders and salt manufacturers. There is debate about whether these and other smaller farmers' scant surplus, modest marketing of agricultural products, and community orientation warrant their classification as "capitalists" (about which, more later). However, on the extreme inequalities in land ownership, there is growing consensus.[14]

There remains room for a Big Ridge, in its economic structure at least, in this historiography. Current research validates the existence of predominantly yeoman farm settlements, along with more stratified configurations, within Southern Appalachia. Communities with relatively egalitarian class structures did not characterize the region, however. Even more, today's researchers tend to view such settlements through a more skeptical, less optimistic lens. They remind us that those who sought a mountain refuge from war, slavery, and industrialization never were able to recreate Eden. From the start, there was trouble in the land.

The Serpent

The Great Depression struck Big Ridge along with the rest of the country. Residents who could read learned about the stock market crash from the newspaper, and all heard rumors of multiple suicides at the opulent Hot Springs resort, but their own lives changed little. By 1934, however, the mountain economy was threadbare. "Public work"—i.e., wage-earning jobs off the farm that brought in much-needed cash—was nowhere to be found.

At Christmas, my father, now a twenty-two-year-old student in his first year of seminary, returned home to Big Ridge. A childhood friend came over to share the happy news of his upcoming wedding, then borrowed a dollar to pay for the marriage license. There was not sufficient money to provide even the traditional present of an orange for each child in the church.

Upon his return to seminary, my father went to eat dinner with friends and swap stories of their Christmas experiences. He sat down at the linen-covered table beneath the chandeliers of the dining hall at Yale Divinity School and stared at the china plates and crystal goblets with a sense of profound dislocation. As he attempted to recount the story of his Christmas on Big Ridge, his fellow students stared at him in disbelief.

If Appalachia once was a garden, at least in natural beauty and abundance, what accounts for the degradation of its environment and the impoverishment of its people? This is the essential question that drives much of the scholarship and debate regarding Appalachia's economic history. For over three decades, the central focus of contention has been the characterization and periodization of Appalachia's relationship with the capitalist economy of the United States and, ultimately, the world.

During the social upheavals of the 1960s and 1970s, competing explanations for regional poverty, from genetic deficiencies of the population to the depredations of capitalism, multiplied; distinctions among the various positions grew sharp, and disagreements intensified. Each position implied the endorsement of a different ensemble of political strategies and public policy interventions to address the region's economic ills. Appalachian studies thus was born not simply as an interdisciplinary academic enterprise, but as part of a political movement.[15]

Each perspective also tended to reflect, sometimes in oblique and unpredictable ways, the social identities and political inclinations of its adherents. Avoiding the intrinsically controversial allocation of blame to a group of human beings, one of the most straightforward and influential positions found mountainous topography at fault; it isolated the region from the markets, communication networks, transportation, and cultural influences of the rest of the United States. The weakness of these linkages led to underdevelopment, which persists to this day. This perspective was enunciated most frequently in the public statements of bureaucrats and politicians in Washington, D.C., such as those in charge of the Appalachian Regional Commission, which funneled millions of dollars into the construction of highways through the mountains.[16]

A counterargument, understandably less influential among policy makers but highly popular among grassroots activists, held that Appalachia was underdeveloped precisely because of strong but asymmetrical linkages with the industrial sector of the U.S. economy. Beginning in the latter half of the nineteenth century, the region's timber and mineral wealth began to beckon outside investors, who rapidly gained control over the land area, especially in the Central Appalachian coalfields. The result was the systematic development of underdevelopment: corporations headquartered elsewhere drained off the region's natural wealth, returning almost nothing in tax revenues and exploiting the people as coal miners.[17] Anyone who has sat at a railroad crossing on a mountain road full of potholes, watching an interminable line of cars loaded with "black gold" rumble toward Chicago, can understand the appeal of this analysis.

The "internal colony" perspective informed an entire generation of academic scholarship and political activism in the mountains. Again, Ron Eller's work is instructive; the contrast between the exploited dependency of the modern period and the dignified self-sufficiency of the preindustrial past became a powerful political trope. The Appalachian Land Ownership Task Force, for example, set out to document, through participatory research, the actual patterns of land ownership in Southern Appalachia. Their collective methods not only validated what many already suspected—

that as much as 85 percent of the land in some coalfield counties was in absentee hands—but also spawned citizen reform movements to address underfunding of public education and other problems associated with regional dispossession. "The Coal Belongs to the People," proclaimed one disabled coal miner's campaign slogan at the time.[18]

However, as activism escalated during the late 1960s and early 1970s, especially in the coalfields, some grew dissatisfied with the thin analytical substance of the internal-colony perspective. It constructed a stark polarity between "us" and "them": the righteous people of Appalachia versus the venal outsiders, especially capitalists. Although a fertile source of slogans and images, this perspective could not account for troubling divisions among Appalachian people themselves. Opposition from conservative forces within the region presented additional questions. If outside capitalists were the problem, would an indigenous bourgeoisie really be better?

Influenced in part by the class conflict in the coalfields, which became astonishingly overt and persistent during this era, some scholars opted for a more classically Marxist interpretation of Appalachia's economy: as a zone of mono-industrial economic activity (especially in the central coalfields), the region represented a spatialized manifestation of the capitalist division of labor. The historically specific context of its industrialization, as a non-union, relatively low-wage competitor to the original, unionized coalfields of Pennsylvania, Ohio, and other northern states, magnified the intensity of regional exploitation.[19]

Today, theoretical and historiographical debates over regional poverty are shifting attention further back in time, to the preindustrial past. Scholars seek to establish continuity, not apocalyptic rupture, between the agricultural and industrial history of Appalachia, and many find it in two related (but contested) developments: the declining viability of nineteenth-century agriculture, which "set free" farmers for industrial wage labor; and the growth of an indigenous but undercapitalized elite, the existence of which ensured that any industrial development would be financed outside the region.[20]

Others, using a world-systems perspective, advocate a more singular theoretical narrative for regional economic history, which suggests that the first European incursions in the early eighteenth century brought with them ineluctable domination by the global forces of capitalism. The work of Wilma Dunaway (1996) provides the most prodigiously researched, theoretically informed exposition of this perspective to date. After winning the struggle for the "first American frontier," the English then parceled out the mountainous land in vast tracts to individuals who rarely settled it themselves. Absentee ownership thus dates back more than two centuries; by 1810, she estimates, 75 percent of the region's acreage was absentee-owned.[21] Those who did settle Appalachia were, from the start, enmeshed in a form of agrarian capitalism that bound them to distant landowners, markets, and political powers (the "core" economy of the world) over which they exercised little influence. Most leased, squatted, or worked as tenants on land owned by the wealthy. This economic configuration yielded low levels of capital available for investment within the region. Industrialization and diversification were therefore stunted, and the region's economic trajectory began to resemble that of the Third World. *By 1860*, she concludes, "Appalachians were much more likely than other Americans to be impoverished, illiterate, and landless."[22]

Others who observe the tendency toward impoverishment within regional agriculture, prior to the onset of industrialization, find different causes. For example, Blee and Billings propose that extremely high fertility rates, combined with equitable partible inheritance customs, gradually led to an imbalance between the population and the land base in the eastern Kentucky community they studied. By 1880, there was a dramatic decline in the average size, surplus product, and livestock inventories of the farms in Beech Creek, as more and more people divided the finite arable land. This rural area contains no coal mines, and its marginal agricultural operations persisted well into the twentieth century, when it became the subject of ethnographic research that fed images of Appalachian peculiarity and backwardness.[23]

[Once again, I must interrupt this narrative. I have long thought of myself (with the perverse pride of leftists) as a descendant of mountain dirt farmers and, on my mother's side, itinerant circuit-riding preachers from the Valley of Virginia. Now it occurs to me that my grandparents may have been, by local standards, part of the elite. Do I need to rewrite my own lineage? Are my family stories of Big Ridge the romanticized, self-validating homilies of the "winners"?

I turn to a list of Big Ridge landowners during the twentieth century, compiled by a woman who taught in the one-room school on the mountain and subsequently married the son of my grandfather's sister. There is a short list of absentee landowners, a longer list of resident owners, including my grandparents, and a slightly shorter list of the landless.[24] Most of the latter are recognizable as the relatives of landowners. A few are not, including Mr. Bill Fogus.

I remember a story my father told. He was called to the Fogus house one night because Mrs. Fogus had hit her husband over the head with a poker, and blood spurted from the wound with each beat of his fading heart. Mr. Fogus is also memorable because he was a socialist and not a churchgoer. A speculative explanation, admittedly simplistic, comes to mind: landlessness + socialism = estrangement from the upright landowners of Big Ridge. Or perhaps landlessness + estrangement = socialism. That he also may have been a wife-beater does not figure into my sympathetic equation of economic position and political affiliation; however, if my grandparents and their associates in the church considered that possibility, it may have had a role. Mr. Fogus survived the poker incident and later moved, with his family, off the mountain. His departure restores my yeoman-farmer image of Big Ridge, but his presence there at all leaves behind a trail of questions.]

There are complicated subtexts (as well as additional positions, too numerous to summarize) in this contemporary debate over Appalachia's economic historiography. Dunaway's world-systems perspective locates historical determinants at a level far removed from the region and its people. In stressing the incorporation of Appalachia's economy into a global capitalist system from the eighteenth century on, she sweeps aside not only romantic images of a preindustrial past but also the behaviors, beliefs, and perhaps countervailing proclivities of various social groups and economic classes within the region. Rhetorically, she asks about the subsistent Appalachian farmer: "Is this a 'peasant' household with roots in the soil and cultural resistance to capitalism? The *mentalité* of the farmer is largely irrelevant, for it would have been almost impossible for such a subsistence producer to be totally free of the capitalist economy."[25] In other words, her insistent economic determinism leaves no room for human agency, except on the part of elites. The inexorability of her historiography resonates with a current mood of powerlessness in the face of global economic forces that seem immune to popular influence.

Others, however, are not so willing to hand over the region's history to the global reach of capital. In 1986, Blee, Billings, and Swanson held out for a categorization of Beech Creek as "noncapitalist" in economic mode and stressed the significance of communitarian social relations in facilitating survival.[26] In later work, these authors modified this appellation to "nonindustrial" and downplayed references to communitarianism.[27] Ironically but purposefully, in attributing regional poverty partially to indigenous social practice, particularly high fertility rates and inheritance customs, Blee and Billings retain the possibility of indigenous agency: Appalachian people's own actions in part caused—and presumably also could help to solve—regional economic problems.

Their sympathetic but carefully historicized analysis contrasts with one other influential perspective on the origins of regional poverty, which should be mentioned before closing this discussion: the derogatory perception that Appalachia was (and is) a retarded frontier inhabited by people who "acquired civilization and then lost it."[28] This rather hackneyed position merits continued analysis because of its amazing capacity for repeated resurrection. Over a century ago was born the image of the mountain barbarian, along with that of its fraternal twin, the noble savage (close relatives of the pure and godly pioneer).[29] Its War-on-Poverty incarnation, which arrived in the garb of social psychology, suggested that Appalachian people's cultural deficits, such as familism and fatalism, were responsible for the region's economic woes. A more vicious variant, featuring laziness, criminality, and sexual licentiousness, underlies contemporary denunciations of the region's (and nation's) poor. The analytic move common to all these images is the ahistorical, astructural apprehension of Appalachian people, which takes impoverishment as evidence of intrinsic deficits.

In all of these formulations, Appalachian people become curiosities. At least the romantic image of the sturdy pioneer is mildly positive, if patronizing, and has a place in America's historical iconography. The barbarian, however, exists only to be eradicated. This latter image connotes profound "otherness" and therefore is especially harmful: the problems of Appalachian people are not our problems; their stories are not part of our (hi)story. Even—of all times—in the worldwide economic cataclysm of the Great Depression, well-intentioned but privileged seminary students received stories of Appalachian poverty with disbelief; surely this attests to the insularity and ignorance that undergird this widespread attitude. It has prompted more than one young migrant to forsake his accent, shed his country manners, and silence his stories of an Appalachian home.

Exile

Over the fifty years that my grandparents lived on Big Ridge, the community they helped to cultivate flowered and then eventually faded away. Although the Depression temporarily brought economic refugees back to the mountain, World War II reclaimed them for the Armed Forces and new opportunities in nearby cities and towns. War, conscription, and industrialization, which many of the original settlers on Big Ridge sought to escape, now beckoned to their offspring. In 1944, the one-room school was closed for good. During the next decade, when my grandfather's health began to fail, the church also ceased its regular services. Today, the U.S. Forest Service owns most of the land on Big Ridge, and those who climb the steep road up to the site of my grandparents' homeplace most frequently are hunters, dirt bikers, and white-tailed deer.

On New Year's Eve, 1971, propelled by forces I have yet to understand fully, I retraced the steps of my ancestors and moved to the mountains of West Virginia. In a sense, I was part of a larger return migration that occurred when portions of Appalachia were teeming with community organizers, social activism, and—for a time—jobs. But in social position and peers, I was part of the influx of outsiders: VISTA workers, Antioch College students (I was one), and Appalachian Volunteers. Like others, I became absorbed in the upheavals of that era, especially the black lung movement.

During the retrenchments of the 1980s, however, the loose community my friends and I had created began to break apart. I watched as, one by one, they moved away; I listened as those who stayed behind talked about how much they wanted to leave. Our lives became more prosaic; I married, had two children, bought a house, and even got a real job in a university. Gradually I began to ponder whether I wanted to commit the remainder of my working life to something that was becoming more a dream of the past than a living experience. In 1995, I sold my ridgetop home in West Virginia, plus seven sweet acres of North Georgia hillside, to finance a move with my two sons to the low-lying riverbanks of Memphis.

The dynamics of Appalachia's political economy have exerted a powerful influence over the migration decisions of its people. During the two decades after World War II, for example, when the coal industry mechanized and hundreds of thousands of jobs were eliminated, over three million Appalachians departed for industrial centers in the North. Today, as the mining, manufacturing, and farming base of the region's economy becomes increasingly anachronistic, another wave of migration, this time to the South, is taking place. The service sector's ubiquitous growth is seen in Southern Appalachia, especially in urban centers and scenic tourist areas, but it does not begin to keep pace with the jobs that are lost. Between 1980 and 1990, West Virginia, the only state that lies entirely within the Appalachian region, lost more of its population than any other state in the country.[30]

What accounts for the richness of memory, identity, and experience binding people so firmly to a region that is, on so many counts, impoverished? The current drive to demythologize Appalachia is in many respects entirely appropriate—indeed, liberating. To dismiss mythology wholesale as ahistorical claptrap, however, may be too hasty. Mythic constructions of the region, especially ones created by those who have lived there, may have something to tell us, not only about the migration saga but also about deeper structures and meanings at stake in the many human experiences that compose Appalachia's past. The larger symbolic systems, of which these regional mythologies are but one instance, involve religious and cultural themes that far transcend this specific place. That they have been so influential in Appalachia's historiographical and ideological construction may be, in part, because they resonate so deeply with certain themes—separation, exile, loss, reunion—in the region's history. That they also have loomed large in the self-concept and expressions of Appalachian people is evidenced not only in the religious traditions documented in this volume, but also in everything from oral histories to the *Foxfire* books to those innumerable sentimental songs about a home in the mountains.

Mythic constructions of place, located either forward or backward in time, may function as profoundly powerful metaphors to organize and motivate human decisions, expressions, and actions.[31] It is evident from self-descriptions and oral retellings, for example, that an Edenic myth was responsible in part for the Fridleys and Smiths' rejection of the potentially lucrative industrialization of southwestern Virginia, and for their flight to the yet more rural, relatively inaccessible peaks of Big Ridge.

Mythic visions may have explicitly political functions and consequences, too—most notably, in recent U.S. history, in the postwar Civil Rights movement, but also in the regional resistance to, for example, environmental degradation. In these contexts, the myths function to encode alternative possibilities, different from what people presently endure, and thereby to nurture a sense of hope. One wonders, then, how those mountaineers who left their dying farms for coal camps and underground work in the mines constructed the home they left behind. Was it as a place of egalitarianism, abundance, and independence that, among other forces, shaped their class formation and militant demands for redress? What visions of place were at work in the actions of retired coal miner Jink Ray, who in 1967 laid his body down in front of a bulldozer to stop the strip mining of his land?

Let me be clear: I am not calling for reinstatement of a romanticism about timeless "mountain people" and their enduring relationship to the land, but rather for a reading of time and place different from that of conventional history (and "common" sense). "Time" in this uncommon sense does not refer to linear or cyclical sequencing, but to desires and possibilities—that which is not presently realized. "Place" locates these dreams in experiences, relationships, and, especially for rural people, specific geographical locales.[32] In our dislocated, uncertain world, "place" may function as a metaphor for the ongoing process of establishing coherent and meaningful social experiences; "time" for the possibility that we can control, protect, escape, change, or return to them.

This is in no way to suggest that the diverse and numerous "places" that people within the region construct as Appalachia (or their home) are empirically more accurate than "externally" generated imagery. That is indeed a false dichotomy on many levels, for Appalachian people, like everyone else in the United States of the late twentieth century, inevitably construct a sense of place out of the flotsam and jetsam of many influences—whether soap operas, sermons, country music, layoffs, advice from the *Farmers' Almanac*, etc., etc. It is to suggest, however, that the examination of these constructions is essential if we are to locate Appalachian people in their rightful roles, along with the coal operators, missionaries, bankers, novelists, and other players, on the center stage of their own written history.

Those who write about the Appalachian past inevitably capture in words on a page only a paltry portion of the infinite complexities of human experience. For three decades now, scholars and activists have tended to focus their analyses on the political economy of the region, apart from its culture, in an understandable response to the victim-blaming denigrations of traditional anthropological accounts. It now may be time, however, to become a little less preoccupied with establishing facts and analyzing economic structures, and a little more concerned with interpretation and meaning.[33] In that manner, we may come a little closer to understanding not only how capitalists, local color writers, ethnographers, and others (including historians) have appropriated Appalachia for their own ends, but also how Jink Ray and other people of the region have constructed it for themselves.

Return

Every year, on the first Sunday in August, the children of Big Ridge return home. On Friday and Saturday, women who deliberately have arrived early open the small, one-room church building, sweep out the acorns deposited by ambitious squirrels, dust off the pews, and chase the field mice out of the pump organ. On Sunday morning, close to two hundred people crowd into and around the church, some listening at the windows, others (mostly men) smoking, chewing tobacco, and talking outside at the door. Most are like me: they never actually lived on Big Ridge, and they have experienced its past only through the stories of their parents and grandparents. Why do they come? What forces pull them there? (More immediately, why do I write this essay?)

Some of the best sermons delivered at these homecoming services address such questions. In one given over twenty years ago, my cousin, who was not a minister but an English professor, said, "We come to remember more vividly our fathers and mothers who toiled this ground and built this church; but in honoring that memory we come to recapture with a vividness more vivid than mere memory, the selves that we are when we are most certain who we are. . . . In this urgency to find ourselves by coming home, we are not unusual. . . . The Old Testament is from the beginning the story of recurrent wandering and coming home again."[34]

[I often think of that sermon when I read or witness impassioned debates over the economic history of Appalachia—distracted by the sense that, in the end, their intensity derives not from conflicting findings about the dead of the eighteenth or nineteenth centuries, but from our own dilemmas and allegiances in the late twentieth. In the midst of those polarized conflicts, I like to believe that we nonetheless are joined together in a common search that is at once mythic, historiographical, and political: to discern what went wrong, driven by a longing to put it right. As people who study and participate in the "making of Appalachia," what we do ultimately may not be so different from the actions of far-flung offspring of a deeply mythologized mountain who come back every year to relocate themselves. Perhaps we all are the children of Big Ridge, or Appalachia, whose past is our home, whose historiography is our difficult, sometimes contentious, effort to return.]

Notes

1. Blue Ridge is located on the border between Greenbriar County, West Virginia, and Allegheny County, Virginia. These historical descriptions are taken largely from my extended family's oral tradition. Written histories of this community are found in Eleanor Fridley, *Saga of the Mountain: A History of Big Ridge* (N.p.: Privately published, 1976; copy in possession of Barbara Ellen Smith); and Joseph M.

Smith, "The Church on the Mountain: A History of Antioch Christian Church on Big Ridge, Allegheny County, Virginia, 1915–1960" (typescript, n.d.; copy in possession of Barbara Ellen Smith).

2. Ronald D Eller, *Miners, Millhands, and Mountaineers: Industrialization of the Appalachian South, 1880–1930* (Knoxville: Univ. of Tennessee Press, 1982), 3.

3. David Whisnant, *All That Is Native and Fine: The Politics of Culture in an American Religion* (Chapel Hill: Univ. of North Carolina Press, 1983).

4. Jane Becker, panel participant, Tenth Berkshire Conference on the History of Women, Chapel Hill, N.C., June 9, 1996.

5. Eller, *Miners, Millhands, and Mountaineers.*

6. Paul Salstrom, "Subsistence Farming, Capitalism, and the Depression in West Virginia," *Appalachian Journal* 11, no. 4 (1984): 384–94.

7. David Whisnant, "Second-Level Appalachian History: Another Look at Some Fotched-On Women," *Appalachian Journal* 9, nos. 2–3 (1982): 122.

8. Eller, *Miners, Millhands, and Mountaineers.*

9. Henry D. Shapiro, *Appalachia on Our Mind: The Southern Mountains and Mountaineers in the American Consciousness, 1870–1920* (Chapel Hill: Univ. of North Carolina Press, 1978).

10. Alessandro Portelli, *The Death of Luigi Trastulli and Other Stories: Form and Meaning in Oral History* (Albany: State Univ. of New York Press, 1991), 2.

11. Whisnant, "Second-Level Appalachian History."

12. Wilma A. Dunaway, *The First American Frontier: Transition to Capitalism in Southern Appalachia, 1700–1860* (Chapel Hill: Univ. of North Carolina Press, 1996; Durwood Dunn, *Cades Cove: The Life and Death of a Southern Appalachian Community, 1818–1937* (Knoxville: Univ. of Tennessee Press, 1988); John C. Inscoe, *Mountain Masters: Slavery and the Sectional Crisis in Western North Carolina* (Knoxville: Univ. of Tennessee Press, 1989); and Mary Beth Pudup, Dwight B. Billings, and Altina L. Waller, eds., *Appalachia in the Making: The Mountain South in the Nineteenth Century* (Chapel Hill: Univ. of North Carolina Press, 1995).

13. Dwight B. Billings and Kathleen Blee, "Agriculture and Poverty in the Kentucky Mountains: Beech Creek, 1850–1910," in *Appalachia in the Making: The Mountain South in the Nineteenth Century,* ed. Mary Beth Pudup, Dwight B. Billings, and Altina L. Waller, 63–88 (Chapel Hill: Univ. of North Carolina Press, 1995).

14. Dunn, *Cades Cove;* Inscoe, *Mountain Masters;* Robert Tracy McKenzie, "Wealth and Income: The Preindustrial Structure of East Tennessee in 1860," *Appalachian Journal* 21, no. 3 (1994): 260–79; and Ralph Mann, "Diversity in the Antebellum Appalachian South: Four Farm Communities in Tazewell County, Virginia," in *Appalachia in the Making: The Mountain South in the Nineteenth Century,* ed. Mary Beth Pudup, Dwight B. Billings, and Altina L. Waller, 132–62 (Chapel Hill: Univ. of North Carolina Press, 1995).

15. Alan Banks, Dwight Billings, and Karen Tice, "Appalachian Studies, Resistance,

and Postmodernism," in *Fighting Back in Appalachia: Traditions of Resistance and Change,* ed. Stephen L. Fisher, 283–301 (Philadelphia: Temple Univ. Press, 1993); and John Stephenson, "Politics and Scholarship: Appalachian Studies Enter the 1980s," *Appalachian Journal* 9, nos. 2–3 (1982): 97–104.

16. David Whisnant, *Modernizing the Mountaineer: People, Power, and Planning in Appalachia* (Boone, N.C.: Appalachian Consortium Press, 1981).

17. Helen Lewis, L. Johnson, and D. Askins, eds., *Colonialism in Modern America: The Appalachian Case* (Boone, N.C.: Appalachian Consortium Press, 1978).

18. Appalachian Land Ownership Task Force, *Who Owns Appalachia? Landownership and Its Impact* (Lexington: Univ. Press of Kentucky, 1983). Walter Burton Franklin, now deceased, used this slogan in his 1968 campaign for the West Virginia House of Delegates. I worked with him in the black lung movement in southern West Virginia. This sentiment was widespread among activists in the era.

19. Richard Simon, "The Development of Underdevelopment: The Coal Industry and Its Effect on the West Virginia Economy, 1880–1930" (Ph.D. diss., Univ. of Pittsburgh, 1978.)

20. Dwight Billings and Kathleen Blee, "Family Strategies in a Subsistence Economy: Beech Creek, Kentucky, 1850–1942," *Sociological Perspectives* 33, no. 1 (1990): 63–88; Billings and Blee, "Agriculture and Poverty: Beech Creek;" Salstrom, "Subsistence Farming, Capitalism, and the Depression"; Mary Beth Pudup, "The Limits of Subsistence: Agriculture and Industry in Central Appalachia," *Agricultural History* 64 (1990): 61–89.

21. Dunaway, *First American Frontier,* 85.

22. Ibid., 21.

23. Billings and Blee, "Agriculture and Poverty: Beech Creek"; James Brown, *Beech Creek: The Social Organization of an Isolated Kentucky Mountain Neighborhood* (Berea, Ky.: Berea College Press, 1988).

24. Fridley, *Saga of the Mountain,* 79–82.

25. Dunaway, *First American Frontier,* 231.

26. Dwight Billings, Kathleen Blee, and Louis Swanson, "Culture, Family, and Community in Preindustrial Appalachia," *Appalachian Journal* 13, no. 2 (1986): 154–70.

27. Billings and Blee, "Agriculture and Poverty: Beech Creek."

28. Arnold Toynbee, *A Study of History* (New York: Oxford Univ. Press, 1947), 149.

29. Shapiro, *Appalachia on Our Mind.*

30. Richard A. Couto, *An American Challenge: A Report on Economic Trends and Social Issues in Appalachia* (Dubuque, Ia.: Kendall-Hunt, 1994); and John Gaventa, Barbara Ellen Smith, and Alex Willingham, eds., *Communities in Economic Crisis: Appalachia and the South* (Philadelphia: Temple Univ. Press, 1990).

31. Stephen William Foster, *The Past Is Another Country: Representation, Historical Consciousness, and Resistance in the Blue Ridge* (Berkeley, Calif.: Univ. of California Press, 1988).

32. Portelli, *Death of Luigi Trastulli*.

33. The deployment of mythic, often religious, symbols and language for political ends is one of the most significant features of contemporary politics, not only in the U.S. but around the world. This article is motivated in part by the conviction that we must go beyond political economy if we are to develop an economic vision worth fighting for and a politics capable of achieving it.

34. Calvin Smith, "Parable" (typescript of sermon delivered in Big Ridge, W.Va., 1975; copy in possession of Barbara Ellen Smith).

Chapter 2

The Church and the Family Farm Ministry in Central Appalachia

BENNETT POAGE

"The days are coming," says the Lord,
    "when grain will grow faster than it can be harvested,
    and grapes will grow faster than the wine can be made.
    The mountains will drip with sweet wine,
    and the hills will flow with it.
I will bring my people back to their land.
    They will rebuild their ruined cities and live there;
    they will plant vineyards and drink the wine,
    they will plant gardens and eat what they grow.
I will plant my people on the land I gave them,
    and they will not be pulled up again."
The Lord your God has spoken.

—Amos 9:13–15

At no other time in history has the case been more compelling, the need greater, for the church to be involved in ministry to, and with, farm families in Central Appalachia. Family farm agriculture, in a threatening transition nationally, is under attack in Central Appalachia. Tobacco is the primary cash crop in twenty-nine of the thirty-five farm-sector counties (for definition of farm sector, see table 2.1; also see

map 2.1), and the uncertain future of domestic tobacco farming is causing a crisis in tobacco-dependent communities and churches.[1]

Tobacco churches are defined in *The Tobacco Church: A Manual For
Congregational Leaders* as "any congregation, rural, small town or county
seat, where the economy supporting that church and community gains
its primary energy from growing, processing and/or marketing tobacco."[2] These churches occupy the unfortunate position of being
caught up in a social and economic calamity which is negatively impacting membership, giving, and programming "at a time when congregations should be reaching out to community needs the most."[3] The
situation is similar to a fire engine's catching on fire. Nonetheless, positive, ongoing ministry is taking place, ranging from traditional direct
services to sophisticated advocacy.

This chapter examines, first, the family farm in Central Appalachia—
where it is located, its economic importance, how it is being affected by
the family farm crisis, and its relationship to the coal and lumber industries; and, second, the church and family farm ministry in Central
Appalachia—issues facing family farms, the church as a resource, examples
of ministry taking place, attitudes toward family farm ministries (from a
survey of social resources related to family farm ministry), and what future
ministries are needed.

The Family Farm in Central Appalachia

Although the Central Appalachian counties produce only 19.3 to 3.2
percent of their states' total receipts in crops and livestock (see table
2.2), these largely family farms are a very important segment of the
subregion's economy. At least thirty-five of the eighty-four counties are
dependent almost solely on agriculture as the principal source of income and jobs (see table 2.3). Agriculture produces significant levels of
income, too (over $942 million annually; see table 2.2). These figures
do not take into account the enormous quantities of food which "subsistence" and "self-sufficient" farms traditionally produce and which is
consumed at home and in local communities.

The economies of Central Appalachian farm-sector counties are
based upon the economic fabric of the family farm. The school system,
banks, Main Street businesses, and churches are inextricably bound together in an economy supported by burley tobacco, corn, and cattle.
This economy is sustained by a very fragile thread, the government-
directed tobacco program.

In a subregion where hungry people already abound (map 2.2), coal-

Table 2.1

Number and Sizes of Central Appalachian Farms

State	Farms in Farm-Sector Counties*	Number of Counties	Average Size (Acres)	Farms in Non-Farming Counties	Number of Counties	Average Size (Acres)
Kentucky[a] (CA Counties)	25,124	24	130	6,280	25	120
Tennessee[b] (CA Counties)	8,000	8	124	6,340	11	125
Virginia[c] (CA Counties)	3,137	3	171	1,615	4	94
West Virginia[d]						
Central Appalachia Totals/ Averages	36,261	35	142	14,235	49	113

SOURCE: U.S. Department of Agriculture, *Agricultural Census for 1992,* (Washington, D.C.: U.S. Government Printing Office, 1993).
[a]In the entire state, 91,000 farms with an average size of 155 acres.
[b]In the entire state, 88,000 farms with an average of 143 acres.
[c]In the entire state, 44,000 farms, with an average size of 198 acres.
[d]County farm numbers not available. No farm-sector counties in the nine CA counties. In the entire state, 20,000 farms, with an average size of 185 acres.
* Farm-sector counties are those with agricultural sales exceeding $3 million in 1993.
CA = Central Appalachia

Table 2.2

Farm Receipts from Crops and Livestock (in thousands of dollars)

State	Year	Total	Total in Central Appalachian Counties	Number of Counties	Percentage of State Total
Kentucky	1994	3,230,277	620,858	49	19.3
Tennessee	1992	2,103,471	253,809	19	12.1
Virginia	1992	2,068,630	66,880	7	3.2
West Virginia	1993	405,500	*	9	*

SOURCES: *Kentucky, Tennessee, Virginia and West Virginia Agricultural Statistics* (1994 and 1995); Kentucky Agricultural Statistics Service, *Kentucky Agricultural Statistics 1994–1995* (Louisville, Ky.: Kentucky Agricultural Statistics Service, Sept. 1995); Tennessee Agricultural Statistics Service, *Tennessee Agriculture 1994* (Nashville, Tenn.: Tennessee Dept. of Agriculture, July 1994); Virginia Agricultural Statistics Service, *Virginia Agricultural Statistics 1993: Bulletin No. 65* (Richmond, Va.: Virginia Agricultural Statistics Service, Sept. 1994); Office of West Virginia Agricultural Service, *West Virginia Agricultural Statistics 1994: Bulletin No. 25* (Charleston, W.Va.: Office of West Virginia Agricultural Statistics Service, 1994).
*County statistics not available.

Map 2.1. Economies of the Central Appalachian Subregion.
SOURCES: *Kentucky, West Virginia, Virginia, and Tennessee see Agricultural Statistics,* 1994; *Coal Industry Annual 1993,* 1994; *Kentucky, West Virginia, Virginia, and Tennessee Divisions/Departments of Forestry,* 1993.

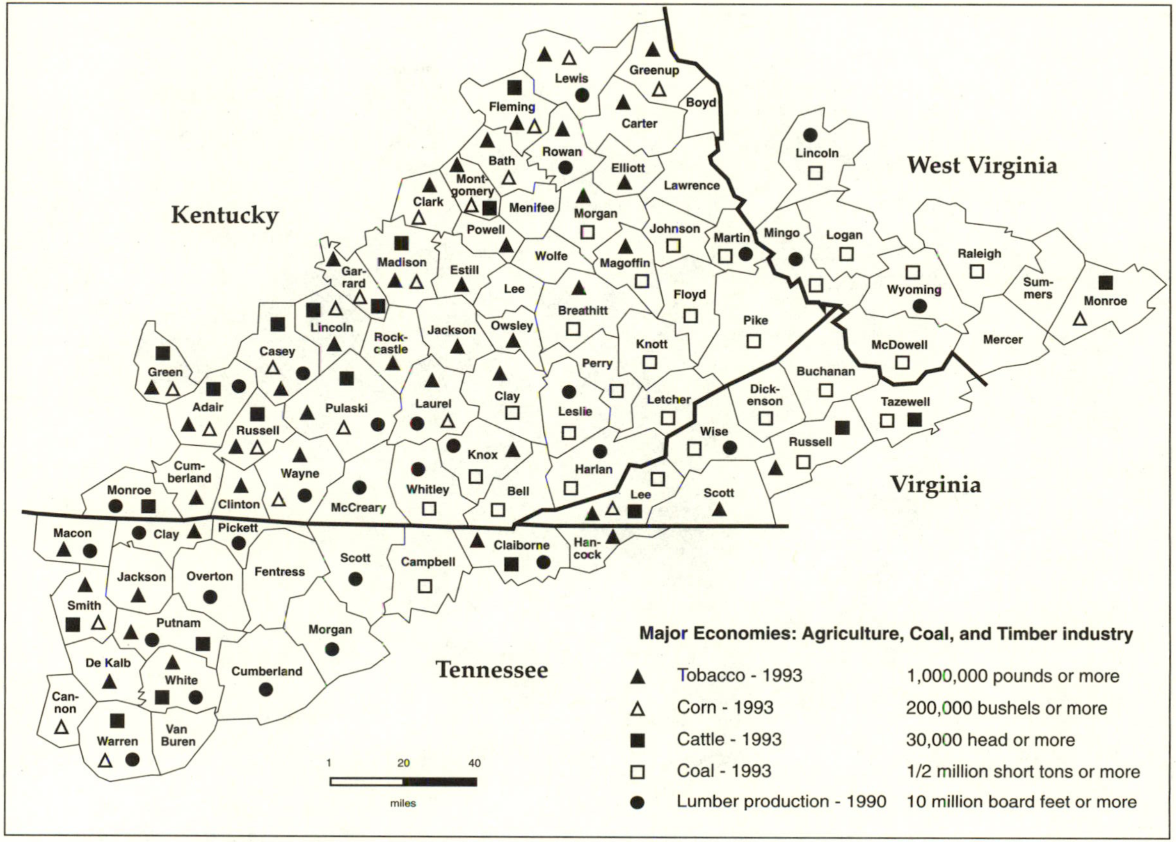

Major Economies: Agriculture, Coal, and Timber industry

▲ Tobacco - 1993 — 1,000,000 pounds or more
△ Corn - 1993 — 200,000 bushels or more
■ Cattle - 1993 — 30,000 head or more
□ Coal - 1993 — 1/2 million short tons or more
● Lumber production - 1990 — 10 million board feet or more

Map 2.2. Poverty Rates in Counties of the Central Appalachian Subregion. SOURCES: *Beyond Distress: New Measures of Economic Need in Appalachia* (Knoxville, Tenn.: Commission on Religion in Appalachia, 1993); Kentucky Cabinet for Human Resources; 1990 Census.

West Virginia
Central Appalachian Avg. Rate 27.1 %
Statewide Avg. 17.9 %

Virginia
Central Appalachian Avg. Rate 23.0 %
Statewide Avg. 9.9 %

Kentucky
Central Appalachian Avg. Rate 31.4 %
Statewide Avg. 18.8 %

Tennessee
Central Appalachian Avg. Rate 21.8 %
Statewide Avg. 15.5 %

1990 Poverty Rate in %
- 25.8 - 52.1
- 15.2 - 25.7
- 13.1 - 15.1

13.1 = Avg. for United States
15.2 = Avg. for Appalachian Region
25.8 = Avg. for Central Appalachia

County labels (poverty rate %):

Monroe	21.0
Summers	24.5
Mercer	20.4
Raleigh	19.9
Tazewell	19.0
Wyoming	27.9
McDowell	37.7
Russell	22.5
Buchanan	21.9
Lincoln	33.8
Logan	27.7
Mingo	30.9
Dickenson	25.9
Scott	20.9
Pike	25.4
Wise	22.1
Boyd	16.5
Greenup	17.6
Martin	35.4
Lawrence	36.0
Johnson	28.7
Floyd	31.2
Letcher	31.8
Lee	28.7
Carter	26.8
Lewis	30.7
Elliott	36.0
Morgan	38.8
Magoffin	42.5
Knott	40.4
Harlan	33.1
Hancock	40.0
Fleming	25.4
Rowan	28.9
Menifee	35.0
Wolfe	44.3
Breathitt	39.5
Perry	32.1
Leslie	35.6
Bell	38.2
Claiborne	25.7
Bath	27.3
Montgomery	21.0
Powell	26.2
Lee	37.4
Owsley	52.1
Clay	40.2
Knox	38.9
Clark	17.7
Estill	29.0
Jackson	38.2
Laurel	24.8
Whitley	33.0
Campbell	26.8
Madison	21.2
Rockcastle	30.7
McCreary	45.5
Scott	27.8
Morgan	20.2
Garrard	18.1
Lincoln	27.2
Pulaski	22.7
Wayne	37.3
Fentress	32.3
Cumberland	18.1
Casey	29.4
Russell	25.6
Clinton	38.1
Pickett	24.9
Adair	25.1
Cumberland	31.6
Overton	17.9
Putnam	16.6
White	17.0
Van Buren	19.2
Green	21.6
Monroe	26.9
Clay	23.0
Jackson	20.0
De Kalb	20.3
Warren	16.8
Macon	19.3
Smith	14.5
Cannon	14.5

1   20   40
miles

related jobs are declining at an ever-increasing rate, off-farm job opportunities are almost totally lacking, real unemployment exceeds 40 percent in many counties,[4] and the poverty rate exceeds 25 percent,[5] it is impossible to overstate the necessity not only of retaining but also of strengthening the family farm. Moreover, the role of "the church" in strengthening farm families, through specifically targeted ministries, is paramount.

Farm Size, Location, and Income

Farms in Central Appalachia range from well-manicured, industrially run, thousand-acre spreads (on the western fringe of Appalachia in Kentucky and along the western rim of the Cumberland Plateau in Tennessee) to traditional "grit and grub" farmers—premodernists—still subsisting (in and around the edges of the Kentucky coal fields and east of the Clinch River in southwestern Virginia). Moreover, a growing number of postmodern sustainable agriculturists are joining this eclectic mix.

Despite the diversity, the most common farm is 125 to 175 acres in size, commercially oriented, growing burley tobacco and beef cattle for cash income, and family run, with farm operators in their fifties or sixties. Dairy farms once were numerous, but decades of low milk prices have taken their toll. These "backbone of America"–style farms are very much oriented toward family and community.[6] Their owners believe in handshake contracts, "down-home cookin'," educating their kids, being good neighbors, and strong churches. The 1992 federal agricultural census documents the numbers and sizes of Central Appalachian farms (see table 2.1). Total net farm enterprise income for the Central Appalachia counties in 1990–94, and the differences between 1990 and 1994, are shown in table 2.3.

An increase of 8.3 percent in five years represents an annual growth rate of approximately 1.7 percent in net farm enterprise income for Central Appalachia. This minimal growth is the result of two factors.

The first is a general rebound in all agriculture, after two subsidy-rich federal farm bills were enacted into law in 1985 and 1990. These subsidies come to farmers as deficiency payments, covering the difference between preset "target prices" on grain (corn and wheat) and oil seed (soy bean) crops and "annual average market prices" (target prices are set annually by Congress and are supposed to cover the costs of producing a given crop). However, as compiled from U.S. Department of Commerce statistics, these subsidies amount to only 2 percent of annual net farm enterprise income in Central Appalachia and are marginal in their impact.[7]

Second, despite quota reductions and price setbacks, tobacco continues to be an income producer for Central Appalachia, especially for family farmers in Kentucky and Tennessee. Moreover, this source of income

Table 2.3

Total Net Farm Enterprise Income for Central Appalachia*

State	Net Income (in thousands of dollars)					Change (%) 1990 to 1994
	1990	1991	1992	1993	1994	
Kentucky	134,049	170,058	197,653	157,699	138,610	3.3
Tennessee	37,517	52,824	59,544	66,677	65,377	57.4
Virginia	19,432	17,544	19,979	10,871	6,839	-64.8
West Virginia	4,476	1,788	3,239	5,287	2,317	-48.2
Farm Sector Central Appalachia (FSA 35 counties)**	172,527	206,703	237,791	206,527	183,951	6.2
Other Central Appalachia (OA 49 counties)***	22,947	35,511	42,624	34,007	29,192	21.4
Central Appalachia (84 counties)	195,474	242,214	280,415	240,534	213,143	8.3

SOURCE: U.S. Department of Commerce, Regional Economic Information System, Bureau of Economic Analysis, June 1996.
Notes:
CA = Central Appalachia
* Cash receipts from all marketing, plus government payments, rent and other income, but not including income from farm wages or other labor income.
Total income reflects the cash position realized from the farm business and the positive or negative value of inventory changes. Total net income figures do not include corporate farms.
** FSA = Farm Sector Appalachia. FSA counties are those with annual cash receipts from all agricultural sales exceeding $3 million in 1993.
*** OA = Other Appalachian. OA counties are those whose agricultural sales are less than $3 million in 1993.

growth is not restricted to farm-sector counties. Tobacco frequently is the sole cash crop of traditional subsistence farmers in the nonfarm (or other) counties.

Finally, when the five-year, nationally compounded inflation rate of 17.5 percent[8] is compared to the subregion's five-year 8.3 percent gain in net farm income, a real loss of 9.2 percent in "purchasing power" is noted.

From this analysis, it is obvious that family farmers in Central Appalachia, as in much of the rest of the country, are not even keeping up with inflation. If the fragile thread of the tobacco program is stretched tighter, or broken (as many forecast it will be), or if Congress reduces farm subsidies to zero over seven years (as was enacted in the 1996 Farm Bill), a massive economic dislocation likely will sweep away many family farms, along with the rural communities they support and most farm income–dependent churches.

Agriculture and Other Key Economic Activities

Aside from oil refineries and a few declining steel mills in Boyd and Greenup counties, in Kentucky; aside from the bright growth of some small industries in communities and corridors along the interstates and major highways; and aside from a small but growing tourism industry around lakes and the more spectacular mountainous areas, the economy in Central Appalachia is based upon these sources, in ranked order: coal, agriculture, and lumber. However, agriculture switches positions from state to state. It is second in Kentucky and Virginia, but in Tennessee it is first, handily outranking both coal and lumber. Moreover, in West Virginia, lumber undoubtedly is second in the nine Central Appalachian counties, since only Monroe County has significant agricultural production (see table 2.4).

Family Farms in Crisis

Since 1980, family farms in the United States have experienced a crisis that has become chronic. The chronic condition is signaled by generally depressed land values; prices for farm commodities below the cost of production; constantly rising prices for fertilizer, fuel, and equipment; a general financial disinvestment in the agricultural sector; and government programs that increasingly favor large industrial farms. Between 1980 and 1994, 375,000 farms were lost nationwide, a decline of 15.4 percent in fifteen years. In the same time period, average farm size in the U.S. increased from 426 to 471 acres, an increase of 9.4 percent.[9]

In Central Appalachia, tobacco is the leading cash crop in forty-five of the eighty-four counties. Moreover, it predominates in twenty-nine of the

Table 2.4

Major Economies in Central Appalachia (in thousands of dollars)

State	Receipts in Crops and Livestock	Value of Coal Produced*a*	Value of Lumber Produced*b*
Kentucky	620,858*c*	2,886,906	2,288
Tennessee	253,809*d*	57,074	1,503
Virginia	66,880*e*	1,053,696	335
West Virginia*f*		1,602,982	605
Central Appalachia Totals	941,547	5,600,658	4,731

Notes:

*a*Average mine prices per short ton of coal in 1993: Kentucky: 113,212,000 short tons at $25.50; Tennessee: 2,096,000 short tons at $27.23; Virginia: 39,317,000 short tons at $26.80; West Virginia: 58,503,000 short tons at $27.40.

*b*Lumber price based on No. 1 common white oak, 4 quarter sawed, per thousand board feet (BF), on January 1, 1994: Kentucky: 427,723,000 BF; Tennessee: 280,958,000 BF; Virginia: 62,641,000 BF; West Virginia: 113,000,000 BF.

*c*Data from Kentucky Agricultural Statistics Service, *Kentucky Agricultural Statistics 1994–1995* (Louisville, Ky.: Kentucky Agricultural Statistics Service, Sept. 1995).

*d*Data from Tennessee Agricultural Statistics Service, *Tennessee Agriculture 1994* (Nashville, Tenn.: Tennessee Dept. of Agriculture, July 1994).

*e*Data from Virginia Agricultural Statistics Service, *Virginia Agricultural Statistics 1993: Bulletin No. 65* (Richmond, Va.: Virginia Agricultural Statistics Service, Sept. 1994).

*f*County receipts not available in West Virginia.

thirty-five farm-sector counties in the subregion. Tobacco, for example, makes up 57 percent of all crop income and 27 percent of farm income in Kentucky, and it accounts for 27 percent of all employment in the tobacco belt counties.[10]

In the early years of the national farm crisis, the tobacco-growing counties were somewhat insulated from the calamities befalling grain farms in the Midwest. Family tobacco farmers have been able to survive by raising tobacco because of its extraordinarily high return from small acreage (two to three thousand dollars net per acre). This return is possible because the federal tobacco program limits production and requires tobacco product companies to pay a fair price for what tobacco farmers grow.

However, by 1985, record crops and tobacco manufacturers' increasing dependence on cheaper foreign-grown tobacco generated a domestic surplus. This surplus eventually led to price-support concessions and reductions in production quotas. These moves had a devastating impact on tobacco farmers in the late 1980s. Moreover, since 1990, tobacco quotas have moved up and down (for example, in 1995) seemingly without explanation, causing confusion and uncertainty, and Kentucky's Long-Term Policy Research Center projected a permanent 40-percent decline in quotas while, surprisingly, quotas have increased in subsequent years.[11]

Nevertheless, increasingly strong public and political pressures to reduce, and possibly ban, the production and sale of tobacco products is threatening to have serious and far-reaching economic, social, political, cultural, and religious effects on family tobacco farmers, communities, and churches in the farm-sector counties of Central Appalachia. A crisis exists.

Because farmers and their families are in the forefront of those affected, tobacco churches in Central Appalachia have been experiencing the impact of this complicated issue for more than a decade. Moreover, there is every reason to believe that the near future holds more stress for churches and people of faith. The pressure already being felt in tobacco communities to grow less profitable crops—crops with uncertain markets—undoubtedly will grow stronger; as this pressure grows, so will the casualties from economic and social stress.

The Family Farm

The last forty years have brought many changes to agriculture and rural America nationally, and the family farms and rural communities in Central Appalachia have been challenged and frequently disquieted by those changes. The very survival of rural community and rural church has been, and is being, threatened. Gentle people have experienced pain, guilt, powerlessness, and economic chaos, frequently without the benefit of understanding or even a sympathetic ear on the part of the leaders and sustainers of their faith. Nonetheless, the church continues to be sought out and held up as a source of support. Current and future rural church leaders must make their family of faith a "safe-place" to share hurts and to receive not only pastoral support but prophetic leadership which will challenge what is unjust, immoral, and evil in our economic and political systems and in our society. Such leadership will honestly question the politics and policies that shape the future of family farming and rural communities in our subregion, and it will point out what the rural and the urban crises have in common.

The Urban Stake in the Rural Farm Crisis

Long-term trends in agriculture favor "big corporate" or "industrial" farming. Corporate "monopolistic" control of food production means: (1) higher priced and lower quality food for the consumer; (2) an increase, reminiscent of the Dust Bowl in the 1930s, in the numbers of bankrupt farmers migrating to the cities in search of ever fewer, highly competitive jobs; (3) rapidly growing dependence upon urban tax-financed welfare programs and an ensuing increase in urban homelessness; (4) a general nationwide decline in civic life and local democracy; (5) an escalating level of environmental damage to our land and water resources; and (6) growing violations of basic justice issues.

For example, food currently is one of the main "weapons" used in U.S. foreign policy to keep Third World countries in the "Western" political camp. In fact, long-term world hunger has been increased by cheap U.S. food exports to Third World countries. Such exports have driven Third World farmers from the land and at the same time bankrupted family farmers in the U.S. Columnist Frank Farmer, writing in the *Springfield (Mo.) News-Leader,* paints this picture of a countryside dominated by industrial agriculture:

> The countryside of tomorrow will not be pretty. Private estates comprising tens of thousands of acres will stretch along major highways. . . . Once-public roads will be closed, too, for bankrupt county seat towns will have no means to maintain the roadways, no funds to fight corporate lawyers in the courts. Food prices will soar. They will demand half or more of your disposable income. [In 1993, 11.1 percent of disposable income was spent on food.][12] The pretty flowers, the interesting rocks across the fence, you dare not touch, for it will have become the property of someone foreign to your way of life, your hopes, and your dreams. You may become their servant. You will never become their equal.[13]

It seems that already we are far down the road to becoming this kind of nation. Many of us who are but one or two generations removed from the land ourselves have lost our roots in the land and among its people. Values and convictions rooted in past generations who lived from the land seem to have no place in contemporary urban and suburban society. Even the term "family farm" is viewed as a nostalgic throwback to a distant past.

Combine the seeming "social acceptance" of family farm losses with the notion that "rural" still equates with "backward," and it is easy to see why failing farmers often are perceived as "inefficient" or "unable to make it in the real world" of today's agribusiness. In the same breath, the people who feed the nation can be condemned and romanticized, judged and praised, put down and lifted up. Usually, they are just irrelevant, outside the scope of our daily experience—even as we trace our own history related to the land, or go to the grocery store, or sit down to eat.[14]

The Tobacco Culture—Positive and Negative Values

The tobacco culture, the tobacco economy, the social structures it supports, its complex marketing system, and the health and ethical issues surrounding its use are systemic to tobacco-dependent family farms in Central Appalachia. The social structure supported by the tobacco economy, for example, is a complex structure of positive and negative values. It is negative in that it supports a "feudal" class structure of low tenants (day laborers with limited education and no capital assets, as well as a rapidly growing number of migrant farm laborers); high tenants (likely to be better educated and frequently owning their own farm machinery—but still landless); small landowners (typically family farmers and the mainstays of most rural tobacco churches); and large landowners and absentee landowners (a growing class and one which spawns yet another class, professional farm managers). It is positive, in that the predominant class—the small landowner—is very much oriented toward family and community, constituting an unusual postmodern social enclave in a modern society still bent on the industrialization of agriculture.[15]

The Tobacco Grower and the Tobacco Industry

Health and ethical issues present another complex set of problems. Noone, not even the tobacco farmer, maintains that the use of tobacco is healthy. But denial frequently is evident regarding the seriousness of health problems said to be created by its use. From an economic perspective, however, with little support for diversification, small family farmers seem to be forced by a monoculture system into growing a never-ending, but less and less profitable, supply of tobacco. This tobacco is being directed by the industry toward vulnerable social groups in the U.S. and toward the Third World. The dilemma is either to grow and keep a strong and worthwhile social system intact; or not to grow, thereby turning the growing of tobacco over to large industrial farms in, and outside, the U.S. Industrial farms, guided by an economic opportunist mentality and benefiting from economies of scale, will continue to supply the tobacco industry and at the same time sign the death warrant of an important and irretrievable segment of the American dream—the small landowner, the economic entity whom Thomas Jefferson called "the most precious part of the state."[16]

Church Resources in Farm Counties

In the face of such disturbing issues among our families of faith, what has "the church" brought to the table"? The answer to this question encompasses national, regional, and local manifestations of "the church."

Nationally, the Presbyterian Church, U.S.A., primarily through its "hunger program"; the United Methodist Church, which has organized and supports a growing cadre of "rural chaplains"; and the Roman Catholic Church, through its "National Catholic Rural Life Conference," are three outstanding examples of funded programming directed toward issues relating to the rural/farm crisis.

However, national church funding programs tend to focus on and support strong national rural advocacy organizations, or organizations primarily serving the Midwest. The number of rural chaplains located in Central Appalachia stays in the single digits, and the National Catholic Rural Life Conference is not active in the subregion.

Regionally, the Kentucky Council of Churches (KCC) has organized and supports a Rural Life Issues Program. The Commission on Religion in Appalachia (CORA), through its Appalachian Development Projects Coalition (ADCP), funds the Community Farm Alliance (CFA; a statewide, chapter-based family farmers organization) and Livingston Economic Alternatives in Progress (a farm-product marketing cooperative), both located in Kentucky. And the Appalachian Ministries Educational Resource Center (AMERC) continues to integrate family farm ministry fully into its January and summer-term curricula. The six-week summer course has a well-developed special-interest-group course on Appalachian Family Farm Ministry, with an experiential learning component.

The KCC Rural Life Issues Program has conducted family-farm-issue workshops, organized workshops for farm women, run a "peer listening program" (funded by the National Presbyterian Hunger Program), and developed a "tobacco crisis" resolution, which was adopted at the KCC annual meeting in 1994. Currently the Rural Life Issues Program is monitoring the increase in Hispanic farm workers and advocating for English-language classes to be sponsored by local faith communities, writes articles on rural life issues for the KCC *Intercom*, and develops state legislative initiatives, in cooperation with the Community Farm Alliance. In the past, legislative initiatives have dealt with expanding agriculture credit, limiting corporate farm ownership, and similar matters. Moreover, the KCC Rural Life Issues Program continues to advocate and lobby for state and national legislation that is pro–family farm, pro-sustainable, and pro-environmental. Finally, this KCC program is the ecumenical home ground for isolated denominational rural-advocacy staff from around the state.

Gifts to troubled farm families locally are, unfortunately, few. Many congregations have, or have access to, community food pantries and clothing banks. Such direct relief would be given freely, if a farm family in crisis could but swallow its pride and ask. Individual counseling also is available, its quality and quantity dependent upon the education, experience, and sensitivity of the pastor.

Too often, however, critical economic situations are ignored or trivialized, or the victim is blamed. David Ostendorf, a rural ministry specialist, writes poignantly of this reality.

> The church's response to this crisis (and others) lies in its ability to deal better with the issues of death than with the struggles of life. In rural areas, in particular, death or disaster brings quick response from the community to the victims. A deadly storm, a fire, or the natural death of a family member engenders widespread church and community support. Within hours, shelter, food, and clothing are provided, or the kitchen table of the grieving family is laden with casseroles, pies, and cakes. But let that same family lose their farm or small business and measure the response. There may well be none, for indeed . . . we do find it difficult to respond in ministry to those life situations that represent economic failure and social decline. It is, in short, the story of a farm couple who attended the same church for thirty years and, when they were broke, were not visited by the pastor or any church member.[17]

Nonetheless, in the farm-sector counties of eastern Kentucky, some more specific and relevant gifts are being offered by fragments of congregations or by groups of cooperating congregations. A majority of the Bethel Christian Church congregation, in Bath County, Kentucky, for example, is composed of activist members of the Community Farm Alliance (CFA). These members do not represent themselves as "the congregation," but they use the sanctuary and fellowship hall for CFA meetings and educational events. Moreover, the bulletin board in the fellowship hall overflows with clippings about CFA legislative advocacy initiatives and Bath County chapter events.

In Garrard County, Kentucky, Christian Church (Disciples of Christ) congregations have formed the Garrard County Cooperative Parish (GCCP) and have recently been joined by a Church of the Nazarene. Along with more traditional direct service, youth, and elderly ministries, GCCP has organized literacy and General Equivalency Diploma (GED) classes at three locations in the county, operates a Job Clearing House, and was the primary mover in organizing a county-wide Habitat for Humanity organization. Related to the tobacco farm crisis, GCCP has written letters and made calls, as a parish, to advocate for legislation supporting family tobacco farms. It also has operated a tobacco labor hotline, in cooperation with CFA.

The potential to activate congregations, parts of congregations, and/or groups of congregations is real and pressing. Fortunately, mainline congregations with resources and, it may be hoped, the inclination to become involved with family farm ministry tend to be found in many counties with high family farm concentrations—that is, along the western edge of Kentucky–Central Appalachia and the eastern edge of Virginia–Central Appalachia (see map 2.3). However, this pattern is not seen in parts of eastern Kentucky or in the Tennessee counties with high family farm concentrations.

The only reluctance found in many communities has to do with attitudes about what the church is supposed to "be" or "do." Does the congregation minister only to the "spiritual needs" of its members, or does it become actively and holistically involved in the lives of its members and their community?

Attitudes Toward Family Farm Ministry

In spring and summer of 1995, a survey of the church and its social response, related to family farm ministry, was sent to sixty broadly selected pastors and laypeople. Thirty-seven responses were received. Table 2.5 compares social response (high, moderate, or low) related to family farm ministry, by category of respondent: farmer versus nonfarmer; living in Appalachia versus not living in Appalachia; CFA member versus non-CFA member; member of mainline denomination versus member of evangelical-Pentecostal denomination; and clergy versus laity. The table also gives the numbers of respondents who thought pastors should, or should not, preach on themes or issues related to the farm crisis.

Analysis of the responses discloses the following. First, farmers, expectably, are more aware than nonfarmers of the economic crisis and stress, and a sizable majority believes that the church should have a strong family farm ministry and that the pastor should preach on themes or issues related to the farm crisis. Second, this was true whether or not the place of residence was Appalachia. Third, the survey showed that the CFA is doing its job in educating its farm members about the crisis and encouraging an appropriate response from the church. (CFA always has had strong professional and lay church leadership on its board and in its membership). Fourth, the social response is not affected very much by the respondent's church membership preference. The percentage of high social responses

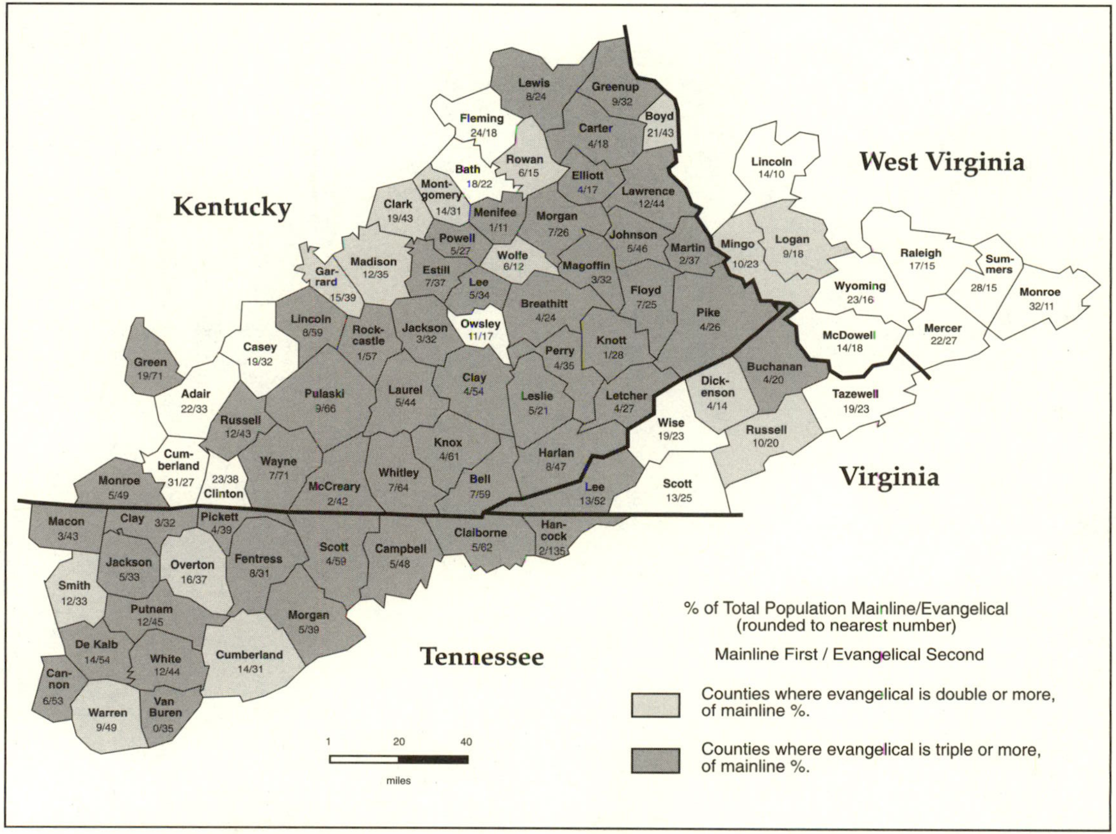

Map 2.3. Mainline and Evangelical Dominance in Counties of the Central Appalachian Subregion. SOURCE: *Churches and Church Membership in the United States, 1990* (Atlanta: Glenmary Research Center, 1992).

Table 2.5

Survey of Attitudes Relevant to Family Farm Ministry

Farmer			Nonfarmer		
Number of Responses	Response Ranking	% of Total	Number of Responses	Response Ranking	% of Total
14	H	70	10	H	58
3	M	15	2	M	13
3	L	15	5	L	29
In Appalachia			Not in Appalachia		
Number of Responses	Response Ranking	% of Total	Number of Responses	Response Ranking	% of Total
15	H	72	9	H	75
3	M	14	2	M	17
3	L	14	1	L	8
CFA Member			Not CFA Member		
Number of Responses	Response Ranking	% of Total	Number of Responses	Response Ranking	% of Total
10	H	79	14	H	58
2	M	16	3	M	13
1	L	8	7	L	29
Main Line			Evangelical-Pentecostal		
Number of Responses	Response Ranking	% of Total	Number of Responses	Response Ranking	% of Total
21	H	66	3	H	60
4	M	12	1	M	20
7	L	22	1	L	20
Clergy			Lay		
Number of Responses	Response Ranking	% of Total	Number of Responses	Response Ranking	% of Total
6	H	50	16	H	73
2	M	17	3	M	11
4	L	33	4	L	16

Should pastors preach on themes or issues related to the farm crisis?
Yes = 27   No = 10

SOURCE: Bennett Page, *Survey of Attitudes to the Church and Family Farm Ministry* (Richmond, Ky.: Christian Church, Disciples of Christ in Kentucky, Appalachian Ministry, Aug., 1995).

Notes:
Based on 37 responses out of 60 surveyed pastors and laypeople, spring and summer, 1995.

CFA = Community Farm Alliance

Social Response Ranking: H = High. Aware of farm-family economic crisis and stress. Aware that the church should minister to farm families in crisis and has some idea of how to do it. Believes that pastors should preach on themes or issues related to the farm crisis. M = Moderate. Somewhat aware of farm-family economic crisis and stress. Aware that the church should minister to farm families in crisis but may not know how to do it. May have reservations about pastors preaching on themes or issues related to the farm crisis. L = Low. Only moderately aware of farm-family economic crisis and stress. Does not believe that the church should single out farm families for special ministry. Does not believe pastors should preach on themes or issues related to the farm crisis.

was almost the same in mainline and evangelical-Pentecostal categories. Finally, the clergy's response was surprisingly conservative, with 33 percent choosing a low social response and only 50 percent choosing a high response. This is partly because the lay response came primarily from farmers and CFA members, while the clergy response came primarily from nonfarmers and non-CFA members. Nonfarmer clergy, unfortunately, may feel that "they don't have a dog in this fight." But it also suggests that a lot of education of the clergy needs to take place, because, in fact, "everyone has a dog is in this fight."

In 1991, Brian Cole, then a student in the Appalachian Ministries Educational Resource Center (AMERC) Summer Program and now an AMERC staff member, surveyed thirty lay and clergy people in the Appalachian farm-sector Kentucky counties of Bath, Clark, and Montgomery. He asked the question: Should pastors preach on themes or issues related to the farm crisis? Responses were both affirmative and negative:

> *No,* preaching should be strictly from the Bible. *Yes,* the prophets spoke with courage about justice issues of their time. Evil must be named and preached against. *No,* it is the clergy's responsibility to preach strictly form the Bible on God's Word, not to use the pulpit as a social or political forum. *Yes,* the land belongs to the people and God speaks of that. The year of Jubilee is an important theme for farmers to hear.[18]

As Cole points out, both yes and no responses point to a high value being placed upon Scripture. However, "those who oppose preaching on farm issues seem to suggest the Bible has nothing to say on the matter [their canon is too limited]. At the same time, those who support such preaching do so because of their beliefs that Scripture speaks directly to the crisis facing rural farms. For these folks, the farm crisis is a justice issue which the Bible is able to address."[19] This suggests that not only do the clergy need educating, but also we have a lot of biblical teaching and preaching to do in our rural churches before we can get congregations to agree on support for advocacy and coalition building around family farm issues.[20]

Future Ministries

First, as the previous section on attitudes toward family farm ministry indicates, clergy education concerning the universality of the family farm crisis—the rural-urban connection—needs to be a part of any planning for future family farm ministries.

Second, intentional teaching and preaching on biblically centered justice needs to take place even in the "most affected" congregations. Mel West, editor of the *United Methodist Rural Fellowship Bulletin,* says, "The church must begin to preach and teach the best of liberation theology. Liberation theology says that God did not create us to be second-class citizens. God has gifted us with the mind and the ability to assess our situation, to set our own priorities, and to work together to achieve common goals that are good for the community and for the kingdom."[21]

Third, any future family farm ministry in Central Appalachia, if it is not founded on the bankrupt belief that industrial agriculture and a depopulated countryside are best for America, must deal with an economic system to support family farm agriculture. This system must have a short-term economic and political strategy—namely, to keep the tobacco program intact. And it must have a long-term economic and political strategy to promote and develop a diversified farm economy and to decrease reliance upon tobacco. A 1985 report from the Rural Advancement Fund, for example, states: "Our goal should not be to save tobacco—but to save those whose livelihood depends on tobacco."[22] And we must promote the development of a federal-state cooperative "commodity transition program" which would "help tobacco growers move into alternative crop/livestock production."[23]

Given the massive nature of the problem, it seems clear that any optimistic future must entail federal and state assistance and federal price support for shifting to a more diversified alternative family economy. Reliance upon the so-called "free market" and the private sector will not produce an optimistic future.[24]

Fourth, family farm ministry planners must look realistically at how those strategies can be achieved. Setting public policy agenda goals, and a lengthy and concerted effort of political advocacy, are required. Moreover, it will be necessary to form coalitions to support such an advocacy effort. What role the tobacco church can and should play in supporting such advocacy and coalition-building efforts also must be determined.

Loretta Picciano, executive director of the Rural Coalition, addresses the role of the community of faith in public policy this way:

> At its best, to stand with the people; hear what they say; and collect them together to create alternate visions, try out models, propose policies, build networks, and renew hope. After all, most policy change occurs because someone has the audacity to make it happen. Social, economic, and environmental justice are simply not priorities of the agribusiness and other interests which have been most aggressive and influential in constructing our

current policies. Our experience of the last decade demonstrates that, most of all, we need the audacity to believe that God is with each of us and together we have the ability to understand, to act, and to make policy which manifests justice instead of injustice.[25]

Fifth, any view of the future which is not grasping nostalgically for a return to the "good old days" must step beyond modernity and grasp a vision of what a postmodern rural America might look like. Harvey Cox sees the breakdown of modernity in all of society—in the collapsing system of sovereignty, in the decline in the power and prestige of science-based technology, in the growing move to decentralization, in a questioning of the spectacular spread of multinational capitalism, and in the beginning of the end of a secularized religion which Cox calls a "trivialized and tamed religion."[26]

The best comparison of modern (or "conventional") agriculture with postmodern ("alternative") agriculture envisions postmodern rural America as including:

Decentralization, with more farmers and a dispersed control of land, resources, and capital.

Independence, with smaller, less expensive production units and technology.

Community, with increased cooperation and the preservation of farm traditions and rural culture.

Harmony with nature, with humans as part of, and subject to, nature; in which nature is respected and not seen as an enemy to be conquered.

Diversity, with multiple crops and integration of crops and livestock.

Restraint in consideration of all external costs, in the use of nonrenewable resources, in consumption, and in the use of science and technology.[27]

Sixth, stepping back from the vision of the larger community, family farm ministry planners need to look at what the church could be in this postmodern future: collegial, open, concerned for community, cooperative, ecumenical, perhaps comprising a union of churches which serves one area, the church working alongside community organizations, open to movement of the spirit, strong on leadership development.

Specifically, David Ostendorf has listed some ideas of what the church could be and do in a postmodern future. He suggests the following modes of ideal response for the congregation:

Education and Training—Helping people understand the farm crisis.

Advocacy—Becoming spokespersons for the movement.

Organizing and Coalition-building—Providing a structure for groups to come together.

Leadership Development and Support—Allowing space for farmers to tell their stories.

Public Policy—Speaking out on the crisis and naming the powers that cause injustice and oppress the rural community.

Public Witness and Direct Action—Becoming visible as a member of the family farm movement.

Use of Church Resources—Using resources wisely and considering the support of rural farm causes.

Support Regenerative Agriculture—Challenging farmers to consider wiser and better ways of farming. Encouraging farmers to take a hard look at how this land is used and often exploited by farmers themselves.[28]

Such direct action responses will not necessarily be comfortable for the church. They will require struggle and sacrifice. But for those who act in the name of a just God, the rewards of a sustainable and growing rural community, and with it a sustainable and growing rural church, await.

Two possible futures exist for family farm churches in Central Appalachia. One is to be empty and quiet in a countryside devoid of people, with boarded-up towns and decaying houses. The other is to be full and alive in a countryside overflowing with farm families, prosperous homes, and growing, progressive communities. The choice is ours to make.[29]

Notes

1. Kentucky Council of Churches, Program Unit on Rural Life Issues, *The Tobacco Farm Crisis in Kentucky: An Action Plan for Churches* (Lexington: Kentucky Council of Churches, Oct. 21, 1994).

2. B. D. Poage, ed., *The Tobacco Church: A Manual for Congregational Leaders* (Richmond, Ky.: Christian Church in Kentucky, Kentucky Appalachian Ministry, 1993), 1.

3. Ibid., 85.

4. W. Kessler, *Jobs and Economic Development: Meeting the Needs of Appalachian People* (Lexington: Univ. of Kentucky, Appalachian Center, 1991), 6.

5. Richard A. Couto, *Beyond Distress: New Measures of Economic Need in Appalachia* (Knoxville, Tenn.: Commission on Religion in Appalachia, Oct. 28, 1992), appendix, pp. 2–3, 6.

6. B. D. Poage, *Farm Income in Kentucky, 1981–1993: Comparisons and Comments*

[compiled from U.S. Dept. of Commerce statistics] (Richmond, Ky.: Christian Church in Kentucky, Kentucky Appalachian Ministry, June 1995), 4.

7. Ibid., chart 2, p. 4.

8. U.S. Dept. of Labor, Bureau of Labor Statistics, *Compounded Annual Inflation Rates* (Washington, D.C.: GPO, Nov. 1995).

9. Kentucky Agricultural Statistics Service, *Kentucky Agricultural Statistics, 1994–1995* (Louisville, Ky.: Kentucky Agricultural Statistics Service, Sept. 1995), 116.

10. B. D. Poage, ed., *The Tobacco Church II: A Manual for Congregational Leaders* (Richmond, Ky.: Christian Church in Kentucky, Kentucky Appalachian Ministry, 1995), 102.

11. Ibid.

12. U.S. Dept. of Agriculture, Economic Research Service, *National Income Spent on Food* (Washington, D.C.: 1994).

13. Presbyterian Church, U.S.A., *The Church Responding to Rural America* (Louisville, Ky.: Evangelism and Church Development Ministry Unit, Presbyterian Church [U.S.A.], June 1991), 49.

14. Poage, ed. *Tobacco Church II*, 3–4.

15. Ibid., 4.

16. Ibid., 4–5.

17. D. Ostendorf, "Toward Wholeness and Community: Strategies for Pastoral and Political Response to the American Rural Crisis," *Word and World* [St. Paul, Minn.] 6, no. 1 (Winter 1986): 57.

18. B. Cole, "A Pastoral Model for the Family Farm Crisis" (unpublished paper, 1991, on file at Appalachian Ministries Educational Resource Center).

19. Ibid.

20. Poage, ed., *Tobacco Church*, 87.

21. M. West, "An Opiate for the People," *The Five Stones: A Newsletter for Small Churches* [Block Island, R.I.], vol. 13, no. 3 (Fall 1995): 21.

22. Rural Advancement Fund, *Uncertain Harvest: A Report on North Carolina Agriculture* (Pittsboro, N.C.: Rural Advancement Fund, Jan. 1985), 11.

23. Ibid., 13.

24. Poage, ed., *Tobacco Church*, 86.

25. L. Picciano-Hanson, "Churches Take Role in Public Policy," *Prairie Journal* [Des Moines, Iowa], vol. 2, no. 2 (Summer 1991): 6.

26. H. Cox, *Religion in the Secular City* (New York: Simon and Schuster, 1984), 186–90.

27. C. E. Beus and Dunlap, R. E., "Conventional Versus Alternative Agriculture: The Paradigmatic Roots of the Debate," *Rural Sociology* 55, no. 4 (Winter 1990): 598–99.

28. Ostendorf, "Toward Wholeness," 62–65.

29. Poage, ed., *Tobacco Church*, 89–90.

Chapter 3

Popular Religiosity in Central Appalachia

CHARLES H. LIPPY

Perhaps no region of the United States has received more attention for its presumably unique religious character than the South. Within that region, Appalachia (the boundaries of which do not necessarily fit into those assigned to "the South") has attracted particular consideration. Whenever newspaper headlines trumpet the death of someone as a result of handling poisonous snakes during worship, as they did during the summer of 1995, prevailing misperceptions of religion in Appalachia are reinforced. Even many with greater sensitivity to the religious pulse of the region have been captivated by an array of images that at best reflect only the outermost layer of Appalachian religiosity: the countless independent churches nestled in the mountains, the many numerically small Baptist congregations representing denominational clusters familiar primarily to the people of Appalachia, the homecomings and foot washings, the shaped-note hymns, the now-declining number of radio broadcasts proffering a simple gospel conveyed through frenzied preaching and the twang of religious "country and western" music.

Long the object of missions spearheaded by those intent upon etching the style of the old-line denominations on this already rich religious landscape, the people of Appalachia repeatedly have found that the primary interest of outsiders was in documenting the quaint and the primitive, the relics of a time long past, thought to endure here in near-pristine form. Convinced that the religious styles flourishing outside Appalachia were superior and closer to the ultimate, precious few of these well-intentioned observers—whether missionaries, government representatives, or scholars—have recognized the internal integrity that marks Appalachian religiosity and the coherent world view that enables the women and men of Appalachia to make sense of their human experience.[1]

Part of the difficulty stems from the understanding of religion that analysts are prone to adopt without probing its implications. Simply put, there is a tendency to equate religion with belief and public practice, and in turn to equate belief with doctrine. Howard Dorgan, who has written extensively and sensitively about numerous facets of the religious life of Appalachia, has called attention to the personal nature of much religion in the region, the emphasis on personal salvation that pervades much of the implicit theology of the region's religious institutions, and the various practices these institutions embody in public worship.[2] But Dorgan's expositions generally stop at the level of formal doctrine and practice. So, too, does the classic collection of interviews found in Foxfire 7.[3] Most of those interviewed were preachers; most of the questions asked them dealt with doctrine and public practice. These are typical of those studies which restrict belief to doctrine.

What this approach cannot hope to discern is what ordinary people make of such doctrine and practice in the course of their daily lives. It cannot begin to see beneath the surface to the dynamics of what I call popular religiosity—the ways in which people themselves construct and maintain an understanding of reality that allows them to explain and interpret their personal and collective experience.[4] For popular religiosity, formal belief (doctrine), and public practice (what transpires "in church") are only part of a personal mix of ideas and actions that comprise the means by which individuals take the pieces of life's puzzle and craft them into a whole. Hence, to explore popular religiosity in Appalachia is, for example, to go well beyond the doctrine of salvation that Old Regular Baptists may be able to discuss with great clarity, or the speaking in tongues and other manifestations of the baptism of the Spirit more common among Pentecostals. It is to look at the contours of daily life more than at what transpires in the context of corporate worship.[5]

Two features of popular religiosity especially recur in much of Appalachian mountain religion, although they are expressed in a variety of ways and often in language different from mine:

1. A sense that the world of everyday life is a realm of power, an arena

where supernatural forces of good and evil are operative. Popular religiosity revolves in part around gaining access to divine supernatural power that assures triumph over the forces of evil.

2.   An understanding that life transpires simultaneously in two dimensions of time, the present and the future, and on two levels of reality, the "here and now" and the hereafter. For those trapped in Enlightenment modes of thinking, in each case the former element is identified with empirical reality and represents all that can be known. But for those imbued with power, the future beyond this life that will come on a higher plane not only transcends empirical reality, but is far superior to it.

Both ideas require explication.

A Sense of Power

Many of those writing about religion in Appalachia have talked about religion as power. Often there has been a faulty assumption behind their reasoning. The traditional argument has been that the feeling of power generated by such ecstatic religious expressions as glossolalia or snake-handling compensates for a deprivation of power in the empirical realm; that is to say, the statistics identifying Appalachia as a region of poverty must mean that people turn to religion as a solace. Deborah Vansau McCauley, in her *Appalachian Mountain Religion*, repeatedly demonstrates that this understanding is a gross distortion. Appalachian popular religiosity has nothing to do with deprivation. But it does have to do with an understanding of the world as a realm of supernatural power—an understanding akin to that which anthropologists have documented in nonindustrial tribal cultures. This perspective also is reflective of the biblical world view of someone such as Saint Paul, for whom the "elemental spirits of the universe," the "principalities and powers," were very much parts of daily life.

In Appalachia, this sense of the world as a realm of power may be most obvious among those attracted to strains of Holiness-Pentecostal Christianity. As Troy Abell noted, among those he studied, life is a highly personal and continual struggle because of the constant threat of temptation attributed to the Devil or Satan. Contemporary society and the present time seem fraught with evil, but such represents the work of the Devil.[6] Indeed, as Abell argued, in the daily experience of ordinary men and women there is a delicate balance of power between God and the Devil. A dimension of mystery surrounds this struggle, particularly in connection with the strength of evil power. Here traditional doctrine creeps into popular religiosity, for the larger belief system of formal Christianity affirms the omnipotence of God. Hence, the daily struggle against the forces of evil and some of its overt manifestations, as in sickness and the necessity of constant hard work, must transpire through the divine will, perhaps as warnings of what may come in the next life should one not be aligned with the supernatural power of God. Life here and now may be a struggle between ordinary people and the Devil, but that is not the whole story.

For those in the Holiness-Pentecostal orbit, the experience of the Holy Spirit introduces one to a superior power, one that assures ultimate triumph in life's battles against forces of evil. Observations from two of Troy Abell's informants are to the point: "The Holy Ghost, he brings into your life—power." "In this day, you need an 'in' with the power of God."[7] Hence the speaking in tongues that often is the initial experience of baptism with the power of the Holy Spirit is both a sign of the presence of supernatural power and an assurance that one now has sufficient control over the forces of evil to emerge triumphant in the next life. So, too, the numerous accounts of faith healing among Holiness-Pentecostal people are indicative, in their view, not only of miraculous cures, but also of a control over evil forces that would impede life as it moves toward its heavenly destiny.

Both glossolalia and faith healing are part of the larger genre of ecstatic religious experience in which the power of the Spirit takes control of the individual. Although it seems for the moment that the individual has lost control in an empirical sense, for the believer it is more an exchange of control. Daily life reveals only too vividly the limits of human power; the baptism of the Holy Ghost allows one to tap into a realm of power far more efficacious. Perhaps because the experience is self-authenticating, it carries with it an assurance not only that this sacred power will manifest itself again, but that it is always available to sustain the individual in the ordinary course of life.

In this context, the significance to their practitioners of such practices as serpent handling, ingestion of poisonous substances such as strychnine, and fire handling becomes much more clear.[8] Debates about whether such phenomena are based on a spurious ending to the gospel of Mark or indicative of a misguided religious fanaticism miss the point altogether. The heart of the matter is that serpent handling, for example, directly draws the believer into a realm of power; one literally has the power of life and death in one's hands. Hence handling serpents is not merely a test of the authenticity or degree of one's faith, but an entrée into the arena of supernatural power. While detractors are drawn more to comment on the cases where persons have suffered adverse effects and even death, some long-time advocates regard the very act of handling the serpents as using the power that God gives to the faithful.[9]

Serpent handlers and those who speak in tongues while in the throes of religious ecstasy represent selected strands of an Appalachian popular religiosity oriented to power. Different approaches may be found among the many strains of Baptists who occupy a vital part of the region's religious landscape. At first glance, the Primitive Baptists and Old Regular Baptists seem farthest removed from those of a Pentecostal bent because of the Calvinistic predestinarian doctrinal base that undergirds their doctrine of salvation.[10] Yet even here a lively sense of power prevails.

On the one hand, the notion of predestination itself revolves around an appreciation of the absolute power of God, who providentially determines who shall receive salvation. What stands out is the contrast between divine power and human helplessness here and hereafter, apart from that power. The hope of election, manifested in holy living, serves as a reminder of the presence of sacred power, although now what Dorgan calls the "bad in life" (hard work, ill health, loneliness, loss of loved ones, suffering, death, and the like) seems to prevail.[11] Even sermons extolling the joys of salvation through God's supreme power often caution the faithful about the constant peril of Satan's temptations, which might cause one to doubt one's own worthiness of election.

On the other hand, among predestinarian Baptists of whatever stripe, the practice of prayer provides a means of access to the supernatural power of God that allows one to cope with the "bad in life." Finite humans indeed are powerless to deal with the vicissitudes that mark the empirical realm. Prayer offers the possibility of ultimate triumph over them. Simply put, God will protect and provide for those whom God has called to salvation.

Prayer provides a point of connection among many strands of Appalachian popular religiosity.[12] The personal testimonies that may be more prevalent in worship among those less directly influenced by Calvinistic predestinarian thinking frequently highlight how prayer works to draw individuals into the orbit of divine power as they meet the situations of daily life. Prayer signifies the willingness of the individual to recognize the superior power of God to resolve problems and to bring victory in the never-ending battle with demonic power. Some who handle serpents point to the centrality of prayer in creating the conditions necessary for the "higher power" of the Holy Spirit to become manifest.[13] For those who espouse predestinarianism in formal doctrine, prayer provides a link to a providential power that works for human good in the present; for others, prayer leads to an optimism about daily life, to be realized at least in part here and now. The many writers who have criticized Appalachian religiosity for its presumed fatalism fail to grasp this understanding of power in prayer and elsewhere.

In this context, one also can appreciate the important role that religious radio, especially, and then television have played in sustaining much Appalachian popular religiosity. Most of the religious radio that has originated in Appalachia has reflected an Arminian, rather than Calvinistic, doctrinal orientation, as well as a strong Pentecostal influence.[14] But central to virtually all these indigenous radio broadcasts are personal testimonies and requests for prayer that come from listeners. The testimonies frequently recount how the power of prayer has brought victory (and therefore a sense of control) in the ordinary course of life. The requests for prayer, often very detailed in sketching specific life situations, assume that prayer will bring results. As a body these communications reinforce the popular conviction that prayer is an effective means of tapping into the reservoir of divine power to achieve mastery over the demonic forces responsible for the travails of life.

Although what has been dubbed "televangelism" lacks the direct regional identification that is vital to religious radio programming that originates in Appalachia, it does serve a similar function. Even if some of the more popular televangelists have suffered disgrace and no longer are on the air, their glamour and their enthusiastic witness buttressed the popular expectation that reliance on the power of God would yield success. As I wrote elsewhere about mass-media religious programming more generally, "All proclaim a message of a God who cares for individuals and their problems. With only minor variation, all proffer a view of the world where the powers of evil are very real and intent on thwarting human happiness. In other words, all support that inchoate understanding basic to popular religiosity of a world where forces of good and evil are constantly engaged in combat for control of human life. All also present exuberant testimonies to the happiness and joy in living that comes from placing ultimate trust in the beneficent power of God, who can bring healing of illness and physical ailments as well as healing of psychological unsettledness. . . . A simple faith becomes a panacea that brings very specific results and grants individuals a sense that they can muster the power to control their own destiny."[15]

Another Plane of Reality

The presence of the power of the Holy Spirit in ecstatic experience, the assurance that a providential God looks out for the elect, and the reliance upon prayer as a way to actualize divine power together constitute one focus of several strains of Appalachian popular religiosity. The other focus has to do with the reality of a heavenly future, but one in which the present allows glimpses into its grandeur. The hope of heaven crosses denominational and theological lines; it is found among Calvinistic predestinarian Baptists, as well as among those with whom the Holiness-Pentecostal approach prevails.

This transcendent dimension of Appalachian popular religiosity, too, has led many commentators astray. Along with the tendency to castigate Appalachian popular religiosity as fatalistic and as compensating for a lack of empirical power by emphasizing an irrational, individualistic emotionalism, there has been a tendency to dismiss it as being excessively "otherworldly" and as perpetuating a personal ethic characteristic of "yesterday's people."[16] To take this stance is to miss the way in which the strong conviction of a heavenly afterlife serves to give meaning to the present. Simply put, the heavenly sphere becomes the plane of authentic existence; present reality pales in comparison. Indeed, even the constant struggles of everyday existence here and now take on fresh meaning when viewed from the perspective of eternity. The triumph in this life over troubles of whatever sort may be transient, but the signs of God's providence and the presence of spiritual power serve as indicators of what will be the ordinary reality in God's heavenly dominion—where adversity, sickness, pain, and death will have vanished. The present may be a time of preparation and testing, yet those whom God has chosen, or those to whom God has given the gift of the Holy Spirit, know that for them there awaits an eternity where all will be well.

Eleanor Dickinson and Barbara Benziger quote a Tennessee evangelist:

> Thank God! One of these days we're going to shout Thank God for ten million years. We're going to keep on shouting and keep on shouting. We're going to sit down at the table of the Lord and eat and eat and eat, Brother Ayers. And when we get through, we can go out and visit around the heavens and, thank God, the table will be ready when we come back. Isn't that going to be a wonderful place? And all the tears shall be wiped from our eyes, hallelujah! No more worries about having a job. No more worries about paying the income tax. No more worries about all those bills coming in because our God, hallelujah, will be the king of that place and all the bills will be paid. Amen.[17]

Little wonder, then, that Troy Abell found that those who had the gift of speaking in tongues were less fearful of death than others; their experience of the power of the Spirit already had introduced them to the heavenly realm.[18] And little wonder that, among those who support evangelistic preaching in revivals and the like, the threat of an eternity in Hell, where the tribulations of the present are magnified, often accompanied visions of a glorious afterlife for those who accepted salvation.

In this vein, one should be sensitive to numerous descriptions of the present as evil times marking the nearness of Christ's return and final triumph, in the interviews conducted by Paul Gillespie and his student associates (and recorded in *Foxfire 7*). These interviews were recorded among persons whose religious affiliations spanned the gamut from the old-line Protestant denominations to independent Pentecostal churches.[19] As the Southern Baptist Bly Owen put it, now is the day of tribulation.[20] Empirical reality becomes the domain of evil in part because of the intrigue wrought by supernatural forces of evil. Equally important, however, present evil can be identified, battled, and conquered because one affirms the reality of a higher realm.

This dimension of Appalachian popular religiosity also illuminates the emphasis on an ethic of individual behavior and personal morality that has intrigued so many observers. It is too easy to see taboos against alcohol, wearing makeup, indulging in certain forms of amusement, and the like as relics of an outdated fanaticism. Indeed, one consciously may avoid behaviors associated with a world where daily existence is characterized by a constant struggle between supernatural powers of good and evil. But one does so precisely because one is already part of another, vastly superior domain. How one lives in the present is a reflection of where one will stand at the Final Judgment.

Much the same holds true for those for whom the Calvinistic notion of predestination shapes personal religiosity. Dorgan, for example, noted how much preaching in Old Regular Baptist churches was focused on the joys of salvation or election.[21] Although individuals could not choose to accept salvation, they could heed God's call to their elect status. At the same time, it is telling that Dorgan subtitled his exposition of the Old Regular Baptists "Brothers and Sisters in Hope." What was the content of that hope but the desire to be worthy of life in God's eternal realm? Although, for these folk, the signs of God's election are not found in the power to handle serpents, to speak in tongues, or to heal the sick, they often are found in personal behavior that befits the saints of God. This behavior in turn is understood largely through contrasting it with the mores that prevail in the larger social order.

More formal expressions of the superior reality of heaven come at homecomings—those times when families return to worship in the churches of their childhoods, to feast on the grounds, and to clean and decorate church cemeteries—or similar occasions. Such gatherings provide opportunities not only to celebrate biological and spiritual kinship (and thus affirming the power reinforced by group identity), but also to validate the links between the present and the heavenly future. Heaven and earth are joined symbolically when the living mingle with the dead ones already rejoicing in the heavens.

Hence the lure of heaven in Appalachian popular religiosity is much more than a reflection of an "otherworldly" style. It represents "a vision of the new world that is hoped to be attained on this earth through conversion."[22] It matters not whether conversion comes through election or free choice. What matters is that heaven replaces earth as the locus of what is truly real.

Sustaining Popular Religiosity in Appalachia

What sustains these strands of popular religiosity? Maintenance of even a very private religious world view requires some external support; individuals must receive signals that confirm the legitimacy and plausibility of their own ways of making sense out of their experience. Several clues about such structures already have been given. Homecomings, for example, help support the rich notion of a heavenly sphere by linking present and future. Kinship is vital to those occasions, as well as to the larger social networks that prevail especially in much of the Appalachian mountain region. Carlene Bryant, for example, noted how the congregations she studied were composed primarily of extended families. Many of those who have explored the phenomenon of serpent handling have called attention to the significance of kinship in sustaining that practice; contemporary serpent handlers are more likely to come from families who have found power in that form of ecstatic expression for two or three generations.

A more subtle form of support for the sense of supernatural power that prevails in much Appalachian popular religiosity is also important. One need not personally handle serpents, speak in tongues, or have any direct confirmation of one's election to receive support for the popular religiosity that sustains them. When one sees another seized by the power of the Spirit, for example, one receives confirmation that the world is indeed a realm of power and that, through faith, one can access supernatural power that will lead to triumph in both this life and the life to come. If one is socialized into a milieu where serpents become symbols of sacred power, then one constantly is receiving validation for a world view that regards the world as an arena of power.

Here, too, we can understand the import of several other features of Appalachian religious life. For several decades, radio broadcasts and then, to a lesser degree, television broadcasts provided validation of personal religiosity. As one heard of others who had conquered the power of Satan as letters were read and stories told over the air, one gained fresh assurance that one's own understanding of reality was legitimate. In a similar vein, the practice of going from church to church, which prevails among some of the smaller Baptists groups and also some of the Pentecostal congregations, offers more than an opportunity to socialize and engage in worship on a more frequent basis. The network of associations they provide by linking like-minded individuals reinforces the legitimacy of individual religiosity, for one realizes that the same basic premises are held by others. The misinformed, who continue to see Appalachian popular religiosity as a relic of a bygone era or as a style that is at odds with the one proclaimed by the old-line denominations, rarely appreciate the depth of support these many structures provide for a way of looking at ordinary reality through a supernatural perspective. As long as there is support to maintain this lively sense of the supernatural and this transvaluation of time because of the hope of heaven, Appalachian popular religiosity will endure.

There is much more to Appalachian popular religiosity. But to begin to understand its dynamics and its pervasive presence, one must have an appreciation for the sense of supernatural power that marks the popular religious world view. One also must appreciate the transformation of empirical reality that results from viewing the here and now from a vantage point marked by all that this world is not. Perhaps the essence of Appalachian popular religiosity is best captured in the words of an old gospel song. It was written by the African American Methodist pastor, Charles Albert Tindley of Philadelphia, but it often is heard in Appalachia:[23]

> We are tossed and driven
>   on the restless sea of time.
> Sombre skies and howling tempest
>   oft succeeds a bright sunshine,
> In that land of perfect day,
>   when the mists have rolled away,
> We will understand it better by and by.

By and by when the morning comes
     All the saints of God are gathered home,
We will tell the story how we've overcome,
     For we'll understand it better by and by.

Trials dark on ev'ry hand
     and we cannot understand,
All the ways that God would lead us
     to that Blessed Promised Land
But He guides us with His eye
     and we'll follow 'till we die,
For we'll understand it better by and by.

Temptations, hidden snares,
     often take us unawares,
And our hearts are made to bleed
     for a thoughtless word or deed,
And we wonder why the test
     when we try to do our best;
But we'll understand it better, by and by.

Notes

1. The most important exception is Deborah Vansau McCauley, *Appalachian Mountain Religion* (Urbana: Univ. of Illinois Press, 1995), a study destined to refocus scholarly understanding of religion in Appalachia in general.

2. Among Howard Dorgan's important studies are *The Airwaves of Zion: Radio and Religion in Appalachia* (Knoxville: Univ. of Tennessee Press, 1993); *Giving Glory to God in Appalachia: Worship Practices of Six Baptist Subdenominations* (Knoxville: Univ. of Tennessee Press, 1987); and *The Old Regular Baptists of Central Appalachia: Brothers and Sisters in Hope* (Knoxville: Univ. of Tennessee Press, 1989).

3. Paul F. Gillespie, ed., *Foxfire 7: Ministers, Church Members, Revivals, Baptisms, Shaped-note and Gospel Singing, Faith Healing, Camp Meetings, Footwashings, Snake-Handling, and Other Traditions of Mountain Religious Heritage* (Garden City, N.Y.: Anchor/Doubleday, 1982).

4. I have probed more deeply both the definition of popular religiosity and the reasons for its neglect by scholars in the opening chapter of Charles H. Lippy, *Being Religious, American Style: A History of Popular Religiosity in the United States* (Westport, Conn.: Greenwood, 1994).

5. One study that moves in this direction, although its focus is on just one strain

of Appalachian religion, is Troy D. Abell, *Better Felt Than Said: The Holiness-Pentecostal Experience in Southern Appalachia* (Waco, Tex.: Markham, 1982).

6. Ibid., 6, 148.

7. Ibid., 4, 5. The first quotation is from Hugo Wilson; the second from Frank Harper.

8. The best analysis is found in David L. Kimbrough, *Taking Up Serpents: Snake Handlers of Eastern Kentucky* (Chapel Hill: Univ. of North Carolina Press, 1995). Thomas Burton, *Serpent-Handling Believers* (Knoxville: Univ. of Tennessee Press, 1993), traces the development of these phenomena and summarizes previous lines of interpretation.

9. Burton, *Serpent-Handling*, 19, quotes serpent handler Perry Bettis of Birchwood, Tenn., as noting that God gives humans power that they are to use.

10. McCauley, *Appalachian Mountain Religion*, and Howard Dorgan's works offer the best expositions of the various Baptist clusters in Appalachia. Dorgan, however, tends to limit his explication of belief to what is found in sermons and rarely explores how people appropriate the ideas articulated in sermons in fashioning their personal religious worlds.

11. Dorgan, *Giving Glory to God in Appalachia*, 198.

12. For first-person accounts that illustrate this understanding of prayer, see Eleanor Dickinson and Barbara Benziger, *Revival!* (New York: Harper and Row, 1974), 117–25.

13. See Gillespie, *Foxfire 7*, 427. The section of this valuable book that treats serpent handling cites the text of a hymn, "Amen, Amen, There's a Higher Power," that is to the point. Ibid., 390.

14. Dorgan makes this point in *Airwaves of Zion*, 7. Dorgan's work is the only book-length description of this phenomenon.

15. Lippy, *Being Religious, American Style*, 200.

16. The phrase comes from Jack E. Weller, *Yesterday's People* (Lexington: Univ. of Kentucky Press, 1965).

17. Dickinson and Benziger, *Revival!* 93.

18. Abell, *Better Felt than Said*, 188.

19. Gillespie, *Foxfire 7*, passim.

20. Ibid., 44.

21. Dorgan, *Old Regular Baptists*, 73–74.

22. F. Carlene Bryant, *We're All Kin: A Cultural Study of a Mountain Community* (Knoxville: Univ. of Tennessee Press, 1981), 116–17.

23. "We'll Understand It All By and By," *Soul Echoes: A Collection of Songs for Religious Meetings, No. 3* (Philadelphia: Soul Echoes Publishing, 1909), no. 30.

Chapter 4

Uneven Ground: Cultural Values, Moral Standards, and Religiosity in the Heart of Appalachia

JANET BOGGESS WELCH

> The better approach to understanding a people's culture . . . the meanings, values, and thoughts that inform their lives—is for the middle-class observer to let the people speak for themselves and to record the results.
>
> —Allen Batteau, 1983

"Where the ground is uneven" is a favorite phrase writers use who want to refer in a dramatic literary fashion to Appalachia. However, the phrase also can be employed metaphorically to apply to states of mind characterizing the Appalachian hills and hollows in the latter half of this century. The ground is indeed "uneven" for West Virginians living in the heart of Appalachia and confronting the inroads of the modern age.

West Virginia is the only state which lies wholly within everyone's physical definition of Appalachia. The Appalachian Regional Commission's "expanded" definition involves thirteen states; the historical "shrunken" version of purists counts, at most, seven states. Thus, the "little

Switzerland" mountains of this heartland state are fertile ground for a researcher asking questions about contemporary currents of feeling in Appalachia. West Virginia is an integral portion of an area of the country which once was referred to as "forgotten" but today finds itself, much like the rest of the United States, caught up in change—change that causes stress and anxiety, change that is unlikely to quit.

Interstate highways now crisscross the Mountain State, and additional connecting sections are being added daily. More important, televisions now blare in every neat hillside ranch house and every dilapidated hollow shanty. This was true when this writer, a native West Virginian, returned to the state at intervals during the 1980s to cross and recross a rural area in the northern part of the state and another in the southern part of the state, listening and recording what the inhabitants had to say about a selected list of topics, dealing particularly with attitudes and beliefs. (This research effort produced 160 hours of taped oral interviews with rural West Virginians and a 345-page report on their stated attitudes, beliefs, and shared values.)

In the 1990s, the in-and-out traffic in the mountains had increased, and the blare from the television sets had intensified when the writer found herself once again entering into extensive conversations with rural people, having moved back to the state to live after residing elsewhere for several years. Thus the following observations are based upon both an earlier, carefully researched study with a purpose, a research plan, and a computer program to assess findings, and a later continuation of that research, with data gathered informally while living in the state and interacting with residents.

Local newspapers also proved valuable sources of current information. The widely circulated state newspapers, the *Charleston Gazette* and the *Charleston Daily Mail,* are among the few newspapers in the country, perhaps, where one reads as much about sin and salvation as about mayhem and murder, primarily because both newspapers devote a great deal of space to readers' letters and readers' "vent columns."

Religiosity of a fundamentalist type is alive and well in the mountains of West Virginia, but the way people feel about their lives, their relationship with their God, and their behavior is very much intertwined with the effects of the modern age on their cultural values. Some of these values the older generation is fiercely trying to retain, while regularly predicting their rapid demise under the stewardship of the younger generation.

The traditional cultural values attributed to Appalachians in general, as identified by earlier researchers, sometimes have been disavowed by those who originally identified and labeled them. Some of the early researchers came to feel that somehow their labels had been misunderstood and had cast Appalachia in a very unfavorable light;[1] still others have lauded these established values and voiced much pride in their distinctiveness. More recent scholars have scorned the persistent emphasis on such values, insisting that, by affirming that they do exist, one somehow is continuing to denigrate the people and the area, thereby heaping additional ridicule upon a people that has suffered enough at the hands of others. All of the above makes for a jarring, provocative body of literature about Appalachia.[2]

One has only to spend a few hours and days among older Appalachian rural folk, however, to conclude that such a sojourn would be somewhat different if spent among Iowa rural people. Opinions expressed, attitudes evinced, and values espoused really are not identical to—or, in some instances, not even similar to—those of rural people elsewhere. They *are* different, *peculiar to the region,* even in an age when television and technology rapidly are transforming many Americans from different parts of the country into facsimiles of each other.

In this essay, West Virginia is the research field, but the writer is venturing to assume that, since rural West Virginians and other Appalachian rural people share a past and a history, their current outlooks also overlap.

A Different Kind of Traditionalism

Rural West Virginians tend to emphasize the past and register a distinct longing for "the way things used to be." This preoccupation with traditionalism, however, seems to stem primarily from a disgust with, and a fear of, the present, more than from a blind loyalty to habit and custom. Encounters with mainstream society currently occur in two major ways, viewed by residents as both progressive advances and Pandora's boxes: television now comes into almost every hollow in the state, no matter how remote, and major interstate and other improved highways, largely the work of the Appalachian Regional Commission, now go out in every direction. The increased contact has had unforeseen results. Such exposure, instead of fostering a determination to emulate mainstream society, has led many contemporary rural Appalachians to voice a desire to withdraw more into the hills and to escape from what they consider to be the unpleasant nature of the world outside.

There seems to be very little envy of the material possessions showcased on television and certainly little desire to imitate the more extreme life styles. Rural people in the less populated areas of Appalachia actually may have less trouble than mainstreamers in distinguishing reality from the unreality of the television world. The settings and confrontations on television bear little resemblance to anything in their daily lives—and almost no relationship to any aspirations they might have. Therefore, television truly is "make-believe" to them, constituting a further indication of the "awfulness" of how people in the outside world think. They are convinced that people today have "too much." Respondents in linoleum-floored rooms in tar-paper shanties talk seriously about people in the U.S. as having "too many *things*." Their attitude is quite sincere and not a rationalization of their own limited means.

A majority genuinely are fearful of, and concerned about, "the direction the country seems to be taking." They are worried about the disintegration of the family. They say: "Young people just don't care about anything, and mothers won't stay home with their kids."

"Teachers should be allowed to paddle more."

"Teenagers are just too lazy and good-for-nothing today."

They mention over and over the widespread use of drugs and alcohol: "Potheads everywhere! and now them crack houses! In the olden days, moonshiners hid out in these hollows. Now the drug dealers have taken over, and the kids can get it anywhere around here."

They are critical of the lack of religious fervor and moral fiber: "What exactly do you mean by the word 'moral,' that we are not as 'good' as we used to be? That's certainly the truth. Why, twenty or thirty years ago, people knew right from wrong."

One tired schoolteacher, living in a seemingly remote valley, said that she was going to retire early because she was suffering from "burnout": "Even the grade-school youngsters are now coming to school under the influence of drugs. Parents are just not caring for their children anymore, and the school can't do it all."

In the 1980s, there were very few newspaper accounts of the proliferation of drugs in the hidden recesses of the hollows, and very few people in the more metropolitan areas knew of the invasion. By the early 1990s, the problem had ballooned to such proportions that most of the state's newspapers had begun carrying daily stories of drug raids, drug rings in small towns, and the attendant escalation of frequent violence and murder. The citizens in the hills were aware, long before the law enforcement agencies, of the growing extent of the problem. Drug operators find the more remote areas to be good hiding places and the interstate highways convenient for distribution. They lure mountain youngsters, impoverished and willing, into becoming runners and addicts—and they sweep up the more middle-class youngsters in the process. It is no wonder that the angry older Appalachians long for an earlier day when they were safe from such terrible inroads (moonshine seems very tame to them). Their remarks are not too different, perhaps, from those heard in our inner cities today, except that, behind their be- leaguered, frustrated tones, there is true puzzlement. They really do not understand how the "bad" aspects of modern life have reached their home area and are flourishing there. They are alarmed that "the hills have not been able to withstand the evil," as one person phrased his concern.

Many rural Appalachians today display a retreat mentality not un- like that of their ancestors, except that, in the past, mountain people were *forced* by a lack of communication and transportation to remain in the mountains in relative isolation. Their descendants *have* access to the outside world but want to retreat from it and what it represents for their future. In a sense, their frustration has doubled. The majority still can- not compete economically, as always has been the case, but now the greater society is encroaching on their way of life and taking *that* away from them, too. In the past, for mountain people, religious faith was a buffer against the harsh realities of a limited existence. Today it is their only buffer against change and outside forces, which some believe threaten not just their economic status but the very value system which sustained them in the past.

Pessimistic and Fatalistic Outlooks

Appalachians often have been accused of being too pessimistic and too fatalistic. It was this attitude that most infuriated aspiring change agents in earlier decades, because it resulted in a negative value cluster: it is best to remain content with your lot and never aspire too high or "try to get beyond others." This rule was passed down from generation to genera- tion, making it very difficult to interest younger Appalachians in pro- gressive education. Even today, one can suggest going on a picnic to an older person born in rural Appalachia, and he or she is likely to gaze out at the bright sunny day and say, "Well, perhaps not, it will probably rain." It is Murphy's Law of the Mountains that things will always get worse, even if presently they are better.

Only the more thoughtful realize that this reflexive way of thinking by some mountain people is a protective device, adopted to stave off hurt. Their parents and grandparents never went out of the mountains, and their days were filled with toil and the constant battle to survive somehow. The older generation today has not had it particularly easy, in a part of the country where economic survival still is a precarious thing. Hard lives have been the norm in these people's history. More often than not, things have not gone right in the life of the traditional mountaineer. If you do not expect too much, you will not have to face disappointment. Pessimism and fatalism are natural consequences of the survival reflex of the human spirit. In an earlier day, parents were lambasted by frustrated social workers because they seemed not to want their children to attend school. Actually, it was not that they did not want Johnny to learn to read; rather, some parents were afraid that, if he did, he would face even greater disappointment when things did not go right for him. It was better to protect him and keep him safe from almost certain hurt.

Even so, despite the worry about the changes occurring all around them, the average person in rural Appalachia today is not abnormally pessimistic. (A few of those interviewed might be termed "rabidly fanatical," particularly in the intensity of their religious views. They were extremely agitated in their responses and voiced the opinion that the world and their fellow men were "beyond redemption.") Certain Appalachian personality types often seem perpetually to be in the grip of an oxymoronic "contented pessimism."[3] They are, for the most part, contented with their own lives and satisfied with the way things have always been, but pessimistic about the upcoming generation's chances for similar contentment.

The older Appalachian often peppers his conversation with a series of complaints about everything in general. Some might label this habit a manifestation of "pessimism." However, complaining is a social ritual in the mountains. Sharing complaints with acquaintances is a neighborly thing to do. Researchers often have expressed amazement at the abundance of health problems that Appalachians in general seem to experience. Talking about these health problems—real or imagined—is an acceptable form of social intercourse, second only to discussions of the weather. At city cocktail parties, the small talk is about business coups, happenings, or personalities. In rural Appalachia, much passing conversation centers on the variety of ailments that people are experiencing. Participants may try to "outdo" each other with vivid descriptions, and everyone is very polite about listening to details. Health problems also are accepted as sure-fire excuses, or rational explanations, for anything that an individual does not want to do. (West Virginians do not place an emphasis on good health practices; statistically, compared to other states, they have a very high level of serious health problems.)

Unfortunately, fatalism about personal abilities and possible advancement still is very much in evidence among some persons, old and young—a consequence, perhaps, of never having known economic complacency or stability. A majority of those interviewed said that they did not expect to change markedly in their lifetimes. Nor were they likely to strive to make changes in their lifestyles. They tended to react with amusement if it was suggested that they might change their situation or move on to other things. It is this attitude, perhaps, more than any other, that explains their one overwhelming fear about the future. They know beyond reasonable doubt that their way of life will *not* remain the same, despite their ardent desire for such stability.

Thus there is an ambivalent air about the so-called Appalachian fatalism. Some tend to live for the moment at hand, caught up in their daily lives and without too much concern about their future personal welfare. Some, overtly, are not particularly hopeful or optimistic and have become less so with their worry about "bad influences" that they cannot control. However, it is safe to say that such persons are not overly morbid; except for a disgruntled few, they do not have a "the world is against me personally" mentality. They do not find the government to be oppressive, and they do not have a "them against us" attitude toward it. There is a quiet acceptance that things don't always turn out well, but they don't really believe that "fate decides lives," or that "God's will" directs their destinies and they personally have no control. In their contentment with things just as they are, they consider themselves to be merely "realistic" about life. (Only a driven outside world, perhaps, has found them too accepting and labeled their less stressful approach "fatalism.")

Religiosity and Moral Standards

Fundamentalism—that intense religiosity, with its emphasis on the necessity of "being saved," its condemnation of human sinfulness and evil nature, its preoccupation with punishment and reward in the hereafter, its distrust of "the world," and its avoidance of contact with mainline church denominations—certainly was in evidence in the homes visited by this researcher in the 1980s. Taped conversations included many moments when voices were raised in thundering condemnation of the sinful nature of the present world and mankind's distance from the true God. In the 1990s, similar voices are heard on local radio talk shows and in the "vent columns" of the newspapers, as well as in the pews of the many small evangelical and Pentecostal churches scattered along the country roads, some in church buildings, others in private homes, and some in store buildings in the hamlets. Some of the buildings are neat and attractive; others reflect the dire economic condition of the surrounding area. Aesthetics are not particularly important; it is the intensity of the spiritual encounter inside the church that counts.

The names that appear on these churches have remained much the same over the decades: typically, "Church of the True Christ," "The Church of Jesus' Name," or "Church of the Living God." According to the local people, the congregations usually are quite small, and each group is very serious about the sanctity of its particular beliefs and practices. Congregations often split into factions when beliefs diverge, and the splinter groups go off to set up their own churches. In fact, it is this very characteristic that bothers the less religiously inclined: "Too much infighting—I just prefer not to have anything to do with any of 'em." Services in the churches often are held on weekday evenings, and upcoming revival meetings or visiting singing groups are advertised via circulars or homemade signs, or, in the case of the larger groups, in the local newspapers. The church is one of the few places where rural Appalachian people traditionally have revealed the leadership talents they usually keep carefully concealed. Services frequently are led by lay people—sometimes by necessity, since preachers may not be readily available.

One woman sitting in her neatly kept living room reported that she and her husband often went out with a group in the evenings "evangelizing"—that is, visiting homes and "talking religion" with people, "trying to bring souls to God." She said that television was their foremost hindrance. "The people just won't turn their sets off for nothing," and it is difficult, she said, to talk seriously with people under these circumstances. (Even as she spoke, her television set was blaring away in a corner, and she frequently turned toward it in order to view the latest turn of events in a popular soap opera.)

This woman happened to live on a heavily populated hillside in a rural area, and she referred several times to the "outlandish" and "sinful" practices going on in neighboring houses. There were questionable "comings and goings at all hours," and some she knew to be "drug-dealing houses." "Drugs in the hills," she said, "are the abomination of our times."

It is easy for a visitor traveling around rural areas in the Mountain State to be deceived into thinking that a majority of the people is totally fundamentalist and extremely religious. This is a mistaken belief, created by the fact that the very religious are very adamant, very emotional, and very vociferous, and tend to make a huge impression. However, a careful researcher is likely to discover that only about one-third of the rural people are strongly religious in belief and practice. Another one-third do not reflect a fundamentalist view of religion at all or are totally indifferent. The remaining one-third show the influence of their environment, in that the intensely fundamentalist people have made an impression on their vocabulary and on their thought processes. Even those who are not personally interested in religion will use phrases such as "born-again Christian," "having salvation," or "getting right with God," in discussing religion— indicating that, in philosophy if not in practice, they believe in conversion and a fundamentalist style of living if one truly "has religion."

At least one-fourth of the rural people in the sampling of interviews said they very much would like to belong to a traditional mainline church if such churches were available to them nearby, and some do drive rather long distances into the more populated towns to attend what they refer to as "regular church." Three lifelong Methodists voiced mild criticism of their neighbors, who were seen as more "emotionally religious" and who seemed to be "addicted to revivals": "Those folks sure do a lot of arm-wavin' and shoutin.'"

When John F. Kennedy came to West Virginia in 1960, the political types made much ado about the fact that Appalachians endorsed the young politician and voted for him in large numbers, despite the fact that he was a devoted Catholic, a faith not widely embraced or understood in the mountains. In later years, the citizens of the state merely laughed about this so-called phenomenon and referred the media to the state's motto: "Mountaineers are always free." What the media never understood is that among Appalachian cultural values is the maxim that a man is also free to choose his own religious beliefs. The fundamentalists may try to convert him, but they will always respect his right to choose his own path. And they do not judge him as a man because of the religious faith he professes.

The majority of rural people would like for their political leaders to be "somewhat religious," but they definitely do not have to belong to a *particular* church. "That's a fellow's own business" said one man, summing up rather well the mountaineer's traditional view on freedom of religion, although another respondent added, "Well, I suppose a Jew might have a problem fitting in around here, but it's still his right to be a Jew." (This remark could have been made only in a very rural area, since West Virginia has a large Jewish population.)

These people definitely equate morality with religion, so they think that it is rather difficult for politicians to be either very religious or very "good." "Politics is just too dirty a business!" one person explained. The majority think that it is wrong for politicians to bend *any* rules: "They should be absolutely honest." They believe in what they are demanding, but they also believe that no politician ever meets these high moral standards. Thus, when they say they would like a leader to be "religious," they mean having a religious faith *plus* high moral standards. However, even the majority of fundamentalists do not insist that leaders should be "born again" or have "the only true salvation."

In an early study, Thomas Ford[4] uses the term "Puritan moralism" frequently in referring to the high moral standards for personal and social conduct which mountain people have advocated since before the early nineteenth century (when the great religious revivals moved through the region and reinforced the emphasis on proper conduct). The Calvinist Presbyterian church was the first influence on the area, but it was swept aside by the more emotionally satisfying and democratic doctrines of the Baptists and the Methodists. These groups, in turn, lost members to numerous small sects when they began to de-emphasize emotional intensity and advocated a more sedate, formalized doctrine. The smaller sects continued to multiply, particularly among the rural folk, while the greater society was engaged in a steady movement toward formally organized churches with central bureaucracies. The smaller sects have continued their emphasis on morality in personal behavior as a hallmark of religious life.

In talking with rural people, one finds that they usually cling to a belief in prayer in the schools ("I just don't see what harm there is in kids prayin' in the schoolhouses"). However, if you ask them if government and religion should be kept separate, they readily say "yes." They do not think of their local schools as a part of "government," so they can't understand why prayer in the schools is such a big issue. One minister, perhaps more thoughtful than most, said, "Everybody just makes too much fuss about the prayer in the schools thing. There are many more important problems for us all to be concerned about."

Surprisingly, a majority of those who discussed religion in the hills did not think that "preachers should meddle in politics": "Jerry Falwell should be out savin' souls, not tellin' folks how to vote!" and "That Pat Robertson doesn't do anything but go around stirrin' things up!" Appalachia really is not a good recruiting ground for the conservative Religious Right. The people resent being told what they should do and how they must behave, politically or otherwise. Their natural inclination is that "people should mind their own business and leave other folks alone." They are troubled, however, by the thought that perhaps it is the duty of Christian people to get somewhat involved in "cleanin' up the country."

Although many of them listen to religious broadcasts or watch them on television, they have grave reservations about the radio and television ministers ("I'm suspicious of those guys constantly beggin' folks for money"). Nonetheless, some of the elderly widows admit that a portion of their Social Security checks regularly goes to one or more of their favorite television ministers ("Insurance for getting into heaven, I suppose," said one irritated nonbeliever when this practice was mentioned).

A majority will take a high moral tone on most issues, but divorce is a thorny problem for them. They really do not approve of divorce, but, as one woman, a local postmistress, said: "Who isn't?" To condemn divorce outright is to condemn too many people to whom one feels close: friends, relatives, and, in some instances, themselves. "I do not believe in divorce at all, but I am divorced," another woman confessed.

If one had interviewed these same people in the 1950s, they probably would have asserted that no political leader should be divorced. It is an indication of how much mores are changing, even for mountain people, that now they say, "Well, I don't condemn the fellow if he's divorced, but a *good* political leader really should be married and have a family—it steadies them and they understand other folks better; and, too, they won't be wanderin' off with their minds on other things." In the final analysis, divorce no longer carries a moral stigma, even among those who embrace a rather strong fundamentalist faith.

Abortion was not a discussion topic raised in the 1980s interviews, because the native interviewer knew that a majority would be embarrassed even to discuss it and almost certainly would condemn it morally. A 1990s interview with a group of rural folk reveals, however, that they are not unaffected by the ongoing controversy in the country: "I do not believe in kids having kids, but . . ." and the voice trails off. "Too many of those folks hooked on welfare have too many kids." They are not completely unworldly in the age of television, but the whole problem just confounds them. They do not believe that abortion should be used as birth control—it is just too morally wrong—but "young people can't be bothered to find other ways not to have babies." Those more fundamentalist in their beliefs see the whole problem as further evidence that "the country has gone to the dogs. This shouldn't ever have even come up!" The older Appalachian is troubled by the existence of the issue, the younger ones far less so. They will tell you that they or their friends have been known to make a trip to a clinic in a metropolitan area.[5]

Religiosity and high moral standards are intertwined value clusters still in evidence in Appalachia. However, most mountain people always have considered themselves to be not pessimists but hard-headed realists, even about their religion: "Well, we older folks know what it means to be truly religious, and we always knowd that most folks don't live like they should—but nowadays, almost *nobody* does."

Familism and Love of Home

A value cluster that is not in question even in the 1990s in Appalachia is the one revolving around familism, love of home, and protection of both. The most nagging worry in the minds of those interviewed, other than economic survival, is what they see happening to the family unit as they know it, or as they have romanticized it based upon memories of the past. They blame the demise on destructive forces coming in from outside the hills more than they do on economic conditions or migration caused by these conditions. "We've always known bad times and have kept on managing to eat—out of our gardens or by cannin' or patch farmin', but there's nothing we can do about the things breakin' up homes today or the influences that mark the kids."

Children have always been important, particularly to the women. The older women generally still insist that young women should be home raising their children, even though they admit that one check doesn't go far enough in some families. They particularly do not approve of women working in the mines or doing men's work. In the 1980s interviews, there was evidence that both women and men often believed that "too much schooling" interfered with actual living, that there was not much sense in encouraging their youngsters toward more education if the jobs weren't there, and that, more than likely, their children were just going to get hurt if they reached too high.

In the 1990s, the tone has changed. There is more conversation about the caliber of the schools and the quality of teachers, as well as subtle stirrings of the idea that, if only youngsters can be made to go to school and really learn, there may be more hope for coping with change and the future. However, many still believe that children should be kept as close to home as possible, and one of the few issues that actually has caused many rural folks to band together and take group action is the movement toward large consolidated schools. No argument about the wise use of limited resources, exposure to better facilities, or greater educational opportunity can convince them to support school consolidation. Children should not be required to travel long distances from home on a daily basis. The scattered rural neighborhood schools will do just fine, no matter how limited they may be in comparison to mainstream schools.

Amazingly, over 90 percent of rural people in West Virginia still repeat the tried and true Appalachian refrain: "No, I will not ever leave these hills, unless I absolutely have to, and maybe not then." A 1990s statistic reveals that a greater proportion of West Virginians own their homes than the inhabitants of any other state.[6] The quality is not as high as in other states, but quantity is higher. When asked if they would consider living elsewhere if a better life were possible, many see only humor in the question: "Why on earth would I want to do that? This is home, and there is no better life than here!" They feel great sympathy for those who are forced to leave the hills to find jobs.

One of the paradoxes associated with this intense love of the hills and home among Appalachians is their inability to articulate it either verbally or, in a physical sense, aesthetically. They are a very verbal people, but they seldom attempt to describe the natural beauty of their environment in poetic terms. There seems to be an assumption that "everyone can see that it's pretty, so why is there a need to talk about it?" They do not rhapsodize about the woods, the streams, the greenness of the hillsides, or the blueness of the mountains; nor do they refer much to their obvious enjoyment of the outdoor life.

Homes often are nondescript, unpainted, and in various states of disrepair, with mini-junkyards surrounding them. In the past, one might argue that the residents' economic situations accounted for these conditions, but this does not quite explain the penchant for throwing trash over the hillsides and polluting their own woods and streams. They are guilty of despoiling one of the most beautiful natural landscapes in the world. An appreciation of the aesthetically lovely never has been a cultural value strongly attributed to the Appalachian.

In the 1990s, however, a generation of craftspeople suddenly has emerged, and their work has come to be lavishly praised and truly appreciated. It is perhaps this very appreciation which has brought out the latent abilities of many Appalachians. For most of their history they have been scorned; it is refreshing and energizing to be recognized finally and to have their work valued highly. Education and the finger of shame pointed at their treatment of the environment have brought results. Appalachians do not like to be "shamed"; they will argue that they should be "free" to do exactly as they please, but embarrassment is a powerful tool for reformers—especially in combination with a sensible system of regular trash pickups. Even rural communities are embracing the need for organized effort on the part of the whole community for the greater good of all. Organized behavior is alien to the nature of the old-time Appalachian, but old habits are bending before the winds of sensible reform.

However, in most rural communities isolationism—provincialism to some—still is preferred and desired, even in the 1990s. The people are devoted to their own families and homes and reveal almost no concern for anyone elsewhere in the world. There is a lingering resentment about the attention that refugees from other countries get from the federal government "when there is so much need among our own people in this country." Curing unemployment among the natives should be a chief preoccupation of the government, in their opinion.

Even when they voice concern for the welfare of the country, the greater concern is that harmful conditions nationally will damage their own lives and families. One gets the distinct impression that, if they could survive economically, they would pull their beloved mountains in around them for the utmost in protection and security, and shut out the rest of the world, watching it only at a distance on their television screens. In the literature about Appalachians over the years, the fluctuating extent of their isolationism is always mentioned; but now there is a new kind of isolationism, a desired one, emerging in reaction to the rampant excesses of a modern age.

The family is still a bulwark, a source of strength. "Kinfolk" matter. If economic conditions allow, larger families will still reside in the same general area, and there will be much dependence on each other. In fact, if the family is large enough, or if generations of neighboring families reside in the same hamlet, there is an almost complete absorption in local or familial matters. The greater world ceases to have much importance in the daily lives of the people.

Sadly, this Walton Mountain type of existence is far from the norm. There is no longer much "coming and going" in a typical rural home; great numbers of relatives do not live together or interact frequently. More prevalent is the nuclear family or the home occupied by one or two elderly people who can survive on their Social Security income. Children or grandchildren are "elsewhere," working or hunting jobs, and families come together only at specified times or on special occasions. Only the older people are likely to ask, "Whose boy are you?" as if clan still mattered.

There is a forlorn aura around many of the rural homes where only one or two people reside. The television set is considered a member of the family and seems to be rarely turned off. Perhaps the ever-present "noise" dispels the loneliness and gives a flavor of having "company" around. It is not considered at all rude to leave the set on when a visitor is present. People simply "talk over it." Rural West Virginians still retain their front porches, and in the summer months these are preferred for sitting and talking. The relieved visitor is assured that this at least is one place where the television set does not encroach upon conversation. The residents welcome conversation with strangers but are justifiably suspicious of non-natives who approach them with an array of questions for "a study." (One elderly lady with twinkling eyes tested this researcher, who was claiming to be a native, by sending her to a side porch to bring back "a poke." When the researcher returned with a paper bag, she indeed had passed the test, and the lady agreed to answer her questions.)

In many households, widows or elderly individuals live very lonely lives. Such individuals do not like to "bother their neighbors much," so their days are spent inside the walls of their homes. They usually do not ask their neighbors for companionship or help unless they are forced by an emergency to do so—even though everyone in the neighborhood may know everyone else. Since there is not much organized social activity, daily living for those alone or left behind can be bleak indeed. One woman running a farm on her own said, "Thank God for television. It gives me and my cats something to look forward to in the evenings."

Individualism, Pride, and Self-Reliance

One of the value clusters associated with Appalachians features a type of self-centered personalism. In the past these people have not been particularly community-minded or turned outward to the community at large if their family is not immediately affected by events there. They are friendly enough and hospitable to both neighbors and strangers if approached, but there is a natural reserve, a point of interaction with others that they will not go beyond. "Hurt feelings" or perceived slights are a frequent result of this lack of communication. In the church groups, the smallest sign of disagreement can result in a splinter group, and one more minuscule church will crop up in the area.

This natural reserve also means that rural mountain people do not consider, as normal routines, going to each other's homes for a social evening or joining together for group activities or pleasure outings. Only families engage in such behavior, and this fact is one more reason why families are so important. Coming together in a church is an accepted group activity. Local high-school sports events generally will attract crowds.

A funeral also is sure to bring out the community. The "wake" always has been a popular social occasion in the mountains, even though, as one old-timer stated, "Most folks stay at the funeral home now and git it over with quick." It is no longer necessary to offer to "sit up with the body" or to "help dig the grave," since the funeral home has taken over these neighborly chores. However, the rural person still feels "beholden" to do something for her or his bereaved neighbor, so food is taken to the household, help is offered in ritual fashion, and a visit is made to the funeral home, sometimes for the whole evening if the deceased was popular. Much socializing occurs, and acquaintances who have not seen each other for months are given a legitimate reason for spending time together. (One woman who was approached for an interview declined, but only because she was in a great hurry to "get ready for the wake." Her neighbor had died that morning, and she was making a cake, "rollin' her hair," and preparing for a social evening with fellow mourners.) As one mountain wag remarked, "Sometimes a fellow gives his neighbors more pleasure dead than alive!"

Some of the behavior patterns discussed above would be seen by some observers as remnants of the old value cluster involving individualism, pride, and self-reliance. Thomas Ford, in a study conducted in 1958, insisted that these values disappeared forever when the governmental welfare system moved into Appalachia to take care of a people who could not take care of themselves. He concluded that the majority of Appalachians had come to think of welfare as "a right" and therefore had forfeited any moral superiority they ever had had over mainstream Americans. Now they were practicing a new form of Appalachian individualism. They came to town to receive their "dole" and then retreated to the hills to procreate and live their lives as they pleased, without any desire to learn new ways so that they and their offspring could live without public assistance.[7]

Ford and others who followed him helped to create still-prevalent stereotypes about welfare types; these ideas have fueled the persistent drive for welfare reform right into the 1990s. Actually, cries for sensible welfare reform have been coming from the Appalachian mountain people themselves for over two decades: "The government is just ruinin' our young people and something has to be done!" Some rural people blame the lavish welfare program for the demise of the ethical and moral value system they always have held dear. They tell many stories about able-bodied men who have become lazy loafers, mountain families who urge their sons and daughters to "have babies quick so more checks will come in," and their own grandchildren who take advantage of the system. The family welfare check also is seen as a main source of drug buying among young people.

To conclude, as Thomas Ford did, that all Appalachians have bought into the welfare mentality is simply inaccurate. In West Virginia, Appalachia's center, three distinct groups exist, at least among the rural people. There are those who live on welfare and have done so for a number of years. At the other end of the spectrum are those who are economically comfortable. This second group is in moral agreement with a third group—those who always have worked hard and who have managed at least a subsistence level of living. These two groups are embarrassed and furious at those West Virginians who have "sold their pride down the river" and have become permanent members of the welfare class ("They bring embarrassment on us all!"). "Fury" is not too strong a term. Emotions run very high over this issue in the hamlets and small towns of West Virginia. It doesn't take very many personal interviews to realize that the majority of these rural Appalachians is very moralistic about welfare abuse. Pride and self-reliance are not forgotten values in the 1980s and 1990s, so far as they are concerned.

Even those participating in the welfare system will espouse, in conversation, the Appalachian value system's emphasis on pride and self-reliance. They readily agree with the statement: "The government does too much for people." However, they also assert that "a person should look after hisself but if there are no jobs, he shouldn't have to starve." They admit that some folks are "gettin' checks who shouldn't," but they dismiss the problem with a wave of the hand: "That's just the way the world is." Some poorer people share in the same value system as the non-poor; they simply "stretch" that value system in order to accommodate themselves to day-to-day circumstances. They no longer reward or punish in the same way, and they tolerate deviations from group values as necessary for survival.[8]

Reserves of real pride and self-reliance are evident among the working class. They surface particularly when the men are out of work or are "laid off" from jobs that they have worked at for many years. Such men are confused by the weakness of the union system, upon which they always have depended to preserve their jobs. They will drive a hundred-mile radius looking for work or doing "pick up jobs"—for miners, this includes "scrabbling," shoveling coal where there are small outcroppings and surface seams. Some are embarrassed even about drawing unemployment benefits while looking for work: "I know it ain't the same as welfare, but to me it seems almost the same." Middle-aged family men who have lost their jobs after years with one company show hurt and bewilderment in their eyes even as they proclaim, "I will never, never resort to welfare like some guys."

Pride and moral courage are not dead in Appalachia, but, as has happened so many times in the past, they collide with economic reality. In this one way, Appalachia has not changed for over a century.[9] However, the world is moving ever faster. There is concern about the older

Appalachian, limited in skills and education, who may be unable to adapt and simply will be swept aside. The younger generation will have to accept abject poverty or acknowledge the absolute necessity for a technologically based education.

The status of Appalachia, once again, is one of paradox and mind-boggling irony. Missionaries, do-gooders, and federal agencies always wanted to take this "strange land" and its "peculiar people" into the world of the mainstreamer, where the people supposedly would live much better lives.[10] They did not count on the world outside becoming less desirable. Just as missionaries often have brought disease and ruin to innocent societies in undeveloped parts of the world, change agents have helped to accomplish similar feats in Appalachia. They promised a great deal but never were able to deliver in substantial quantity the most important need of all: economic succor. Often, what they did bring were some of the most harmful of outside influences.

The Future: A Blessing or a Curse?

Driving through the Appalachian Mountains and finding breathtaking beauty around every curve, the visitor today may pause on a misty mountaintop and, in the peaceful surroundings, speculate that Appalachia once again is suspended in time. Alas, it is not so. Change is everywhere.

There is further, almost humorous, irony. At one time the greater society wanted nothing to do with Appalachia's way of life or its value system. Approaching the end of the twentieth century, however, over-whelmed and stressed-out mainliners look with interest at the lifestyle advocated by rural Appalachians for over two centuries. Millimeter waves and the Internet, computers and technology, increasingly enable urban dwellers to pursue their economic goals anywhere. The workplace is no longer necessarily in the cities. They look with interest and greed at the beautiful and rugged landscape of Appalachia.

Futurists currently are predicting national trends that hold particular interest for Appalachians. Coinciding with the opening of the new century, technology will enable many people to live where they please and to pursue lifestyles of their own choosing. For a growing segment of the population, commuting to workplaces or entertainment facilities no longer will be necessary, since for them the home will take on multiple roles and become work site, entertainment center, and communications base. Machines in the home will be able to provide visual and vocal contact with almost anyone in the world. It is predicted that some current city dwellers will move toward establishing low-density, "people-friendly" communities, with strict zoning laws, in environmentally safe locations of great natural beauty. They will view minimal transportation outward to interstate highways and inward to their communities as both satisfying and desirable.[11] Obviously, Appalachia is made to order for this type of expansion, since it is one of the last bastions of unspoiled, sprawling green areas in the eastern United States that is comparatively unoccupied. (A perusal of real estate records reveals that the eastern edge of West Virginia, particularly its eastern panhandle, already is experiencing the impact of the New-Age search for alternative homes. Metropolitan residents from Baltimore and Washington have "discovered" the area.)

The rugged Appalachian terrain, always an impediment to economic development in the past, may become the region's greatest asset. Even the early Indian tribes did not attempt to live in the more mountainous areas but used them as hunting preserves. Now twenty-first-century technology will make an almost inaccessible land, labeled "forgotten" a century ago, highly valued living space for modernists.

Contemporary Appalachians may redefine themselves to welcome and profit from the coming influx, imposing the best of their retained mountain values on the newcomers; or they may allow the outsiders to take advantage of them and siphon off their birthright. It has happened to them before. The next quarter-century will reveal their destiny: as shrewd beneficiaries of the change that threatens them, and which they cannot forestall, or as victims who must suffer a final and complete loss of their heritage.

Notes

1. The core values identified in Jack Weller's *Yesterday's People: Life in Contemporary Appalachia* (Lexington: Univ. Press of Kentucky, 1965) long since have become accepted as discussion facilitators, despite the fact that Weller and others initially were accused of advancing a "culture of poverty" stereotype and thus adding to Appalachia's problems.

2. See Allen Batteau, *Appalachia and America: Autonomy and Regional Dependence* (Lexington: Univ. Press of Kentucky, 1983); David Walls and John Stephenson, *Appalachia in the Sixties: Decade of Reawakening* (Lexington: Univ. Press of Kentucky, 1972); Frank Riddel, ed., *Appalachia: Its People, Heritage and Problems* (Dubuque, Ia.: Kendall/Hunt Publishing Co., 1974); Helen Lewis, Linda Johnson, Donald Askins, *Colonialism in Modern America: The Appalachian Case* (Boone, N.C.: Appalachian Consortium Press, 1978); David Whisnant, *Modernizing the Mountaineer: People, Power and Planning in Appalachia* (New York: Burt Franklin and Co., 1980); John Gaventa, *Power and Powerlessness: Quiescence and*

Rebellion in an Appalachian Valley (Urbana: Univ. of Illinois Press, 1980); Bruce Ergood and Bruce Kuhre, *Appalachia: Social Context Past and Present* (Dubuque, Iowa: Kendall/Hunt Publishing Co., 1983).

3. The Appalachian's complacency extends to accepting natural disasters as a way of life. In West Virginia, repeated flooding of some areas is viewed as a kind of "recurring sport," with community inhabitants joining together to clean up homes and businesses. This occurs with a frequency that would be the despair of others. Disaster as tradition may seem strange to some, but not to Appalachians accustomed to accepting life's blows and dealing with them. See "For Some, Flooding 'A Way of Life,'" *Charleston (W.Va.) Daily Mail*, Jan. 22, 1996, p. 1.

4. Thomas R. Ford, ed., *The Southern Appalachian Region: A Survey* (Lexington: Univ. of Kentucky Press, 1962), 23.

5. In 1993, West Virginia had 5.3 divorces for every 1,000 residents, the thirteenth highest rate in the nation. Not surprisingly, the Mountain State had one of the nation's lowest rates of abortions: 134 abortions for every 1,000 babies born, compared to the national rate of 379. See "Vital Statistics: W.Va. Lags," *Sunday Gazette-Mail*, Dec. 3,1995, p. 2C. The statistics in this newspaper report also indicate that, despite an increase in drug-related problems, West Virginia still is a relatively safe state to live in. It was sixth lowest among states in violent crime in 1993. The report also reveals that this most Appalachian of the states still has difficulty promoting education. Despite the state's ranking as seventeenth highest in spending on each public school student, in 1990 more than a third of all West Virginians had failed to finish high school. The state has a number of fine public and private colleges and universities, but in 1994 only 7.5% of residents over age 25 held college degrees.

6. See "State Is First in Home Ownership, Census Says," *Sunday Gazette-Mail*, Jan. 21, 1996, p. 7C.

7. Ford, *Southern Appalachian Region*, chap. 2.

8. This is, in reality, an earlier scholar's theory of "value stretch." See Hyman Rodman, "The Lower Class Value Stretch," *Social Forces* 42 (Dec. 1963): 209.

9. From 1979 to 1984, the State of West Virginia lost nearly twenty thousand jobs a year. In November 1995, economists predicted that the state's economy would grow, but at a slower rate than in the previous five years, when growth had been moderate. See "Economist Predicts Slower Growth," *Charleston Daily Mail*, Nov. 14, 1995, p. 1D.

   As of January 1996, the state was spending $183 million a year for job training for the unemployed but admitted to making very little progress in rural counties. West Virginia's thirty-eight rural counties—those which lacked a city of ten thousand or larger population—contained 39% of the state's population, but only 28% of the state's jobs. See "'Workfare's Efforts May Be Fruitless," *Charleston Gazette*, Jan. 13, 1996.

In June 1997, as the deadline for enforcement of new federal welfare rules approached, private companies in West Virginia were being asked to "pick up some of the slack" in a state where the unemployment rate was among the highest in the nation. By mid-1997, the new rules decreed, a quarter of the state's welfare recipients heading single-parent households had to be working twenty hours per week. Three-quarters of two-parent households had to have one parent working thirty-five hours per week. The numbers added up to nine thousand West Virginians who suddenly were expected to obtain work. The new rules further indicated that welfare recipients must be in work programs or working after two years of receiving benefits and must be off the welfare rolls after five years. See "W.Va. Firms Wrestle with Welfare Laws," *Charleston Daily Mail,* June 4, 1997.

10. Lest the reader think that the wave of outside interest in "helping Appalachia" has receded, it was reported in late 1995 that the Roman Catholic Church had unveiled a pastoral letter calling for the creation of sustainable progress in combating the "poverty-stricken region's environmental problems and the abandonment of its people." The letter offered suggestions that Appalachians might employ in "building sustainable communities and warding off outside corporations who are taking the area's natural resources in permanently destructive and environmentally unsafe ways." See "Catholic Church Reaches Out," *Charleston Daily Mail,* Dec. 16, 1995, p. 7B.

11. See: Mary Pipher, *The Shelter of Each Other* (New York: Grossett/Putnam, 1996); Witold Rybczynski, *City Life: Urban Expectations in a New World* (New York: Touchstone/Simon and Schuster, 1995); Gerald Celente, *Trends 2000* (New York: Warner Books, 1997); issues of *Trends Journal* from Trends Research Institute, 1996 and 1997; and, in the popular press, "Looking Ahead to 2012," *Home* magazine, Mar. 1997, pp. 60–86.

Chapter 5

The Church College in Central Appalachia

IRA READ

Small Protestant colleges in America—the colleges attended by Ronald Reagan (Eureka), Richard Nixon (Whittier), and Dan Quayle (DePauw)—are a well-known but infrequently studied part of American life. The attention of historians typically has focused on the Ivy League or the major state universities. When these scholars have deigned to study small colleges, they have been more likely to study schools like Amherst or Williams.[1] Most of the small schools, however, probably were never more than academies and some hardly more than dreams.

The first colleges in the South and in Southern Appalachia were started by the Presbyterians. They drew their inspiration from the "log colleges" founded in Pennsylvania, where prospective Presbyterian ministers were trained in the classics and in divinity. Presbyterian patriarch William Tennent's Log College in 1746 became the College of New Jersey (later Princeton University). To garner added support, the college would expand its curriculum beyond ministerial training. The governor of New Jersey would be chairman of the trustees, the state would have four additional trustees, and no sectarian tests would be applied to trustees, faculty, or students. Had the rules been otherwise, it is highly doubtful that the college ever could have been chartered. This rather amorphous church-state college formed the general pattern for most schools in the eighteenth and early nineteenth centuries. The tradition of the preacher-president would insure reasonable conformity to denominational principles, while at the same time allowing the Protestant colleges reasonable latitude in seeking students and funds.[2]

With Anglicanism still the established religion of Virginia, and the College of William and Mary more or less under its control, Presbyterians began establishing academies, beginning with Augusta Academy (later Washington and Lee) and following, by 1776, with Hampden-Sydney. The primary purpose of these early Presbyterian ventures was to provide for an educated ministry, but at the same time the schools were to provide "a place where young men could learn to become gentlemen, versed in the classics—but not scholars; acquainted with contemporary knowledge; and, if they desired, trained in law or medicine."[3] Early statements by these colleges disavowed sectarianism and mentioned nothing about the training of ministers, yet ministerial training clearly was intended.

The creation of Hampden-Sydney stemmed from a suspicion that the College of William and Mary had Tory sympathies. Republican sympathies were as important as denominational considerations. Moreover, the desires of the denomination (be it Presbyterian, Methodist, or Baptist) were tempered by the need for students—of whatever denomination—and by a desire for state funding. Washington and Lee College continually faced this dilemma: if the college minimized its Presbyterian connections, it lost support from Presbyterians; yet an overemphasis on denominational affiliation could limit financial support and hamper student recruitment.

The Presbyterians, many of them involved in the creation of both Washington and Lee and Hampden-Sydney, crossed the Appalachian Mountains in 1780 and established Transylvania Seminary in Lexington, Kentucky. Transylvania's later notoriety for intra- and inter-denominational disputes began early, with the appointment of its first president, Harry Toulmin, described thus: "By profession a Baptist preacher, but in sentiment he was unitarian . . . a sycophantic satellite of Thomas Jefferson."[4] Transylvania ultimately would be controlled by the Disciples of Christ, and out of all the bickering eventually would emerge the University of Kentucky.

Tusculum College in Greeneville, Tennessee, was an amalgam of two, or perhaps three, different schools. Hezekiah Balch, a Princeton graduate and Presbyterian missionary, founded a Greeneville College in 1794 and received a charter for it from the legislature of the Southwest Territory. Samuel Doak, another Princeton graduate and Presbyterian minister, established Washington College a year later and then founded Tusculum Academy. Greeneville was inoperative for awhile and offered no college work until about 1805. Washington College never was really a college, although it has retained that name to the present. While both men were Presbyterians, their schools never were formally controlled by the presbytery. Indeed, Balch attempted to secure a fifty-thousand-acre land grant that Congress had allotted for a college in Tennessee.

Also in 1794, Blount College in Knoxville, Tennessee, was established by another Presbyterian minister, Samuel Czare (an ominous middle name for a college president!) Carrick, a friend of Balch who had attended Liberty Hall in Virginia. Eventually Blount College received the state appropriation coveted by Balch, although Blount failed to take advantage of it. By 1807, the school had been transformed as East Tennessee College; later it became the University of Tennessee.[5] Presbyterians also were instrumental in founding the primarily African American institution, Knoxville College.

A few miles down the road from Knoxville, one of Carrick's pupils, Isaac Anderson, another Presbyterian preacher-president, acted independently after receiving neither encouragement nor funding in his attempts to create a theological seminary in the Southwest. Presbyterians capable of supporting such a project saw little need for it and contended that they still had Princeton to support. Maryville College was not chartered until 1842 because the Tennessee Legislature feared that Presbyterians were planning to infiltrate the state government. Maryville was one of the more diverse frontier ventures, because it admitted both blacks and Indians. With the founding of Maryville Presbyterian, collegiate expansion came to a temporary halt in Appalachia.[6]

Five more colleges in the Appalachian region were created before the Civil War. Methodists founded Emory and Henry in southwestern Virginia in 1836, and in 1857 Tennessee Wesleyan, in Athens, Tennessee. Baptists started Carson-Newman College (originally Mossy Creek Baptist Seminary) in 1851, and in 1856 North Carolina Baptists opened the French Broad Baptist Institute (its name was formally changed to Mars Hill College in 1859). Berea College began in 1855 as a one-room schoolhouse established by John G. Fee, an abolitionist from Lane Seminary. It was located on land given by a William B. Wright, with considerable encouragement from Cassius Clay and limited help from the American Missionary Society.

None of these schools began as a college. All were academies existing precariously and often disappearing for periods of time. Name changes were frequent, and, until well into the second half of the century, there was unending talk of relocation. While Richard Hofstadter argues that a Great Retrogression (in enthusiasm for education) resulted from a reaction against the Enlightenment, in Appalachia it appears more likely that sectarian rivalries created more colleges than were needed.

Insofar as the Southern Appalachian region is concerned, the period between 1865 and 1918 was the period of greatest growth in the number institutions. Presbyterians created King College in Bristol, Tennessee, in 1867; Pikeville College in Pikeville, Kentucky, in 1889; Warren Wilson near Asheville, North Carolina (1894); Lees-McRae in Banner-Elk, North Carolina (1897); and Montreat-Anderson in Montreat, North Carolina (1916). The Baptists established Alderson-Broaddus (1871), an amalgamation of two different colleges ultimately located in Philippi, West Virginia; Virginia Intermont in Bristol, Virginia (1884); and Cumberland College in Williamsburg, Kentucky (1889). Whatever national and southern tendencies may exist for Baptist colleges to proliferate, they showed a great deal of restraint in a region considered heavily Baptist. The Methodists established only three more schools: Union College in Barbourville, Kentucky (1879); Sue Bennet in London, Kentucky (1897); and West Virginia Wesleyan in Buckhannon, West Virginia (1890).[7] Milligan College was founded by the Christian Church in East Tennessee in 1866; Seventh-Day Baptists established Salem (now Salem-Teikyo) in 1888; Seventh-Day Adventists started a college near Chattanooga called Southern in 1892; Congregational Christians began Piedmont (1897) in North Georgia; and the Christian and Missionary Alliance established Toccoa Falls (1907), also in North Georgia. Another school that perhaps should be mentioned is Lincoln Memorial University (1897), which never had any specific denominational affiliation.

In 1918, the Churches of God founded Lee College in Cleveland, Tennessee. Alice Lloyd, another independent college, financed partially by religious interests in the East, was started in 1923 as Caney Creek Junior College in Kentucky. Finally, three more fundamentalist colleges were established in the twentieth century: Bryan in Dayton, Tennessee (1930); Tennessee Temple in Chattanooga (1946), affiliated with a local independent Baptist congregation; and Covenant College on Lookout Mountain, Georgia (1995), associated with conservative Presbyterians. There also are a number of Bible colleges in the region. Two of these are large enough and sufficiently well accredited to be included in *American Universities and Colleges* or *Peterson's Guide*: Johnson Bible College, affiliated with the "independent" wing of the Christian Church; and Clear Creek Baptist Bible College in Pineville, Kentucky.

Besides the University of Tennessee in Knoxville, there also is the University of Tennessee at Chattanooga. The latter began as a Methodist College in 1886. The University of Charleston, in Charleston, West Virginia, originally was Morris-Harvey College, also Methodist (1888). Certainly many more colleges exist, too.

Location and Organization

The late Grady Nutt—Baptist preacher, humorist, and member of television's *Hee-Haw* cast—often spoke at colleges where attendance at chapel still was required. He usually would start out: "I knew the moment we arrived at campus this was a Christian college—it is located about seven miles from the nearest sin." Occasionally he may have been wrong. After all, Pikeville is much farther away from sin than seven miles, as are Emory and Henry and the schools of upper West Virginia. Such locations sometimes may have been selected by accident. Some preachers owned farms, and these became campuses after the preacher decided to become a president and start his own school. Bethany College, almost in Pennsylvania and not in the region included this study, is the best example of this process. Alexander Campbell bought a farm and then started the college there. Samuel Doak did the same with Tusculum.

At other times, the selection of a rural location was quite intentional. The Jeffersonian and American distrust of urban areas, still evident in certain persons and regions today, affected the way people thought about colleges. A prospectus for West Virginia Wesleyan called it "an ideal location, a beautiful country town, near the centre of the state, free from saloons, well supplied with churches, and probably as free from evil influences as any town of the size in the state." The Tusculum College catalogue boasted in 1847 that its "distance from Greeneville and Rheatown is such as gives it all the advantages of a location in a town, and also guards it from all the ensnaring and demoralizing influence of a town on the minds and morals of youth."[8]

Some colleges born in rural locations were absorbed into urban areas as nearby towns experienced population growth. A railroad running through or close to campus later proved a godsend. Berea College even campaigned for a railroad for the benefit of the town.[9] The standard joke about Tusculum College in the 1950s was that students from New Jersey, then short of colleges, ran out of money in Greeneville and were compelled to attend Tusculum. Since all colleges accepted the principle of *in loco parentis*, a rural environment was thought to allow greater seclusion and control.

The best metaphor for a nineteenth-century college is the prototypical Victorian family, with the president as father figure, a man whose loyal wife often functioned as both first lady and counselor to students. Many small church colleges still refer to themselves as families, or at least communities, of staff, faculty, and students. A more precise analogy for many colleges today might be the corporation, with the president acting as chief executive officer and faculty-staff linked in the "chain of command."

The early college president was, almost without exception, a minister. This was true even at state colleges until late in the century. The president received a higher salary than faculty members, although in times of financial difficulty his salary might go unpaid. He raised money, often with limited success, wrote innumerable letters to parents, served as chief disciplinarian, gave most of the chapel talks, and often taught classes, including a capstone course for seniors.

Faculty members were poorly paid, had less status than ministers, and were forced to exercise considerable discipline in matters of student behavior. However, student violence—characteristic of schools of the Lower South—seem to have been less evident in Appalachia, possibly because the students were poorer. At many schools, a disproportionate number of faculty were ordained ministers. The curriculum consisted of the standard classical fare of the day, with occasional efforts to broaden offerings by including more practical subjects. Small Appalachian colleges, like most small colleges, were not highly innovative.

Financial problems plagued these colleges from the very beginning. All too often a school relied primarily on tuition for funding, and that was not always sufficient to cover costs. Lotteries were attempted, with little success. Prepaid tuition, guaranteeing a student a set fee for four years, created more complex problems, as the college seldom charged enough. Almost without exception, college histories are bleak tales of financial hardship and sacrifice, of faculty underpaid or unpaid for long periods, of fires that obliterated facilities, endowments that existed only on paper, and ruthless demands by wealthy donors. All this made survival of the college uncertain from year to year.

Church-related colleges in the Appalachian region neither could nor would charge enough tuition to cover the costs of instruction, let alone of constructing and maintaining buildings. As a result, they continued to depend upon special financial gifts that lowered the deficit but often were insufficient to meet annual needs. Inadequate income made it impossible to respond to unexpected financial crises, such as a decline in outside giving, reduction in student enrollment, fires, or other destructive events, and to the inevitable deterioration of facilities. Consequently, colleges borrowed money and deferred applying funds to endowments. As late as 1960, Georgetown College (in Kentucky) had both a building debt and an endowment, each amounting to one million dollars.[10]

Funding from churches or increased enrollment was rarely sufficient. The alumni could be expected to provide some funding, but ultimately financing relied heavily upon wealthy benefactors' contributions. Few millionaires remained in the South after the Civil War and fewer still in Appalachia, but as the twentieth century approached, certain Yankee philanthropists were willing to give large sums of money. D. K. Pearsons of Chicago was one of the more generous patrons. He gave significant sums of money, some five million dollars in all, to nearly forty southern and western colleges. Some of his gifts required matching funds, while others were direct grants with no strings attached.[11]

More often, the terms for large gifts were very specific. For example, West Virginia Wesleyan received a gift of one hundred thousand dollars in 1946, earmarked for building programs. The funds, however, actually were available only after construction began, and at least two other buildings of equal cost had to be constructed simultaneously.[12] Moreover, upkeep costs seldom were written into building costs.

The wealthy could try to control college life in other ways, too. Nettie McCormick, the widow of Cyrus McCormick, gave substantial sums to Tusculum College over the years but always dictated how the money should be used. She included stipulations that the president, a percentage of the faculty, and two-thirds of the trustees must be Presbyterian. All of this came at a time when Tusculum was competing for money and students with King College, another Presbyterian school, only fifty miles away. The president of the college could only register his concern.[13] Unfortunately, this dependence upon the generosity of wealthy benefactors to establish endowments and pay for buildings all too often caused administrators and fundraisers to ignore other potential sources of income.

Life with philanthropists was no easy matter, but it was further complicated by uncertainty over the exact amounts the school might receive upon the death of the benefactor. Administrators lived in the anticipation of large bequests that rarely occurred. Nettie McCormick, for example, left only $75,000 to Tusculum College.[14] Sometimes the benefactor simply assumed that the family would continue to support the college. Senator Elkins never provided for Davis and Elkins College in his will, suggesting that the family would continue to provide funds. Such funding was only sporadic, however. Likewise, the college failed to receive funding anticipated from the Davis estate.[15] Even when benefactors meant well and made specific provision, their gifts often were less than anticipated. Union College was given a building in Louisville valued at $206,000 and counted in the college's endowment at that amount, but the building finally sold for only $53,000.[16]

Another method of securing support was a specific campaign to pay off debt, build a building, or bring endowment up to a certain level. Financial campaigns usually began when operational deficits caused concern among creditors and endowments already had been borrowed against. These financial campaigns rarely were successful; the all-time record for lack of success must belong to Mars Hill College, which managed to raise only $99.50 out of a goal of $20,000 in one of its drives.[17] While most drives were a bit more successful, there was no guarantee that even trustees would contribute.[18] College historians often are unable to trace the precise results of such campaigns. Few fundraising efforts appear to have been entirely successful, however, and those that succeeded often did so by drawing on funds that normally would have gone for other purposes.

Endowments remain the most common method of assessing the financial status of a college, but their dollar values are difficult to determine precisely. Endowment totals may reflect real assets that provide steady income, or simply wishful thinking. Union College in Kentucky owned stock in Louisville Cement listed at four times its actual value.[19] The use of endowments to grant mortgage loans also confuses the value picture. In 1930, almost two-thirds of Maryville College's endowment was in mortgage notes. This was a bad time to have major funds concentrated in any one investment. Another endowment problem, attributable to local trustees, was aptly expressed in a plaintive cry from the president of Tusculum: "It is not uncommon for us to have $50,000 to $75,000 in the bank drawing no interest at all. Furthermore, loans are made from our endowment funds to men in Greeneville who are business associates of our Greeneville trustees."[20]

The Church and the Denomination

The relationship between the church and its colleges began in a rather dubious manner and usually remained ambiguous. Today, many schools have dropped, or at least downplay, their religious affiliations, and most Protestant colleges confront the issue of whether to sever their ties with the church completely. Early on, when no college contemplated leaving its denomination altogether, the problem always existed of how much authority the denomination should have over the college. Cooperative and amicable relationships did exist in particular cases between churches and colleges, but such examples were less noticeable because less newsworthy. Contributing toward cooperation were the considerable number of students who came from the denomination. Foundations might provide money, but Appalachian schools depended heavily—in some cases almost solely—on tuition, a reality that demanded extensive efforts at student recruitment. Recruitment at the local level had its limitations, especially once the land-grant colleges and normal schools became competitive. Thus denominations became the best sources of future students. Toward this end, colleges often developed choir tours and traveling gospel teams, usually sent out with recruiter in tow. Moreover, the college president almost always was a minister from the denomination, as was a sizable proportion of the faculty. No matter how illusory denominational support might be, there was an understandable reluctance to move away from its protection and security.

It is tempting to describe the relationship between church and college as entirely a matter of finances. Especially when colleges were desperate for money and church bodies were reluctant to provide additional funding, it could seem as if that were the case. Whatever the problem might be, money always seemed to be at the root of the difficulty. However, numerous other reasons for these conflicts existed. First, whatever their denominational affiliations, the majority of colleges advertised and considered themselves to be nonsectarian. Second, there were numerous local constraints. With transportation poor in the nineteenth and early twentieth centuries, students, trustees, and financial supporters were more likely to come from the region close to the school. Later in the century, philanthropy became a factor. The truly wealthy could provide more support in a single gift than churches could or would give over decades. A fourth reason is less well documented in college histories. In many cases alumni were more difficult to please, yet more crucial to the school's well-being, than denominational bodies. Fifth, since schools depended so heavily upon tuition for survival, they were more likely to cater to student needs. These included practical and vocational programs and, later, accreditation. As a result, too, some schools overlooked questionable student conduct. Finally, many denominations were located in regions where their strength was insufficient to maintain predominantly denominational schools. Often colleges were located in regions where there were too many colleges chasing too few denominational dollars.

The role of philanthropy was another source of conflict between church and college. Occasionally the philanthropist supported the denomination. As noted earlier, the president of Tusculum College complained that Mrs. Cyrus McCormick's stipulations required that the president, a percentage of the faculty, and two-thirds of the trustees must be Presbyterian. This was unusual, however. At Vanderbilt University, for example, the power of the philanthropist acted to dilute church control. While Richmond College, now the University of Richmond (Virginia), today is affiliated only loosely with Virginia Baptists, as early as 1920 a Richmond newspaper editorial stated that "the University of Richmond is no more a Baptist school than the College of William and Mary is an Episcopal school because it was founded by and partly supported by the Church of England."[21] Earlier, when the Baptist General Association suggested that the university should report to it annually, the chairman of the trustees replied that the General Association had made no effort to increase funds since 1873. Ultimately, however, it was a substantial gift of sixty million dollars by the Robins family that required the university to change its charter and free itself from any direct control by the Baptist General Association. As a concession, one-fifth of the trustees were to be elected from a list supplied by the Baptist General Board.[22]

There is nothing in any college history to suggest that a denomination ever bought a school a building. Occasionally there would be denominational drives for endowment, but these were few. For buildings and substantial increases in endowment, the philanthropist usually was a necessity.

The role of alumni rarely is noted in college histories unless the alumnus happened to be a philanthropist. However, a substantial percentage of the alumni either were not members of, or only nominally were affiliated with, the particular denomination with which their school was connected. As early as 1859, alumni associations were formed;[23] while rarely as powerful as denominational bodies, they represented another countervailing force. The college could and later would go directly to its alumni for financial support and for student recruitment aid. One suspects that the alumni, especially local alumni, were a major factor in the overemphasis on college athletics.[24]

A struggle between colleges and the church, expectably, ensued when colleges wished to become major universities. This was clearly the case at places like Duke and Vanderbilt. Most schools, however, had no aspirations to become major universities. However, accreditation generally was considered desirable, and the search for it led to innumerable conflicts between church and college.[25] Even before accreditation, schools began to break out of their classical curricular mold in order to secure more students. Survival, whether it involved broadening the curriculum or pursuing accreditation, often meant hiring outside the denomination. Indeed, in many cases these changes radically diminished the academic uniformity characteristic of small Protestant colleges. Often there was no-one available from that denomination or that school to teach, say, business or sociology. Most schools never had formal denominational quotas for hiring faculty, but those that did learned to make exceptions. At Carson-Newman in Tennessee, 75 percent of the faculty were to be Baptists, but the school was permitted to modify this in the Department of Fine Arts.[26]

At many small colleges, the need for a qualified professor with a doctoral degree, as accrediting boards often required, far outweighed denominational loyalties. Most colleges accepted hiring outside the denomination but continued to hire only Protestants, not Jews, Catholics, or Unitarians. At other colleges, the process could be slow. Davidson College moved from requiring teachers to be members of the Presbyterian Church (as required by its 1887 constitution) to requiring that all "inaugurated" (i.e., full) professors be Presbyterian (1928). By 1945, 75 percent of inaugurated professors and professors of Bible had to be Presbyterian, but others needed only to be a member of some evangelical church. By the 1970s, faculty positions were open to non-Christians.[27] For most schools, the process was more rapid. Usually only members of the religion department retained denominational uniformity.

Yet other conflicts occurred when denominations themselves were quite weak, when there was denominational antagonism toward higher education, or when denominational quarrels erupted over the allocation of limited funds. Catawba College in North Carolina, a Reformed college; and Salem College (now Salem-Teikyo College), a Seventh-Day Baptist school in West Virginia, never had enough students or potential faculty from their denomination to be church-related other than in name. The problems of Baptist colleges, apart from the denomination's small membership, always were exacerbated by strong pockets of anti-intellectualism within the churches. This resulted in poor support for higher education.[28] Among Baptists, it never was a foregone conclusion that ministers needed college training. For Washington College (later Washington and Lee), the keenest competition at times was its fellow Presbyterian institution, Hampden-Sydney.[29] Methodists recommended in the 1920s that Ferrum College close its doors in order to provide more support for Blackstone College and the Randolph-Macon schools.[30] It was quite common for church bodies to close a college or merge two or more.[31]

The vast majority of Protestant colleges, of course, stayed within the denominational fold. There was sporadic denominational pressure on colleges to conform to denominational attitudes, especially concerning matters such as drinking, smoking, dancing, and, less often, theological questions.[32] Some of the pressure for denominational conformity eased in the twentieth century, when evangelical and fundamentalist groups, some of which split off from their denominations, formed new schools, most of which were Bible colleges. Dissident elements in the same denomination focused their energy on these new colleges and generally left the older colleges alone.[33] The vocational emphasis of the Bible college precluded any emphasis on the liberal arts.

David Potts, president of Judson College in Alabama, who has studied the problems of denominational relationships extensively, concluded that colleges became more denominational after 1850 and that the overall effect of funding by the Carnegie Foundation for the Advancement of Teaching was minimal. The program was founded primarily as a pension fund in 1906, but it turned to emphasizing academic standards and minimal requirements as prerequisites for financial aid. Potts noted in his study that only fifteen colleges severed their denominational relationship over a twenty-year period in order to benefit from Carnegie's pension plan.[34] It must be noted, however, that the vast majority of southern schools qualified for assistance from neither Carnegie nor Rockefeller. The Carnegie Foundation stipulated that a college have six full-time professors and certain entrance requirements—features clearly beyond the scope of financially beleaguered southern schools. Simply put, most southern colleges retained their denominational relationship because they had few, if any, alternatives.

Some schools, such as King College and Tusculum College, waffled in their denominational affiliations. In 1979, King College, in severe financial difficulty, opted to accept conditions by a committee of conservative Presbyterians to "make the school unapologetically and enthusiastically an evangelical institution of higher Christian education."[35] In 1953, eight trustees of Tusculum College filed suit in what proved to be a futile effort to prevent the college from forming stronger ties with the Presbyterian Synod of the Mid-South.[36]

Religion and the Student

The focus of religious life on campus was built around mandatory chapel attendance and various prohibitions on sin. Sin, of course, usually included tobacco, alcohol, and sex. The fact that a college was church-related did not necessarily mean that a particular degree of religiosity existed on campus. Diversity of religious traditions—between Baptists and Episcopalians for example—meant that campus spirituality varied considerably. There are nineteenth and even twentieth-century visions of well-scrubbed young men and women carrying Bibles and filing silently into chapel services several days each week, living lives of chastity and eschewing tobacco, alcohol, drugs, and dancing. College administrations encouraged that image, but in reality the diversity was much greater.

As American society changed, so did the disciplinary and religious ethos of Appalachian colleges. The strictness of pre–Civil war rules in

Appalachian colleges never provoked the violent responses they elicited elsewhere.[37] Compulsory chapel may have remained a requirement at some state universities as late as 1940, but by then some of the church colleges already had either dropped it or reduced it to a weekly, religious "convention."[38] Normally dancing was prohibited in the nineteenth century (any kind of unchaperoned contact between the sexes was discouraged), but gradually, over the years, the majority of church colleges either sanctioned social dancing or pretended not to notice that dances were being held off campus. West Virginia Wesleyan in the 1920s followed the more common procedure of allowing dancing off campus while prohibiting it on campus, then made parents who wished to allow their children to dance to indicate this by writing to the dean.

The social changes that occurred in small Appalachian colleges rarely were publicized and often are not chronicled in college histories. It was clearly safer not to allow either the local or the denominational constituency to know what was going on. When Georgetown College lifted its ban on dancing, the Kentucky Baptist Convention expressed great regret but made no move to censure the college or deny it funds. The University of Chattanooga (at that time a Methodist college) allowed dancing at the beginning of the century but changed its policy when ministers threatened to halt church support; then the college quietly allowed dancing to resume.[39] At Morris-Harvey, the president agreed that students had the right to dance at public places and private homes; but, since the college was subject to church discipline, dances were not allowed at college functions. Students got around this policy by organizing dancing clubs.[40] Students used enormous amounts of energy in getting around the rules at small Protestant colleges.

College histories give less attention to policies concerning drinking and smoking, practices which usually were prohibited by school rules but were enforced only sporadically. These histories also omit references to sexual scandals or the responses of students and faculty to the social upheavals of particular eras. To his credit, Thomas Richard Ross records the efforts of Davis and Elkins College to end racial discrimination against students by local barbers and beauticians. He also notes that three Davis and Elkins students went to Selma, Alabama, to march as civil rights protesters. He even discusses the presence of women on the faculty as early as 1914 and acknowledges that there was a suffragette in the student body.[41]

Such campus regulations were standard on campuses in the nineteenth century. Yet it is hardly surprising that student (and faculty) discipline problems lasted even into the 1960s. A particularly fascinating case occurred at Tusculum College in the mid-sixties, when the school temporarily was denied accreditation by the Southern Association of Colleges and Schools, owing to a paucity of terminal degrees on the faculty. This, as usual, reflected limited funds to hire better-trained teachers. But the accreditation crisis stimulated further discontent, especially among the students. At the time, a couple was fined for sitting together on a bench, girls were fined fifteen dollars for kissing their dates goodnight at the dorm door, and an embrace could result in expulsion. Boys and girls could not wash clothes together at the laundromat, for fear that girls would see boys' underclothing, and boys and girls no longer could swim together in the campus pool. All this led to demonstrations, finally resulting in the president's departure.[42] Curiously, Tusculum was considered rather liberal by other nearby colleges.

It may be said of many of the colleges under consideration that they are "in" Appalachia, but not "of" Appalachia. Berea and Alice Lloyd[43] most certainly are identified with Appalachia, however, and other Kentucky schools—Union, Cumberland, Pikeville, and perhaps two or three others—are, too, to some degree. However, other colleges in the region made few, or at best sporadic, efforts to identify themselves with the surrounding region. Moreover, some denominations strong in the region—the Primitive and Old Regular Baptists, for example—did not establish any colleges.

Colleges always recruited locally, but as time went on, they expanded their geographical base in an effort to secure more tuition-paying students and more potential benefactors. In time, Maryville College recruited less from its geographical area, partly because local students commuted to the University of Tennessee, which had a greater range of academic offerings. Generally, "Maryville never has had among Presbyterians in the area either a financial or student clientele comparable to those of Presbyterian colleges in the strong synods."[44]

Given that money is rather important if a school is going to have a continued existence, it is understandable that many colleges would not focus strongly on their home regions, but in Appalachia this practice meant that church colleges played a relatively small role in educating the region. Another factor was the failure of work programs that might have provided an incentive for mountain children to come to the campuses. Except for those at Berea College, such programs as existed were poorly conceived and poorly executed. However, the major problems seem to have been denominational identification and the ability to find either enough money or enough students locally to make the college a viable enterprise. Only Berea College, with its nondenominational status, could manage to attract both sufficient funding and adequate student enrollment.

Notes

1. In West Virginia alone, Rector College existed in Pruntytown, Weston College was founded in 1858, and Levelton Male and Female College and Allegheny College were founded in the southern part of the state in 1860. In 1865, the Free Will Baptists established West Virginia College near Pruntytown, and Shelton College was begun by Baptists at St. Alban's. Each of these finally was taken over by private owners and failed by the turn of the century. Powhatan College was opened in Charles Town and eventually became an Episcopal girls' school. A Presbyterian girls' college, Greenbrier College, finally became private in 1929. Charles H. Ambler, *A History of Education in West Virginia: From Early Colonial Times to 1949* (Huntington, W.Va.: Standard Printing and Publishing, 1951), 107–29, 184–86, 737–40, 758–60.

2. For a balanced and readable account of the founding and early days of Princeton University, see Thomas Jefferson Wertenbaker, *Princeton, 1746–1896* (Princeton, N.J.: Princeton Univ. Press, 1946), 3–152.

3. Robert Polk Thomson, "Colleges in the Revolutionary South: The Shaping of a Tradition," *History of Education Quarterly* 10, no. 4 (Winter 1970): 400. See also Herbert Clarence Bradshaw, *History of Hampden-Sydney*, vol. 1: *From the Beginnings to the Year 1856* (Durham, N.C.: Privately printed, 1976), 11–24. Earnest Trice Thompson, *Presbyterians in the South* (Richmond, Va.: John Knox Press, 1963), 1:254–57. Olinger Crenshaw, *General Lee's College: The Rise and Growth of Washington and Lee University* (New York: Random House, 1969), 23–31.

4. John D. Wright, *Transylvania: Tutor to the West* (Lexington: Univ. Press of Kentucky, 1975), 25–26.

5. James Riley Montgomery, Stanley J. Folmsbee, and Lee Seifert Green, *To Foster Knowledge: A History of the University of Tennessee* (Knoxville: Univ. of Tennessee Press, 1984), 3–14.

6. Ralph Waldo Lloyd, *Maryville College: A History of 150 Years, 1819–1969* (Maryville, Tenn.: Maryville College Press, 1969), 3–28.

7. I have used the dates and places reported in *American Universities and Colleges*, 13th ed. (New York: Walter de Gruyter, 1987). Most schools used the earliest date which reflects their beginnings as an academy or junior college. Many moved, and I have used the final location.

8. Kenneth W. Plummer, *A History of West Virginia Wesleyan College: 1890–1965* (Buckhannon, W.Va.: West Virginia Wesleyan College Press, 1965), 31. See also Joseph T. Fuhrmann, *The Life and Times of Tusculum College* (Greeneville, Tenn.: Tusculum College, 1986), 82–108, 124–25.

9. Elizabeth S. Peck, *Berea's First 125 Years: 1855–1980* (Lexington: Univ. of Kentucky Press, 1982), 36.

10. Robert Snyder, *A History of Georgetown College* (Georgetown, Ky.: Georgetown College, 1979), 143–56.

11. Merle Curti and Roderick Nash, *Philanthropy in the Shaping of American Education* (New Brunswick, N.J.: Rutgers Univ. Press, 1965), 158–59.

12. Plummer, *History of West Virginia Wesleyan,* 77–97.

13. Fuhrmann, *Life and Times of Tusculum,* 82–108, 124–25.

14. Ibid. It is not clear what the college had expected, but it had received $350,000 over the years. The author knows of one Appaclachian school where the rather optimistic college president fully expected several million dollars upon the death of a potential benefactor and instead received nothing at all.

15. Thomas Richard Ross, *Davis and Elkins: The Diamond Jubilee History* (Elkins, W.Va.: Davis and Elkins College, 1980), 40–55.

16. Erwin S. Bradley, *Union College, 1879–1954* (Barbourville, Ky.: Union College, 1954), 93.

17. John Angus McLeod, *From These Stones: Mars Hill College: The First Hundred Years* (Mars Hill, N.C.: Mars Hill College Press, 1955), 207–34.

18. Fuhrmann, *Life and Times of Tusculum,* 155. In one study of giving, it was noted that less than half of the trustees actually contributed to the college. Trustees most often are selected for the position because it is thought they have money to contribute.

19. Bradley, *Union College,* 93–108.

20. Fuhrmann, *Life and Times of Tusculum,* 275.

21. Reuben E. Alley, *History of the University of Richmond, 1830–1971* (Charlottesville, Va.: Univ. Press of Virginia, 1977), 190.

22. Ibid., 73–74, 248, 257–58. When drinking finally was allowed on campus in 1970, the Baptist General Association protested, but to no avail.

23. David Duncan Wallace, *History of Wofford College, 1854–1949* (Nashville: Vanderbilt Univ. Press, 1951), 62.

24. George J. Stevenson, *Increase in Excellence: A History of Emory and Henry College* (New York: Appleton-Century-Crofts, 1963), 193–96. The alumni believed that a college was judged almost solely by its athletic program.

25. It led to other kinds of conflicts as well, especially when it threatened athletics. In the 1930s, trustees sometimes elected to lose accreditation rather than give up a winning football team. Stevenson, *Increase in Excellence,* 193–96.

26. Isaac Newton Carr, *History of Carson-Newman College* (Jefferson City, Tenn.: Carson-Newman College, 1959), 63–67.

27. Mary D. Beaty, *A History of Davidson College* (Davidson, N.C.: Briarpatch Press, 1988), 353, 394.

28. The Baptist preachers of southern West Virginia simply ignored mail they re-

ceived from Alderson-Broaddus. The college finally learned that it got a much better response when mail was sent directly to church clerks. Ervin Peter Young Simpson, "A History of Alderson-Broaddus, 1812–1951," unpublished manuscript, written at Phillippi, W.Va., 1983, pp. 381–82. Copy in Alderson-Broaddus Library.

29. Crenshaw, *General Lee's College,* 92–93. It must be added that Washington College was upset about the number of Episcopalians associated with Virginia Military Institute and also about the fact that Washington's president preached in Episcopal churches.

30. Frank Benjamin Hurt, *A History of Ferrum College: An Uncommon Challenge* (Roanoke, Va.: Stone Printing Co., 1977), 71, 92.

31. There were constant efforts to unite Tusculum and King colleges.

32. It is hardly surprising that the major theological question facing colleges concerned evolution.

33. The Bible college movement has given rise to scores—perhaps hundreds—of small and large colleges. They range in size from fewer than 10 students to more than 3,000 students. The ultra-conservative wing of the Disciples of Christ (independents, called the Christian Church in the South and both Christian Church and Church of Christ in the North), with perhaps a million members, at one time had some forty Bible colleges and only one liberal arts college. The most famous Bible college is Moody Bible Institute, in Chicago, but probably the majority of these colleges is located in the South. This phenomenon never has been studied fully by either educational or church historians. For an inadequate treatment of the movement, see S. A. Witmer, *The Bible College Story: Education with Dimension* (Wheaton, Ill.: Wheaton College Press, 1970), or William C. Ringenberg, *The Christian College: A History of Private Education in America* (Grand Rapids, Mich.: Christian Univ. Press, 1984), 157–73. More recent and much more complete is Virginia Lieson Brereton, *Training God's Army: The American Bible School, 1880–1980* (Bloomington: Univ. of Indiana Press, 1990).

34. David B. Potts, "American Colleges in the Nineteenth Century: From Localism to Denominationalism," *History of Education Quarterly* 11, no. 4 (Winter 1971): 374.

35. Ringenberg, *Christian College,* 105.

36. Fuhrmann, *Life and Times of Tusculum,* 273–81.

37. On college violence, see G. C. Coulter, *College Life in the Old South* (Athens, Ga.: Univ. of Georgia Press, 1951).

38. Student resistance to required chapel attendance ordinarily is not discussed in college histories, but subtext suggests that chapel often was eliminated or changed radically whenever it was deemed necessary to recruit more students. In the summer of 1938, Davis and Elkins reduced chapel to once a week; at roughly the same time, after the move to Charleston, Morris-Harvey dropped chapel. Ross, *Davis and Elkins,* 112–41; Frank J. Krebs, *Where There Is Faith: The Morris-Harvey College Story, 1888–1970* (Charleston, W.Va.: Morris-Harvey College, 1974), 166–67.

39. Snyder, *History of Georgetown*, 143–56. Gilbert Govan and James W. Livengood, *The University of Chattanooga: Sixty Years* (Chattanooga, Tenn.: Univ. of Chattanooga Press, 1947), 128–29, 235.

40. Krebs, *Where There Is Faith*, 165–67.

41. Ross, *Davis and Elkins*, 244–314, 40.

42. Fuhrmann, *Life and Times of Tusculum* , 300–310.

43. For a recent and informative history of Alice Lloyd, see P. David Searles, *A College for Appalachia: Alice Lloyd on Caney Creek* (Lexington: Univ. of Kentucky Press, 1995).

44. Lloyd, *Maryville College*, 39.

Chapter 6

Mountain Religion: An Overview

Loyal Jones

Mountain religion is a search for meaning. Mountain people, like all people, ask the big questions: Who are we? How did we come to be? If we were created, what is the nature of our Creator, and what power does the Creator hold over our lives here and beyond? Why is there evil in the world and within ourselves? What is our nature and our purpose, and how can we change our nature, fulfill our purpose, and face eternity? Most of the answers, for us in the Southern Uplands, come from the Bible (King James version). Some answers, of course, come through the oral tradition—ancient ballads and folk tales in which small boys face the devil in a standoff, or in which supernatural happenings take place. Mostly, however, even in oral tradition, the Bible is the singular source.

The Old Testament is read for its revelation of creation, the fallen condition of humanity, the nature of God, and how God dealt with His chosen people and their enemies. The New Testament is the authority on the human condition and what is necessary for salvation from it. The letters of the Apostle Paul most often are perused in the quest for meaning.

The issues that divide us Christians in the mountains are the nature of God and the nature of the human condition. The heavy hand of John Calvin is felt throughout the mountains, particularly among the Old-Time Baptists (Primitive, Old Regular, United, and others), stressing the Almightiness of God and the fallen human condition, and emphasizing some degree or form of predestination, limited atonement, salvation through grace, and eternal security. The theology of Bishop Jacob Arminius and the Reverend John Wesley also has found ready acceptance. Arminianism stressed free will, the possibility of universal atonement, human preparation for grace, salvation, and dramatic human improvement through salvation and sanctification. Both First and Second Great Awakenings brought struggles over these conflicting theologies, after producing new communities of faith.

The early immigrants, who left political, economic, and religious turmoil to come to this new land, found even more disorder in the wilderness, and thus they held onto the Calvinistic system, with its assurance that God was in charge of their destinies. As frontier people gained a modicum of control over their lives, they yearned for a more hopeful gospel. It came with the Methodists. The revivals that they energized, especially in the Second Great Awakening, won many to the hope that all may achieve salvation and, beyond that, may improve human nature through sanctification. Many Baptists and Presbyterians forsook their Calvinism for the more optimistic theology of the Methodists.

These two sets of theological beliefs—Calvinism and Arminianism—continued to divide religious people throughout the nineteenth century. Splits took place among the Presbyterians and Baptists, which led to the formation of such communions as the Cumberland Presbyterians and Restorationists (Christian Churches), and, by the century's end, the Holiness-Pentecostal movements. In addition, political and economic issues connected with slavery and the Civil War contributed to the schisms that split almost all the mainline denominations into northern and southern factions, each split having theological ramifications. The major black denominations resulted from the war, the abolition of slavery, and black people's wish to escape white domination in the realm of religion.

Today, the Primitive, or Old-School, Baptists are the most Calvinistic of Appalachian Christians. They embrace the classic points of Calvinism: election, limited atonement, the total depravity of humankind, irresistibility of grace, and perseverance of the saints, although all would disclaim Calvin and instead cite appropriate scriptures to justify their beliefs. As Howard Dorgan has written, the Regular, Old Regular, United Baptists, and other subdenominations are Calvinistic in a limited way.[1] They have modified the doctrine of election to include any who hear the Word and repent. The relatively small number calling themselves Grace Baptists (Sovereign) have reasserted Calvin's tenets but have modern church houses and instrumental music, as well as promoting some missionary activity. The Southern and American Baptists, Missionary and Free Will, have accepted most of the Arminian doctrine, while retaining Calvinistic ideas regarding the corruptible human nature and the perseverance of the saints. Presbyterians and Christian groups, too, have modified their Calvinism.

The Church of God (Cleveland, Tennessee), was the first of the Pentecostal denominations in the mountains. It grew out of a concern that the basic idea of Holiness coming out of Methodism had been watered down. Like the Methodists, they believed in an act of grace that lifts converts above sin, but they emphasized a third act of grace when the Holy Ghost descends and enables people to do extraordinary things, such as speaking in unknown tongues. The Church of God of Prophecy resulted from a split in the Church of God, Cleveland. The Church of God, Mountain Assembly, headquartered in Jellico, Tennessee, apparently was called the Church of God even before the Cleveland denomination was established. Many locally autonomous churches of various names also sprang up throughout Appalachia as parts of the Holiness-Pentecostal movement. These churches were embraced particularly by beleaguered people, those who had little economic security or affirmation of their worth by the larger society. Their beliefs, stressing the work of the Holy Ghost, affirmed their basic dignity. Of course, many other people who have security and worldly acclaim still feel the need of a strong Spirit-filled religion.

The sociology of Appalachia dictates many kinds of churches and nuances in theology. Robert Penn Warren, in *All the King's Men,* has Gov. Willie Stark comment on the law, "It's like a single-bed blanket on a double bed and three folks in the bed and a cold night. There ain't ever enough blanket to cover the case, no matter how much pulling and hauling, and somebody is always going to nigh catch pneumonia."[2] In contrast, the blanket of Christian theology is wonderfully ample and covers all who tug at it. People who hold conflicting opinions about God, the devil, human nature, salvation, death, the resurrection, and eternity find scriptural authority for their beliefs.

We mountain Christians, even while holding firm beliefs across the theological spectrum, nevertheless usually are humble human beings, holding open the possibilities that we might be wrong and that we are not capable, with our limited minds, of understanding the magnificence of God and His eternal plan. For example, some Old Regular Baptists are hesitant to say "I know," in regard to their or others' guaranteed place in Heaven, but instead will say "I feel," "I believe," or "I hope."

Perhaps this humble stance, which is amply supported in the Scriptures, is what sets mountain "fundamentalists" apart from the "Christian Right," so prominent in today's media, who seem immune to doubt about their political and religious stances. While many mountain Christians may be uneasy about such issues as abortion, most would be reluctant to promote governmental solutions to religious and moral problems. In many churches there is a profound belief in the separation of "the World" from the spiritual realm. Government is seen as part of the World, which is manipulated by Satan. The perilous task of the Christian is to remain "unspotted from the World." Most heed the dictum, "Render therefore unto Caesar the things which be Caesar's; and unto God the things which be God's" (Luke 20:25). For many mountain Christians, church is a place to worship God, not a place to organize committees, establish budgets, and advance social causes. There is fear that doing good works may entice us away from the worship of God. This is not to say that mountain Christians do not become involved in social issues. Many have participated in labor unions, poverty and environmental programs, efforts to reform government, and the like, but have remained reluctant to make such efforts part of the Church's mission.

Mountain people, of course, have been affected by political events. Many who settled the region were part of religious groups fleeing control over their spiritual lives by both Old and New World church-state forces. The Civil War made many mountaineers into Lincoln Republicans, and they spoke out against slavery, supporting the Union. All mainline churches had members with northern sympathies, and several of the smaller groups, too, were outspoken against slavery, among them Primitive Baptists, Wesleyan Methodists, and Holiness Methodists (those in the South who were associated with northern Methodism).[3] Baptists in western North Carolina and East Tennessee who had joined the Union League were chastised for joining a secret society, so they formed the Union Baptist Church, which assisted slaves and freedmen in various ways.[4]

Politically, conservatives in the mountains are different from conservatives elsewhere, because mountain conservatism came out of Lincoln Republicanism. Most have modest incomes and material resources and thus are not necessarily in sympathy with the efforts by modern Republicans to cut government and social programs while providing tax cuts and other benefits for well-to-do people and corporations. Because they have radical roots, mountain conservatives at times are as radical in politics as in religion. For example, the United Mine Workers of America, though largely Democratic, has had many Republican members. Also, in the coalfields, there are communities where race relations have been mostly cordial, and in eastern Kentucky there are at least three churches which always have held racially integrated services.[5]

The above statements are generalizations about churches that stand in contrast to mainstream religion. Many differences exist within the region, however. Larger cities and towns have Catholic churches and Jewish syna-

gogues. Moslems also are present in the region, and mosques are beginning to appear in various places. Hindu groups also are represented, the
best known being the Hare Krishnas in West Virginia. There also are
Buddhist monasteries in West Virginia and western North Carolina. Large
cities and county seats include most of the Protestant churches that would
be found throughout America. Even the rural areas may include Southern,
American, or National Baptist churches; Episcopal; United Methodist; Af-
rican Methodist Episcopal (A.M.E.), Zion; Presbyterian or Cumberland
Presbyterian; Disciples, Church of Christ; Independent Christian;
Lutheran; Seventh-Day Adventist; Church of the Brethren, Mennonite;
Church of God, Cleveland; Church of God of Prophecy; Church of God,
Mountain Assembly; as well as Saints of Christ, the Church of God in
Christ, Pentecostal Holiness, Assemblies of God, and Church of the
Nazarene.

There are numerous other churches and their associations, sometimes
referred to as sects by denominational people. Among the Baptists are
Primitive, Regular, Old Regular, Union, United, Free-Will, Two-Seed-in-
the-Spirit Predestinarian, General Six-Principle, Seventh-Day, and Duck
River. There are Wesleyan and Holiness Methodists, as well as Bible and
Full-Gospel churches. In addition to Pentecostal-Holiness groups already
named, there are many locally autonomous churches or smaller associa-
tions, such as Church of God, Jerusalem Acres, and Church of God, Zion
Hill (both of these split from the Church of God of Prophecy); Fire Bap-
tized Holiness Church; Pentecostal Church of God; Apostolic Church of
God; Church of God in Jesus' Name Only; and Church of God Militant
Pillar and Ground of Truth. These lists are far from exhaustive.

The names and worship practices of these churches imply the variety
of their distinct views on God, the human condition, Satan, Heaven and
Hell, salvation, baptism, sacraments, death, the Resurrection, and the
Hereafter. The following are opinions, sometimes colorfully and always
sincerely expressed, on subjects of primary concern by mountain Christians.
It is important to let Appalachian Christians express their views for themselves. These comments are representative, not definitive.

God

Pastor Henry T. Mahan, a Grace Baptist minister from Ashland, Kentucky, had this to say about God:

> His throne is the throne of sovereignty. . . . Is anything too hard for God?
> The Scriptures say that the Lord rules over all. God is God! He declares the
> end from the beginning. . . . God's rule is an everlasting dominion, and all

the inhabitants of the earth are reputed as nothing . . . , dust, a drop of water left in the bottom of a bucket, and He doeth His will in the armies of Heaven and among the inhabitants of the earth. . . . He worketh all things after the counsel of His own will, and that's in creation, and that's in providence, and that's in salvation. . . . None can stay God's hand. If He sets out to save, He'll save. If He sets out to damn, He'll damn. He has the key to Hell and death, and the One who carries the keys is in charge. [6]

On God and salvation, Elder Squire Watts, an Old Regular Baptist, believed that one has to cooperate with God in order to be saved:

If you don't want God to speak to you, He sure won't. If you don't want to do His will, you never will. . . . This voice speaks to your heart today. If you want to do what that still small voice bids you do, you'll wind up in Heaven.[7]

Will Igon, an Alabama Pentecostal, touched on God and the work of the Holy Spirit:

We cannot be real Christians without the Holy Ghost with us. I will say that when we are converted and love comes in, why that's the Holy Ghost, and it makes us have a feeling that nothing else has. There's nothing can cause the feeling to come in your body, your soul . . . like that of the Holy Ghost. That's the thing that comes from God.[8]

Brother Ozell Bunch, a Pentecostal preacher from LaFollette, Tennessee, spoke of God as a shield against Satan:

Brother, I'm not afraid of the devil. . . . I'm not afraid of him because the Man that lives in me is greater than he is. I know God. I am here . . . to preach a great God to a great people, and I believe that when people get their minds on God, and God puts His mind on the people, there are not enough devils in Hell to keep them from growing, to keep them from building, to keep them from shouting, to keep them from going forward in the name of Almighty God.[9]

Satan and the World

Mountain people take the Bible at its word and believe that Satan is roaming the world today, tempting people, turning them away from God, just as in biblical times. As they see it, Satan is all too real, not just a metaphor for evil. An unidentified radio preacher said this about the devil:

If you want to have an effective warfare against Satan, then you must have the right equipment. You don't go against your enemy who has a .50-caliber machine gun with a derringer. You must have the whole armor of God, and you don't get that from a rock concert. . . . You get that from the Word of God. People's problems today is that they have not put on the whole armor of God.[10]

The Reverend Buell Kazee, a Baptist minister, described the devil not so much as a combative being but rather as a beguiler:

Religion's . . . got a lot of good things in it, but there's a lot of difference between "good" and that which is from God. Keep in mind, a Christian must never ask, "Is it good?" He must ask, "Is it from God?" You understand . . . [the devil's] a counterfeit god. He's going to be as much like God as he can. He wants you to have religion. . . . He wants everybody to have religion. He wants to divide and have all sorts of religion for everybody. It's good religion. It has humanitarianism in it; it's got morality in it; it's got all the marks that we are looking for as good in it. But godliness, that's something else. He's working on good honest people, the most consecrated religious people . . . , but the deception lies in the devil getting them to believe something other than the Word of God.[11]

Sue Cox Cole, from Harlan County, Kentucky, now a minister and gospel singer, linked the devil to things of "the World":

Some people think that if something is going big, God is in it. Well, if it went that way, the Superbowl, the Cincinnati Reds, the Kentucky Wildcats, and all that kind of stuff is big. I doubt that God cares who wins. I figure it is a bunch of foolishness to Him—that a nation could get with something like that, so frivolous. People care more about pleasure than they do God.[12]

Concerning the tension between worldly success and spiritual matters, Buell Kazee said:

There isn't a man or woman who can appear on Billy Graham's program who hasn't been a "success" *in the world*. That is to say, his success in the world qualifies him to appear in the crusade program. He has to be a headliner in the world. . . . They had a fellow who was the champion yo-yo artist on a program in Lexington. Now he came not because of his great Christian life—he was a Christian maybe. The point is, he was there *because he was a champion yo-yo artist*. As you can see, this is pure sham, because most of the people who are dedicated to Christ in the real sense wouldn't have any time for any of this other stuff.[13]

Brother Herman B. Yates, another Grace Baptist, returned to topic of the militant and forceful Satan:

Christ has never tolerated any truce with the Evil One, and He never will. There is a deadly, implacable, infinite, eternal enmity between Christ and sin, of which Satan is the representative. In this battle no compromise can ever be thought of, and no quarter can ever be given. The Lord will never turn from His purpose of casting Satan into the Lake of Fire.[14]

The Human Condition

Most Appalachians see humankind as the object of God's love and of the devil's work and wonder what our true nature and our destiny are. Audrey Wiley, an Eastern Kentucky woman, said, "God created Adam and Eve to replenish the earth. That is the sole purpose. . . . He put us on earth to get glory out of us."[15]

Elder Mike Smith, a Primitive Baptist, said:

Man in his best state is nothing, less than nothing. We've got nothing to plead. We've got no righteousness to plead. The only righteousness you and me have is the imputed righteousness of Jesus Christ.[16]

The Reverend Fred Lunsford, a North Carolina Southern Baptist, had this opinion of human nature and salvation:

Man has fallen into a sinful state, and he is by nature a sinner. His inclination is in that direction. When a man trusts the Lord and becomes a Christian, he still has fleshly inclinations. This is his nature, and there comes a constant warfare in his life. This takes him back to priorities, and he must decide which he must put first.[17]

The Reverend L. O. Johnson, pastor of a Church of God of Prophecy congregation, agreed that the fleshly part of us is subject to sin, but he talked also of the spiritual side of human beings and how, through salvation, one can be cleansed of sin:

That which is born of flesh is flesh; that which is born of the Spirit is spirit. Man himself is spirit clothed in the flesh of the body. The body shall be destroyed . . . , but the spirit lives forever. . . . When we speak of saving the soul, we are thinking of that person being delivered from the bondage of sin and being set free from it so he will not have to go to Hell forever.[18]

Salvation

For mountain people, as for other Christians, the object of religion is salvation. As one member of the Church of God, Mountain Assembly, wrote, "The acceptance of the Savior brings a glow of perfect peace, perfect love, perfect assurance."[19] For others, salvation may require a long travail in achieving and retaining it. Elder Frank Fugate, an Old Regular Baptist, commented, "The prime cause of Baptist people is the doctrine of repentance. Repentance is a Godly sorrow in the heart. . . . We all repent, but whether or not we repent to the extent of satisfying God's wrath and receive God as our strength is the thing about it."[20] Brother Alfred Carrier, a Pentecostal preacher, said this:

> There has to be a conviction of the Spirit, because man is a fallen creature and has to be converted. He's got to have a complete total change within his heart. . . . He must have an altar somewhere and give a total, complete repentance and confession before the Lord, and we say definitely a public confession must come before you can fully please the Lord. . . . The blood of Christ is the only atonement for sin today, and when the blood is applied through the Spirit, we are aware of the fact that we have been made free from sin and that we are now a child of God and qualify for entrance into Heaven.[21]

While some people talk about salvation to gain Heaven and to avoid Hell, others talk of how, though salvation, they have become better in this life. Sue Cox Cole, the Kentucky Pentecostal minister quoted previously, said, "I feel honored to work for God. You know, when you are a Christian, you hear that you are a special creation of God, and that you are important, that you are somebody, and that God has a place for your life. It's certainly going to make a difference in your behavior."[22] William Addison, a West Virginia coal miner, a leader in the United Mine Workers of America, and a Pentecostal, testified:

> I used to be a man that had these great inferior feelings. . . . After I committed myself to Christ thirty years ago, He's done these things for me. He's set me free, and He has showed me what a man really is. . . . It's like John L. Lewis came along and told the miners what they really were, and

they began to lose their inferior feelings. . . . The greatest thing that happens to a Christian is that He makes a person out of you. It doesn't make an overbearing person, or a person that is going to hurt somebody, but it makes a person who will stand. . . . When I look at death, I'm not concerned, but what I am concerned with is what I can do in the world before I die.[23]

The gospel is interpreted in different ways by the people of the mountains, then, but their similarities of belief are greater than their differences. Their similarities to mainstream Christians also are greater than their differences from such people. Some mountain people may be largely unchurched, or salvation may come when they are "up in years," in the Calvinist tradition.[24] Most, however, seek God at some point in their lives and see Jesus Christ as their way to Him. They believe in the Holy Spirit and believe that this Spirit is with them. They yearn for a life beyond this one. Some speak more eloquently and with more certitude than others, but those quoted above and others like them are fervent in their beliefs and in their quest for God and salvation. They want to become better persons here on earth than they actually are now, although some are more optimistic than others about their ability to do so. However, they believe that a religious conversion will improve them here and give them "sweet hope in their breasts" for Heaven.

Some mountain people are as intensely Christian as people elsewhere. The Christian faith and the King James Bible have been their teachers, their sources of solace and inspiration; and religion has permeated the culture and influenced even those who nominally are not a part of the Christian Band. Yet in the past some denominational missionaries have been too caught up in their mission to notice the quality of faith already present in mountain people. Some, no doubt, will make the same mistake in the future. Therefore it is important to help missionaries to understand mountain people and their religion. It also is important to suggest, and to hope, that they will adopt one of the cornerstones of Appalachian theology—humility. One *may* be right, but, on the other hand, one may not be—especially about such mystical matters as belief, faith, and hope. Those who come to the mountains to work need to realize that they will not be successful with mountain people if they do not respect them and the faith they already posses.

Mountain people are changing. Farming, coal, and timber no longer are the mainstays of the economy, yet as new industries move in, unemployment remains high and family income low, and governmental support payments supply a large portion of income. A great deal of

land, minerals, and other resources still are controlled by absentee owners. Richard Couto, writing for the Commission on Religion in Appalachia, suggests the ups and downs of the economy in Central Appalachia. Some counties gained from 10 to 18 percent in family income in
the 1970s and then lost as much as 18 percent in the 1980s; the coalfield
counties have been left behind as Sunbelt Appalachia prospers.[25] However, the region in most ways is changing for the better. There is more
native activism in regard to government, the economy, and the environment. New economic enterprises, both home-grown and imported, are
developing; except for Central Appalachia, the region has made great
progress. State government, schools, and local initiatives are becoming
more effective. Good roads and new communications systems have
made a great difference.

As mountain people change, so will their religion, although perhaps
not always for the better. Mountain people will continue to find meaning through their faith as both they and their religion change. Perhaps
in the future they will be influenced by mainstream religion, but perhaps not so much as some expect. In whatever ways their faith evolves,
I believe it will be sincere and appropriate for their lives. Therefore they
should be accepted and respected for their perseverance in the faith.

Notes

Unless otherwise noted, audiotapes of all interviews cited are in the possession of
the author and are to be deposited in the Special Collections Department of the
Berea College Library.

1. Howard Dorgan, *Giving Glory to God in Appalachia: Worship Practices of Six Bap-
tist Subdenominations* (Knoxville: Univ. of Tennessee Press, 1987); and Howard
Dorgan, *The Old Regular Baptists of Central Appalachia: Brothers and Sisters in Hope*
(Knoxville: Univ. of Tennessee Press, 1989).

2. Robert Penn Warren, *All the King's Men* (New York: Harcourt, Brace, 1946),
145.

3. J. Lawrence Brasher, *The Sanctified South: John Lakin Brasher and the Holiness
Movement* (Urbana: Univ. of Illinois Press, 1994).

4. See Richard Alan Humphrey, "The Civil War and Church Schisms in Southern
Appalachia," *Appalachian Heritage* 9, no. 3 (Summer 1981): 38–51.

5. These churches are: The First Baptist Church of Town Mountain, near Hazard,
Ky.; the Little Home Old Regular Baptist Church in Red Fox, Ky.; and the
Church of God Militant Pillar and Ground of Truth, in McRoberts, Ky.

6. Henry T. Mahan, "The Throne of Grace," sermon recorded at Thirteenth Street
Baptist Church, Ashland, Ky., n.d.

7. Squire Watts, sermon at Cedar Grove Old Regular Baptist Church, Letcher County, Ky., Oct. 23, 1993.

8. Will Igon, transcript of interview, June 11, 1959, Southern Appalachian Studies, series V, box 71, folder 5, in Berea College Special Collections.

9. Ozell Bunch, sermon on an unidentified radio station, 1975.

10. Unidentified radio preacher, sermon recorded by Garner Hargis in a Pentecostal Church, Lincoln County, Ky., 1975.

11. Buell Kazee, interview by Loyal Jones, Winchester, Ky., 1975.

12. Sue Cox Cole, sermon, Berea, Ky., Jan. 2, 1987, recorded by Stephen Burgess.

13. Buell Kazee interview, 1975.

14. Herman B. Yates, "The Battle for the Elect of God," sermon preached in the Grace Baptist Church, Dingess, W.Va., n.d. Audiotape in Berea College Special Collections, AC-CT-363-001.

15. Audrey Wiley, interview by Gary King, Estill, Ky., summer 1975.

16. Mike Smith, interview by unidentified Berea College student, 1975.

17. Fred Lunsford, interview by Loyal Jones, Vengeance Creek, N.C., 1976.

18. Transcript of interview, June 25, 1959, Southern Appalachian Studies, series V, box 73, folder 7, in Berea College Special Collections.

19. "Does It Pay to Be a Christian?" *Gospel Herald* 31, no. 8 (Aug. 1970): 10.

20. Frank Fugate, interview by Herb E. Smith, Letcher County, Ky., 1976, in Appalachian Film Workshop Archives.

21. Alfred Carrier, interview by Garner Hargis, McKinney, Ky., 1975.

22. Sue Cox Cole, sermon.

23. William Addison, interview by Mike Yarrow, Beckley, W.Va., Oct. 8, 1986.

24. Because strict mountain Calvinists believe that salvation is wholly the work of God, they often emphasize that salvation comes on God's time, not ours. Thus elected individuals may not be "brought to grace" until late in life.

25. For more on the Appalachian economy, see Richard A. Couto, *An American Challenge: A Report on Economic Trends and Social Issues in Appalachia* (Dubuque, Ia.: Kendall/Hunt Publishing Co., 1994).

Chapter 7

Mountain Holiness

Deborah Vansau McCauley

In the early 1990s I taught a gender studies course at Columbia University on women and Appalachian mountain religion. With the help of dozens of slides and photographs, along with tapes of interviews and worship services, the people enrolled began to learn the features of mountain religion's oral and material culture. Largely undocumented up to that time, apart from my work with the Appalachian photographer Warren Brunner over a period of several years, was the mountain church tradition of independent Holiness, thousands of whose tiny, often unmarked one-room church houses are scattered throughout Appalachia, especially in its central regions. Most of these church houses or worship structures are all but invisible to the untrained eye, escaping attention and eluding any awareness on the part of the outsider of their prominence, history, and importance in mountain religious culture. Since leadership roles are especially common for women in much of mountain Holiness culture, we focused a lot of our attention in the course on mountain Holiness and its relationship to other mountain church traditions—how they are alike, how they are different, and how they influence each other. The summer after the course ended, one student enrolled in the class, a third-generation Russian Jew who had always lived on the East coast, made a two-week car trip throughout the areas the course had highlighted. Later he called me and said, "You're right! Holiness churches are *everywhere*. I didn't really see them at first, because they are hard to spot until you know what to look for."

All of mountain religion mirrors this openhearted young man's encounter with mountain Holiness churches. Unless you are part of the landscape, it generally escapes your notice "until you know what to look for." Mountain religion has an invisibility for those not part of it in some way or another. Such invisibility belies mountain religion's importance in the overall religious life and culture of the Appalachian region. In this chapter, I concentrate on Appalachian *mountain* religion, "mountain religion" being the distinguishing term accepted by Appalachian Studies scholars such as Loyal Jones and American religious historians such as Catherine Albanese.[1] Mountain people also accept the term without pause when they hear it but do not use it themselves. They often talk about "mountain churches" when speaking in general. I distinguish between those church traditions that are in the Appalachian region but not largely of it, mostly the denominations of American Protestantism, and those church traditions that exist predominantly—or almost exclusively—in the region and are very special to it. The historical echoes of what is unique to religious life in Appalachia are much weaker in the Appalachian churches of American Protestantism in general, but they are there. Several denominations in Appalachia, particularly the United Methodists and Southern Baptists, have a long and significant history in the region. Unlike most of their urban, county-seat, or larger-town churches, many of their small mountain churches have been profoundly affected by the distinctive religious culture of the region. It is precisely the defining configuration of land, people, history, and traditions that constitutes Appalachian mountain religion as a regional religious tradition.

Appalachian mountain religion is one of the very few uniquely American, regional traditions to which Protestantism in the United States can lay claim. It is made up of church traditions found almost entirely in the region's mountains and small valleys. Generally, these mountain churches do not exist beyond Appalachia, except through outmigration. These church traditions, nearly invisible to the outside world and to much of the Protestant mainstream even within Appalachia, make up what is exclusive to religious life in Appalachia. Moreover, they have had a profound impact on the overall religious character of Appalachia, extending their influences even into large, urban, and broad-valley mainline Protestant churches in subtle, indirect ways. However, mountain church traditions are scarcely influenced by the presence of American Protestantism in Appalachia today. Mountain religion embodies the distinctive religious ethos of

Appalachia. The Appalachian churches of American Protestantism are affected by that ethos, for it permeates Appalachian culture well beyond the doors of the mountain "church house." When we focus on those church traditions in the mountains which most densely concentrate within themselves the characterizing features of mountain religious life, mountain Holiness stands with them at the forefront.

Historically, in the American consciousness, Appalachian mountain religion has been portrayed in stereotypical terms that focus on an archetype called the "mountain preacher" who oscillates between two extremes with unfortunate and unrealistic characterizations: as either a strict, suffocating Calvinist or an emotionally unstable fanatic with a penchant for serpent handling. In fact, mountain religion, like the mountain preacher, exists only as a range or spectrum of worship life and traditions sharing "regional" characteristics. From Old Regular Baptist to independent Holiness, the most basic and the most significant of these characteristics is a predominant emphasis on grace and religious experience, mediated by the Holy Spirit. These features are at the core of Appalachian mountain religion.

Any claim of shared "regional" characteristics, at the outset, can be a thorny issue in terms of methodology. But Catherine Albanese incisively helps us out of this apparent dilemma. Regional religion may be looked at primarily through the interplay of what Albanese calls *creeds* (what people believe), *codes* (how people live), *cultuses* (how people worship), and *communities* (the people who are bound together by shared traditions, history, and place).[2] Regional religion, writes Albanese, is "religion born of natural geography, of past and present human history, and of the interaction of the two."[3] By the second half of the nineteenth century, especially after 1850, Appalachia's regional character had become sharpened and clearly defined. Well before that time, the variety of church traditions making up Appalachian mountain religion were already firmly established as having more in common with each other—notwithstanding theological differences—than with the large denominations and religious movements, both within and outside of Appalachia, with whom they shared their earliest roots.

If we depict Appalachian mountain religion as ranging across a spectrum (a linear, two-dimensional model useful only for purposes of discussion), the independent nondenominational church stands at the center of that spectrum. Very often Baptist, more often Holiness-Pentecostal, these churches today carry on the worship practices and belief systems of pre-1850 plain-folk camp-meeting religion more fully than any other mountain church tradition. Indeed, plain-folk camp-meeting religion was localized almost exclusively in the Appalachian region of the Upland South. Dickson

D. Bruce defines "plain-folk" as a term descriptive of the vast majority of southerners, most of whom were farmers and were not of the planter class of society that came to dominate the economic, political, and social fabric of the South. Instead, Bruce writes, "The small farms and domestic economy of these plain-folk therefore came to dominate certain upland areas of the South—the uplands and highlands of middle and western North Carolina, poorer lands in the Valley of Virginia, the northern parts of Georgia and Alabama, the foothills and mountains of Tennessee and Kentucky, and the mountainous regions of west Virginia."[4] In other words, the plain-folk of the Upland South, whose camp-meeting religion Bruce writes about, were overwhelmingly the people of Appalachia.

The independent nondenominational church—part of a long heritage beginning with the first years of settlement in the eighteenth century and crystallized especially through plain-folk camp-meeting religion—is perhaps the most common form of religious organization in many areas of rural Appalachia, especially Central Appalachia. It is also the least visible and least considered in writings on mountain religious life—with a few notable exceptions. Some social scientists insist that such churches epitomize a "subculture of poverty" model and models of powerlessness and alienation.[5] Commentators also have pointed to such churches as their premier example of mountain religion as sectarianism-run-amok. It follows that many believe a church-sect typology is the most appropriate lens for looking at mountain religious life.[6] Despite their bad reviews in the available literature, the foundational, shared characteristics of independent nondenominational churches nonetheless serve as a benchmark for looking at other mountain church traditions and discovering what they have in common, how they influence each other, and how they may be influenced by traditions nearer the ends of the spectrum, or—far less likely—by church traditions and religious movements clearly beyond the spectrum.

On the surface, this may seem to be an extraordinary claim: that not only does mountain religion have a church tradition consisting of churches that are invisible yet exceedingly numerous, widely scattered, totally autonomous from each other, as local and grassroots as possible, and almost always extremely small (often limited to a single room, either as a free-standing structure or in a private home); but that this church tradition is exceptionally significant. Indeed, such a tradition is indispensable to our understanding of mountain religion and its history. Autonomy and free church polity expressed in varying degrees are two of the most basic threads found throughout mountain church traditions. Embodying a radical autonomy and a highly spontaneous free church polity, independent nondenominational churches epitomize many of the normative institutional features and qualities of popular piety defining mountain religion throughout its history. This interpretation negates the church-sect typology model. It means that each of these churches does not constitute a random, discrete "sect," unconnected and peculiar unto itself, but that each is part of a large, intelligible church tradition.

These churches, in apparent contradiction, constitute a major mountain church tradition created *solely* by a myriad of totally "disconnected" churches. Yet this organizational dispersion can be a very misleading perception, as the long-standing and highly valued tradition of "fellowshiping," or constantly traveling around to worship at each other's churches, firmly attests. Mountain churches represent a tradition that lacks any kind of subregional institutional framework like the associational systems of such traditions as the Old Regular Baptists. These churches are also unremittingly characterized as highly "individualistic" (and therefore "sectarian"), because each church exhibits personal, freely self-determined variations on the firm foundation of shared worship traditions. Such traditions range from shared styles of preaching, singing, testifying, and praying, to expressive and ecstatic behaviors in worship centered on the episodic experience of conversion that is not merely an individual event but a *communal* event and a hallmark of mountain religion. Variations in worship life, whether pronounced or quite subtle, make independent nondenominational churches all the more obscure as a clearly differentiated mountain church tradition. However, these churches' shared worship practices and beliefs long have been faithfully transmitted with an uninterrupted integrity through the oral tradition of a regionally specific culture of popular piety that historically has infused all of mountain religion.

We cannot understand mountain religion without beginning to understand and appreciate its independent nondenominational churches. Like the history of the elemental forces creating the universe, the traditional history for independent nondenominational churches—converging into a church tradition indispensable to the creation of Appalachian mountain religion and crystallizing many of its normative features—is not entirely lost in the mists of time, despite the apparent randomness and chaos of these tiniest of forces on the religious landscape of Appalachia's mountain regions. An earlier, though most immediate, heritage is the essentially oral tradition of plain-folk camp-meeting religion. In the following paragraphs I outline a tradition history for mountain religion's independent nondenominational churches identified as Holiness. This conceptual framework should make it easier to understand these churches as part of a long-lived, organic religious *movement* in the mountains, while simultaneously they constitute a definable *church tradition* that is one of the largest—if not *the* largest—in Appalachian mountain religion.

"Holiness" is the universal generic term for the presence of the Holiness-Pentecostal movements in the mountains of Appalachia through independent nondenominational churches. The Holiness-Pentecostal movements in the mountains are represented only secondarily, albeit with a significant presence, by denominations whose national identity and national institutionalism define them, rather than their being defined primarily by their spiritual character or religious ethos, as mountain religion's independent nondenominational churches are. The Holiness and Pentecostal movements on a national level both have numerous denominations and church traditions and submovements, as well as thousands of loosely affiliated or unaffiliated churches throughout the United States—churches that also are nondenominational. Unlike mountain people who make up Appalachia's nondenominational church tradition of independent Holiness, Holiness and Pentecostal *denominations* use the terms "Holiness" and "Pentecostal" in the manner of organized religion, as terms that clearly differentiate them from each other, referring to a denominational institutionalism defined by codified creeds, doctrines, and polity, whose institutional life is bureaucratic and therefore quantifiable by statistics.

When mountain people use the term "religion" to make an all-important distinction between "religion" and "faith," they invariably mean *organized* religion, as represented primarily by the mainstream denominations of American Protestantism. These include the Southern Baptists, Presbyterians, and Methodists, *as well as* Holiness and Pentecostal denominations. The latter denominations range from the Church of God (Cleveland, Tennessee), the second largest Pentecostal denomination in the South; to the Church of the Nazarene, the largest Holiness denomination in the United States. Outsiders invariably designate as "Pentecostal" mountain people who align themselves with mountain religion's independent Holiness tradition, primarily because speaking in tongues is widely practiced in these churches. That practice served to differentiate decisively the Holiness and Pentecostal movements—as well as their denominations—from each other in the first years of the twentieth century. When asked if they are Pentecostal, people who worship in mountain Holiness churches will often say yes, but they refer to themselves almost universally as Holiness. Their usage of the term "Holiness" eschews the organizational categories distinguishing Holiness and Pentecostal denominations, and points to a very different formulation of the Holiness-Pentecostal movements in the mountains through a distinct tradition history for independent Holiness churches rooted first in mountain religious culture.

Albanese confirms the central place of the independent nondenominational church in mountain religion, which she describes more poetically as "the fruit of the mountain spirit and the mountain religious tradition" that "carried the tendencies within mountain religion to their *logical* conclusion" (emphasis added):

> [N]ondenominational churches . . . carried the tendencies within mountain religion to their logical conclusion, as one individual or another (usually male) among the people became convinced that God was calling him to preach and exhort. So he would set about establishing a church of his own, often on his property, either in his house or a separate building he might construct. Like a patron to his neighbors in a lonely mountain hollow, he invited them to join with him in seeking the Word and will of God. Here all the characteristics of mountain religion came together at their fullest expression: the uneducated preacher, the independent church, the primacy of the Bible, and the strong emotionalism of religious worship. The nondenominational church was the fruit of the mountain spirit and the mountain religious tradition.[7]

How accurate is Albanese's portrait? The field notes or schedules completed during 1931 for Elizabeth R. Hooker's social science survey of mountain religious life[8] provide some important clues to the continuity of the tradition that became mountain Holiness. The field notes supply limited but precise information on native ministers, sermons, and worship services not included in the published studies. Some of the ministers were born in the 1850s and 1860s, and thus the data provide a glimmer of religious life in the Appalachian region during the second half of the nineteenth century and into the early twentieth. However, the field notes are fraught with the biases of the field workers; education and cleanliness seem to have been of paramount concern.

One handwritten summary describing a mountain preacher stands out in particular, because it is a good example of much of what the survey uncovered. W. H. Callaway of Avery County, North Carolina, was born in 1858. A farmer with no schooling, he had been pastor of the "Independent Church of God," the name he gave to the church house he built on his own property, for nearly twenty-five years at the time of his interview:

> Mr. Callaway is an elderly farmer who has spent his whole life in this place. He has no education and could not read until after he was grown. He has spent a great deal of time reading the Bible, which he regards as inspired in every detail, and as a result knows it remarkably well. Feeling

called upon to preach the Gospel, he set up a building on his own land, at his own expense and with his own hands, and established a church independent of other denominations. At present the church has only 12 resident members, mostly relatives or life-long friends of his. For 24 years he has served as the pastor to the best of his ability, and received almost nothing in return. He is a kindly, lovable old man, always ready to help any who need it, and sometimes is imposed upon. Although his own beliefs are very definite, he very often allows men who differ with him to preach in his building.[9]

The parallels between Albanese's 1981 composite portrait and this short sketch from fifty years before are striking. Other preachers and religious leaders continuing in the tradition of mountain Holiness, whom I have met along the way, have embodied this portrait in their lives at the end of the twentieth century and are part of a large host of people.

In all writings about Appalachian mountain religion, the independent Holiness church has been the church most ignored, even though it distills many of the defining features of mountain church life in Appalachia. It has been the most ignored largely because its churches are extremely small and radically autonomous, with an anti-organizational structure and an almost complete absence of a clearly defined doctrinal tradition, making them amorphous, difficult to pin down and examine. However, mountain religion's numerous independent Holiness churches have a great deal in common with each other in worship practices and belief systems, even though each is marked by its own freely determined individuality or particularity. Indeed, they form a unique genre within mountain religion, one with common roots linked to the era of plain-folk camp-meeting religion during the first half of the nineteenth century.

Mountain religion retained the traditional expressions of emotional piety that characterized earlier revival religiosity, along with the ideology of grace and the Holy Spirit that they embodied. This religious ethos flourished through mountain religion long before, and well after, the rise of the Holiness-Pentecostal movements. Almost everywhere else in the U.S., the centrality of religious experience had disappeared decades prior to the clear emergence of these movements, which began to take form in gatherings such as Phoebe Palmer's "Tuesday Meetings for the Promotion of Holiness" held in her Manhattan parlor beginning in 1835, and culminating in the first "National Camp Meeting for the Promotion of Holiness" convened at Vineland, New Jersey, in July 1867. Finally, the 1906 mid-April meetings at the Azusa Street Mission in Los Angeles are nearly universally designated as the decisive events in the maturation of the Pentecostal movement. These earliest landmarks in the history of the Holiness-Pentecostal movements did encircle in geography and at a great distance the mountain religious culture of Appalachia, suggesting an over-all isolation from mountain religion. The Holiness-Pentecostal move-ments, however, did not simply emerge on their own, totally outside the perimeter of the distinctive religious culture of a region that seemingly did not touch them directly. They were, in reality, part of an organic move-ment embracing the sweep of American religious history that was not only highly concentrated but *uninterrupted* in the mountain regions of Appala-chia. That uninterrupted history in many ways made possible what became the Holiness-Pentecostal movements, although that history, like Appala-chian mountain religion itself, remained virtually unrecognized due to its essentially oral character and almost exclusively regional context.

Mountain religion directly contributed to what became many fea-tures of the Holiness-Pentecostal movements evident in such founda-tional components as worship practices, strong emotional piety, and an emphasis on the Holy Spirit. These contributions historically were not exclusive to mountain religion but were strongly identified with it, due to the integrity of its uninterrupted transmission process and the clear affinity of its distinctive religiosity. To what extent and in what ways—directly and indirectly, through its *oral* and *material* culture—mountain religion influenced the Holiness-Pentecostal movements, especially in their formative years, remains a question mark. To what extent moun-tain religion, at the level of popular religious culture, continues to in-form the development of the Holiness-Pentecostal movements—espe-cially as they are manifested within Appalachia itself—is yet another area awaiting exploration.

The issue of Appalachia's geographical isolation, and Methodist-based theological contributions of perfectionism or sanctification, were integral to what initially distinguished the religiosity of the Holiness-Pentecostal movements from mountain religion. Nonetheless, many of the defining features of mountain religion were grounded in earlier re-ligious movements—from pietism and Scots-Irish sacramental revival-ism, to early Baptist revival culture in the Mid-South, all of which were infused by a strongly pronounced and thriving Calvinist heritage em-phasizing grace and the Holy Spirit. That Calvinist heritage created the specific theological cast for the central role of religious experience in the normative revival religiosity crisscrossing mountain church traditions, despite their ideological distinctions that otherwise served to differen-tiate them within mountain religion.

Mountain religion's normative religiosity, conjoining its variety of church traditions, came to be further reconfigured in the regionally specific movement of plain-folk camp-meeting religion, born in the Great Revival on the Appalachian frontier, that dominated much of early- to mid-nineteenth-century popular religious culture in the Upland South, most of which Appalachia encompassed. These earlier, defining religious movements—pietism, Scots-Irish sacramental revivalism, Baptist revival culture, plain-folk camp-meeting religion—and the extent to which they are relevant to the most distant echoes still heard in the Holiness-Pentecostal movements introduce historical *and* theological components yet to be taken into account in understanding the tradition histories and symbol systems of Holiness-Pentecostal culture. Given the myriad of today's sociocultural, ethnic, and geographical variations on the Holiness-Pentecostal movements' basic building blocks in American religious history, the question arises, "Where might they still be best 'preserved?'"

Through historical echoes that persist today in their worship life, mountain Holiness churches provide major clues to the tradition histories and earlier symbol systems of many of the most important worship practices and the beliefs that became identified with the Holiness-Pentecostal movements in the national consciousness, often expressed in such crude terms as "holy rollers." These carefully nurtured clues point most immediately to an earlier (and little recognized) heritage crystallizing in the predominantly oral culture of plain-folk camp-meeting religion, whose influences did not remain confined solely to the large expanse of the Upland South, where it ostensibly "died out" by the mid-nineteenth century. The heritage of plain-folk camp-meeting religion—germinating in the piety of a popular religious culture outside of denominational or official institutional church structures—continued to thrive in the mountains. That heritage also extended, in less apparent ways, far beyond the Appalachian ridges and valleys into the national religious culture. Though submerged for some time throughout the rest of the nation's Protestant religious culture and later reconfigured in other theological terms by the Holiness-Pentecostal movements, the centrality of a type of religious experience defined by the emotional piety of expressive and ecstatic worship practices would not be thwarted. What had been predominantly a regionally specific religiosity, centered on religious experience itself, began to reemerge elsewhere, now asserting itself far beyond the Appalachian region where the heritage of that religiosity not only had persisted without interruption but would continue to thrive. Indeed, Appalachian religion defined a large and theologically diverse regional religious tradition.

Although we lack clear evidence at this time, it is probable that, in the

mountains of Appalachia, the appellation "Holiness" was appropriated, beginning no later than the 1890s, by Baptists of various backgrounds, as well
as by Methodists less closely aligned to Methodism's connectional system.
At the least, it was a term applied to newly created church communities by
people who came out of Baptist and Methodist churches that had perpetuated the traditions of plain-folk camp-meeting religion. Many churches
had institutionalized in their worship life the revival traditions distilled in
plain-folk camp-meeting religion—which, though a religious movement,
had quickly established itself as a nondenominational church tradition of
popular piety. These revival traditions were intensely expressive, egalitarian, and nonsectarian. They were the progeny largely of the institutionalized revival traditions that entered the worship life of many Appalachian
Baptists churches—widely ranging from Old Regular, to United, to Missionary, to Free Will—through the eighteenth-century Great Awakening
in the Mid-South whose church-based worship traditions found their
home predominantly in the mountains of Appalachia. As a church tradition, plain-folk camp-meeting religion had characterized the worship life
of numerous mountain Baptist and Methodist churches since the camp-
meeting days of the Great Revival. For the members of these churches who
either remained with their churches or parted to form new ones, "Holiness"
served better to describe their traditional, customary worship identity, for
the first time clearly distinguishing their worship life within mountain religious culture.

It is likely that the term "Holiness" thus was appropriated in the late
nineteenth century as a fitting description of a long-popular variant of
mountain religion's normative revival religiosity. That variant embodied a
style of worship life now fully differentiated from other, more theologically
conservative, Baptist church traditions (from Old Regular Baptist to Free
Will Baptist) which in turn were differentiated by their own variants of the
revival religiosity normative to mountain religion. "Holiness" also served to
distinguish the churches of former mountain Baptists and Methodists
steeped in the heritage of plain-folk camp-meeting religion from the now
fully "denominationalized" Methodist and Southern Baptist churches, also
found throughout Appalachia in the mountainous rural countryside, but
especially in the valleys, county seats, larger towns, and urban centers. They
themselves once had been an integral part of plain-folk camp-meeting religion that had given them their biggest boost in numbers in the very early
nineteenth century. However, the Methodists and the churches that were
identified as Southern Baptist after 1845 eschewed, soon after the ebbing of
the Great Revival on the Appalachian frontier, the centrality of religious
experience for the national institutionalism of denominationalism. By the

1890s, they had been separate from mountain religious culture for decades. The exceptions were many of their small mountain churches.

The appropriation of a name should not confuse our understanding of the Appalachian origins of its nondenominational tradition of independent Holiness churches. My thesis is that a well-established movement of popular religious culture in the mountains, present long prior to the clear emergence of the Holiness-Pentecostal movements, quickly and early took on the word "Holiness" to characterize itself, once the term had been elevated to such prominence in the Holiness-Pentecostal movements. If so, it would strongly indicate that mountain people perpetuating plain-folk camp-meeting worship life in their churches *recognized* the fundamental similarities, long normative to their distinctive variant of mountain religious culture, that they shared with emerging Holiness-Pentecostal culture outside Appalachia.

The emergence of the nondenominational tradition of independent Holiness churches, like the earlier emergence of other mountain church traditions, is a testimony to the vitality and ongoing development of mountain religion as a regional religious tradition. Mountain Holiness churches are, in many respects, set quite apart from the larger Holiness-Pentecostal movements outside Appalachia, belonging much more to mountain religion than to these larger national movements. Indeed, they belong to mountain religion first—apart from which they cannot be understood—and to the Holiness-Pentecostal movements only secondarily. Usage of the term "Holiness" by mountain churches indicates that, if the Holiness-Pentecostal movements reached into the mountains of Appalachia in such an instrumental way in the late nineteenth century, they did so *not* by introducing into mountain religion a new tradition that reconfigured it. Instead, the Holiness-Pentecostal movements provided a term that created a consensus of self-recognition. The term "Holiness," in effect, gave mountain people who, in their church life, were perpetuating the traditions of plain-folk camp-meeting religion, the means to "name" for themselves, and thus clearly set apart, the traditions that had, over time, come to differentiate them within mountain religious culture. This consensus of self-recognition, identifying Holiness with a variant of mountain religion stemming from the camp-meeting days of the Great Revival, reinforces the premise that the traditions consolidated and transmitted without interruption almost exclusively by mountain religion helped to shape the earliest foundations of the Holiness-Pentecostal movements, apart from their later and more self-defining theological formulations.

These multifaceted theological formulations stand as the single principal contribution of the Holiness-Pentecostal movements to many of the large host of churches, in all of their variety, making up the tradition of mountain Holiness. When present, the form such theological influences may take, and their extent, differ considerably from church to church. The worship practices and fundamental belief systems—centered on grace and religious experience mediated by the Holy Spirit—which today exemplify mountain Holiness remain rooted in the heritage of plain-folk camp-meeting religion and its own heritage in the streams of historical influences that coursed together in the creation of Appalachian mountain religion.

Notes

1. See Loyal Jones, "Mountain Religion: The Outsider's View," *Mountain Review* 2, no. 3 (May 1976): 43–46; and Catherine L. Albanese, *America: Religions and Religion* (Belmont, Calif.: Wadsworth Publishing Co., 1981), on "mountain religion" in the "Southern Appalachians," 226–29, 233–34, 237, 241–42.

2. Albanese, *America: Religions*, 8–9.

3. Ibid., 222.

4. Dickson D. Bruce, *And They All Sang Hallelujah: Plain-Folk Camp-Meeting Religion, 1800–1845* (Knoxville: Univ. of Tennessee Press, 1974), 24.

5. See Nathan L. Gerrard, "Churches of the Stationary Poor in Appalachia," in *Change in Rural Appalachia: Implications for Action Programs,* ed. John D. Photiadis and Harry K. Schwarzweller (Philadelphia: Univ. of Pennsylvania Press, 1971), 99–114. Gerrard's essay illustrates this genre of social science writing on mountain religion. He uses a subculture-of-poverty model for understanding the independent nondenominational Holiness churches in Appalachia, and the language he uses to describe them is extremely condescending (for example, he refers to Holiness mountain people as "contemporary primitives"). Gerrard does recognize the preponderance of such churches in rural areas (103–4) and that mountain people, more often than not, identify themselves as "Holiness," even though outsiders would call them Pentecostal (see esp. p. 112, n. 5). See the critique of Gerrard's essay in Jones, "Mountain Religion," 44.

6. Gerald Keith Parker, "Folk Religion in Southern Appalachia," Th.D. diss., Southern Baptist Theological Seminary, Louisville, 1970. Parker's study traces the development of church-sect typology in academic research, from Ernst Troeltsch to H. Richard Niebuhr to Earl D. C. Brewer. Parker argues *against* using church-sect typology for describing and analyzing Appalachian mountain religion. Brewer, an ordained Methodist minister and sociologist, directed the religion survey of the 1959 Southern Appalachian Studies, sponsored by Berea College and the Council of the Southern Mountains and funded by a Ford Foundation grant. His findings are summarized in Earl D. C. Brewer, "Religion and the Churches," in *The Southern Appalachian Region: A Survey*, ed. Thomas R. Ford (Lexington: Univ. of Kentucky Press,

1962), 201–18. This was the first survey of the Appalachian region since the 1935 USDA study (see below, n. 9). The Brewer summary and research data set the direction for most of the social science doctoral and postdoctoral research on Appalachian mountain religion for the next fifteen years and still is cited.

7. Albanese, *America: Religions,* 234.

8. Elizabeth R. Hooker, *Religion in the Highlands: Native Churches and Missionary Enterprises in the Southern Appalachian Area; With a Section on Missionary and Philanthropic Schools by Fannie W. Dunn* (New York: Home Missions Council, 1933). Field research for this study was conducted during 1931.

9. "1935 Religious Survey," Box 5, Series VII, 11–5: Avery County, North Carolina, Survey of Ministers; in Southern Appalachian Archives, Special Collections, Hutchins Library, Berea College, Berea, Ky. This 1931 Hooker survey is dated 1935 in the Berea College Archives because that was the year the USDA study on Appalachia was published. Hooker had used her field data on religion for *Religion in the Highlands* (1933). See Elizabeth R. Hooker, "The Church Situation," in U.S. Department of Agriculture, *Economic and Social Problems and Conditions of the Southern Appalachians,* Miscellaneous Publication no. 205 (Washington, D.C.: U.S. Department of Agriculture, Jan. 1935), 168–84.

Chapter 8

Old-Time Baptists of Central Appalachia

Howard Dorgan

For persons unfamiliar with Baptist diversity, it is confusing enough just to encounter what might be called the mainline divisions of this denomination—American Baptists, National Baptists, Southern Baptists, and the General Association of Regular Baptist Churches (not to be mistaken for the Regulars of Appalachia). It becomes increasingly perplexing when the following Baptists are added to the picture: Primitive, Missionary, Regular (the Appalachian groups), Old Regular, Separate, United, Free Will, General, German, Seventh Day, Six Principle, and Two-Seed-in-the-Spirit Predestinarian, to name a few. Indeed, the mix becomes even more baffling when one of these divisions is subdivided into Old School Primitives, Original Old Line Primitives, Regular Primitives, United Baptist Primitives, Predestinarian Primitives, and Primitive Baptist Universalists—an inventory that is by no means exhaustive. The frustration of dealing with such variety was expressed by an audience member, who, after hearing a lecture on this list, asked, "Why can't a Baptist just stay a Baptist?"

This discussion examines only Central Appalachian Baptist subdenominations that—with one exception—fall under the informal title "Old-Time Baptists," those direct descendants from the first movement of Baptists into the Appalachian Mountains at the close of the eighteenth century. These groups have maintained all or most of the following traditions: (1) lined *a cappella* singing, rhythmically chanted impromptu preaching, congregational shouting, and warmly tactile worshipping behavior; (2) foot washings and "natural water" (or "living water") baptisms; (3) governance rules that preserve Pauline gender mandates and articles of decorum dating from the earliest history of colonial Baptists; (4) restrictions on divorce and "double marriage" (remarriage after divorce while the original spouse still lives); and (5) common liturgical formats that make the typical Appalachian Primitive Baptist service appear remarkably similar to those of Regular, Old Regular, United Baptists, and others. Most of the region's Missionary Baptists, along with some Uniteds and Separates, have moved away from several of these old-time practices; but a majority of the subdenominations mentioned in this essay still hold to all or a significant portion of these traditional ways. Indeed, so uniform is this adherence that no observer would experience difficulty imagining the history shared by these groups.

This essay also examines Free Will Baptists, the one exception, because that subdenomination is so strong in Appalachia; however, this group usually is not considered "Old-Time," since they do not preserve many of the traditions mentioned above, and since they did not splinter from Separate Baptists or Regular Baptists or one of their several schisms. Free Will Baptists (frequently called "Freewill") trace their origins to a movement largely separate from the Great-Awakening Baptists who split to form the Separates and the Regulars.[1]

When detailing memberships for these Appalachian Baptist groups, I draw heavily upon statistics supplied by Clifford A. Grammich Jr., who worked for the Glenmary Research Center, Atlanta, Georgia, during that agency's most recent church-affiliation census.[2] Glenmary's 1980 canvass had indicated that Central Appalachia residents were substantially "unchurched," a finding driven by the fact that many small groups were overlooked in the 1980 effort. This problem was only partially corrected in 1990.[3] Nevertheless, I benefited from Grammich's work, including 1989 or 1990 data on a large number of Old-Time Baptist associations.[4] Grammich also produced—for the Commission on Religion in Appalachia (CORA)— his *Appalachian Atlas*, its tables and maps depicting the Appalachian presence of many of the formally constituted religious denominations and subdenominations.[5]

The Beginnings of Baptist Diversity in Appalachia

Any answer to that question—"Why can't a Baptist just stay a Baptist?"— must go back at least to the Great Awakening, a three-decade era, roughly 1726 to 1756, during which (as some see it) the American colonies were swept by successive waves of intense revivalism. The movement was led by a mixed group of exhorters. Although the Awakening is known for the work of itinerant evangelist George Whitefield, pastor-theologian Jonathan Edwards, and preachers such as Gilbert Tennent, it also influenced two early Baptists, Shubal Stearns and Daniel Marshall. Converted as "New Light" (pro-revival) Congregationalists, Stearns and Marshall accepted Baptist views, carrying them to frontier North Carolina by the 1750s. Known in part for its confrontational methods, its impassioned evangelism, its itinerant clergy, its populist following, and its frenzied emotionalism, this revival split three denominations—Presbyterians, Congregationalists, and Baptists.[6]

Concerning the Baptists, "Separates" fell in line with the tone and temperament of the Great Awakening, while "Regulars" defended the established churches, especially the Philadelphia Association, established in 1707, and the Philadelphia Confession, adopted in 1742 as a revision of an earlier London Confession of Particular (Calvinist) Baptists.[7]

The Separates

During the last half of the eighteenth century, when Baptist families— sometimes entire congregations—migrated toward the western frontier, they brought with them this division between Separates and Regulars. Shubal Stearns and his brother-in-law, Daniel Marshall, are credited with pointing the Separates westward. By 1755—in what is now Randolph County, North Carolina—Stearns and Marshall had established Sandy Creek Church, from which Separate Baptists would expand into regions of southwestern Virginia, move deeper into the Carolinas, cross the Blue Ridge into eastern Tennessee, and eventually establish a number of churches along forks of the Cumberland River in both Tennessee and Kentucky.[8] By 1785, 1787, or 1788 (the exact date is in dispute), the South Kentucky Association of Separate Baptists was formed, thus instituting the Separate Baptist alliance that today claims the most direct tie to Shubal Stearns's initial movement.[9] Stearns began preaching in the late 1740s, influenced by the Calvinism of George Whitefield; but it was not until 1751 that he embraced the Baptist faith, that same year becoming ordained by a Connecticut church of that persuasion. Four years later he led sixteen Separate Baptists to the North Carolina spot where he and Marshall founded Sandy Creek Church.[10] Stearns and his followers had not initially called themselves "Separates." Indeed, on his way to North Carolina, he had, for a brief time, labored among those Regular Baptists of northern Virginia who were, in 1766, to found the Ketocton Association, a group of churches influential in the Regular tradition.[11] However, the Baptist congregations within the Stearns-Marshall movement quickly distinguished themselves through their "New Light" leanings, particularly by their impassioned worship services.[12]

Largely as a result of Whitefield's influence, Separate Baptists at first were more staunchly Calvinistic than the Regulars, holding to a limited atonement doctrine. However, their evangelistic zeal and suspicion of written creeds led them to modify their Calvinism toward greater emphasis on human free will and the general atonement, doctrines advocated today by their heirs, the South Kentucky Association of Separate Baptists and other affiliates of the General Association of Separate Baptists in Christ.[13] Separates also differed—then and now—from the Regular tradition: they allowed women to lead in worship, offering public prayer and even preaching.[14] That greater acceptance of female participation in worship activities and church governance today remains one of the differences between Separates and Regulars. Neither group ordains women, however. In attendance at the 1991 annual session of the General Association of Separate Baptists in Christ, in Russell Springs, Kentucky, I observed extensive female participation. Such public involvement, in either church governance or congregational worship, is not typical of most Old-Time Baptist subdenominations.

Five associations of Separate Baptists are located in or near Central Appalachia: South Kentucky, thirty-seven fellowships in Kentucky and Ohio; Nolynn, nineteen churches in Kentucky; Christian Unity, six congregations in North Carolina and Virginia; Mount Olive, three churches in Tennessee; and Southwest West Virginia, only one fellowship, located in that state.[15] These Separates have become one of the most Arminian of the Old-Time Baptist groups, practicing open communion and advocating a general atonement doctrine. At one time, some South Kentucky Association elders even preached a version of Universalism labeled "Hell Redemption" or "Restoration from Hell" doctrine.[16] This theology, similar to that of Universalist Elhanan Winchester (1751–1797), proclaimed that sinners spend time in a purgatory state, suffering for all their earthly transgressions, before eventually being reunited in heaven with all of the purer-in-soul brothers and sisters.[17]

The Regulars

In his *History of the Baptists in Virginia*, Robert Baylor Semple noted that Regular Baptists began their movement into northern Virginia in 1743, coming first from congregations in and around Baltimore, Maryland, and then from fellowships in Pennsylvania. Both groups brought with them a connection with the Philadelphia Association.[18] By 1766, Virginia's Regular Baptists were able to "arm off" from the Philadelphia Association and form the Ketocton Association. These eighteenth-century Regulars moved steadily down the Shenandoah corridor and into frontier regions that now constitute southwestern Virginia, northwestern North Carolina, eastern Tennessee, and eastern Kentucky. In 1785, the Elkhorn Association was founded, the first alliance of Regular Baptists west of the Alleghenies,[19] and the following year the Holston Valley Baptist Association was instituted. This second alliance contained many Separates who had migrated across the Blue Ridge from North Carolina, but it immediately adopted the Philadelphia Confession and a constitution modeled after that of the Philadelphia Association.[20]

Although the two earliest Appalachian Regular Baptist associations have changed over the last two centuries, with Holston moving into the Southern Baptist tradition and Elkhorn entering the Primitive Baptist camp, many have retained their original "Regular" delineation. This is particularly true in Allegheny, Ashe, Avery, Wilkes, and Yadkin counties, North Carolina, and in Grayson and Smyth counties, Virginia, where a number of Old-Time fellowships belong to Little River Association of Regular Baptists (three churches in North Carolina, one in Virginia, and one in Maryland), Primitive Association of Regular Baptists (fifteen churches in North Carolina), Mountain Union Association of Regular Baptists (two churches in North Carolina, two in Maryland, and one in Pennsylvania), and Original Mountain Union Association of Regular Baptists (nine churches in North Carolina and one in Virginia).[21]

Union Baptists

The last two associations listed above—the latter split from the former in 1961—often are called "Union Baptists," a title that initially was used because the churches that instituted the initial 1867 alliance had been pro-Union during the Civil War.[22] Nevertheless, the articles of faith and the practices of these two associations clearly place them within the Regular camp. In writing *Giving Glory to God in Appalachia,* I treated Union Baptists as a discrete subdenomination. I no longer am willing to separate them from the rest of the Regulars.

Two additional Regular Baptist associations have churches in the Appalachian region. Indeed, one of these is the largest of the present Regular Baptist clusters: Enterprise Association of Regular Baptists has thirty-five congregations in Kentucky, thirty-four in Ohio, and one in Indiana. The second, on the other hand, is the smallest: Mud River Regular Baptist Association has only three churches, all in West Virginia.[23]

Although considerable variety exists within the Regular Baptist family, the tendency is for these churches to be less Old-Time than their more traditional cousins, the Old Regular and Primitive Baptists. Only on special occasions do these Regular Baptist churches practice lined singing, and they depart from the traditionalism of Old-Time Baptists by including musical instruments in some of their services, particularly for midweek or Saturday night sings. In addition, they allow "Sabbath Schools," a practice that staunchly Calvinistic Baptist subdenominations reject. Elder Earl Sexton, recent moderator of the Original Mountain Union Regular Baptist Association, for years even had a radio program on WKSK, West Jefferson, North Carolina,[24] an activity rejected by the Old Regulars and Primitives. Likewise, Regular Baptists, especially in North Carolina, are more open in their relations with other religious groups, and their ministers are willing to "share the stand" with preachers from divergent Baptist subdenominations.[25]

The Free Will Baptists

The origins of the Free Will Baptists coincide with those of the Separates and the Regulars. Frank S. Mead states that this group of Baptists had its American beginning in the South in 1727 (about the time the Great Awakening was commencing) and in the North in 1780 (fourteen years after Ketocton Association was organized).[26] Norman Allen Baxter's *History of the Freewill Baptists: A Study in New England Separatism* accepts the 1780 organizing efforts of Benjamin Randall as constituting the official American start of the faith;[27] but both Elmer T. Clark and Paul Woolsey place the subdenomination in eastern North Carolina, under the leadership of Paul Palmer, well before the middle of the eighteenth century.[28] H. Leon McBeth, however, notes that Palmer, while certainly preaching a free will doctrine, did his organizing under a General Baptist title.[29] Formal establishment of this faith in Central Appalachia, nevertheless, can be traced to the Toe River Association of Free Will Baptists, organized November 15, 1850, at Jack's Creek Church in Yancey County, North Carolina.[30] Today, the Appalachian presence of this faith is evident in two organizations. The larger is the National Association of Free Will Baptists, headquartered in Nashville, with roughly 94,000 members in the Appalachian Regional Commission (ARC) counties of Ohio, Pennsylvania, West Virginia, Kentucky, Virginia, Tennessee, North Carolina, South Carolina, Georgia, Alabama, and Mississippi;[31] and the smaller is the John-Thomas Association of Freewill Baptists, with approximately eighty churches in the ACR counties of Virginia, Kentucky, and Ohio. John-Thomas Association held its 1981 annual session in Coeburn, Virginia, and that year reported a total of

7,483 individual members.[32] In addition to these two associations, there are numerous independent Free Will congregations within the Appalachian region, generally unified in doctrine but considerably diverse in practice.

As their name suggests, Free Will Baptists accepted a doctrine of the general atonement, that Christ died for all persons. Sinners receive grace by freely trusting Christ. For most Appalachian "Freewillers," that faith includes the rudiments of a creedal statement first adopted in 1916 by the North Carolina State Conference of Free Will Baptists: "We believe, as touching Gospel Ordinances, in believers' baptism, laying on of hands, receiving of the sacrament in bread and wine, washing the saints' feet, anointing the sick with oil in the name of the Lord, fasting, prayer, singing praise to God and the public ministry of the Word, with every institution of the Lord we shall find in the New Testament." A free-will acceptance of these tenets, however, also implies the possibility of a later free-will rejection of the same, suggesting that the "saint" can easily "backslide" to become the "sinner."

The Great Western Revival and the United Baptists

At the beginning of the nineteenth century, a religious movement sometimes called the Second Great Awakening, or the Great Western Revival, swept the Appalachian frontier, characterized by camp meetings attended by Presbyterians, Methodists, Baptists, and others.[33] Three important effects of the revival on Baptists were: a renewal of individual conversionism, increased membership, and the unification of certain Baptist associations. Beginning in Virginia and then extending into Kentucky, many Separate and Regular associations consolidated or agreed to "correspond." For Appalachian Baptists, the most significant of these unifications occurred in 1801, between South Kentucky (Separates) and Elkhorn (then Regulars).[34] Although this particular union did not remain firm, the initial union constituted the beginning of the Appalachian region's United Baptist subdenomination.[35]

By 1801, South Kentucky Separates already had adopted a general atonement position. Elkhorn Regulars, on the other hand, were "particular" Baptists, stressing Christ's death only for the elect. Thus the union required this statement: "We the committees of the Elkhorn and South Kentucky, do agree to unite on the following plan . . . , that . . . preaching Christ tasted death for every man shall be no bar to communion."[36] The two stopped short of assuming the same name; nevertheless, individual fellowships referred to themselves as "united Baptists," perhaps for a while with the "u" remaining in the lower case. However,

Spencer credited the agreement with creating harmony among Kentucky Baptists and with establishing a statewide use of the title "United Baptists."[37]

This harmony did not last; it was disrupted by more than two decades of missionary-antimissionary debate. Still, the nineteenth century showed a steady proliferation of Uniteds, with most of this movement occurring in Kentucky, and with a majority of the United Baptists adopting general atonement. "We believe," declares Mount Zion Association of United Baptists, "in the free atonement of Jesus Christ, and that he tasted death for every man and that salvation is offered to all men and women upon the terms of the Gospel."[38]

In 1990, in the ARC areas of Kentucky, Tennessee, and West Virginia, Grammich identified 176 United churches with a total of 20,147 members. Kentucky houses the largest number of Uniteds, 130 congregations, with a total of 13,193 members, distributed over a region bounded by Greenup County in the north, Pike County in the east, Whitley County in the south, and Rockcastle County in the west. In Campbell and Scott counties, Tennessee, Grammich identified 27 United churches containing 4,528 members; while in Cabell, Lincoln, Logan, Mingo, and Wayne counties, West Virginia, he located 19 churches representing 2,426 members.[39]

Most United Baptists of Appalachia can be called "Old-Time," by virtue of having preserved the traditions identified earlier. However, these associations are a mixed lot in terms of precise doctrines and relations with other groups. Mount Zion, for example, has the liberal atonement theology mentioned above, but disavows the practice of Sunday schools and "corresponds" with the Old Regular Baptist association, Thornton Union.[40]

The Old Regular Baptists

I treat the Old Regular Baptists extensively in *The Old Regular Baptists of Central Appalachia*; therefore only the basic characteristics are presented here. Readers are reminded, however, that Old Regulars—at least in terms of worship practices, rules of governance, and behavioral codes—are arguably the most traditional of the Central Appalachian Old-Time Baptist groups, preserving not only the nineteenth-century absolutes relative to lined singing, natural water baptism, impromptu preaching, male-dominated church hierarchies, and a host of other liturgical or governmental issues, but also dress and hair codes, many directed especially toward women.

Old Regulars began as Uniteds, when, in 1825, New Salem Association organized under that title before gradually evolving to become the mother association of Old Regulars. In terms of atonement doctrine, Old Regular theology stands roughly midway between the deterministic double-predestination doctrine (discussed later) of some Primitive Baptist groups and the freewill atonement tenet of the more Arminian groups. Since publication of my 1989 volume on Old Regulars, the subdenomination has increased its number of associations from sixteen to seventeen, with the addition of the Little Dove Association (two churches in Kentucky).[41] However, there appears to have been no significant change in the total number of formal members—approximately 15,000, with as many as another 10,000 to 15,000 regularly attending nonmembers.

At church services, members sit in the "stand area," those pews immediately to the right, left, or rear of the pulpit. Usually this section of the church is elevated, and it becomes a region of clear gender separation, in contrast to out-front sections in which nonmembers sit, often with no attention to gender. The symbolism in this arrangement involves the idea that nonmembers are awaiting their "calls," recognizable moments of religious exhilaration when individual celebrants receive their personal summons to redemption. Eschewing even child baptism, Old Regulars do not anticipate this "call" until at least young adulthood, preferring a later age for conversion. As a result, Old Regulars frequently "go down to the water" when they are in their mid-thirties or older.

Old Regulars cluster in some two dozen counties of eastern Kentucky, southwestern Virginia, and southern West Virginia, with a small number of "outmigration" fellowships in Arizona, Florida, Illinois, Indiana, Michigan, North Carolina, Ohio, Tennessee, and even Washington State. The annual late-summer or early-fall "Association Times," however, all are held in Central Appalachia and regularly draw hundreds—probably thousands—of these outmigrants back to "Old Regular country" for these three-day events. Two of these association meetings are quite large: Union Association holds its session the third weekend in September at Ash Camp, Pike County, Kentucky, and draws up to three thousand people; and New Salem Association meets the fourth weekend in September at Minnie, Floyd County, Kentucky, attracting up to four thousand people. Each owes its large crowds to the fact that so many Old Regulars belonging to one of the other associations try to attend one or both of these more heavily populated gatherings—for the singing, preaching, association-business debates, and general socializing.

After my 1989 book appeared, some radical realignments of the associations occurred, with Indian Bottom Association and Old Indian

Bottom Association essentially exchanging positions in the networks of "corresponding" Old Regular groups. Until recently, New Salem and Union did not recognize the legitimacy of the Old Indian Bottom alliance of churches. Now New Salem and Union, in conjunction with several other smaller associations, reject Indian Bottom and correspond only with Old Indian Bottom.[42] Such shifts frequently occur in Old-Time Baptist circles, making it difficult to remain current on the intricate maze of associational alliances.

The Missionary-Antimissionary Split: Beginning the Missionary Baptists

The first quarter of the nineteenth century saw an intense growth in American missionary activity, as eager evangelists and Christian teachers were sent to such far-away places as India, Burma, and the South Pacific, in addition to home mission spots in the American Indian territories and the Appalachian Mountains.[43] When this effort touched frontier Baptist communities in Central Appalachia, either to raise money for foreign missions or to establish home missions, it generated two hostile responses. Home missionary action disturbed Old-Time Baptists by implying that their own religious institutions were not seen as adequate. Foreign missions activity led the more Calvinistic subdenominations to scorn the idea that human activity could increase the number of God's chosen.[44] From the 1820s to the end of the century, many Appalachian Baptists distanced themselves from missionary organizations, tract societies, Sunday school boards, and all mission-related endeavors. Thus a major split developed within Baptist ranks of Appalachia and elsewhere, dividing churches and associations into two sides, "missionary" and "antimissionary."

As their name suggests, Missionary Baptists promoted a theology of evangelism. Since these churches held that new converts could be "won to Christ," revivals, missionary work, and other forms of evangelism were sanctioned. Sunday schools were accepted as a method of nurturing the young into the faith; the doctrine of freewill was avowed, as the individual's power to accept or reject the faith; and "backsliding" usually was recognized: he or she who chooses can also reject, then eventually choose again.

At the beginning of the controversy, some Baptists were designated "missionary" purely as a generic classification. Indeed, the period was characterized by great confusion concerning which titles would be assumed by which groups. There was even a controversy between the two sides as to which should inherit the term "primitive," a term used early on to link certain Baptists directly with the New Testament church. With time, many of the early "missionary" Baptist fellowships affiliated with those general-atonement Baptists who became (after 1845) either the Southern Baptists or the Northern Baptists (today American Baptist Churches, USA). Others used the term "missionary" to delineate independent Baptist churches which funded missionaries directly. Presently, southern and central Appalachian Missionary Baptists roughly fall into three categories: (1) those congregations affiliated with one of the larger Missionary Baptist associations, (2) those purely independent fellowships which label themselves "Missionary," and (3) those more "old-fashioned" Missionary Baptists who, in addition to being "missionary," have preserved most of those Old-Time Baptist ways mentioned at the beginning of this essay.

Grammich found 9,749 Appalachian Baptists belonging to the Baptist Missionary Association of America, which claims 290,000 adherents nationwide.[45] Examples of the third category include both the Enon Missionary Baptist Association and the Old Missionary Baptist Associations, each with churches well within the Appalachian region.[46] The second category is represented by the hundreds of independent Missionary Baptist churches found throughout southern and central Appalachia. These include the Mount Paran Missionary Baptist Church of Deep Gap, North Carolina, featured in *Giving Glory to God in Appalachia*.[47] Grammich notes that membership statistics for these "second category" Missionary fellowships are difficult to discover. Nevertheless, these small congregations play a significant role in the religious life of Appalachia, while remaining largely uncounted in church affiliation canvasses.

Primitive Baptists

The missionary-antimissionary split was not the sole cause of the Primitive Baptist movement. The term "Primitive," along with such terms as "Old School" and "Old Line," also had been applied to those Baptists who adhered to a more deterministic theology. Nevertheless, after the split began, titles became more important, with implications for both lineage and theology. In Fulton, Kentucky, a four-day debate in July 1887 pitted Elder Lemuel Potter of the "Regular Old School Baptists" against Elder W. P. Throgmorton of the "Missionary Baptists." The formal question for debate was "Who are the Primitive Baptists?" Each spokesman claimed the title for his particular faction.[48] Throgmorton argued that, among Missionary Baptists, such practices as paid ministers, funding mission boards, operating Sunday schools, and even adherence to certain interpretation of Calvinistic doctrines (as in the Philadelphia Confession) were not issues, since some of their churches followed these practices and some did not. What was critical, he argued, was the broader principle "that the gospel should be preached to every creature, and that every sinner should be exhorted to repentance and faith; that repentance and faith are duties as well as graces; and that the reading, and especially the preaching of the word, is a means of conviction and conversion of sinners."[49] For Throgmorton the preaching of the gospel to humankind was a Christian mandate.

Potter disagreed, proclaiming that no element of humankind could play any role in the salvation of any other element of humankind, since the entire process of redemption was in God's hands: "We claim it is the duty of all people to repent of doing wrong, of sin, and that it is right for them to believe the truth, and accept it, wherever they find it. But we do not think that the salvation of sinners is on condition of their hearing the Gospel. That is what makes the issue between us. We deny that repentance is a condition of salvation. [Throgmorton] . . . believes that heaven depends on the sinner voluntarily repenting and believing. We deny that."[50] Thus, Potter drew a distinction drawn by many old-line Primitives: Whether the condition in question is identified as "salvation," "redemption," or "election," or all three, it is a product solely of God's doing, not man's. Potter believed his deterministic theology to be the pure gospel pronounced by Christ and Paul, warranting the term "Primitive" for the Missionary Baptists.

The battle for this title, however, was short-lived. In later rhetoric, general atonement Baptists let the term slide into a pejorative mode, along with "Hard-shell," "Old School," and "Old Line."

These struggles over titles, missions, and lineage legitimacy were further complicated by controversy engendered by the Campbellite movement, with its disdain for all extra-gospel creeds and ecclesiastical structures, and with its own emphasis upon the restoration of the Pauline church.[51] The result was a division of nineteenth-century Old-Time Baptists into two broad camps, the one now occupied by various Primitive groups, and the other occupied by the less deterministic Regulars, Old Regulars, Uniteds, and Separates. Baptist records are replete with chronicles of battles waged, as association after association divided relative to issues of atonement, predestination, evangelism, extra-gospel organizational structures, various gender-related mandates of the Pauline church, and questions of traditionalism in worship styles and congregational behaviors.

By 1900, so much doctrinal diversity had developed among Primitives that an attempt was made by elders from Alabama, Arkansas, Georgia, Indiana, Illinois, Kentucky, Mississippi, Missouri, Tennessee, and Washington State to write a confession of faith with which they all could agree. Thus was born the Fulton Confession, adopted November

18, 1900. This document essentially restated the 1669 version of the Particular (Reformed) London Confession. Added, however, is a Primitive Baptist interpretation of that original particular-election body of doctrine, including clarification of such troublesome questions as divine sovereignty, biblical infallibility, the Fall, the particularity of election, immersion baptism, closed communion, and the acceptability of divorce and remarriage. However, there is no evidence that this document ever had a significant effect upon the Primitives of Appalachia. Indeed, as yet I have found no Central Appalachian Primitive elder who was aware of the confession prior to my mentioning it.

Primitives generally share the following beliefs: (1) some version of the elect doctrine, which proclaims that this "elect" (the Church) is composed of individuals identified before the beginning of time as the true followers and beneficiaries of Christ; (2) some version of the predestination doctrine, at least as applied to the elect; and (3) and some version of the "never finally fall away" doctrine, which proclaims eternal "justification" for the elect, meaning that these individuals (if truly elected) will never finally fall from grace. Few doctrines disturb Primitives more than the idea that a cycle of backsliding, regeneration, backsliding, and perhaps a culminating end-of-life return to the fold can produce redemption.

Four Major Subdivisions of Primitive Baptists

Elder Robert Webb, founder and director of the Primitive Baptist Library of Carthage, Illinois, has classified Primitives in three categories:

Group I, often called single-predestinationists, includes Primitives who believe in the predestination of election, while rejecting the idea that God has predestined all things.

Group II, often called double-predestionationists, encompasses churches and associations who pronounce a doctrine of eternal, absolute, and unconditional predestination of all things.

Group III is comprised of Primitives who, although they have an anchoring in the faith, have moved their practices (and sometimes their doctrine) towards more Arminian semblances, accepting one or more of the following: Sunday schools, paid ministers, evangelism, instrumental church music, radio ministries, and other elements of a nondeterministic religious expression.[52]

A fourth group, the Primitive Baptist Universalists, is not recognized by Elder Webb as part of the Primitive Baptist family.

Grammich adopted Webb's classifications, finding that the vast majority of Appalachian Primitives belong to either Group I or Group II, with the former being the larger of the two. The Webb-Grammich list of Appalachian Group I Primitive Baptist associations includes such alliances as Burning Spring (nine churches in eastern Kentucky), New River (five churches in southwestern Virginia), Original Mates Creek (twelve churches in eastern Kentucky and two churches in southwestern Virginia), Mount Zion (ten churches in West Virginia), Sandlick (ten churches in southwestern Virginia), Saint Clair's Bottom (one church in northwestern North Carolina and two churches in southwestern Virginia), and Senter (six churches in northwestern North Carolina). The Webb-Grammich classification includes the following Group II Primitive associations with churches in Appalachia: Mates Creek (one church in eastern Kentucky and one in West Virginia), not to be confused with Original Mates Creek; New River, the total-predestination side (two churches in southwestern Virginia); and Smith River (seven churches in southwestern Virginia).[53]

Webb and Grammich list no Group III associations in Appalachia, but they do include a handful of independent Primitive Baptist churches in this category, three found on the western edge of Tennessee's Appalachian counties (one each in Coffee, Franklin, and Hamilton counties) and four found in northern Alabama counties (two in DeKalb, one in Elmore, and one in Madison).[54] Neither Webb nor Grammich classified the Eastern District Association of Primitive Baptists (eight churches in eastern Kentucky, six in eastern Tennessee, and twenty-six in southwestern Virginia), but my observations of this Primitive alliance place it either squarely in Group III or on the cusp of it, simply because of the Eastern District's liberal attitude toward associations with non-Primitive Old-Time Baptists, particularly Mountain Liberty Association of Old Regular Baptists and Thornton Union Association of Old Regular Baptists, both constituting a more progressive faction of this particular subdenomination.[55]

There is also a fourth group of Appalachian Primitives that Elder Webb does not recognize as legitimate members of the subdenomination: Primitive Baptist Universalists, four small associations with congregations in eastern Tennessee, eastern Kentucky, southwestern Virginia, and southern West Virginia, in addition to minor representations in Indiana, Ohio, Pennsylvania, and Maryland. In Appalachia, these Primitive Baptist Universalists (PBUS) usually are called "No-Hellers," since it is alleged that the faith does not believe in hell. That allegation, however, is incorrect, since this doctrine includes "hell" as a feature of the temporal life. What specifically is rejected is the idea of an afterlife divided into heaven and hell. Instead, the faith expounds a "universal" atonement doctrine, arguing that "Christ tasted death for all men" and that, following "Resurrection," all humankind will share the same eternity, an egalitarian heaven in which humankind will be restored to the sinless unified-with-God state that existed prior to Adam's transgression.

PBU theology advances the following tenets: (1) Because of Adamic sin, all humankind is inherently sinful, making sinfulness a standard characteristic of "natural man"; (2) Satan is nothing more than natural man, warring with "spiritual man," and thus will have no existence beyond the temporal world; (3) Adamic transgression also instituted temporal-world punishment (that absence-from-God's-blessing "hell" of the earthly life) and "death" (humankind's ultimate punishment for Adamic sin); (4) humankind's self-extrication from this natural sin-state is impossible, thus requiring Christ's atonement; (5) that atonement, nevertheless, was for *all* humankind, and at "Resurrection" will irrevocably come to pass for *all*, just as irrevocably Adam's transgression had earlier condemned *all*; (6) however, there is the "Elect," Christ's church (the Primitive Baptist Universalists, and perhaps others not known to the movement), that has been "separated from the rest of God's people here in time," chosen to be the earthly witness of Christ and the earthly preserver of his righteousness, "kept by the power of God through faith" and destined never finally to fall away; (7) still, elected individuals can sin and temporarily suffer the hell that a separation from God's blessing institutes, probably feeling that hell more intensely than the nonelect; (8) at "Resurrection," however, all temporal existence will terminate, bringing an end to "sin," "punishment," and "death"; (9) then *all* humankind will go to a wholly egalitarian heaven, the culmination of Christ's universal atonement; (10) and, since punishment is a factor solely of the temporal world, there will be no hell after Resurrection.[56]

PBUs cluster in thirty-three Central Appalachian churches, plus three in Ohio and one in Pennsylvania, each fellowship affiliated with an association: Regular Primitive Baptist Washington District (two churches in eastern Tennessee, ten in southwest Virginia, one in West Virginia, two in Ohio, and one in Pennsylvania), Three Forks of Powell's River Regular Primitive Baptists (eight churches in southwestern Virginia, one in eastern Tennessee, and one in eastern Kentucky),[57] and two Elkhorn Primitive Baptist alliances (the first with two churches in southwestern Virginia, one in West Virginia, and one in Ohio; and the second with eight churches in West Virginia). The PBU heartland stretches along the Virginia side of the Cumberland Divide, beginning in northeastern Tennessee and closing out in southern West Virginia; but the most southwestern church sits on the west side of Cherokee Lake in Grainger County, Tennessee, and the most northeastern one rests near the Susquehanna River in York County, Pennsylvania.

Universalism accompanied Appalachian settlers from Boston, Baltimore, Philadelphia, and elsewhere;[58] but the first Universalist church established west of the Blue Ridge was Consolation Universalist Church, begun in 1819 in what is now Christian County, Kentucky.[59] From there the theology may have spread back through Tennessee, as Universalist societies organized in Glimpsville, Knoxville, Harriman, Chattanooga, and Free Hill in Washington County.[60] It was in the Washington District Association of Primitive Baptists that PBU theology first appeared, the earliest association debate on the doctrine being generated in 1907, when Elder M. L. Compton of Hale Creek Church in Buchanan County, Virginia, was admonished for having preached Universalism.[61] By 1924, the doctrine had split Washington Association into the "Heller" and "No-Heller" sides, with the "No-Heller" camp soon joined by three other Primitive associations of the region: Elkhorn, Stony Creek, and Three Forks of Powell's River.[62] Aside from Stony Creek—which slowly disintegrated between 1941 and 1946 during debates over physical versus spiritual resurrection—these are the alliances that still constitute the Primitive Baptist Universalist movement.

Imbued with their doctrines of universal atonement, no after-life hell, and a totally egalitarian heaven, these particular Old-Time Baptists are remarkably open and accepting of outsiders, believing that all humankind will share that ultimate glory. In addition, they are wonderfully joyous in their worship, having removed from their beliefs that entire dark side of Christianity focusing on an eternal horror of fire and brimstone, into which all the impure in soul are cast, with the entire process being ruled over by a gleefully sadistic Satan. They are, nevertheless, insistent that Resurrection will lift both the physical and spiritual body, producing a heaven of recognizable loved ones, somehow devoid of the imperfections of age and infirmity.

PBU worship is remarkably similar to that of other Old-Time Baptists, so much so that one could stumble into a PBU church and not realize the denominational distinction involved. Lined singing, chanted impromptu preaching, highly tactile fellowship, foot washings, natural-water baptisms—all these PBU practices compare strongly with what one finds in Old Regular, United, or Primitive churches. However, there are differences. Aside from not having the freedom to preach, PBU women face few restrictions in their worship behaviors, hairstyles, and dress. Furthermore, there is little gender separation. The more Calvinistic songs of the Goble hymnal will not be sung, and—as mentioned before—worship expression probably will be far more joyous. In tone, these are Old-Time Baptists; in theology, they are followers of a nineteenth-century Universalist, Hosea

Ballou, who, through his "happifying of God" theology, sought to redeem the deity from all harshly unloving, mean-spirited, and vindictive imagery.[63]

A Closing Comment

Old-Time Baptists have done their share to create the richly diverse patchwork quilt that constitutes Appalachian religion; if there is no other consequence, an awareness of this diversity should dispel the stereotype of Appalachian religious life as a monolith fixed in either the serpent-handling phenomenon, the Holiness-Pentecostal movement, or the Old Regular tradition. Indeed, variegation has always been a feature of the Baptist picture, especially in Appalachia, where this denomination's historic emphasis has been on hair-splitting theological debate, local church autonomy, and spirited confrontation. A traditional joke about Baptists—often told by Baptists—is that if two of these brethren engage in doctrinal discourse, they end up with four theologies. During the late 1970s, when Richard Humphrey chaired the Department of Philosophy and Religion at Appalachian State University, he occasionally asserted that he had discovered twenty-seven subdenominations of Baptists in Appalachia, a count I privately viewed as suspect. No longer does such skepticism pervade my thinking: Depending upon how finely the divisions are drawn, one might end up with well over thirty.

Notes

1. Howard Dorgan, *Giving Glory to God in Appalachia: Worship Practices of Six Baptist Subdenominations* (Knoxville: Univ. of Tennessee Press, 1987), 36–41; H. L. McBeth, "Free Will Baptists," in *Dictionary of Baptists in America*, ed. Bill J. Leonard (Downers Grove, Ill.: InterVarsity Press, 1994), 122. The northern branch of the Free Will movement, instituted in 1780 by Benjamin Randall, did have a connection with George Whitefield and the Great Awakening, but in 1911 that division of the faith merged with the Northern Baptists, later to become the American Baptists. The southern branch of the movement came out of the General Baptists, a faction that in its origin predates the Great Awakening.

2. Martin Bradley et al., *Churches and Church Membership in the United States, 1990* (Atlanta, Ga.: Glenmary Research Center, 1992).

3. In Appalachia there are many wholly independent churches, particularly of the Baptist, Holiness, and Pentecostal faiths, that are not affiliated with any larger organizational unit. Indeed, it is not unusual for some of these churches to maintain no membership roll. Therefore, it is extremely difficult to canvass the memberships of these churches.

4. Hereafter cited as Grammich Notes, in private collection of the author.

5. Clifford A. Grammich Jr., *Appalachian Atlas: Maps of the Churches and People of the Appalachian Region* (Knoxville: Commission on Religion in Appalachia, 1994).

6. Maloy Alton Huggins, *A History of North Carolina Baptists, 1727–1932* (Raleigh: North Carolina Baptist Convention, 1967), 50–51; Robert Baylor Semple, *History of the Rise and Progress of the Baptists in Virginia* (1810; rpt. Cottonport, La.: Polyanthos, 1972), 11–13.

7. Huggins, *History of North Carolina Baptists*, 23–24; Glenn A. Toomey, *The Centennial History of the Holston Valley Baptist Association and Its Affiliated Churches, 1884–1983* (Rogersville, Tenn.: Holston Valley Baptist Association, 1983), 4–5; George Washington Paschal, *History of North Carolina Baptists* (Raleigh: North Carolina Baptist State Convention, 1930), 44–45.

8. Huggins, *History of North Carolina Baptists*, 51–52; Semple, *History of the Rise*, 12–14; Morgan Scott, *Separate Baptist Church* (Indianapolis, Ind.: Hollenbeck Press, 1901), 108–35, 158–229; William Warren Sweet, *Religion on the American Frontier: The Baptists* (New York: Cooper Square Publishers, 1964), 8–9.

9. Howard Dorgan, "Separate Baptists of Central Appalachia: Followers of Shubal Stearns," *Journal of the Appalachian Studies Association* 5 (1993): 110–16.

10. Semple, *History of the Rise*, 12–14; Sweet, *Religion*, 8–9.

11. Semple, *History of the Rise*, 375–87.

12. Deborah Vansau McCauley, *Appalachian Religion* (Urbana: Univ. of Illinois Press, 1995), 203; Scott, *Separate Baptist Church*, 111; Sweet, *Religion*, 10–11.

13. Dorgan, "Separate Baptists," 110–16; McCauley, *Appalachian Religion*, 92; J. H. Spencer, *A History of Kentucky Baptists* (1886; rpt. Layfayette, Tenn.: Church History Research Archives, 1967), vol. 1:482–83.

14. J. T. Spivey, "Separate Baptists," in *Dictionary of Baptists in America*, ed. Bill J. Leonard (Downers Grove, Ill.: InterVarsity Press, 1994), 246; Scott, *Separate Baptist Church*, 111.

15. General Association of Separate Baptists in Christ, *Minutes*, 1990, pp. 19–38, in private collection of the author.

16. Spencer, *History of Kentucky Baptists*, vol. 1:483–84; 2:93, 2:138–40. In some Baptist association minutes, this theology was also referred to as the "Short Hell Doctrine."

17. Ernest Cassara, *Universalism in America* (Boston: Skinner House, 1971), 114–17; Glenn T. Miller, "Elhanan Winchester," in *Dictionary of Baptists in America*, ed. Bill J. Leonard (Downers Grove, Ill.: InterVarsity Press, 1994), 291.

18. Semple, *History of the Rise*, 375–85.

19. Spencer, *History of Kentucky Baptists*, vol. 2:1.

20. Toomey, *Centennial History*, 4–5.

21. Dorgan, *Giving Glory to God*, 28–31; Grammich Notes.

22. Dorgan, *Giving Glory to God*, 31–36; J. F. Fletcher, *A History of the Ashe County, North Carolina, and New River, Virginia, Baptist Association* (Raleigh, N.C.: Commercial Printing, 1935), 31–38.

23. Grammich Notes.

24. Dorgan, *Giving Glory to God*, 69.

25. Ibid., 34.

26. Frank S. Mead, *Handbook of Denominations in the United States*, 5th ed. (Nashville: Abingdon Press, 1970), 42.

27. Norman Allen Baxter, *History of the Freewill Baptists: A Study in New England Separatism* (Rochester, N.Y.: American Baptist Historical Society, 1957), 25.

28. Elmer T. Clark, *Small Sects in America* (Nashville: Abingdon Press, 1965), 204; Paul Woolsey, *God, a Hundred Years, and a Free Will Baptist Family* (Chuckey, Tenn.: Union Free Will Baptist Association, 1949), 4.

29. McBeth, "Free Will Baptists," 12.

30. Woolsey, *God, a Hundred Years*, 165, 193.

31. Grammich, *Appalachian Atlas*, 32.

32. John-Thomas Association of Freewill Baptists, *Minutes*, 1981, p. 37, in private collection of the author.

33. John G. Boles, *The Great Revival, 1787–1805* (Lexington: Univ. Press of Kentucky, 1972); Catharine C. Cleveland, *The Great Revival in the West, 1797–1805* (1916; rpt. Gloucester, Mass.: Peter Smith, 1959); Fredrick Morgan Davenport, *Primitive Traits in Religious Revivals* (New York: Macmillan Co., 1917), 73–86; Sweet, *Religion*, 615–16.

34. Sweet, *Religion*, 23–25.

35. Dorgan, *The Old Regular Baptists of Central Appalachia: Brothers and Sisters in Hope* (Knoxville: Univ. of Tennessee Press, 1989), 29–31; Dorgan, "Separate Baptists," 113–14.

36. Sweet, *Religion*, 23–24.

37. Spencer, *History of Kentucky Baptists*, vol. 1:16.

38. Mount Zion Association of United Baptists, *Minutes*, 1991, p. 13, in private collection of the author.

39. Grammich Notes; Grammich, *Appalachian Atlas*, 38–39.

40. Dorgan, *Old Regular Baptists*, 43; Thornton Union Association of Old Regular Baptists, *Minutes*, 1992, p. 7, Belk Library, Appalachian State Univ., Boone, N.C.

41. Little Dove Association of Old Regular Baptists, *Minutes*, 1989, in private collection of the author.

42. Union Association of Old Regular Baptists, *Minutes*, 1994, pp. 4, 6, Belk Library, Appalachian State Univ., Boone, N.C.

43. Sweet, *Religion*, 58–62.

44. Ibid., 61–76. See also McCauley's thorough discussion of attitudes toward Appa-

lachian religion as expressed in the home mission movement: McCauley, *Appalachian Religion,* 392–464.

45. Grammich Notes; Grammich, *Appalachian Atlas,* 30.

46. Grammich Notes.

47. Dorgan, *Giving Glory to God,* 1987.

48. W. P. Throgmorton and Lemuel Potter, *Who Are the Primitive Baptists? The Throgmorton-Potter Debate,* Stenographically reported by Joseph Losier and Laura Potter (St. Louis: Nixon-Jones Printing, 1888).

49. Ibid., 2–3.

50. Ibid., 19–20.

51. Sweet, *Religion,* 70–72.

52. Grammich Notes; Robert Webb, interview by Howard Dorgan, Carthage, Ill., Aug. 9, 1994, in private collection of the author.

53. Grammich Notes.

54. Grammich Notes.

55. Dorgan, *Old Regular Baptists,* 43.

56. Regular Primitive Baptist Washington District Association, *Minutes,* 1994, pp. 12–13; Three Forks of Powell's River Regular Primitive Baptist Association, *Minutes,* 1994, p. 15; Elkhorn Primitive Baptist Association, *Minutes,* 1994, pp. 8–10, in private collection of the author; Charles F. Nickels, *Salvation of All Mankind* (Nickelsville, Va.: Published by the author, 1937); and over a hundred interviews of PBU elders and regular members, conducted by Howard Dorgan, July 1991–Sept. 1995. A detailed examination of these tenets is provided in Howard Dorgan, "Salvation for All," chap. 4, *In the Hands of a Happy God: Primitive Baptist Universalists of Central Appalachia* (Knoxville, Tenn.: Univ. of Tennessee Press, 1997).

57. At the time of this writing, a minor split appears to have occurred in Three Forks Association. If the split becomes final, three churches may withdraw from the alliance.

58. Cassara, *Universalism in America,* 1–38. See also Russell E. Miller, *The Larger Hope: The First Century of the Universalist Church in America* (Boston: Unitarian Universalist Association, 1979).

59. Russell E. Miller, *Larger Hope,* 734.

60. Ibid., 731–33; Ida Metz Hyland, *Unitarian-Universalism in East Tennessee* (Johnson City, Tenn.: Holston Valley Unitarian Universalist Church, 1979); D. B. Clayton, *Forty-Seven Years in the Universalist Ministry* (Columbia, S.C.: Published by the author, 1889); and Russell E. Miller, *The Larger Hope: The Second Century of the Universalist Church in America, 1870–1970* (Boston: Unitarian Universalist Association, 1985), 193–96.

61. Washington District Primitive Baptist Association, *Minutes,* 1907, p. 5, in private collection of the author.

62. Old Constitutional Washington District Association, *Minutes,* 1924, pp. 3–11, in private collection of the author; Washington District Primitive Baptist Association, *Minutes,* 1924, pp. 1–3; Elihu J. Sutherland, *Regular Primitive Baptist Washington District Association: Short History* (Clintwood, Va.: Published by the Association, 1952), 20–22.

63. Cassara, *Universalism in America,* 21; Hosea Ballou, *An Examination of the Doctrine of Future Retribution, on the Principles of Morals, Analogy and the Scriptures* (Boston: The Trumpet Office, 1834), 36; Hosea Ballou, *A Treatise on Atonement; in which, The Finite Nature of Sin is Argued, Its Causes and Consequences as Such; The Necessity and Nature of Atonement; and Its Glorious Consequences, in the Final Reconciliation of All Men to Holiness and Happiness* (Randolph, Vt.: Sereno Wright, 1805), iv.

Chapter 9

Serpent Handlers: When the Sacrament Comes Alive

MARY LEE DAUGHERTY

And he said unto them, "Go ye into all the world, and preach the gospel to every creature. He that believeth and is baptized shall be saved; but he that believeth not shall be damned. And these signs shall follow them that believe; In my name shall they cast out devils; they shall speak with new tongues; They shall take up serpents; and if they drink any deadly thing, it shall not hurt them; they shall lay hands on the sick, and they shall recover."

—Mark 16:15–18 KJV

A Typical Service of the Serpent-Handling Christians in Southern West Virginia

The year is 1982. It is sunset, between 7:30 and 8:00 o'clock on a Sunday evening. I have arrived at a meeting at the Camp Creek Holiness Church in West Virginia. Joe Turner is pastor of the Jesus Church. For the past half-hour, cars have been arriving from nearby towns, and from as far away as three hundred miles. Those with instruments—accordions, guitars, drums, and tambourines—have gone inside to get ready for the evening service. Kathy, Preacher Joe Turner's daughter, is already inside, playing "Well, Holy, Holy, Holy." The large loudspeakers and open church windows carry the music down the mountain. The words being sung are a favorite among serpent handlers in West Virginia. They are:

Chorus:
Well, holy, holy, and that's alright.
Well, holy, holy, and that's alright.
Well, holy, holy, and that's alright.
Oh, if you're livin' holy, that's alright.

Verse One:
They call us holy rollers, but that's alright.
They call us holy rollers, but that's alright.
They call us holy rollers, but that's alright.
Oh, if you're livin' holy, that's alright.

Other verses begin with additional refrains:

Verse Two: They call us serpent handlers . . .
Verse Three: They say we worship serpents . . .
Verse Four: They say we're of the devil . . .
Verse Five: They say we've all gone crazy . . .
Verse Six: They call us "Jesus Only" . . .
Verse Seven:
There's just no understanding, but that's alright.
Oh, if you're livin' holy, that's alright.

The church building is a simple white frame structure on the side of a hill. It was constructed by Joe Turner in 1955. The church is small, 25 by 100 feet, and plain. Over the past thirty years, it has undergone major renovations. In 1960, the interior was paneled; carpeting, custom-made pews of oak, and a heating stove were installed. Bathrooms replaced the outhouses, and an air-conditioner was added in 1979.

Boxes of snakes are hand-carried or brought in cars. Each box has a hinged door which is opened from the top, and screened openings that allow air to circulate inside. Painted on, or burned into, the wooden sides is the scriptural citation of Mark 16:17–18. The snakes most commonly used are copperheads and rattlesnakes, since they are the ones most easily found in this part of the country. Usually, the snakes are brought to the church

only during the warm months of May through October. The boxes of serpents are placed near the pulpit, along with a jar of strychnine or another
poison.

A typical service at Joe Turner's Holiness church during the snake-
handling period begins with a spontaneous sermon. As the Spirit moves
them, the saints approach the altar area and give testimony or speak of
their own conversion. Throughout the service, there is singing, dancing, laying on of hands, praying aloud together, serpent handling, and
fire dancing. There is an occasional poison drinking and, once or twice
a year, foot washing. Foot washing is not practiced after the celebration
of the Lord's Supper, as in most other foot-washing churches, but is
simply part of a typical service. Often no offering is taken, since the ex-
penses of the church are small and Joe is paid no salary. There is no
church roll. A specific Bible text is not read; rather, the Bible is quoted
from memory during the preaching of a sermon, during testimonies, or
at any other time during the services.

During the singing of the second hymn, Kathy Turner, her two
brothers, Donnie and Mackie, and others begin to play "God's Not
Dead, He's Alive," on guitar, accordion, drums, and electric organ. As
Kathy begins singing, the congregation and the leaders and musicians
sitting on the raised platform spontaneously join in. No hymnbooks are
present; all instruments are played by ear, and hymns are sung from
memory. Kathy sings a line or two of the chorus; the others, recognizing the song, join in.

Music

The music in serpent-handling churches is lively and usually in 4/4 time.
Even a popular hymn like "Amazing Grace" is sung to a different tune
in 4/4 meter so that believers can dance to it.

A great variety of music is used—traditional gospel music, old bal-
lad hymns of biblical stories from both Old and New Testaments, bal-
lad hymns such as "Noah Picked Up a Hammer and Saw," "Mary and
Martha," and "Ananias." Still other musical forms are the traditional old
white spirituals of the mountains or black spirituals from the South.
Such hymns were sung at the Great Revival at Cane Ridge, Kentucky,
and the camp meetings which followed. Spirituals and choruses are still
to be heard in churches in the region where the old forms of mountain
religion persist. Antiphonal singing, during which believers may answer
each other across the aisle of the church house, can be heard today.
Amplified, rhythmic, and chantlike, the music carries believers into the
spirit of the service.

Preaching

Joe begins to preach. He uses no notes or outline. His preaching is typical of the Holiness or Pentecostal style. A sermon may last thirty minutes to an hour. His preaching is extemporaneous, filled with anecdotal, everyday life experiences. In one sermon, Joe quoted from twenty-six different books of the Bible. Seven references were made to the Old Testament and nineteen to the New Testament. Joe does not give chapter and verse, but his knowledge of Scripture is evident. Joe quotes the nugget of truth from the Bible passage, not the exact words in their exact order. This is how the oral tradition functions in these mountain churches.

Joe's preaching always "lifts up Jesus." He encourages his people to count their many blessings, and the service of worship celebrates the goodness of God. He is always concerned that people be saved and receive the gifts of the Holy Ghost. He readily admits his failings but always proclaims that God is able to overcome all obstacles. His preaching is, on the whole, positive and uplifting.

Reverend Turner's sermons are also sprinkled with glossolalia. Examples of this follow from this service:

Joe Turner:

> I get lonely. . . . Amen. Hama kolamaha shandamaha kiya.
>
> Jesus called me to preach. Honey, I was backslid when He called me. I did not want to do that . . . praise the Lord! I wondered, how did He call somebody like me? But when it got in me and I got in it, I'm glad I accepted it.
>
> Ho ho luh shandamahi ha ma sa.

During the healing portion of the service, Joe says:

> You've got to move against the powers of Satan, through the name of Jesus. Halamaho shandamaha kiya.
>
> In the name of Jesus. Halamaho seetalaho . . . shanda.
>
> Thank God in the name of Jesus.
>
> Halamaha shanda. In the name of Jesus.
>
> Halama seetalaho shanda.

Glossolalia

Glossolalia speech, or tongue speaking, is heard frequently in these churches. In my study, I did not record any foreign tongues (zino glossolalia), only syllables like those in Joe Turner's sermon.

The gift of tongues is usually the first and easiest gift of the Spirit to receive. There is no requirement that tongues be interpreted. Believers constantly speak of feeling healed inwardly after speaking in tongues. Members of these churches know little or nothing of the modern "charismatic movement." They have always spoken in tongues or sung in tongues, as long as anyone can remember.

Group Prayer

After preaching, group prayer begins. Men and women kneel; some are lying on the floor, jerking in the Spirit, praying, or speaking in tongues. It is the custom to kneel on the floor and for all to pray out loud together. Shouts of "Hallelujah!" are heard. Some members pray softly; others rise to shout "Glory to God." After five or ten minutes, the guitar starts up; the tambourine joins in; then the electric organ and drums. The music builds to sustained crescendo as the serpents are removed from the box. Kathy Turner begins singing "Noah Picked Up a Hammer and Saw" (a ballad-type hymn), followed by "Keeping Me Alive."

Serpent Handling

Joe Turner begins to handle serpents. After several years, I came to understand that the ritual of serpent handling functions sacramentally for him. As he dances with the serpent, while constantly calling on the name of Jesus, he is celebrating the central message of Christian faith in this ritual—that of victory through Jesus over death, and of belief in the Resurrection, or eternal life. Dancing ecstatically and praising God, he lifts out of the box two rattlesnakes and a copperhead, handles them and then passes them to his son Donnie, his daughter Kathy, and others. Serpents are shared only among those who feel they possess the "anointing of the Spirit." The energy engendered by the handling of serpents is almost beyond description. The entire congregation is ecstatic. As the snakes twist and slither against the air, there is a sense of expectancy and awe. The name of Jesus is chanted over and over: "Jesus, Jesus, Jesus, Jesus, Jesus." The believers ask for protection and power from the Holy Ghost as they pass the snakes among themselves.

The serpents are now returned to the box, and Kathy leads the singing of "Jesus Is on the Main Line" and "I'm a Soldier in the Army of the Lord." By this point, almost everyone is praying ecstatically, dancing, clapping hands, or playing a musical instrument. The sensations of sound and rhythm are pervasive. High energy flows throughout the bodies of believers, who tell me that their hands and feet tingle and they feel an intense warmth when filled with the Holy Ghost. Those who experience it most profoundly are those who pick up serpents, handle fire, or drink poison.

Dancing with Fire

As the music continues in full swing, Donnie Turner has lit a home-made torch—a soda bottle filled with kerosene, with an old rag for a wick. (Sometimes a propane torch is used.) He holds the fire to his hands, arms, and under his chin. Sometimes fire is even held against clothing. This is the most difficult gift of the Spirit to attain, requiring the greatest concentration and surrender of the self to God.

Donnie Turner does not experience pain and is not burned. "Long as I keep in the Spirit, I keep my mind on God, then I'm okay. If some-body bothers me, you know, if I get my mind off God, start thinkin' about people, then I get burnt.

"One time in particular, we had a coal stove, a potbellied stove. We reached inside and got some hot coals; it didn't burn our hands. But when we dropped one, it burnt the floor; it sure did."

Sister Kathy Turner tries to handle fire, but she cannot gain the anointing tonight. A man sings "Jesus Is on the Main Line." Kathy dances ecstatically; then she and Donnie dance together. Another hymn begins: "If You Want the Holy Ghost, Call Him Up and Tell Him What You Want." Donnie dances across the front of the church with his hands and fingers in the flame. Joe Turner, as he dances, waves his hands, his palms outstretched to God. More hymns are sung. Believers dance only in their churches, never in the outside world.

Foot Washing

After the dancing subsides, Kathy Turner takes a small tin washbasin and fills it with water from a larger water cooler. She then kneels in front of her father. She helps him remove his shoes and socks. She then places her father's feet in the basin and with her hands gently pours cold water around his feet. As the woman in the Bible dried Jesus' feet, she wipes each foot dry with her long, blond hair.

Others in the church have removed their shoes and socks and join in the dancing, singing, and foot-washing service. Since there is only one basin, it is shared by all. When the water runs dry, it is refilled from the large metal water jug. Men, women, boys, girls, teenagers, black and white, family and non-family—all wash each other's feet and exchange the Holy Kiss. Joe Turner takes the basin and kneels in front of a young black girl about twelve years old. He gently washes her feet and dries them with a towel. Joe then kisses first her feet and then her mouth and gives her a hug. These churches were never segregated in southern West Virginia (although they were in Kentucky).

Holy Kiss

The Holy Kiss is a real kiss on the mouth, although it is always done with discretion. Men kiss other men; women may kiss other women; men and women may kiss each other, but perhaps less so today than in the past. The Holy Kiss symbolizes the deep belief that all believers are members of one big family, the family of God. All are brothers and sisters in Christ Jesus.

"Praying Through" at the Altar

At the altar, some people are now "praying through" for salvation. The altar is usually a short partition which separates the pulpit and platform from the rest of the church, where the congregation sits. Getting saved is the most important experience in a person's life. When anyone is seeking to "pray through," the service usually comes to a halt. The entire church will then lay hands on and pray for the one seeking salvation. The seeker may weep and even wail, and then confess to God all her or his sins of the past. Others will kneel beside the seeker and help them by praying. Often after "praying through" and thus feeling forgiven, the seeker may fall into a swoon, break forth into tongues, shout, dance, and jerk in the Holy Spirit.

It is important that salvation be a total experience, bringing about real change in one's life. The authenticity of this experience is demonstrated by receiving the gift of tongues or jerking in the Spirit. In most cases, believers are able to recall the exact day and hour of their salvation. After salvation occurs, baptism by immersion soon will follow in a nearby creek or river. Joe uses a branch of the Little Coal River (the baptism ritual I filmed was held here).

Healing

Prayer at the altar is not only for salvation, but also for healing. Two men lay their hands on Brother Johnson, who has come to the altar to pray for healing. Others are prayed for: a woman who has an ear problem, another woman with a foot problem, and a woman who wants to be healed of her desire to smoke. They come forward, bowing their heads for men and women to lay on their hands. Still other believers raise their faces and stand with arms raised toward the heavens.

Whatever the concern, each believer is prayed for separately. Olive oil may be used for anointing the body that is ailing. Prayer cloths with the name of Jesus printed on them have been used in serpent-handling churches. Serpent-handling Christians tend to believe that cancer healing may be accomplished only through the most fervent, audible prayers, which are prayed in tongues. Today, some may choose to seek medical help.

Every person who desires a special prayer for healing is prayed for. Church members believe that the spiritual energy of those who lay on hands flows into the body of the one who is seeking healing. Men and women exercise discretion when practicing the laying on of hands with members of the opposite sex. The preacher usually lays his hands on the head of the one being prayed over.

Believers do go to the hospital for surgery and medical treatment, but they believe that healing also can take place through prayer and fasting. Faith healing is an old custom in mountain churches with both spiritual and pragmatic implications. It was at once an act of faith and a response to the scarcity of medical insurance and medical treatment facilities.

Testimonies

The final segment of the evening's service is the giving of testimonies. It provides an opportunity for any person present to tell of his or her Christian experience. This may be a speech concerning a unique faith experience, an especially painful concern, an expression of victory in the faith. Kathy Turner's testimony was particularly moving to me that night. Kathy testified, saying:

> You know, about two years ago, bless His name, I was in a car accident. I was a-drivin' this little Volkswagen, hallelujah; you know there was a truck, bless His name, a truck was in front of me, a-carryin' a grader, or end-loader, and it fell off and hit me [it tore the car in half]. And you know, I was knocked out for about fourteen days before I knew anything. While I was out, I flew in the Spirit with Jesus. And He carried me out in the Spirit, halleluyer. You know, I stayed with Him for many days; I flew in the Spirit with the Lord. Above all these trees and everything, Jesus took me to Paradise. It was a beautiful place. . . . He took me to Hell. It was like a gulf, the gulf was under me. When the doctors would come in, I'd tell them that there wasn't anything the matter with me, but they thought I was crazy, because, you know, I'd tell them what I'd seen. You know, there's a lot of people don't believe in God. But hallelujah, I know He is. He walks with me, He answers me in my prayers. You know, God give me life.

Joe Turner now calls the service to an end by welcoming everyone present. It is 11:30 P.M. The congregation leaves after exchanging goodbyes. Some of the men have to get up by 4:30 or 5:00 A.M. to go to work in the mines. Children must go to school; many young ones already are asleep on pews or in the arms of their parents. The boxes of serpents are collected, the untouched poison jar closed and removed, and the musical instruments packed. Everyone leaves, "happy in the Spirit."

Historical Roots

The Symbolism of the Serpent

The symbolism of the serpent is found in almost all cultures and religions everywhere and in all ages. It suggests the opposition of good and evil, sickness and health, life and death, mortality and immortality, chaos and wisdom. Because the serpent lives in the ground but often is found in trees, it conveys the notion of transcendence, a creature that lives between earth and heaven. And because it sheds its skin, it seems to know the secret of eternal life.

In the Bible, the serpent is associated most obviously with the temptations of Adam and Eve (Genesis 3:1–13), but we also read of the rod that Moses and Aaron turned into snakes (Exodus 17:8–12), and of Moses' bronze serpent standard (Numbers 21:6–9). The two entwined snakes in the ancient figure of the caduceus, symbolizing sickness and health, have been widely adopted as the emblem of the medical profession. And sometimes, in early Christian art, the crucifixion is represented with a serpent wrapped around the cross or lying at the foot of the cross (cf. John 3:13). Here, again, good and evil, and the victory of life over death are symbolized.

In early liturgical art, John, the Evangelist, often was identified with a chalice from which a serpent was departing, a reference to the legend that when he was forced to drink poison, it was drained away in the snake. Among the early Gnostics, there was a group known as the Ophites who were said to worship the serpent because it brought "knowledge" to Adam and Eve and so to humanity. They were said to free a serpent from a box; it then entwined itself around the bread and the wine at the Eucharist, changing it into the body and blood of Jesus.

Of course, this ancient history and symbolic lore are unknown to the mountain serpent handlers in West Virginia, and when I shared with them some of this history, they really were not very interested. Their own tradition is rooted in their literal acceptance of what they regard as Jesus' commandment at the conclusion of Mark's gospel. The problem of biblical textual criticism, relating to the fact that these verses upon which they depend are not found in the best manuscript evidence, does not bother them. Their Bible is the King James Version, and they know, through their own experiences, that their faith in the healing and saving power of Jesus has been tested and proved beyond question and doubt. It still functions sacramentally for them as a "sign." It is a ritual about life, death, and resurrection through faith in Jesus.[1]

Protestant Revivalism

The serpent-handling Holiness church grew out of a patchwork of religious beliefs developed in the isolation of the rugged Appalachian mountain terrain and the economic instability of a rural subsistence farming and mining economy. Well into the 1990s, those grassroots religious forms and folk theologies persist.

Between 1700 and 1776, approximately half a million Protestant Irishmen, who actually were Lowland Scots, settled the Appalachian Mountains. Others who came were German, Welsh, and English. They immigrated inland because they were too poor to buy land along the seacoast; then they moved into what is now West Virginia. The Scots-Irish moved into what is now West Virginia as early as 1719. For the next hundred years, they came from Pennsylvania, Virginia, North Carolina, and Europe.

It was the period between 1800 and 1850, called the "Great Revival" era, that had the greatest formative impact upon the region. By 1830, the Scotch-Irish Presbyterian influence began to wane, as the church no longer could supply enough ordained ministers for the growing numbers of people immigrating to the Appalachian region. Nonetheless, by this time, the Presbyterian Calvinistic tradition was deeply embedded in Appalachian culture.

During the first half of the nineteenth century, camp meetings and grassroots revivals proliferated throughout the region. Mountain people became Baptists and Methodists. The Baptists, who, like the Presbyterians, were Calvinist in their theology, were one of the most important and influential religious groups on the frontier. During the Civil War, when West Virginia broke away from Virginia over the issue of slavery and established statehood in 1863, there were approximately ten thousand Baptists in West Virginia.

In West Virginia, however, the Methodist Church was the denomination with the largest membership.[2] Central to Methodist teaching was the notion that holy, or pious, living and God's salvation were not reserved for the clergy, but were available to all.

The Methodist church gained a foothold between 1789 and 1816 in the area that later was to become West Virginia, largely due to the efforts of circuit-riding missionaries. The circuit riders preached, baptized, married, buried the dead, and brought news of the outside world to these isolated mountain people. At night, they slept on the trails or stayed with mountain families.

The Holiness movement sprang from the dissatisfaction of certain Methodists at the increasing modernism of the Methodist ministry. Methodist numbers continued to expand, but debates arose over worldliness, materialism, and holiness.

The Christian Union

Inspired by the renewed revivalism marked by the First General Holiness Assembly in 1885, Richard G. Spurling Sr., a seventy-two-year-old pastor of a small Baptist church in Coker Creek in Monroe County, Tennessee, and his son, Richard Spurling Jr., called a meeting on August 19, 1886. In the Barney Creek Meetinghouse, a rough log building which was about two miles from the joint border of Tennessee and North Carolina, they established a new group, which they called the Christian Union.

The Christian Union is important for our understanding of the origin of serpent-handling groups. The union eventually evolved to become the Church of God and the Church of God of Prophecy, both of Cleveland, Tennessee. George Hensley and his wife Amanda were the first modern-day serpent handlers. They were part of the early movements that became the Church of God (Cleveland, Tennessee).

Oral tradition suggests that, during the revival of 1896 at Camp Creek, North Carolina, more than one hundred people received the baptism of the Holy Ghost, but how many became members of the Christian Union is not positively known. The revival was soon persecuted unmercifully by other church people from both far and near. The Christian Union's schoolhouse was barred; the log church was burned; and individuals were threatened, beaten, and shot at. But persecution only stimulated greater fervor. Between 1890 and 1926, a total of twenty-five small churches formed which preached tongues-speaking. Hundreds of smaller religious groups, each with its own self-appointed leader, later sprang up in the surrounding areas of Tennessee and North Carolina. The most extreme of these was the serpent-handling group.

Taking Up Serpents

In December 1904, A. J. Tomlinson (originally a Quaker who distributed Bibles throughout the mountains) moved to Cleveland, Tennessee. He was then fifty miles from Camp Creek, North Carolina, and to pastor the church there he often rode through what is now the Cherokee National Forest. By 1906, several other prominent members had moved to Cleveland, Tennessee. A Second Assembly was held in 1907, and a new name was chosen. "The Church of God" was agreed upon by all as a more suitable designation for the church than "the Christian Union."

The doctrine of the Church of God began to spread throughout the city of Cleveland. Among those attracted was George W. Hensley, a poor subsistence farmer who believed that he was called by the Holy Ghost to preach the gospel. George W. Hensley is believed to have been the first preacher to take up serpents.

Church of God members have debated who exactly was the first to handle serpents. Some assert that A. J. Tomlinson, and not George Hensley, was the "father" of serpent handling. Church of God leaders dispute this. Tomlinson's son, M. A. Tomlinson, stated in interviews with me on October 20 and 21, 1981, that neither he, his father, nor his brother Homer ever had handled serpents. He explained that both he and his father had observed those who did, but Tomlinson maintained that most were rural ministers and were not among the main leadership of the Church of God in Cleveland, Tennessee.

In the early days of the Church of God movement, Hensley and his followers did not pose a challenge to Tomlinson's leadership. However, as Hensley's influence on rural pastors grew, divisions developed. By 1914, the Church of God's official newspapers and other publications began to debate serpent handling.[3] Until 1989, numerous articles appeared, as church leaders questioned, praised, and denounced the unfolding movement.

Historians have given George Hensley credit for founding serpent handling in 1910 in Grasshopper Valley, Tennessee, some thirty-five miles from Chattanooga. George Hensley was a Church of God evangelist who could neither read nor write. However, his first wife, Amanda, was literate. She probably filled out his license to preach, while he made an "x" in the place for his name. This license is in the Church of God archives in Cleveland, Tennessee.

In an interview on August 21, 1991, in Cleveland, Tennessee, Hensley's youngest son (by his first marriage), James Roscoe Hensley, made it clear that it was George's wife who read the Scriptures to the family every night and who gave theological interpretations of the Word of God to the family. According to her son, it was she who taught George most of what he knew about the Bible immediately after his conversion. She was a Christian before he was converted. One wonders if Amanda Hensley's insights as reader and exegete did not provide the foundational principles of the original serpent-handling legacy. Historian David Kimbrough suggests that Hensley had seen a man handle a snake during a preaching service.[4] Amanda Hensley handled serpents early in the movement's history.

Nevertheless, it is remembered that Hensley, "brooding over" the statement in Mark 16:17–18, read to him by Amanda, climbed White Oak Mountain, which rims Grasshopper Valley on the east; prayed for a sign; and spotted a large rattlesnake in the rocky gap. He put it in a gunny sack and took it to the revival meetings. A few days later, he began his evangelical work. In a religious meeting at Sale Creek, he cited these Bible texts, handled the serpent himself, and thrust the rattlesnake at the people, asking them to prove their faith.

George Hensley later deserted Amanda and her five children and married three additional times before his death from a serpent bite in Altha, Florida, at the age of seventy-five. Amanda, with the help of her daughter Esther, raised the children, continuing to instruct them in the Scripture and the doctrines of holiness. Roscoe Hensley recalled that his mother supported the family through work at a Chattanooga hosiery mill. She remained steadfast in her faith and provided the children with spiritual nurture.

Amanda is buried in the cemetery beside the Dolly Pond Church of God near Birchwood, Tennessee, home of the original serpent-handling Christians. As I stood by her grave, I wondered if she, like so many women of faith, had been denied her rightful place in the history of her own religious movement.

As for George Hensley, he traveled extensively, preaching and wrestling with the demon of alcoholism, often returning home drunk. His son recalled that, prior to his conversion, George Hensley brewed whisky, served time in jail, and gained first-hand experience of the sin-filled life.

In his theological beliefs, George, like most of the early serpent handlers, was a strange amalgam of Calvinism and Arminianism. As serpent handling moved northward in the late 1920s and the early 1930s, it found a ready reception among miners in Kentucky and West Virginia.

Hensley believed that if he wanted to receive eternal life, it was imperative that he handle serpents. He died of snake bite on July 25, 1955, in Florida. While the idea that salvation is dependent upon handling serpents is not stated in the text of Mark 16, Hensley understood that it was imperative to his faith and his salvation. His followers are divided over this question today. While most do not feel their salvation is dependent upon handling serpents, some still insist that it is necessary.

In West Virginia, few of the early serpent handlers ever met George

Hensley, and even these knew little about his life and work. Their "prophet" was Kentuckian Raymond Hayes. Hayes visited Elsie Preast in 1941. In 1946, Preast began serpent handling regularly in Fayette County, West Virginia, at the Church of All Nations. Preast told me that he knew serpent handling had been practiced seventeen or eighteen years earlier (early 1930s) in southern West Virginia, up Cabin Creek outside of Charleston, West Virginia. Today, the most active serpent-handling church in southern West Virginia is located near Jolo, where Robert and Barbara Elkins and Dewey Chapin, her son, are leaders.

What the future holds for serpent handlers is unclear. Outmigration from the Appalachian region threatens to weaken the family-church communities and connections. Although young people in the past have tended to stay in their local communities, the temptation is to move out to nearby cities to find work. It appears likely that this temptation will escalate as job opportunities continue to shrink in rural areas. Mobility means loss of the family and religious ties which have held the serpent handlers together.

Better education and greater economic opportunities are testing the loyalty young people feel toward the religion of their snake-handling parents. Some already have chosen to become part of the more mainline Holiness and Pentecostal churches. This may be due largely to the fact that in most urban areas they do not have easy access to churches that continue to practice the ritual of serpent handling. A few, however, have practiced the ritual in nearby cities, to which serpents are taken from the rural churches. Many of the once-active serpent-handling churches have closed as the older leaders have died. For example, Preacher Joe Turner's church has been converted into a family dwelling for one of his sons.

Donnie Turner, another son, has moved deeper into the mountains; and when I last spoke with him was still handling serpents. Turner acknowledged that Joe's grandchildren would never handle serpents, but he wanted them to remember their religious heritage with great pride. For those who remain in the mountains, serpent handling will, I believe, remain a very important part of their lives in the immediate future. There are about one hundred to two hundred practicing serpent handlers in West Virginia today. They know, through their own experiences, that their faith in the healing and saving power of Jesus has been tested and proven beyond doubt.

While a fundamental ritual can be lost forever, it may also lie dormant for generations. Time alone will tell what will happen with snake handling in the mountains. It is my prayer that history will remember the deep spirituality of these sturdy snake-handling Christians whom I have been privileged to know and love. [5]

Notes

1. Thomas L. Harvey Jr., " A Sacramental Approach to Snake Handling" (unpublished paper, fall 1995, Church of God School of Theology, Cleveland, Tenn.), 5. See also Mary Lee Daugherty, "Serpent-Handling as Sacrament," *Theology Today* 33 (Oct. 1976): 232–43; Thomas Burton, *Serpent-Handling Believers* (Knoxville: Univ. of Tennessee Press, 1993; and David L. Kimbrough, *Taking Up Serpents: Snake Handlers in Eastern Kentucky* (Chapel Hill: Univ. of North Carolina Press, 1995).

2. In 1980, there were 17,000 in the United Methodist Church. John Price, director, West Virginia Council of Churches, interview by Mary Lee Daugherty, July 29, 1981. Records in the West Virginia Council of Churches offices, Charleston, W.Va.

3. Church of God, *Minutes of the Thirteenth Annual Assembly*, 1917, p. 297, in Archives, Lee's College, Cleveland, Tenn. Qtd. also in *White Wing Messenger*, Oct. 11, 1930, in Archives, Church of God, at Lee's College, Cleveland, Tenn.

4. Kimbrough, *Taking Up Serpents*, 9–40.

5. "Saga of the Serpent Handlers—A Typical Service," videotape, West Virginia Cultural Center, State Capitol Complex, Charleston.

Chapter 10

Mountain Preachers, Mountain Ministers

GARY FARLEY AND BILL J. LEONARD

Wounded and left for dead, a casualty of the Baker-Howard feud that alternately simmered and erupted in Clay County, Kentucky, James Anderson Burns recovered and asked himself why God had spared his life. The answer came that he was to bring an end to the feuding by becoming a preacher, by teaching the children of feudists the truth of the Christian faith. Already in his late twenties, he left the mountains in 1892 for training at Denison University.

After less than a year of college, he returned to Clay County to teach in its remote schools and serve as pastor of rural churches. His work in the ministry proved to be so effective that he was invited to teach at Berea College in the 1896–97 term. However, the feud flared again. So in 1899 Burns invited fifty of the feudists, an equal number from each side, to a meeting at the grist mill on the Red Bird River a few miles north of Manchester. They came, not only because they believed in him, but also because they genuinely desired peace. The feudists trusted Burns both because he once had been a fierce fighter in the Baker clan and because they had come to know him as a man of integrity and vision during the several years he had ministered among them. They listened as he shared his vision of a school where their children could prepare themselves for life in the emerging new world of the twentieth century. This vision struck a responsive chord. Most wanted a more peaceful life for their children.

Burns offered these Appalachians a new challenge, the founding of a residential school to serve their children. Oneida Institute was begun in 1900. Its Board of Trustees was comprised largely of leaders of the warring clans. The school, located in eastern Kentucky, continues today with an expanded mission to serve an even broader regional constituency.

Burns was aided in the founding of the school by another minister, H. L. McMurray, a pastor in Berea. A native of Kansas and well connected in the urban church circles across the North, McMurray enabled Burns to tell his story in large churches and on the Chautauqua circuit, where he could raise funds to support his educational enterprise. McMurray was the product of leading educational institutions of the day. Undoubtedly he saw the mountains as a place much in need of both the gospel and modern education. He saw in Burns a person with character, connections, and the vision to accomplish this mission. Together they formed an effective alliance—one a native son of Appalachia, the other a concerned outsider. While they came from different subcultures and did not always agree, apparently they were able to work together on common endeavors.[1]

Burns and McMurray can be viewed as particular "types" of the many preachers/ministers who continue to labor in the Appalachian Mountains. Burns lives on in many of the indigenous preachers of the region. Like his, their stories often feature a wild and reckless youth, followed by a personal and spiritual crisis in their middle or late twenties. As these preachers "testify," an illness, accident, addiction, or family crisis can precipitate a spiritual transformation and the "call" to preach. This call then is tested within and among specific congregations, and, if confirmed by the community of believers, often will result in ordination to the gospel ministry. While many of these preachers have limited formal education, they may be extensively self-taught and in most instances are closely related to a "mentoring" pastor who provides counsel and assistance along the way.

The more effective, or "successful," of this type of preacher usually is distinguished by a certain charisma—gifts of spiritual insight, homiletical flourish, and pastoral concern. His skills also may include the ability to perform the "manly" tasks of the mountain culture, such as hunting, fishing, various sports, woodcraft, agricultural knowledge, and strenuous manual labor. Abilities in music and story telling also are prized. The preacher is expected to be a person of deep integrity, loyalty, good counsel, and courage. His hands must be hard, their grip firm; his "fly must be closed" (no sexual immorality); and, as some will say, there must be "no lace on his pants."[2] Added to this is an ability to perform in worship according to the standard expectations regarding good gospel preaching: colorful sermon content, the ability to touch the deepest emotions, and the recognition that he is merely an instrument of the Holy Spirit. All these are expressed in sermons which will elicit audience responses of "Amen," "Praise God," and other verbal declarations from the answering congregation.

For these preachers in the Burns tradition, the "call" from God is essential to genuine mission and ministry, authenticating spiritual authority, motivation, and power. In much of Central Appalachia, these "called" preachers often are more ambivalent about the need for, and place of, ministerial education than was James Burns. On the one hand, they want to know more so that they can be effective, "studying to show themselves approved unto God," as the biblical text admonishes. On the other hand, many insist that a little education can be detrimental to vital faith—i.e., it can "put out the fire" of the Spirit. They also know that certain "educated" ministers can be scornful and critical of their indigenous brothers. Even among those mountain preachers who have more formal education, it is the Divine call, more than educational credentials, that energizes their ministry. As some will say, education is the "sharpening of the axe," but it must never be confused with the axe itself.[3] Often the rhetoric of the mountain pulpit reflects a colorful response to the question of an educated ministry, as when a preacher declares, "God gave me a B.A.—Born Again!" Yet another preacher may insist, "The only graduation I claim is from 'knee university.'"

Most of the rural churches, many village churches, and various independent congregations in the cities of Appalachia are pastored by persons of the James Burns "type." These individuals typically are bi-vocational—that is, they maintain a second (secular) job, which probably provides their primary economic support. Many see this as normative for all God-called preachers and are critical of pastors ("hirelings") who are paid a salary by their churches. Others may understand their current bi-vocationalism as temporary, looking to the time when the church they serve grows enough to be able to support them, or the time when they will be called to a larger congregation which can provide full-time financial support. Many preachers make a clear choice to be bi-vocational, so that they can serve a congregation which otherwise might not be able to have a pastor.[4]

H. L. McMurray represented another "type" of minister, one whose background and orientation are essentially alien to the Appalachian culture. These ministers reflect the denominationally-oriented or home-mission-board approach to ministry in Appalachia. Most were reared outside the region and often have received ministerial training in colleges or seminaries. Those who are from the region run the risk of becoming alienated from their culture and their people due to their educational background or their changing approach to ministry.[5]

Like McMurray, many ministers have come to Appalachia with a genuine sense of mission. They have come with a desire to call persons to faith in Jesus Christ, to worship of God, and to challenge conditions, culture, or unjust social systems. These ministers face twin dangers. On the one hand, they must avoid paternalism and the tendency to look down on the persons they have come to serve. They must also deal with the temptation to be unduly critical of their mountain-preacher counterparts. On the other hand, they may be tempted to "go native" in an attempt to adapt to the religious culture of the region. Such an effort may turn into simply another form of paternalism, and it may lead to an uncritical acceptance of many problematical ideas and practices.

Origins of Appalachian Ministry

Burns and McMurray personify two "types" of Appalachian preachers or ministers. We should not suppose, however, that these are the only two ministerial "profiles" to be found in the region. Local religious leaders reflect the complexity and diversity of the communities of faith they serve. In fact, clergy in the region long have been a diverse lot, and any individual embodies elements of various pastoral profiles. This essay is an attempt to clarify the tasks facing preachers and ministers in Central Appalachia.

Today, some clergy remain mountain preachers—self-educated, serving without pay, exercising their gifts of proclamation and practice in independent congregations spread throughout the region. Others are "imported" pastors linked to denominational systems and structures. Some are lay preachers carrying out ministerial functions without benefit of full or formal ordination. Some have Bible school or seminary training, others do not. Some consider themselves "bi-vocational," working a "secular" job while serving a church which does not or cannot provide financial remuneration. Others think of themselves not as bi-vocational, but rather as self-supporting, choosing not to distinguish between elements of their Christian service.[6] Some are men, but a growing number are women, functioning amid controversy over their place in the church.

In some sense, the mountain preachers—unpaid, self-supporting, people's pastors—are the heirs of some of the earliest clergy to find their way to the western and southern frontiers in the late eighteenth and early nineteenth centuries. Some reflect the work of itinerant Methodist circuit riders, associated with the early Wesleyan awakenings in England and the U.S. These circuit riders traveled widely, linking congregations. They were part of a conference of ministers and churches which followed John Wesley's Arminian theology and methodological organization. In a day when churches were spread out across a huge region and ministers were few, the circuit-rider system was a dynamic and creative ministerial solution.

Baptists and other evangelical groups often relied on the "farmer-preacher" as the model for preaching and ministry. These individuals came from the land, working farms and otherwise supporting themselves but taking up Bibles on Sundays to proclaim the gospel in assorted churches throughout the region. Each supported himself through the "sweat of his brow" and carried on his ministry alongside the laity in the churches.

Later models combined elements of the circuit rider and the farmer-preacher. Many Appalachian churches in rural areas and small towns had half- or quarter-time preachers who lived in a given geographical area, supported themselves, and served multiple churches in the region. They might receive "love offerings" from the congregation, or be paid in sundries such as vegetables, beef, chicken, eggs, and butter, all given by church members.

The Holiness-Pentecostal movements introduced another element into Appalachian ministry: women preachers. While women exercised various roles in Appalachian churches, the Holiness-Pentecostal churches understood early that women, like men, could receive the Spirit and exercise gifts of proclamation and ministry. In those congregations, women could serve as evangelists and preachers, and often as pastors. (Some Pentecostals permit women to preach as evangelists but not to serve as pastors; others make no such distinction.) The admonition in Acts 2, "My spirit is poured out on all flesh," was taken as a mandate for both men and women who received the "call."

Deborah McCauley profiles such a Holiness woman, Sister Lydia Surgener of Cranks Creek, Kentucky, who preaches in two churches in the region. Of Sister Lydia, McCauley writes that she began preaching in her thirties and later took in her nephew, Junior, a man in his twenties, who became her apprentice. McCauley concludes that the two "share a symbiotic ministry, Junior supporting and helping the ministry of his now aged aunt through the skills and talents he has developed by working with her, and Sister Lydia continuing to provide Junior mentorship, access, and opportunity to exercise his call."[7]

The sense of "call" was extremely important to churches seeking ministers. Mountain congregations and other evangelical communions made the call from God the primary requisite for ministry and preaching. At ordination and before joining a congregation, potential preachers were asked to describe their conversion experience and call, the latter often an additional or accompanying spiritual experience. This call to preach might accompany conversion, or the baptism of the Holy Spirit (particularly strong in the Pentecostal tradition), or it might come as a separate experience of the divine presence. This declaration is evident in the statement of a young Baptist candidate in Kentucky during the 1830s. In his account of the call as preparation for ordination, he acknowledged his conversion, noting, "Soon after this I think I enjoyed more of the sensible presence of God in my soul than ever before; and my mind was more deeply exercised to the duty of Preaching Christ. . . . I did not feel it my duty to engage immediately in trying to Preach; but that this duty was before me, & that I ought to use every means in my power to qualify me for it. My Brethren advised me to cherish this impression of duty prayerfully, and to be free in exercising my gift in exhortation when I felt it my duty. Elder W. advised me to try to go to School as soon as I could."[8]

In his work, *Powerhouse for God: Speech, Chant, and Song in an Appalachian Baptist Church*, Brown University professor Jeff Todd Titon recounts the "call to preach" of a more contemporary mountain preacher. It is part of the "testimony" of Brother John Sherfey, pastor of the Fellowship Independent Baptist Church, located near Stanley, Virginia. Brother John recalled:

> So I—I kept fighting it off and going you know with this I don't know, it was a burden seemed like or a heavy feeling on me . . . so one evening I was working the three-to-eleven shift and I was coming home from work and it just got so heavy upon me I just couldn't stand it. And I pulled an old '42 Studebaker car I had oh it was about eleven-thirty in the night . . . I just fell down over the steering wheel. And I said, "Lord, if it's preach, I'll go. If you'll lift this burden." And, believe me, it left. Just like that it was gone.[9]

Calls often involve a sense of hesitancy, or of bearing a heavy burden, until the decision is made. Some preachers insist that the calling is so awesome that it can be accepted only if there is no way to relieve the burden other than by fulfilling the divine mandate. Some declare, "If you can do anything else in this world, then you are probably not called!"

In earlier eras (and in many communions today), the ordination process often began with a "license to preach," whereby a specific congregation vouched for the person's initial call and agreed to oversee his progress in the ministry. Many of these preachers served several small congregations which were led by local lay leaders. Ordination was the ultimate event leading toward pastoral ministry. Its practices varied in the early congregations. Baptist churches usually utilized an ordaining council composed of laity and visiting clergy. That council's recommendation, along with acceptance by the church, was required before a service of ordination could be held.

In the Methodist system, ministerial candidates moved through an orderly process involving ordination as deacon, a internship period, and ordination carried out by the bishop and other members of the conference. Presbyterian ordination was directed by the presbytery of the church and the regional synod. Mountain Holiness churches might or might not utilize formal ordination, but the spiritual ordination of the Spirit was an absolute necessity.

The experience of being "called" often seemed to give rural Appalachian Baptist pastors, for example, both power and prestige. And while their holy role often subjected them to ridicule by unbelievers and other skeptics, this seemed a small price to pay for being a spiritual leader and a warrior for God. In fact, it is possible to understand the rural Appalachian Baptist pastor as inheriting the role of the Highland clan chieftain. This is particularly true of the moderators of Baptist associations (regional church confederacies) in the mountains. This authority can be (and no doubt has been) used both to exploit and to bless. Discord and schism often has resulted as congregations debated this aspect of the ministerial office. These observations regarding Baptist pastors also may apply to other Appalachian religious traditions.

More recently, divisions have occurred over the role of women in all denominations, with some churches among the Methodist, Presbyterian, Lutheran, and even a few Baptist traditions calling women as pastors. This is a great challenge to some churches which read quite literally biblical texts regarding the silence and submission of women in the churches. Still others point to the liberation of Christ for all persons, suggesting that conversion and baptism represent great equalizers, opening possibilities for preaching and ministry for all persons, "Jew and Greek, slave and free, male and female." The Reverend Marcia Myers, a contributor to this volume, is a Presbyterian minister in West Virginia and Kentucky who illustrates the changing role of women preachers in the region.

Education for ministry is as diverse as the ministry itself. Some faith communities remain suspicious of formal education, viewing it as detrimental to the Spirit. Yet these traditions often have preachers who are self-taught through personal reading and study and who have imbibed the oral tradition of preaching passed on from one preaching generation to another. Others have attended Bible schools or institutes throughout the region. (Baptists, for example, founded schools such as Fruitland Bible Institute in North Carolina, and Clear Creek Bible College in eastern Kentucky.) Some have college and seminary degrees. Indeed, ordination in some denominations—Disciples of Christ; Presbyterian Church, USA; United Methodists; Lutherans; and Episcopalians—is contingent upon seminary education. (Some exceptions may be made in selected cases.) Debates over the necessity for, and use of, seminary-trained ministers continue to characterize certain traditions in the region.

Strong norms also apply to the performance of the Appalachian ministerial task. Mountain preachers are expected to be emotional, motivating speakers who declare their unequivocal opposition to all manner of personal sin. There are certain sermonic terms or expressions which must be sprinkled throughout sermons. These include references to such images as: "Calvary's cross," "a Devil's hell," "the precious blood of Jesus," and the like. One finds in these sermons a standard form of delivery, a style probably rooted early in the nineteenth century. It is interesting that this "holy form" has been maintained as normative among rural sectarians for so long.

In such homiletical forms, the preacher begins his remarks calmly and in a normal tone of voice. "As he proceeds, his voice becomes louder, faster, and, many times, harsh. Soon he is speaking in a rapid, chanting manner. Phrases are punctuated by a 'haa' sound, called variously the 'holy grunt or holy hack.' His diction often takes on the qualities of a tobacco barn auctioneer. He will frequently emphasize his point by striking the pulpit stand. He may remove his coat and tie. He may jump up and down, come down from the pulpit, run up and down the aisles."[10]

This set of expectations concerning appearance, manner, and performance developed in the region during the first half of the nineteenth century. Some of the forms may have their roots in the revivals characteristic of the First and Second Great Awakenings, as well as the revivalistic environments of American evangelical life.

The discovery of iron ore and of large deposits of coal, both needed for the industrialization of the nation, resulted in very significant changes throughout much of Appalachia in the second half of the nineteenth century. Miners and other workmen were imported from Europe and placed in company-built and -operated villages, often referred to as "coal camps." This was particularly true in northern Appalachia. Company-funded churches were among the amenities offered to mine workers. One or more might cater to the workers—Roman Catholic Italian, Polish, or Irish; Welch Baptist, Russian Orthodox, or German Lutheran. Another congregation—Presbyterian, Methodist, or Episcopal—was more likely to be provided for the management. In Central Appalachia, many of the miners were indigenous to the region, so the company might furnish a Baptist, Holiness, Methodist, or Presbyterian church for the workers. The immigrant Catholic churches tended to replicate the parish concept of the church which had informed life in Europe. The American mountain congregations tended to be more like the covenanted congregations described above. In many cases, the minister in these villages was a missionary from a national denomination or a Roman Catholic order. Often some of the support for these ministers came from the mining corporation.

The Present Situation

Industrialization often was intertwined with modernity—that effort to bring new science, knowledge, and theology to the culture. Initially, science and technology seemed to join Calvinism in the call to conquer the natural world.[11] Yet modernity also implied a natural, even a secular, explanation of the human condition—an explanation which many Christians believed undermined the presence of the supernatural and the doctrine of divine sovereignty. In mainline society, causal explanations no longer relied on demons, angels, or other spirits, nor did they always attribute causation to God. Rather, the laws of nature and of reason dominated. Preachers often denounced "modernism," "liberalism," and other "isms" predicated upon unbelief and unorthodoxy.

The spiritual and theological implications of modernism were addressed by Appalachians in several different modes. Some ignored it, while others embraced it. Among certain Calvinists and other evangelicals, two forms of fundamentalism emerged. Many mountain preachers chose to attack education. As many articulated it, education was destructive to genuine faith, substituting human reason and intellect for divine sovereignty. Another fundamentalist response came from educated Calvinists who attempted to utilize certain rational categories to establish the truth of revelation. Another response involved a mediating position and attempted a synthesis of modernist thought with the affirmation of the Sovereignty of God.[12] This latter position was common among seminary-trained Baptist pastors and college professors in Appalachia, as well as among employees of various denominational agencies.[13]

Looking to the Future

As we look to the future, we need to listen well to the mountain preachers who have devoted their lives to calling people to a Christian world view. Certainly they have insights that can enrich the Body of Christ. Too often we have operated with a linear view of change which promoted the "modern" at the expense of the "traditional." Many have tended to look down upon the mountain preachers and have scorned their premodern, "traditional" views as out of date and inadequate—as seriously in need of rejection or at least significant change. But now it seems that we were wrong. Change is more Hegelian in nature. The premodern and the modern were but the thesis and the antithesis of the emerging postmodern world. We now need a renewed effort to unite in response to the challenges and opportunities of Christian mission in the postmodern world. Some of us need to confess that we approached ministry in Appalachia more as missionaries of modernity than as missionaries of the gospel. Others of us need to confess that our faith in God was so small that we did not seek God's truth honestly and openly. Some of us need to confess our paternalism toward our colleagues in ministry, while others among us need to confess our unwillingness to change.

If rapprochement can occur among the various ministry types, then the next decades will be exciting times for ministry in Appalachia. These years might involve several important projects. First, mountain ministers might inform our understanding of Christian spirituality, given that these ministers have retained a strong emphasis upon spirituality—the life of prayer, study of the Scriptures, religious experience, and the "practice of the presence of God." This spirituality has been nurtured in the communal life of the Appalachian congregation, or what some now might call an "accountability" group. Such a group is evident in "base community" church-renewal groups in South America and is an intimate part of the Appalachian mountain church tradition.[14]

Second, at its best, contemporary mission endeavors understand the importance of cross-cultural communication. Basic to this is the concept of translating the gospel, as much as is possible, into the world view of a particular people.[15] For the next several generations in Appalachia, three world views will be present: premodern, modern, and postmodern. The initial presentation of the gospel was in a premodern culture much like that of the traditional Appalachian culture. Mountain preachers have been working at presenting the gospel to premodern people for generations. This must be affirmed. Conversely, the town preachers have been effective in presenting the gospel to modernized people. Our problem is that these approaches have alienated Christians from one another.

Third, we must become as honest as the Apostle Paul and declare that we also "see through a glass, darkly." Culture always diffuses the truth of the gospel. Our corrections will need correcting sometime later.

Fourth, there is much for ministers to do yet in Appalachia. The land has been abused, and so have the people. Those who compare the region to a Third World Country are sometimes correct. Justice issues must be addressed alongside traditional themes of sin, redemption, and personal morality.

Finally, ministry in Central Appalachia, like the churches themselves, is a mosaic of persons paid and unpaid; with and without formal education; in mountain and rural churches; in small towns, suburban environs, and urban areas. Whatever their setting, these persons can claim no greater calling than that articulated by Jesus himself: "The Spirit of the Lord is upon me, because he hath anointed me to preach the gospel to the poor; he hath sent me to heal the broken-hearted, to preach deliverance to the captives, and recovering of sight to the blind, to set at liberty them that are bruised, to preach the acceptable year of the Lord" (Luke 4:18–19 KJV).

Notes

1. Darrell C. Richardson, *Mountain Rising* (Oneida, Ky.: Mountaineer Press), 1986.

2. Paul F. Gillespie, ed., *Foxfire 7: Ministers, Church Members, Revivals, Baptisms, Shaped-note and Gospel Singing, Faith Healing, Camp Meetings, Footwashings, Snake-Handling, and Other Traditions of Mountain Religious Heritage* (Garden City, N.Y.: Anchor/Doubleday, 1982).

3. Gary Farley, "The Working Minister: A Study in Role-related Stress," M.A. thesis, Univ. of Tennessee at Knoxville, 1974.

4. Ibid., 103–5.

5. Tex Sample, *Blue-Collar Ministry* (Valley Forge, Pa.: Judson Press, 1984).

6. Deborah Vansau McCauley *Appalachian Mountain Religion* (Urbana: Univ. of Illinois Press, 1995), 60.

7. Ibid., 59–60.

8. "The 'Religious Experience' of a Candidate for the Ministry as Related before the Church," in *Early American Christianity*, ed. Bill J. Leonard (Nashville: Broadman Press, 1983), 124.

9. Jeff Todd Titon, *Powerhouse for God: Speech, Chant, and Song in an Appalachian Baptist Church* (Austin: Univ. of Texas Press, 1988), 317.

10. Farley, "Working Minister," 77.

11. Peter Berger, *Facing Up to Modernity* (New York: Basic Books, 1977).

12. George Marsden, *Fundamentalism and American Culture* (London: Oxford Univ. Press, 1980).

13. Grady C. Cothen, *What Happened to the Southern Baptist Convention?* (Macon, Ga.: Smyth and Helwys, 1993).

14. Gary Farley and D. G. McCoury, *We're Family* (Nashville: Convention Press, 1992).

15. David J. Hesselgrave, *Communicating Christ Cross-Culturally* (Grand Rapids, Mich.: Zondervan, 1978).

Chapter 11

The Commission on Religion in Appalachia: Empowering the People

JAMES SESSIONS

The 1960s began with the election of John Kennedy or, perhaps more important for Appalachia, with the West Virginia Democratic primary which pitted Kennedy against Hubert Humphrey. That regional election tested the "electability" of a Roman Catholic in West Virginia, the most Protestant of states. The story goes that Kennedy discovered poverty in West Virginia, made a campaign pledge to attack it, and won the primary. Thus the seeds of the War on Poverty in Appalachia were sown.

In 1962, W. D. Weatherford and Earl Brewer published their *Life and Religion in Southern Appalachia* and admonished national denominations to give up their superficial and competitive approaches to underlying life issues in Appalachia. They noted, for example, that in Appalachia there were "hundreds of subsidized but undersubscribed[,] substandard [and] struggling agencies and churches . . . many of which broke away from their founder or denomination . . . resulting in more sectarianism and competition than in effectiveness or Christian cooperation or strategy." They went on to describe the persistence of human need in Appalachia, suggesting that the churches' penchant for subsidizing substandard parishes, agencies, and surface activities on a competitive basis . . . "had to give way to more effective strategies and designs cast in a more ecumenical and cooperative framework."[1] This important call to the churches raised questions concerning their seriousness about ministry in the region and their faithfulness to their mission. Heartwarming but cosmetic services, hampered by denominational rivalries, failed to touch the real life and work issues of Appalachian communities.

In 1965, responding to the analysis of Weatherford and Brewer, to the federal government's initiative, and to the broader social movement that was burgeoning throughout the country, the Commission on Religion in Appalachia (CORA) was launched, exactly one year after War on Poverty projects began to be funded. CORA's first meeting, which included numerous bishops and other regional and national church leaders, was held in November 1965, in Morgantown, West Virginia. The organization was incorporated for the purpose of dealing "with the religious, moral, and spiritual implications inherent in the economic, social, and cultural conditions in the Appalachian region." At that initial stage, the organizers understood that the general purpose would be achieved through consultations and sharing information with churches and other agencies at work in the region; through research, study, and education to expand knowledge of conditions in the region; by coordination of staff and programs; and by engaging in projects.

The founding member organizations included seventeen Christian denominations, the Council of Southern Mountains, and councils of churches in the Appalachian states. This group came together to organize what the members hoped would be a more effective, less competitive, less sectarian, more cooperative mission strategy.

Today, each of CORA's nineteen member denominations elects three commissioners, who join representatives of ten councils of churches, five other ecumenical organizations, and eight at-large community representatives to form the Commission of CORA. It accepts the boundaries of Appalachia as defined by the federal Appalachian Regional Commission: segments of twelve states from New York to Mississippi and all of West Virginia. While headquartered in Knoxville, Tennessee, with a regional office in Kentucky, the staff of CORA tries to be faithful to the whole region by recruiting representation from northern, central and southern Appalachia. It instituted a creative special initiative in northern Appalachia in the 1980s, when deindustrialization produced massive unemployment and economic dislocation there.

The commission meets twice a year over long weekends, alternating between northern and southern locations. Its smaller board of directors is elected from the commission, serves three-year terms in three classes, and meets quarterly, usually in Central Appalachia. The board shares the same elected officers as the commission and includes the chairpersons of each program unit. CORA has an annual budget of about $800,000, over half of which goes to grassroots projects. Approximately three-quarters of the funding comes from national denominations.

In 1996, the following were CORA members, with representation designated according to each communion's own procedures:

American Baptist Churches in the USA
Roman Catholic Church
Christian Church (Disciples of Christ)
Christian Methodist Episcopal Church
Christian Reformed Church
Church of the Brethren
Church of God (Anderson, Indiana)
Cumberland Presbyterian Church
Episcopal Church
Evangelical Lutheran Church in America
Friends United Meeting
International Council of Community Churches
Lutheran Church—Missouri Synod
Mennonite Central Committee
Presbyterian Church (USA)
Reformed Church in America
Southern Baptist Convention
United Church of Christ
United Methodist Church
National Catholic Rural Life Conference
National Council of Churches of Christ in the USA
Christian Associates of Southwest Pennsylvania
Interfaith Consortium of Greater Cumberland, Maryland
Virginia Interfaith Center for Public Policy

and the State Councils of Churches in Georgia, Kentucky, New York, North Carolina, Pennsylvania, Ohio, South Carolina, Tennessee, Virginia, and West Virginia.

Historically, CORA has implemented a variety of special programs. These include a program in "Cooperative Congregational Development," an effort to create ecumenical cooperative congregational ministries. This program supports dozens of emerging and ongoing ecumenical cooperative congregational ministries, whose work encompasses such ministries as clothing, food and job banks, community advocacy programs, Hispanic ministries, shelter programs, and community organizing projects. CORA raises around half a million dollars a year for some fifty community-based organizations in the region which work together in the Appalachian Development Projects Coalition (ADPC). Following ADPC's lead, CORA now holds an annual regionwide assembly that focuses on bringing networks, groups, and grassroots organizations together to exchange and create ideas, visions, strategies, and skills; to celebrate cultural heritages; and to help develop and support leadership from the communities of Appalachia.

The "Volunteer Program" coordinates work camps and volunteer placement of more than three thousand volunteers annually from over 150 churches, universities, and colleges. A conservative estimate suggests that CORA volunteer groups contribute over $1,140,000 in actual funds and in-kind labor in the communities where they work.

CORA offers advocacy assistance through its public policy committee on such issues as black lung compensation, health care, toxic dumping, small farms, land use, and workplace health, safety, and representation.

CORA periodically revises, updates, and publishes volumes of *Atlas of the Church in Appalachia* and *Trends and Issues in Appalachia*, each based on the latest available census data. CORA also publishes the monthly news sheet *CORAlation*, going to about three hundred church leaders. A quarterly newsletter, the *CORAspondent*, goes to over seven thousand friends and supporters; it focuses on the stories of real people in Appalachia and celebrates the victories of their efforts in specific communities.

In addition to its constituent denominations, CORA works in local contexts with leaders and members of churches that are not official participants in the CORA board. The independent nature of many Appalachian churches sometimes means that cooperative work occurs when and where it can, often in response to a specific need or crisis. A goal of CORA over the years has been to develop closer ties and missional relationships with what sometimes are called the indigenous or independent churches of Appalachia.

As CORA looks to the future, its attention focuses on (1) developing and implementing ecumenical and cooperative strategies to engage the churches through their judicatory leadership, national and regional, as well as congregations in their communities; (2) allocating human and financial resources to community and regional organizations to insure their stability and viability; (3) developing networks of community organizations and congregations in various locations throughout the region that will be committed to social and economic justice; and (4) creating an active network and social movement, as a Christian witness and commitment to issues of justice and public policy advocacy.

Occasionally, CORA members pursue those goals through the organization's governing commission and its program units. The commission is composed of representatives from each of the nineteen partner denominations and from its other partner groups, plus members at large who represent community organizations. The program units also have representation in the Appalachian Development Projects Coalition, the Volunteer Program, and the Cooperative Congregational Development Program.

CORA began with a sort of Lady Bountiful perspective, buoyed by some professional paternalism and energized by an era of social activism, much of it underwritten by government funding. Over a period of time, church leaders learned from grassroots leaders, local communities, and some activists within their own ranks that it was imperative to move beyond their well-intentioned programs, their comfortable pews and offices, to ministry "in the trenches" with Appalachian communities. There were difficult, tense times with well-intentioned, middle-class church folks who had little experience of rural poverty in a culture different from their own. Early on, CORA often seemed more accountable to bishops and church agencies than to the region, more at home in management churches than in miners' chapels, more adept in worship with county-seat congregations than in foot-washing services and ridge homecomings, and more anxious about agency accountability than about community aspirations and desperation. Coming together was not easy. Staying together over the long haul required a stretch of the moral imagination.

That tension is an ever-present reality at CORA. Questions include: Who is the prime constituency? Whom do we serve? Who makes up the governance of the organization? Often the standard response meant: "We serve the people of Appalachia . . . but we make decisions over here with these other people." How will CORA link its Appalachian constituency to its support constituency in denominations, judicatories, and national ecclesiastical organizations? That always has been a serious dilemma for CORA. It is a profound question for the organization and the churches, one that never really has been resolved and perhaps should not be. Over time, supporting church leaders have appointed as CORA representatives persons who also have struggled with this question of constituency. Many understood the significance of the question and were willing to live and work within that tension. Many have accepted it is a continuing dynamic of CORA's existence.

Questions about CORA's constituency and overall identity have not been lost on certain grassroots coalitions in the Appalachian region.

Many of CORA's founders envisioned its mission as centered in producing programs, studies, and service projects for and with religious communities in the region. Others perceived CORA primarily as a source of financial and technical support for Appalachian ministries. Still others saw it as a program of advocacy and information, presenting the "Appalachian situation" to the rest of the nation and acting as the "peoples' advocate" when legislative, union, or natural crises arose. Discussion and debate over these questions of mission led to continuing efforts by community and regional groups to gain greater voice and control in the CORA system. These dynamics again raised questions for the CORA board and staff regarding the organization's role in Appalachia. To this day, CORA's leaders continually must seek to encourage and facilitate grassroots leadership, while also relating closely to CORA's institutional support system in the denominations and churches. This balancing act inevitably creates tension and occasional conflicts within the CORA program. These struggles, however, have kept the organization in continuing dialogue with multiple groups as to its purpose, its work, and its identity.

As CORA gained valuable and sometimes painful and instructive experience in the region, leaders sought to develop an overall church-community coalition as the foundation of CORA's activity for the future. Processes were created for more intentional involvement of individuals and groups from specific Appalachian communities. This became the Appalachian Development Projects Coalition (ADPC).

The evaluation, funding, and review mechanism CORA developed for and with ADPC community organizations was known as the Screening and Allocations Committee (SAC). It provided for an equal number of elected representatives from community organizations and churches, in order to insure democratic and participatory decision making. Over a period of two decades, SAC evolved into a sophisticated funding and review mechanism—one which, through CORA's members, provided funds for establishing annual organization-building support for some thirty to forty organizations, in grants ranging from five thousand to twenty thousand dollars. At the same time, SAC consistently demonstrated accountability on the part of CORA and its grassroots constituency to the church-related funding agencies. This process forged an important relationship between CORA participants inside and outside Appalachia. Long-time Appalachian researcher Richard Couto commented in 1993, "CORA's support of grassroots organizing and development is the slow tedious pace of democratic change. . . . Over the past decade, CORA has emerged as the only region-wide organization with a total and enduring commitment to social and economic justice. . . . No other organization can or does speak as well as CORA about the moral resources of social capital, especially the gifted leaders and determined common ties, of the entire region."[2]

Over time, CORA has become a more intentionally church-community-based program promoting issues of economic justice in Appalachia. With its roots in the 1960s antipoverty movement, which impacted both church and society in Appalachia, issues of economic justice always have been, both explicitly and implicitly, its reason for being. A turning point for CORA was the development in 1980 of a study document entitled *A Theological Reflection on Economic and Labor Justice*, issued by the Social, Economic, and Political Issues (SEPI) task force. CORA members struggled for several years with this more explicit and biblically based call for economic justice in the region. The church members of SEPI held hearings in communities and engaged CORA with many community struggles throughout Appalachia. Through this grassroots exposure, community experiences of struggle, and continual examination of the Scriptures, SEPI tenaciously brought CORA members to deeper understandings of the churches' mission in the region.

With its primary emphasis on justice and its mission of service and charity, CORA has worked in a variety of ways to aid people in gaining control of their lives. For example, it has supported fair employment practices, along with land ownership and fair taxing policies. It has emphasized the struggles of women and minorities in the region, while serving as advocate for workers rights and good-faith bargaining between labor and management. CORA's efforts have highlighted environmental problems and the health predicaments created by toxic wastes and other ecological abuses. It also has supported local cooperatives and advocacy groups working for institutional change and economic alternatives.

Found in many CORA publications and descriptions is this statement: "The strategy of the churches through CORA is directed at more than symptoms; it is a holistic approach which focuses on the *causes* of Appalachia's problems. There are religious and moral implications inherent in the economic, social, and cultural conditions in Appalachia." CORA seeks to highlight those conditions, to explore them through consultations, dialogue sessions, and study, while using them to challenge and educate its own members, churches, and the community at large. CORA representatives often say: "The purpose and philosophy of CORA is to bring the churches together in partnership with the people to help people become powerful enough to control their own lives."

CORA leaders learned in profound and sometime difficult ways the importance of sustaining a church base while creating practical partnerships with grassroots communities in Appalachia. For the sake of its commitment to Appalachian communities, CORA enabled certain national church bodies to provide needed resources through accountable, democratic, reliable, and productive processes, all aimed at facilitating the empowerment of Appalachian people. In cooperation with both church and community representatives, it developed the mechanisms for establishing accountability, organizations, and programs for ministry by and for Appalachian individuals and groups. Couto notes: "As mediating structures, CORA, the church groups with which it works, and the many projects it supports go between the large, faceless social, political, and economic forces and the small communities and individual human beings that these forces impact. Whatever else the future brings, it will bring more and more need for mediating structures in the public life of America."[3]

In the late 1970s and early 1980s, ecumenical associations around the country were in decline. Their networks in the United States related more to the North, East, and West than the South. Membership and financial crises characterized their organizational life. It was during this period, however, that CORA gained significant strength and self-confidence, was compelled to deal with the continuing tensions of its existence, and linked its Appalachian and denominational constituencies. In addition to its fidelity and willingness to work within its tensions, it has survived partly because of its credible and functional national ties, because it always has worked in numerous states and across church boundaries, and because it always has been able to make a well-documented, persuasive, strong moral claim on the churches, contrasting the condition of the poor and working people of Appalachia with the relative wealth of the main-line churches.

Through its efforts to serve as a moral force providing material resources to grassroots communities, and its willingness to confront some of the toughest political and economic issues of the times, CORA has managed to remain effective and useful in a time of dramatic social change. Over time, it has gained credibility through partnership with community groups. This credibility was hard-won and not without periods of struggle and conflict. CORA has earned the trust of participants through its perseverance and accessibility. Its idealism and commitment have been sustained, on the one hand, by remaining focused on the priorities of the region; and, on the other hand, by the people in the mountains, whose courage and needs always exceed the churches' vision. These people are an enduring source of cultural and religious insight.

Whenever CORA convenes its members and friends, it is always in collaboration with local constituencies. Wherever the meeting takes place, the gatherings are significant occasions. The meetings are characterized by music and stories, faith and spirit. Participants express themselves freely in affirmation and argument, all in an effort to inspire and empower. CORA's denominational and community representatives alike seem to anticipate the gatherings which nurture their sense of ministry and mission. For example, meetings may bring together an ecclesiastical executive from New Jersey with a coal miner from Kentucky. Another person whips out a banjo and sings a song about activism and injustice in the coalfields. Music, dialogue, and ethical imperatives, at their best, link representatives in a common call to action and service.

For many denominational representatives, CORA meetings provide opportunities for acquiring information about Appalachian ministry through interaction with persons from the region. These encounters bring denominational staff from their national offices—dare we say ghettoes?—into the active environment of Appalachian life and ministry.

As cumbersome and complicated as CORA's nineteen denominations, sixty community organizations, hundreds of work camps, its board, its commission, and its staff may be, the organization is amazingly effective in its activities. Its success requires involvement of multiple constituencies—denominational officers, community leaders, and grassroots participants—in order to maintain its vision and its financial support. CORA continues to forge new links in Appalachia by building on the gifts of all its partners. Its work continues to promote the empowerment of people. It also advocates inclusivity, creating efforts to move beyond the barriers of race, sex, and class. It seeks to be faithful in its work in Appalachia in cultivating a society committed to justice and equality.

In a study of CORA's historical development, written in 1983, Judy Morelock identified three themes evident throughout CORA's development: (1) "the degree to which CORA recognizes structural causes of Appalachian problems; (2) the extent to which CORA accepts a role for the Church in fostering systemic change; and (3) the extent to which CORA works cooperatively with indigenous people."[4] Morelock discusses those themes in terms of CORA's progress toward achieving goals for fulfilling the church's prophetic role and developing a partnership with Appalachian people. Part of CORA's organizational health, she says, stems from the fact that it has continued to develop and advance toward the achievement of those goals. She noted that CORA's strengths include the "commitment and cooperativeness of the staff, the open style of leadership and functioning, and the ability to resolve conflicts and to change."[5] Like Appalachia itself, CORA continues to change, to develop, and to live.

Notes

1. W. D. Weatherford and Earl D. C. Brewer, *Life and Religion in Southern Appalachia* (New York: Friendship Press, 1962), 83–84.

2. Richard A. Couto, *An American Challenge: A Report on Economic Trends and Social Issues in Appalachia* (Dubuque, Iowa: Kendall-Hunt, 1994).

3. Ibid.

4. Judy Morelock, *The Historical Development of the Commission on Religion in Appalachia* (Knoxville, Tenn.: Commission on Religion in Appalachia, 1983).

5. Ibid.

Chapter 12

Southern Baptists

BILL J. LEONARD

The Southern Baptist presence in Appalachia once seemed rather easy to describe. While local and regional diversity was always evident, rural and "county seat" churches often shared certain similarities in their ecclesiastical profiles. A certain kind of "Southern-Baptistness" distinguished these churches from other Baptist groups in the region. Sundays meant church, all-day church. Off you went to Sunday school, armed with the three great symbols of Southern Baptist faith: (1) a King James Version of the Bible (zipper edition);[1] (2) a Sunday school "Quarterly" published at denominational headquarters in Nashville, detailing the Bible lesson for the day; and (3) an envelope containing the weekly "tithe or offering," and on which elements of one's weekly spirituality were recorded.[2] After Sunday school came morning worship, where an "order of service," written or unwritten, included hymns, prayers, and preaching, as well as the "Sunday school report" describing the day's attendance and offerings. (Statistics might also be listed on a board located near the front of the church.) Hymns might be taken from denominationally produced resources—the Broadman Hymnal or Baptist Hymnal—or from paperback gospel hymnbooks with shaped notes or "Stamps-Baxter" harmony.[3] While sermon styles might vary—due, often, to the educational background of the preacher or the context of the congregation—each began with a Bible text and ended with a call to Christian conversion. An "invitation" hymn was sung as people were asked to "come forward" or "walk the aisle" to profess faith in Christ, to move their membership from another congregation, or to "rededicate" their lives to Christian discipleship.

After a big Sunday dinner, church members returned for "Training Union," a small-group experience which provided instruction in church history, doctrine, and ethics, through lessons published in yet another resource book provided by the denomination. Evening worship followed, ending with another invitation hymn and, on some nights, a church "fellowship" for food and conversation. Wednesday nights were set aside for "Prayer Meeting," in which congregational concerns were taken to "the throne of grace," as the believers invoked God's intervention in human affairs.

The annual calendar of most Appalachian Baptist churches included such events as summer "Vacation Bible School," in which children were instructed in the Scriptures and handicrafts, and encouraged to "accept Christ as Lord and Savior." (Bible School materials, too, were published by the Southern Baptist Sunday School Board.) Seasonal revivals usually were held after spring planting and fall harvest. These easily became major community events, often lasting for several weeks, and were conducted by a visiting evangelist. Indeed, in some Appalachian churches, revivals were known as "protracted meetings," begun at a specific time in the agricultural season and ceasing only when the Spirit had run its course. Revivals were followed by baptisms, usually in rivers or creeks, with the congregation gathered around receiving the newly baptized with open arms, drying them off, and welcoming them to membership in the church and citizenship in the Kingdom of God. In many rural churches, a mural depicting the Jordan River was painted on the wall behind the indoor baptistery, linking that local congregation with Jesus and the earliest Christian baptisms. (Paintings often resembled the terrain of eastern Kentucky or western North Carolina more than the arid regions of ancient Palestine.) Well into the twentieth century, these were among the identifying marks of rural and small-town Southern Baptist churches across Central Appalachia, uniting elements of frontier religion with denominational cooperation in the region's most public faith.

Indeed, as the largest single religious tradition in Central Appalachia and the largest Protestant denomination in the United States, the Southern Baptist Convention (SBC) often seems to dominate the ecclesiastical landscape. Claiming some four million of the convention's seventeen million members, Appalachian Southern Baptist churches can be found today along mountain roads and in county-seat towns, as well as in urban and suburban areas. Their presence in the region is evidence of a complex diversity in history, belief, and practice. In fact, convention-related churches now are so diverse as to make generalization about them extremely difficult. Some congregations wear their denominational commitments loosely, exhibiting qualities present in independent mountain churches. Others, particularly county-seat or large urban congregations, maintain strong ties to the convention, remaining ever loyal to its programs and policies. Still others now participate in multiple groups and societies outside the SBC system. Some pastors are bi-vocational mountain preachers with limited formal education, who receive little or no financial support for their ministry. Others are college and/or seminary graduates, some serving churches with "multi-staff ministries" in music, education, or youth. Some churches give minimally to the Cooperative Program, the denomination's system of collective funding, while others contribute a large percentage of their annual receipts to enhance the SBC's missionary endeavors worldwide. Whatever their responses to the denomination at the end of the twentieth century, SBC churches are an illustration of denominational and congregational transition.

Southern Baptist religion in Appalachia dates from the early days of settlement in the region. Churches which became part of the Southern Baptist Convention were born of the revivals in New England and on the western frontier in the early nineteenth century. They participated in, and contributed to, the early religious ethos of Central Appalachia. Through the life of its churches, the SBC functioned within the religious culture of the mountains. As a denomination, however, it "targeted" the region as an important home mission field, "planting" churches, schools, and settlement houses, and appealing to the broader convention for funds to carry out specific organizational programs. That mission effort represents what historian Deborah Vansau McCauley calls the "colonizing forces" in the region.

In a sense, the SBC presence in Appalachia is both a people's movement and a denominational system. Southern Baptist theology, as expressed in the "Baptist Faith and Message," the denomination's official confession of faith, represents something of a *via media* in the Baptist family, lying somewhere between the Calvinism of the Primitive Baptists and the Arminianism of the Free Will Baptists.[4] During the last quarter of the twentieth century, the denomination itself, at every level of its organizational life, has been affected by a controversy between fundamentalists and moderates over theological identity and denominational control. More recently, churches urban and suburban have been drawn to certain so-called "mega-church methods," utilizing marketing techniques to facilitate church growth. In short, Southern Baptists in general, and Appalachian Southern Baptists in particular, have been, and continue to be, impacted by innumerable beliefs and trends on local, regional, and national levels.

Although the Southern Baptist Convention was formed in 1845 as a result of a schism with northerners over the questions of slavery, missions, and other sectional issues, its theological and historical roots in the South may be traced to the 1690s and the founding of First Baptist Church, Charleston, South Carolina. These Regular Baptists, who came from Maine and spread their gospel across the South, were staunch Calvinists who supported an educated ministry and orderly worship in the Reformed tradition. They sang the Psalms as divinely inspired hymns, and their ministers, sometimes numbered among the South's "gentlemen theologians," preached organized and erudite sermons with evangelical fervor.[5] As evangelical Calvinists, Regular Baptists called all persons to conversion, believing that God would use gospel preaching to awaken the hearts of those elected to salvation before the foundation of the world. They were, however, less enthusiastic about the revival methods that would characterize the First and Second Great Awakenings. Regular Baptists were more likely to be found in the population centers of the region than in rural or mountain areas.

The Separate Baptists represent a second tradition whose influence is evident in Appalachian churches. They entered the region by the 1750s, influenced by the First Great Awakening, which had impacted various churches in New England and the Middle colonies. One well-known group of settlers, led by Shubal Stearns and Daniel Marshall, New England Congregationalists who had accepted Baptist views, established a church at Sandy Creek, North Carolina, in the 1750s. This church became the mother church of more than forty churches throughout the Appalachian region.

These Baptists readily supported the religious enthusiasm of the First Great Awakening. While utilizing the language of Calvinism, they entertained the possibility of salvation for all who would repent and believe in Jesus. Their ministers often were men of the people, sometimes known as "farmer-preachers," who received no salaries, worked the land or otherwise supported themselves, and preached in camp meetings and revivals or pastored churches organized in newly settled regions. Most served several churches, in what sometimes were known as "half-time" or "quarter-time" ministries. Many were suspicious of education, seeing it as a detriment to spiritual religion. (A Baptist deacon once told me, "We were a little worried about educated preachers, we saw what it did to the Presbyterians!") Separate Baptist worship services were characterized by lively hymns and revival songs, extemporaneous preaching, and emotional outbursts from the people. Their converts "got saved hard" and did not hesitate to weep, sing, and shout when God's grace descended upon them. The Separate Baptists were particularly strong in the Appalachian mountain churches that became affiliated with the Southern Baptist Convention.

A third tradition evident among Southern Baptists in Appalachia was found in a movement known as Old Landmarkism, and represented an attempt to trace Baptists directly to Jesus and the New Testament church. Begun in the 1850s by J. R. Graves of Tennessee and J. M. Pendleton of Kentucky, the movement took its name from Proverbs 22:28: "Remove not the ancient Landmarks which thy fathers have set." Its proponents declared that Baptist churches alone bore the "marks" of the true church and could trace their lineage through an unbroken succession of faithful congregations—represented in the Montanists, Donatists, Cathari, Waldenses, Anabaptists, and other sects—all the way back to Jesus as baptized by John (the Baptist) in the River Jordan. Since other denominations lacked such pristine lineage, they were not churches but "societies." Landmarkists insisted that local Baptist congregations alone were the sole expressions of the church, so they opposed mission boards and other denominational "hierarchies." No other ecclesiastical organization had authority over local communities of faith.[6]

Try as they might, Landmarkists never were able to impose their doctrines upon the entire Southern Baptist Convention. Nonetheless, many of their views became part of popular Baptist piety and practice, evident in SBC churches throughout Appalachian. Two of the most common Landmark practices related to "alien immersion" and "close (or closed) communion." The former meant that Baptists rejected baptism, even immersion, performed by non-Baptists, necessitating rebaptism for those who joined a Baptist congregation. Close communion was based on the idea that the local Baptist congregation alone had the authority to administer the Lord's Supper. This meant that the Lord's Supper could be distributed only by the local church and then only to its specific members. Even members of other Baptist churches were refused communion when worshipping outside their own congregation.

The Landmark movement flourished at a time of active competition among Protestant denominations involved in elaborate debates regarding the nature of the church, with each claiming the strongest connection to the church of the Apostles. Baptist Landmarkism was a particular response to the restorationism of the Stone-Campbell movement and its claim to have reconstituted the New Testament church, long lost among the multiple denominations of human creation. Landmark leaders insisted that they needed to restore nothing, since they had maintained an unbroken connection to Christ and his teaching across the centuries. To this day, many Appalachian Baptists—related or unrelated to the SBC—are convinced that they belong to the only church which has maintained direct links with the New Testament Christians. They insist that Baptists are not Protestants, since they began not with Martin Luther or John Calvin, but with Jesus and John the Baptist.

Historically, these traditions—Regular, Separate, and Landmarkist—shaped Southern Baptist understanding of faith and doctrine in many ways. They account for the great diversity of Southern Baptist churches and individuals in Appalachia and throughout the South. They informed the way in which Baptists understood those specific "distinctions" around which the diverse theological and regional groups were united. These distinctions identified Southern Baptists with the broader Baptist tradition. While many are not unique to Baptists, their uniqueness may be found in the way in which Baptists apply them to ecclesiastical and theological issues.

First, Southern Baptists affirm the authority of Holy Scripture as well as the freedom of the individual to interpret Scripture according to the dictates of conscience. Differences over the meaning of Scripture and the role of individual interpretation continue to lead to debates and schisms among and within Southern Baptist churches.

Second, Southern Baptists are conversionists. They insist that all church members must be "regenerate," testifying to a personal experience of divine grace. While they often sound as if this salvation experience involves a dramatic conversion, they also seek to nurture children through various developmental stages of faith. While most nineteenth-century Southern Baptists were Calvinist in their understanding of election and predestination, twentieth-century SBC churches generally reflect a more Arminian approach to free will and the possibility of redemption for all humanity. In short, contemporary Southern Baptists often talk like Calvinists but act like Arminians in their response to conversion.[7]

Third, the Southern Baptists observe two "ordinances": baptism by immersion and the Lord's Supper. Few practice foot washing.[8] Baptism is a symbol of identification with Christ and membership in the church ("buried with Christ in baptism, raised to walk in new life"). The Supper is generally viewed as a memorial in remembrance of Christ's death.

Fourth, they maintain an ordained ministry, while also emphasizing the priesthood of the laity. Like other congregationalists, they recognize two officers: pastors (sometimes called elders) and deacons. Conflicts over the nature of ministerial and lay authority in the church continue to impact SBC churches.

Fifth, Southern Baptists cling tenaciously to the idea of congregational autonomy, while affirming the need for associational relationships among churches. Sixth, they promote religious liberty while declaring their loyalty to the state.

In Appalachia, Southern Baptist churches reflect something of a paradox. On the one hand, some of their churches mirror many of the mountain Baptist congregations—Primitive, Old Regular, Free Will, and Independent—in their fierce concern for the autonomy of the local church, the freedom of the individual conscience, and the need for conversion. On the other hand, their churches are linked to the denomination in programmatic ways which shape their identity and distinguish them from other more independent Baptist congregations.

In Appalachia, many Southern Baptist churches are characterized by a strong sense of individualism, "soul liberty," and congregational autonomy—all of which contribute to a powerful populism in church life. Individualism is informed by the need for personal conversion. Like other Baptist groups in the region, Southern Baptists preach that all persons must be "born again." A direct encounter with divine grace is necessary for church membership. Although contemporary Southern Baptists have institutionalized conversion in assorted plans, roads, and laws, many Appalachian churches require believers to give "testimony" to their faith, both as a prerequisite for baptism and as a continuing sign of Christian witness. For generations of Southern Baptists in the mountain and town churches, conversion was linked closely to revival meetings in which sinners were saved, Christians "rededicated," and potential ministers called out "for full-time Christian service."

Individualism also was nurtured by "soul liberty," an idea which united the priesthood of all believers with the trustworthiness of individual conscience in religious matters. Not only could sinners come directly to God with no other mediator save Jesus Christ, but also they were free to interpret the Scripture for themselves.

Soul liberty for the individual was closely connected to congregational autonomy, a belief that primary ecclesiastical authority rested with individual churches, not national denominations. Southern Baptist churches generally exercise a strong democratic congregationalism, voting on everything from calling a new pastor to the color of the church building. They sometimes split over both. One common practice, continued in most Appalachian SBC churches, involves voting on new members. The tradition of voting members into (and out of) the church has its roots in radical congregational government. In an earlier era, new members knew that such votes were a way of affirming their testimonies of faith and reminding them of the possibility of church discipline. Members caught in sin—dancing, drinking, gambling, sexual immorality, or other peccadilloes—could be "disfellowshipped" or "churched" by majority vote. One need only read the minutes of Appalachian sbc churches to know that discipline was swift and sure. In fact, many of these churches often seemed to have three distinct purposes: to preach the gospel, to lead sinners to repentance, and to throw people out of the church.

Local autonomy also meant that sbc churches in Appalachia were inherently suspicious of denominational encroachment on congregational affairs. As the sbc took shape after 1845, its leaders continually acknowledged that the convention was not to dictate policies to local congregations. Even today, it is theologically incorrect to speak of the sbc as the Southern Baptist "Church." Rather, local autonomy requires the term Southern Baptist "churches," indicating that no denominational entity can claim primary authority above the local community of faith.

At the same time, Southern Baptist churches, even in Appalachia, chose to participate in various denominational programs and organizations—local, regional, and national. It was their support for the denomination, its agencies, and its activities that came to distinguish Southern Baptist churches from other Baptist and independent mountain congregations in the Appalachian region.

Those Appalachian Baptist churches which became associated with the sbc were, in most respects, ones which supported the missionary imperative of the church in the classic debates on that subject in the late eighteenth and early nineteenth centuries. One early controversy was sparked by Daniel Parker (1781–1844), a frontier populist preacher who denounced missionary activities, Bible societies, and theological schools, as "human efforts" at spreading the gospel.[9] Parker's brand of Calvinism led him to promote the "two-seed-in-the-Spirit" idea that each person was born with one of two spiritual seeds which inevitably produced regeneration or damnation. Since he could find no evidence of mission boards in the New Testament, he denied that a true New Testament (Baptist) church should participate in such heretical movements.[10] Parker's ideas influenced antimission Baptists from Appalachia to Texas.

Parker's views were echoed by John Taylor (1752–1835), another Appalachian Baptist who opposed mission boards, theology schools, and "hireling" (paid) preachers. He rejected all "human societies" as signs of "works righteousness" and attempts to usurp the divine prerogative in salvation of the elect. Undergirding the theological debates was an inherent opposition to the interference of outside agencies and bureaucracies in individual or local church affairs.

In Appalachia, the designation "missionary Baptist" may be applied to those churches which support the sending of missionaries, home and foreign, and are willing to join with other churches in funding such endeavors through mission boards—in this case, the boards and agencies of the Southern Baptist Convention. Southern Baptist Churches in Appalachia may call themselves missionary Baptist as a way of distinguishing themselves from the more Calvinist or independent churches.[11]

Missions also played a part in the schism between Baptists North and South when the SBC was founded. When the Triennial Convention, the missionary society funded by Baptist churches throughout the U.S., refused to appoint a known slaveholder as a missionary, the southerners charged that the terms of their agreement had been violated. Meeting in Augusta, Georgia, in May 1845, representatives of southern churches and state conventions instituted a new denomination for "the extension of the Messiah's kingdom" though missions. By combining their limited funds with the resources of others in funding the missionary cause, SBC churches in Appalachia and elsewhere in the South could feel that they were furthering the "Great Commission" made by Jesus to his disciples in Matthew 28:19–20 to preach the gospel to all nations.

It was through the development of the Home Missions Board that Southern Baptists initiated specific denominational efforts in Appalachia. Historian Robert Baker noted that, during the period between 1877 and 1917, Appalachia was one of the regions targeted for home missions ministry. This was particularly evident in the founding of schools. Baker wrote: "In cooperation with Baptists of western North Carolina the board carried on a joint mission program in the mountainous areas in the 1880s, and in addition, began the development in 1905 of a system of mountain schools in cooperation with other Baptist groups."[12] The 1917 Home Mission Board report claimed an enrollment of 5,190 in mountain schools in Virginia, Kentucky, Tennessee, North and South Carolina, Georgia, Alabama, Arkansas, and Missouri.[13] The board, along with state Baptist conventions, long has provided funds to support new churches and "mission pastors" in the region.

On a more grassroots level, the association, a gathering of churches in certain geographical proximity, constitutes the most basic local alliance of SBC churches. Associations date to the earliest Baptist groups in seventeenth-century England and are intended to provide fellowship, doctrinal affirmation, and interchurch participation for like-minded congregations. While associational relationships are declining among many urban and suburban Southern Baptists, they remain important among many Appalachian SBC churches, some of which maintain certain nineteenth-century practices. For example, some Appalachian associations continue to require that only men speak publicly at the annual meeting, mandating that even the report from the associational Women's Missionary Union be given by the president's husband.[14]

Southern Baptist churches also relate to the Baptist convention in the state where they are located. These organizations have their roots in the nineteenth century, and most antedate the founding of the SBC itself. It is through the state conventions that the earliest Baptist colleges and universities in Appalachia were founded. These include Mars Hill College and Gardner-Webb University in North Carolina, Furman University in South Carolina, Shorter College in Georgia, and Carson-Newman College in Tennessee.

In the Central Appalachian states, West Virginia is a curious anomaly for Southern Baptists. In 1845, many of the mission-supporting Baptist churches in West Virginia chose to remain identified with Baptists in the North, rather than join the new Southern Convention. While there is a strong Southern Baptist presence in West Virginia today, the state also has a large number of churches affiliated with the American Baptist Churches in the USA, the former Northern Baptist Convention.

By contributing as little as $250 per year to the "Cooperative Program," a common funding program for the denomination, local SBC churches may be considered "cooperating churches" in the national SBC, eligible to send messengers to the annual meeting. The SBC governs denominational operations though the Home and Foreign Mission boards, theological seminaries, the Sunday School Board, a Christian Life Commission, and other entities. It is through these organizations, particularly the Home Mission Board, that the denomination initiated other kinds of ministry in Appalachia beyond and alongside the local, more indigenous congregations.

Since 1979, Southern Baptists have been embroiled in a controversy over biblical inerrancy and denominational control which has reached almost every level of church life. The controversy began with the election of a series of convention presidents committed to using their appointive powers to create a majority on all SBC boards of trustees, dedicated to promoting the doctrine of biblical inerrancy in all convention agencies. "Inerrancy" was defined as the doctrine that all Scripture—doctrine, ethics, astronomy, history, or any other topic—was without error. Supporters insisted that the convention (not unlike other "mainline" denominations) had become "soft on liberalism" and was headed down the "slippery slope" to heresy. An opposition group, later known as "moderates," charged that theological debates were merely a smoke screen for a denominational takeover by right-wing political and doctrinal "fundamentalists." Fundamentalists gained control of the denominational system and succeeded in redirecting the convention toward their conservative agenda.

The issue of biblical inerrancy is significant for understanding Southern Baptist churches in Appalachia. Clearly, many of those churches affirm the doctrine of biblical inerrancy. Yet applying and interpreting the meaning of that doctrine is another matter. Popular Baptist preaching often proclaims: "The Bible says it; I believe it; and that settles it." The Bible stands at the heart of the Southern Baptist ethos. Church members are encouraged to bring their Bibles to every church occasion and to study them daily. Southern Baptist laity, male and female, particularly the older generations, have extensive knowledge of the Bible, committing large segments of the King James Version (KJV) to memory. While many Appalachian Southern Baptists continue to use the KJV and honor it as the most significant, if not the only, appropriate translation, the use of other versions—*Living Bible,* the *New International,* and the *Good News Bible,* among others—is gaining in popularity. Some churches continue to debate the issue of translations and the use of the "authorized" KJV text.

Controversy over biblical authority is evident in specific issues such as the role of women in the church and the question of divorce in Christian marriages. Concerning the role of women, Southern Baptists in Appalachia are at once literalists and pietists. As literalists, many insist that "women are to keep silent" in the church and are not to "have authority" over men in the home or the congregation. Since qualifications for pastors include being "husband of one wife," SBC literalists insist that women cannot hold the ministerial office. As pietists, Southern Baptists long have looked to women as the spiritual and moral centers of the church. Likewise, Southern Baptist piety led to such declarations as "Do whatever God calls you to do," or "Surrender yourself to God's will wherever it takes you." Inevitably, many Southern Baptist women, like their Holiness counterparts, have heard and applied such spiritual demands to their own callings.

For SBC families, the issue of divorce also challenges the literal and pastoral approaches to family problems in the church. Many Appalachian Southern Baptists (particularly preachers) remain adamant in their belief that all divorce is unacceptable, except in cases of adultery (see Matthew 5). Many preachers continue to view the remarriage of divorced persons as a violation of Jesus' teaching. Yet, as divorce has spread throughout the culture, even into rural and mountain churches, pastoral concern for families and individuals has led to a struggle over biblical interpretation. Volatile controversies continue as to the role of divorced members—pastors and laity—in church life. May divorced preachers and deacons continue in serve the church? Is divorce a disqualification for Sunday school teachers and other church leaders? These questions remain matters of extensive debate and division in churches rural and urban.

Equally significant is the growing trend toward marketing techniques utilized by an increasing number of churches in Appalachia and impacting many more. City and suburban churches, along with some congregations in more rural locations, have begun to promote methods which market religious services to "seekers," those who are religiously nonaffiliated. These churches may reflect certain charismatic worship styles, multiple services for target segments of the constituency (youth, seniors, young married couples) and fast-paced programs. There is some indication that rural churches may be impacted by these trends, as members leave those congregations and drive to the "full-service" churches. Most of the towns in the region have congregations utilizing some of these "mega-church" methods of reaching the public. That trend demands further study and analysis.

Southern Baptist churches in Appalachia are facing major transitions in denominational and cultural life. Old mechanisms for uniting the constituency are disappearing or being reorganized. A theological-political controversy over denominational orientation and control has shaped the convention's life and activities for almost two decades. While elements of the old convention system remain intact, the future certainly will be characterized by changing local, regional, and national alignments. Old identities are giving way to uncertainty as to what it means to be Southern Baptist and how the fragmenting denomination can find ways to cultivate unity and cooperation. Southern Baptist churches in Appalachia reflect these transitions. Those which have maintained greater localism and autonomy may be better suited to confront the challenges of the future and the need to articulate a specifically Baptist identity and pass it on to succeeding generations.

Notes

1. Editions of the Bible often were given to SBC young people at about the age of 8 or 9. The cover of the Bibles—black for boys, white for girl—was enclosed by a zipper. See Bill J. Leonard, *God's Last and Only Hope: The Fragmentation of the Southern Baptist Convention* (Grand Rapids, Mich.: Eerdmans Publishing Co., 1990).
2. Printed on the front of the offering envelope was the famous "six-point record sys-

tem," on which the individual Christian could record his or her spiritual activities for the week. One was asked to check boxes for: "Bible brought (to church), offering, studied lesson, staying for church (morning worship), on time, and visitation (inviting others to church)." The tithe was one-tenth of the individual's or family's income. Children were encouraged to tithe any money they might receive from allowance or chores.

3. Shaped-note hymnals represent a particular method for teaching singers to read music. "Stamps-Baxter" music was a form of gospel singing associated with the famous Stamps Quartet and other groups known for their harmony. See Paul F. Gillespie, ed., *Foxfire 7: Ministers, Church Members, Revivals, Baptisms, Shaped-note and Gospel Singing, Faith Healing, Camp Meetings, Footwashings, Snake-Handling, and Other Traditions of Mountain Religious Heritage* (Garden City, N.Y.: Anchor/Doubleday, 1982).

4. Southern Baptists had no official confession until 1925. The "Baptist Faith and Message" was revised in 1963. It has been the center of extensive debate and unofficial revision as a result of recent debates over biblical inerrancy, election, free will, and academic freedom. See Leonard, *God's Last and only Hope*; and Nancy T. Ammerman, *Baptist Battles* (New Brunswick, N.J.: Rutgers Univ. Press, 1990).

5. E. Brooks Holifield, *The Gentlemen Theologians: American Theology in Southern Culture, 1795–1860* (Durham, N.C.: Duke Univ. Press, 1978).

6. Leon McBeth, *The Baptist Heritage* (Nashville, Tenn.: Broadman Press, 1987), 447–61.

7. In the latter twentieth century, signs of a revival of Calvinism are evident among many Southern Baptists. How extensive this movement has become and its ultimate influence on the sbc have yet to be documented. See Bill J. Leonard, "Southern Baptists and Conversion: An Evangelical Sacramentalism," in *Ties That Bind: Life Together in the Baptist Vision*, ed. Gary Furr and Curtis Freeman (Macon, Ga.: Smyth and Helwys Publishing, 1994), 9–22.

8. Some mountain sbc churches have a tradition of foot washing, as affirmed by North Carolina preacher Ben Cook in Gillespie, *Foxfire 7*, 39–40. (Since 1976, I have conducted foot-washing services among Southern Baptist students at the Southern Baptist Theological Seminary, Louisville, Ky.; at Samford University, Birmingham, Ala.; and at the summer program of the Appalachian Ministries Educational Resource Center, Berea, Ky.

9. McBeth, *Baptist Heritage*, 373.

10. Ibid., 374.

11. The designation "missionary Baptist" sometimes is applied to those independent Baptist churches which reject denominational affiliation and accompanying support of mission boards, but send out their own missionaries funded directly by the congregation. Thus, not all Appalachian churches using the appellation "missionary

Baptist" should be considered to be affiliated with the sbc. See Bill J. Leonard, "Independent Baptists: From Sectarian Minority to Moral Majority," *Church History* 56 (Dec. 1987): 504–17.

12. Robert A. Baker, *The Southern Baptist Convention and Its People, 1607–1972* (Nashville, Tenn.: Broadman Press, 1972), 290.

13. Ibid., 294.

14. Walter B. Shurden, *Associationalism among Baptists in America, 1707–1814* (New York: Arno Press, 1980).

Chapter 13

The Presbyterians in Central Appalachia

H. Davis Yeuell and Marcia Clark Myers

History of Presbyterians in the Region

People of a Presbyterian-Reformed persuasion were among the first settlers to enter the Southern Appalachian Region in the 1750s.[1] By the time the Revolutionary War ended, the Ulster-Scots (Scotch-Irish), who had immigrated from Northern Ireland to middle and western Pennsylvania, had pushed their way down the Ohio River into western Virginia and Kentucky and up the Shenandoah Valley, branching off into the Piedmont sections of North and South Carolina and into southwestern Virginia and through the mountain passes into Tennessee and Kentucky.

As families and entire congregations moved westward, Presbyterian-Reformed churches followed their own. Congregations sprang up quickly in the mountains, and petitions were made to presbyteries to send clergy. The primary concern was to prevent those who already had gathered from being lost to the wilderness. Frederick Jackson Turner asserted that "the wilderness masters the colonist."[2]

At first, it seemed that ways were available to the Ulster-Scots and other Reformed Christians to prevent complete mastery by the frontier. They brought with them a mission-oriented polity which surrounded struggling congregations with a presbytery (classis), the presbyteries with synods. A General Assembly (Synod) represented and coordinated the whole. The settlers carried creeds (the Westminster Confession, the Larger and Shorter Catechism) linking doctrine with moral and religious conduct.

These creeds were accompanied by a tradition which not only required a literate and trained clergy (an asset which, from some perspectives, was to become a liability) but also espoused the use of the three *R*s by the people.

The minister-missionaries brought a message based in a theology forged in the fires of the Great Awakening (mid-eighteenth century). Contrary to the popular stereotype of Presbyterian-Reformed clergy as being cold and overly intellectual in person and message, the evidence suggests a caring identification with their people and passionate proclamation of the gospel. Grounded in Evangelical Calvinism, they called sinners to conversion—"the transition from nature (sin) to grace." Such conversion performed at least five functions: (1) It brought forgiveness of sins. (2) It communicated the intellectual content of Christianity. (3) It required a credible profession of faith as a qualification for the Lord's Supper. (4) It appears to have been a means of recruiting new members. (5) It played an important role in the socialization process. It represented one of the ways in the individual came of age in the new land. This station then would be celebrated ritually through the formal elements of confession and admission to church membership.[3]

This approach to conversion may have originated in the understanding of the Evangelical Calvinist that intellectual conviction and not an uncertain emotional experience served as the foundation for the new life in Christ. The minister would provide the means for a rational appropriation of Christian truth.

In summary, the Presbyterian-Reformed churches entered the region with a people, a mission-oriented polity, a discipline, a commitment to education, and an evangelical message which had the potential for subduing the frontier. What they lacked, however, was an adequate number of minister-missionaries. Finding persons with the "call" who would confront the frontier and the Presbyterian educational regulations was no easy task.

There were notable native-born Appalachians who went away to be educated and came back to found churches. These include: the "Apostle of the Kanawha Valley," Rev. Henry Ruffner, ordained in 1818; and the Brown family, which produced at least six Presbyterian ministers who served in West Virginia in the nineteenth century.[4] Such faithful evangelists served in county-seat towns and forested hills, preaching, administering the sacraments, and encouraging congregations.

By the 1830s, the Presbyterian Church, U.S.A., was torn apart over issues in theology and polity, revolving around how the church should organize itself for missions. Schism came in 1837–38, when the church divided into two Assemblies (Old School and New School).The mission effort, especially in the Appalachian region, was badly fragmented.

Most of East Tennessee went with the New School. Eastern Kentucky was about evenly divided between New School and Old School. Churches in western North Carolina were Old School, as were those in southwestern and western Virginia.

By the outbreak of the Civil War, migration into the Appalachian Highlands had practically ceased. The frontier had moved across the Mississippi River onto the Great Plains, into the far Southwest, and along the Pacific Coast. The people who remained in the Highlands were pretty much forgotten. The missionaries and ministers available were being sent to serve a more numerous population to the west. But while the people may have been forgotten, their land and its resources—timber and minerals, especially coal—were not. Prior to the outbreak of the Civil War, the lumber industry had entered the region. Surveyors, lawyers, and engineers of the coal companies were staking out the land. The railroads were laying plans to enter the region. With the cessation of war, the land was opened.

The Home Mission Era

In the 1870s, Presbyterians began to turn their attention to "mission work among mountain whites."[5] Neither the northern churches (Presbyterian Church in the United States of America, Reformed Church in America, and the United Presbyterian Church of North America) nor the southern churches (Cumberland Presbyterian Church, and the Presbyterian Church in the United States) entered the region with a grand design for mission. The beginnings resulted from individual initiatives by persons caught up in the Protestant zeal for mission that marked the latter part of the nineteenth century. They soon were able to elicit the support of particular congregations, wealthy acquaintances, and eventually denominational mission agencies.

The theology undergirding Presbyterian-Reformed missions in this period was not uniquely Reformed. Rather it was a theology that crossed denominational lines, born of both frontier and urban revivalism. The emphasis was on a highly individualistic and personal relationship with Jesus Christ. The Christian life was a state to be achieved rather than a response to God's grace. Of particular importance for the mountain mission enterprise was an understanding of conversion as a means for assimilating "exceptional populations" into the American mainstream. The missionary periodicals of the era speak of the establishment of a unified Protestant Christian nation. As church leaders sought to Christianize the nation, the people of Appalachia became a critical "problem" to be dealt with.

On the one hand, the people were described as quaint, strange, or peculiar in their speech, customs, and dress. Or they could be horrifying in their ignorance, feuding, drinking, and lack of personal cleanliness, in this way constituting a threat to the ideal of a Christian nation.

The Appalachians also were described as a people of promise, however. Although outpaced by the more fortunate segments of the population, these people were in no way inferior. Rather they possessed superior Scotch-Irish, Anglo-Saxon virtues—the sort upon which the nation was founded. For members of Presbyterian-Reformed churches, their Scotch-Irish, German, and Huguenot ancestry made them especially worthy of the church's concern. They were "kith and kin," members of the family, "bone of our bone and flesh of our flesh, and should be special objects of our sympathy, of our interest and our labors."[6]

If the Appalachian people were understood as threat or promise, the response of the Presbyterian-Reformed churches was to counter the first and enhance the second. The dynamics of this missionary enterprise led to a culture of natives and outsiders, the latter being leaders who, with all good intentions, created churches, schools, and agencies in which Appalachian people were ministered *to* rather than *with*.

While there was no overall design for missions in the region, there were different emphases on the part of the northern and southern churches. For the northerners, the goal was "uplift," with primary emphasis on the establishment of an educational and health care system, and the organization of congregations through evangelism as a by-product. For southerners, churches began with evangelism, and an educational system was to follow.

The Northern Churches

In Appalachia, Presbyterian-Reformed mission efforts on the part of the northern churches were to become an essentially feminine enterprise.[7] Women entered the mountains as teachers in the mission schools and serving as Bible readers and Sunday school and community workers. Women's missionary boards assumed responsibility for raising money, establishing curriculum for the teachers and schools, and promoting their publications and missionary conventions.

Samuel Tyndale Wilson writes proudly of an "Appalachian Triple Uplift System."[8] At its base were "day schools" and smaller community centers. As the system developed, certain of the day schools evolved into "boarding schools." These usually were located in a county seat and were referred to in the literature as "presbyterial academies." At the top of the system were "normal schools," which provided a senior high school level of education, plus teacher training.

The overall goal for this educational system was expressed in the purpose enunciated for establishing the Asheville Home Industrial School in 1887: to give "mountain girls mental, physical, industrial, and spiritual training to be future homemakers." To the profession of homemaker could be added that of teacher. For mountain "boys" (who in most cases were at least in their teens and in many cases were mature men), the training was directed toward farming or the trades and leadership in the community and church. One objective was the preparation of persons to serve as ministers, missionaries, and evangelists, who (it was hoped) would serve their own people and build up the church in the region. With some notable exceptions, the mission schools seem never to have produced large numbers of ministers and missionaries. Young men[9] were not necessarily introduced to the more "classical" forms of knowledge that were prerequisites for a theological education.

The contribution of the mission school and community center system to community building is difficult, if not impossible, to measure. The chronicles of the schools, however, do list with pride the names of those students who made a mark in county, state, nation, and church. For a generation of mountain youths, their access to positions of leadership and participation in community life would have been impossible but for the "Appalachian Triple Uplift System."

Southern Churches

The involvement of the Presbyterian Church, U.S., in a mission to the Southern Highlands was initiated by the Synod of Kentucky at its annual meeting in 1881. The action was unprecedented, since the home missions plan adopted by the General Assembly in 1866 lodged primary responsibility for the enterprise in the presbyteries. Many believed that a synod had no role to play. In fact, some leaders of the church argued that a synod had no constitutional right to engage in home mission activities.

However, Dr. Stuart Robinson, a respected minister in Louisville, Kentucky, was convinced that if the Presbyterian Church was ever to penetrate certain sections of Kentucky, the synod would have to do it. He died on October 5, 1881, with his vision unrealized. A few days following his death, the annual meeting of the Synod of Kentucky received a telegram from two men in Louisville offering to double any amount between $2,500 and $5,000 which might be raised by the synod for evangelistic labors. The offer was accepted, and an appeal was made to the churches. The $5,000 was quickly oversubscribed, and five evangelists were appointed. One of these was E. O. Guerrant, a physician turned minister, who resigned a prominent Louisville pastorate to begin work in eastern Kentucky.

Guerrant labored four years as a synod evangelist but was forced by broken health to return to a more settled pastorate. During his four years in the mountains, twelve churches were organized, and evangelistic services were held in mining and lumber camps.

Although relinquishing his work as synod evangelist, he continued to serve as organizer and interpreter of mission in the region. By 1887, convinced that denominational resources were not adequate to meet the needs of the region, Dr. Guerrant organized the Society of Soul Winners. Beginning with $360 and one missionary, the work of the society grew until 1910, when the annual report lists fifty-nine day schools, 239 teachers, and 1,343 pupils. In addition to the school program, the society supported some 70 evangelistic workers, on a budget of twelve thousand dollars a year.

Southern Presbyterians developed work in other parts of the mountain region. The Synod of North Carolina adopted a synodical plan for home missions in 1888, followed by the Synod of Virginia in 1892. The work in western North Carolina received impetus with the organization of Asheville Presbytery in 1896. Two evangelists were appointed to survey the mission potential within the presbytery's bounds.

Transition and Decline

By the early 1920s, the mountain mission enterprise had reached its peak. The Presbyterian-Reformed churches, by this time, had completed their work in founding schools. While churches would continue to be organized and evangelistic work carried on, this activity, too, leveled off. Certain hospital facilities would be expanded, but few, if any, new ones established.

In 1959, Professor Robert Handy of Union Theological Seminary in New York posited the concept that American Protestantism experienced a religious depression and spiritual lethargy from the mid-1920s to the mid-1930s.[10] This critical period was a time of transition, in which Protestant evangelical consensus gave way to religious pluralism. As a result, the missionary motive decayed and financial support for the benevolent work of the church declined markedly. Most noticeable in the foreign mission enterprise, the religious depression also was evident in support for home missions. The evangelical zeal for Christianizing America had lost its steam. The Presbyterian-Reformed mission in Appalachia was not immune. The reports of Home Mission Boards and Committees alarmingly report deficits and loans for missionary salaries.

In addition to the financial stress, the fundamentalist-modernist controversy that broke out in the Presbyterian Church, U.S.A., during the 1920s dissipated the church's energy for mission. Many of the missionaries in the mountains were sympathetic with the more conservative wing of the pcusa and often were suspicious of the New York–based Home Missions Board.

As public education developed with the support of Presbyterians, the centerpiece of the mission enterprise—the mountain mission school— began to disappear. In 1931, the General Assembly adopted a resolution "that no graded or high school would be continued unless it was needed for some special form of training which was not provided by the state, and which was necessary to the permanence and progress of the church in the regions served."[11]

Of significant consequence for Appalachian missions was the decision of the Presbyterian Church, U.S.A., to reorganize its national boards. The women's boards were dissolved and their work given to the Boards of Foreign and National Missions. Without the energy and financial support of the women, mission efforts were weakened.

From the early 1930s through the 1940s, the role of Presbyterian-Reformed churches in the Central and Southern Highlands was essentially one of maintenance. The work was reduced in scope but was to continue through the presbyteries. Some centers—such as the West Virginia Mountain Project in the Coal River Valley and the "Shack" near Morgantown; at Frenchburg and Ezel; and in Jackson County, Kentucky—continued to be a focus for mission concern from Presbyterians beyond the mountains.

Rediscovery and Renewal

In the 1950s, America discovered in its midst a "ravaged land and a dispossessed people." As the demand for coal decreased in the postwar era and new mechanized mining techniques were developed, a great outmigration began, as people in search of work moved to the urban centers on the periphery of the region—Atlanta, Cincinnati, Cleveland, Chicago, Detroit, and other cities. Among those involved in the outmigration were members of Presbyterian-Reformed churches, and this reduced the already small number of constituents and potential leaders.

One of the significant contributions of Presbyterians during this period of distress came in response to a health care crisis. In 1947, a report commonly called *The Boone Report* found the health care system available to coal miners and their families to be "very poor" and its acceptance "a disgrace to a nation to which the world looks for pattern."[12] In response, the United Mine Workers of America's Welfare and Retirement Fund constructed ten new hospitals, dedicated in 1956—at Hazard, Harlan, Whitesburg, Middlesboro, McDowell, South Williamson, and Pikeville,

Kentucky; at Beckley and Man, West Virginia; and at Wise, Virginia. Health care workers with a missionary philosophy were recruited into the region.

The undertaking was so successful that the hospitals were unable to keep up with the demand for services—not only from miner's families, but also from many others who could not pay for care. This demand for services, the drop in coal production, related loss of income from the Welfare and Retirement Fund, and damage from a 1957 flood combined to put the "Miner's Hospitals" on the brink of bankruptcy. In 1962, plans were announced to close four of the hospitals.

Presbyterian ministers and lay leaders sprang into action to save the hospitals. The Reverend Samuel McMaster Kerr of Harlan, Kentucky, urged church leaders to consider purchasing the hospitals. The Board of National Missions and a variety of political leaders, including Franklin D. Roosevelt Jr.; Daniel Patrick Moynihan; President John F. Kennedy; and Kentucky's Gov. Bert J. Combs, worked together to create Appalachian Regional Hospitals, Inc., formed on June 28, 1963, as a not-for-profit corporation. This was a significant and controversial step for the Presbyterian Church. Some health-care professionals argued against unfair competition. It was a risky step when the church invested approximately $2 million of its own funds toward the $9.6 million purchase cost. The Appalachian Regional Heathcare system survived some precarious years and now boasts eleven hospitals and eleven clinics, serving Appalachian people without regard to race, national origin, religion, or ability to pay.

From the 1970s to the present, presbyteries in the region have been strengthened to take on the legacy of "mission projects," evaluate them, and help them evolve to meet contemporary needs, as perceived by residents. Through changes in policy and leadership style, the Presbyterian Church, recognizing local congregations as the primary agents of mission, has empowered local churches through their sessions (governing boards) to call pastors of their own choosing, to hold former mission property and manage it, and to set ministry and mission agendas as they discern human need and the will of God.

Presbyterians have utilized connections with the larger church and ecumenical partners to support congregations in their ministries. As outmigration continued, mission workers and denominational leaders recognized the inadequacy of their ministries, when faced with the serious economic, social, and cultural conditions in the Appalachian region. Studies and surveys were commissioned; and, in 1962, *The Southern Appalachian Region: A Survey* was published.[13] Leaders of the mainline denominations began a series of consultations exploring ways to deploy the church's resources in response to the needs revealed in the survey.

In 1964, the Appalachian Presbyterian Council (APC) was formed to bring together the resources of the Presbyterian-Reformed family and to work with the region as a whole. By 1973, APC had evolved into the Coalition for Appalachian Ministry (CAM), which took on the task of coordinating and unifying the work of Presbyterian-Reformed churches in Appalachia. In 1975, six functions were affirmed as CAM's special responsibilities: (1) To devise strategies for the church in Appalachia; (2) To heighten the region's visibility to the judicatories and the church at large; (3) To highlight the needs of the small church; (4) To help recruit, train, and support the Appalachian pastor; (5) To offer united strength, through ecumenical channels, to Appalachian missions; (6) To address pressing social and economic issues facing the region.

In 1982, a cooperative study of mission strategy in Appalachia was commissioned by the member bodies of CAM: the Christian Reformed Church, the Cumberland Presbyterian Church, the Presbyterian Church in the United States, the United Presbyterian Church in the USA, and the Reformed Church in America. It recommended that, in Appalachia, the member churches emphasize mission, theological exploration, leadership development, congregational development, and community development.[14]

In 1983, the "northern" (UPCUSA) and "southern" (PCUS) Presbyterians reunited to heal the wounds of one hundred years of separation and strengthen their witness for generations to come. Because Appalachia was the region where these two denominations overlapped, reunion has had significant impact. While Kentucky Presbyterians blazed the trail of union in 1971 with the formation of the Presbytery of Transylvania, other presbyteries have been born since reunion. Presbyterians found new vitality in the blending of traditions and mission.

Today's Presbyterian Congregations in Appalachia

Diversity

While the Presbyterian label might denote a homogenous congregation of middle-class people carrying on denominational programs much like those of churches elsewhere, in truth Presbyterian congregations reflect the diversity of the region. There are large urban or suburban program-oriented churches and very small worshipping congregations with five faithful worshippers on most Sundays. There are churches with three choirs, and churches which sing *a cappella*. Despite Scotch-Irish leanings, Presbyterians welcome an ethnic mix—including Italian, African American, and Korean congregations. A Sunday morning tour of churches would demonstrate liturgical diversity; some churches use denominational hymnals and pipe organs, while others prefer the "Jimmy Davis Song Book" and guitar music. Some congregations celebrate the Lord's Supper at the table every other week; others celebrate it once a quarter. Within the Presbyterian family are churches which baptize frequently in the river and Presbyterians who believe such practice is forbidden. (It is not.) While the little church in the country looks forward to annual revival services, a county-seat church down the river cherishes the practice of placing ashes on foreheads on Ash Wednesday. Elders who do not read share pews with college professors. They all love John Calvin's church and sing "Amazing Grace" with gusto!

When asked about the future, most Appalachian Presbyterians would share concern about the impact that outmigration of the young has had on congregations. This trend has left behind aging congregations who struggle to survive and fondly remember better days when pews were full.

Empty pews mean sparse offerings. Some Presbyterians are unemployed. Most are affected by the sluggish economy. Many Presbyterians are professionals or own small businesses. Due to the state of the economy and the popularity of a Wal-Mart over the mountain, many a family-owned hardware store has been forced to close.

The region continues to be dominated by small churches. Many communities are overchurched yet underdiscipled. The Presbyterian Church has witnessed to God's faithfulness by its long-term commitment to people, regardless of congregational growth. The church has stayed in small communities to provide a ministry of presence, sometimes providing the only seminary-trained pastor, who then becomes "community pastor." Such a pastor may care for a flock many times larger than the number who appear on Sunday morning.

Pastoral Leadership Issues

For most Presbyterians in the mountains, the educational requirements for clergy continue to be a problematical issue. Standing firm on the requirement of a baccalaureate degree plus a master of divinity degree, the Presbyterian Church, U.S.A. (and its antecedents), created difficulties for itself. Most Presbyterian seminary students come from large congregations in urban areas and attend urban seminaries. Many have spouses who want professional employment. Rising educational costs leave new ministers with high debts. These factors work against a call to a small rural church. While the Presbyterian Church has a bountiful supply of ministers, applicants for small Appalachian churches are scarce. If a minister does accept such a call, there is great potential for rough spots in the relationship. Though the minister may feel that the salary is very low, it may be higher and provide more benefits than members of the congregation receive. Relatively few Presbyterian ministers are native Appalachians, so they must learn quickly to adapt and to appreciate rural and small church life. There is often a gap between congregational and clerical expectations of ministry. Congregations expect "servant ministry," which involves a great deal of contact with people; Presbyterian ministers generally are trained for a specialized, professional ministry with a strong emphasis upon study and administrative tasks. The Reformed understanding of vocation fits with Appalachian egalitarianism, but the practice of ministry does not always uphold this.

New Ministry Models and Emerging Ministries

Declining budgets and rising costs make it difficult for churches to obtain their ideal of having an ordained Presbyterian minister for every church. A typical Presbyterian church in Appalachia must have an annual budget of about fifty thousand dollars in order to support a full-time pastor at minimum salary and carry on the work of ministry. In response to financial realities, Presbyterians are developing new models for vital ministry, based upon support of community life, strong ecumenical ties, and less pastor dependency. Today there is a general strengthening of lay leadership and an excitement about lay preachers. The denominational Constitution was changed in the 1980s to allow presbyteries to train and commission laypersons for preaching, administration of the Lord's Supper, and other pastoral duties.

Seeking ways to pool resources, small churches are forming new cooperative parishes, often involving joint worship services and youth ministries. Cooperative ministry helps small congregations get beyond survival to reach out to their communities and the world in the name of Christ.

The Presbyterian Church is rediscovering "tent-making" or "bi-vocational" ministry, long the norm for other denominations which dominate the region. Clergy who are able to earn income outside the church are freed to serve small congregations who cannot afford full-time pastor support.

The increasing number of women clergy serving in the area is reflective of the high percentage of seminary students who are women. Though their presence requires an adjustment for many congregations, this trend is good news for churches, as women have been quite effective as nurturing leaders of small churches and are supportive of lay colleagues. Since missionary couples have been common in Appalachia, some small churches have adjusted easily to ordained minister couples. Such "clergy couples" sometimes are able to serve several small churches with various part-time arrangements that fit their budgets. As Appalachian couples take on new roles, clergy couples may provide helpful models for work and marital relationships.

Like Presbyterian churches elsewhere, urban Appalachian churches struggle for a specific ministry niche, often developing new ministries to single parents, Alzheimer's patients, persons with AIDS, and issues of environmental activism.

Like other Americans, many Appalachians voice mistrust of institutions and professionals. "Outsider" organizations, from corporations to government agencies, have left scars. Long the benefactor of Appalachian missions, the national Presbyterian Church has left its share of hurt, as well-intentioned people enforced rules better suited to other settings, set the agenda for missions, promoted a sometimes controversial social agenda, and applied measuring tools that rate Appalachian churches as deficient. Small churches everywhere tend to feel unappreciated and neglected, as American culture promotes "bigger is better." Throughout the denomination, strong efforts have been made to strengthen small congregations. One prominent effort is in the Presbytery of Greenbrier (now West Virginia), but others also have been intentional about the support of small churches, recognizing the relational nature of the small church and structuring presbyteries in response to expressed congregational needs.[15]

Changes in the economic base of the region and resultant demographic changes present significant challenges for Presbyterians personally and for Presbyterian congregations. Many churches manifest a decline of missionary zeal, as congregational energy is focused upon survival. There is much grieving over "what used to be" and anxiety in the present, mixed with some expectancy that perhaps new opportunities lie ahead. As budgets throughout the Presbyterian Church are strained, fewer mission dollars flow into Appalachia. Presbyterian congregations across the nation are spending more money locally for community ministries, personnel, and capital improvements and putting less into missions elsewhere.

This financial squeeze is both a difficulty and a blessing, as Appalachian Presbyterians are challenged to rely upon their own resources and creativity rather than depending upon outsiders. There are no longer "mission churches" and "mission presbyteries," only "churches and presbyteries in mission." The primary funding for ministry comes from within the region now, and mountain Presbyterians are sharing generously with others in need. Judging from a sample of 1994 giving patterns for eight presbyteries in Central Appalachia, total annual per-member contributions are slightly lower than the national average for Presbyterians, but annual per-member giving to missions averages twenty dollars above the national average![16] Long on the receiving end of workcamp groups, Appalachian Presbyterians now head south to work on hurricane-devastated homes in Florida or to aid villagers in Mexico. The Presbytery of West Virginia has established a partnership with the Presbytery of Nyeri in Kenya; Kentucky Presbyterians partner with Cuban brothers and sisters in Christ.

Presbyterian Theology

In recent years, Presbyterians sometimes have been objects of ridicule because of theology and lifestyles. Appellations such as "the frozen chosen" and comments like "If you need help, go to the Presbyterians. If you want religion, go anywhere else" have hurt. These images continue to challenge us. The Presbyterian Church is a "prayer-book church" in a "foot-washing culture." Presbyterian worship style and government have appealed to educated, middle-class people, while many neighbors prefer more emotional worship and more congregational polity.

Finding their beliefs to be an alternative—in some communities the only alternative—to Pentecostalism or fundamentalism, Presbyterians offer a perspective unique in the Appalachian theological landscape. The result of this distinctiveness may be smaller congregations which are faithful to their theology and tradition. As struggling Presbyterian congregations see the growth of independent churches, it is difficult for them to resist the pressures of the Appalachian religious milieu to imitate more "successful" churches. To do so would result in "a mushy blend, rather than an offering of our unique gifts" to the table of Christian community.[7] In Appalachia and elsewhere in modern America, Presbyterians must adapt the "prayer book" liturgy in ways that make it more attractive, but must retain the essential Reformed content nevertheless.

Major theological emphases of Presbyterianism which are especially significant for Appalachians include these beliefs:

God is Creator and sovereign over all of life.

Salvation by grace, forgiveness.

God endows gifts to every person.

God's care is for the whole person.

The Kingdom of God as present and future—not only a comforting hope, but a present possibility in Christian relationships.

"The Holy Spirit goes beyond carrying on in church, to carrying on into the world."

Covenant theology which stresses God's faithfulness in the journey of life on which we walk together, all "sinners in need of forgiveness"; yet all have a responsibility for service and praise.

Activism which values God's management of human destiny, yet rejects fatalism.

The value of theological inquiry.

A look at Presbyterians in the Southern Appalachian region in the 1990s shows a people of faith, continuing many of the positive contributions of their ancestors. Presbyterians continue to have an impact upon their communities far beyond their numbers. They are leaders in education, in business, in community development. As forefather John Calvin felt called by God to build schools, hospitals, houses, and sewer systems in Geneva, so twentieth-century Calvinists do the same in Hazard, Kentucky, and Spencer, West Virginia. Presbyterians active in the PTA, on college faculties, and as campus pastors continue the tradition of nurturing the minds and hearts of God's children. Generous Presbyterians, deceased and living, bless the youth of their communities with scholarship funds for technical schools, health-care training, and college. New leaders are given opportunities to learn and lead through Presbyterian Women, youth programs, and presbytery committee assignments.

Youth ministry continues to be a significant priority. Even very small churches sponsor nursery schools, Head Start, after-school programs, gym programs, or park-like recreation space. Facilities begun as orphanages or schools now serve as temporary homes for troubled children.[18] Church programs to teach sex education, parenting skills, and budget management are aimed at improving the quality of life for children and their parents. Camping programs with an environmental focus are built around bountiful natural resources.

Presbyterians have been leaders in housing ministries. Pastors slept on the courthouse lawn in Huntington, West Virginia, to initiate a community response to homelessness; other Presbyterians built scores of Habitat for Humanity houses with their hands, sweat, and dollars.

Both individually and ecumenically, Presbyterian churches provide direct relief services to thousands of needy Appalachians every day. Such ministries of compassion are a witness to Christ to all persons, irrespective of church affiliation.

The Future of the Presbyterian Church in Appalachia

Evangelism is a great concern, and the challenge is great. As professional and managerial people have migrated out of Appalachia, leaving a very low percentage of college graduates, Presbyterians attempt to reach people who are not traditionally or easily Presbyterian—blue-collar, laboring folk. Class differences make it very hard to change perceptions and patterned behavior. Presbyterians have the money to do wonderful ministry, but those resources and its power distance them from those of limited resources. The challenge is to welcome all strata of society and not be identified solely as the church of professionals.

Always leaders in education, Presbyterians naturally will support the growing community concern for educational issues. They remain strong in college-related communities and should continue to support programs in campus ministry. A leader in affirming the gifts of women for leadership, advocating for women's concerns, and welcoming women into professional ministry, the Presbyterian Church is likely to attract modern Appalachian women.

Presbyterian sociologist James Cushman points out that Appalachia, as the economy shifts away from resource-based industry, already is seeing significant changes in education to meet the growing demand for skilled labor. The rapidly expanding community-college system is producing what Cushman calls a new kind of blue-collar person who has a high degree of technical skill in electronics, communication, and health care. He suggests that such young adults in their twenties and thirties are likely to be receptive to Presbyterian evangelism efforts, if there is an adjustment of worship style.[19]

As mainline Christians—accustomed to urban culture and large church organizations—migrate to Appalachia, some clash of cultures is inevitable as they connect with small, rural Presbyterian churches.

Unless there is a significant intentional effort to adapt and reach out beyond traditional Presbyterian groups, it is unlikely that Presbyterian churches will see tremendous growth in Appalachia. While caring for the aging faithful, Presbyterians need to refocus on a new generation. Traditional middle-class Presbyterians may not want to change, but they must, if they are to be effective witnesses in the twenty-first century.

Building on Diversity

In the twenty-first century, Presbyterians will be challenged by diversity to cross racial, cultural, and class barriers to build a strong church and a strong witness to Christ. As by-products of Presbyterian mission efforts in Asia, Korean Presbyterian churches are growing in many U.S. communities, including Appalachia. Educational centers in the region are attracting Asian and Eastern European immigrants. Appalachia, which long has been very homogenous, will see nonwhite outsiders continue to move in, especially Asians in motel and restaurant businesses and migrant farm workers from Central and South America. At its best, the Presbyterian Church can be the welcoming family, the prophetic voice, and the academy where tolerance is taught. The presence of new immigrants will force more diversity in worship.

Congregational Strategy

It is inevitable that some churches in dying rural communities will close within the next decade. Some presbyteries estimate that significant numbers of their churches will not be viable long into the next century. If the Presbyterian Church is to minister to Appalachians, it must be cautious in its assessment of "viability." It must walk the narrow ridge between wasting scarce funds and overlooking great opportunities to support significant ministries which may not fit familiar models or national standards. One of the hallmarks of Presbyterian ministry in Appalachia has been the willingness to invest resources in people without regard to a "return on the investment."

When congregations must end their ministry, the larger church must assist in that process in a pastoral manner, without abandoning Aunt Tillie and Elder Buck, the faithful saints of the church who have taught generations of Christians and sent them forth from these mountains, who have turned the heat on and shoveled the walk, who have endured long pastoral vacancies and short pastorates, who have been spiritual models as they prayed heartfelt prayers and preached eloquent sermons. Congregational strategy must be more creative and flexible, if mainline churches are to have a presence in Appalachia. As the mall attracts shoppers away from small family-owned stores, the large-program church may be more attractive to religious consumers than the small community church. There will be a trend toward parish clusters which can offer the kind of programs that modern "consumer Christians" want, while maintaining the intimacy of the small church.

Presbyterian churches in the region will call fewer full-time pastors, engaging instead more commissioned lay preachers, bi-vocational ministers, retired ministers, clergy couples, and student interns. Since five Presbyterian seminaries ring the region, it is natural that a symbiotic relationship should develop in which small churches obtain relatively inexpensive leadership and students are nurtured in life-changing ways by wise Christians who know much about pastoring pastors. James Cushman challenges the seminaries to "teach pastors to serve the entire community—not be office-sitters."[20]

The revival of ministry by laity is expected to grow in the years ahead. Presbyterian leader George Aichel suggests that this resurgence has its basis in liberation theology—paralleling the Civil Rights and Women's Liberation movements: "Now we are seeing liberation of the laity from a clerical mind-set; able to acknowledge their own gifts and calling."[21] As this movement continues, lay-inspired ministries will replace professional-directed ministries.

Mission

The legacy of Presbyterian mission involvement will continue. Important work will build upon past strengths in the areas of education, community development, housing, health care, and ministries with children, youth, and senior citizens. Mission concern leads Presbyterians into the public policy arena. Paul Rader, director of CAM, stated, "The relevance of the Presbyterian Church is being put to the test in Appalachia."[22] Rader quoted Richard Couto: "72 percent of the 200,000 square miles of Appalachian surface land is absentee-owned. 80 percent of minerals are absentee-owned. Taxation on such land has historically and traditionally been low. As long as government services continue to be funded by property taxes, Appalachia will always be behind. To remedy this, we need land reform and tax reform."[23] Such reform is likely to have a consequential negative impact upon Presbyterian business people.

These are just some examples of the vested interests which make public policy discussions difficult for Presbyterians. Theirs is a church of miners and millionaires. Too often, local church leaders have chosen the easy road of silence and let Synods, General Assembly, or ecumenical groups take the heat for providing the prophetic witness. Can Presbyterians make a new path that is neither silent nor adversarial? As communities deal with issues of religious pluralism, such as prayer in the public schools and educational curriculum, or issues of environment and health, or community development strategy, can Presbyterians find a new role as catalysts for dialogue?

Highways and Technology

Historically, geography has posed a challenge to a connectional church, as it took all day to travel to meetings. This heightened the tendency for churches to act independently, losing unique Presbyterian identity to the religious culture of their neighborhood. Never again will Appalachian people be geographically isolated. The completion of the Appalachian highway system will give access into and out of the mountains. New highways will bring new businesses, create new jobs, and stabilize the economy. They also will bring a new wave of outsiders and facilitate loss of cultural identity to "malled" America. Cable and satellite television give the opportunity to see ministry models from around the globe in our living rooms, and they dispel stereotypes, as Appalachians "star" in national programs demonstrating positive ministry models. The Internet and the Presbyterian computer network, PresbyNet, are proving to be quick and inexpensive communication tools to link pastors and laity with each other and with ministry resources. This new medium may empower Presbyterian laity as never before, offering direct access which does not rely upon hierarchical flowcharts. While it will appeal most to the educated and those who can afford home computers, even the most rural communities have computers in their schools and businesses. Presbyterians will benefit from the computer world in many ways. The faith of John Calvin may be more attractive to technologically trained Appalachians who are comfortable with words and at ease on the Information Superhighway.

Toward the Future

From the beginnings of Appalachian settlement, the challenges to Presbyterianism have been geography, lack of clergy willing to serve in the area, and identification with educated, middle-class people. With the growth of highways and technology, geography will not be a significant problem in the years ahead. With the rise of lay preacher programs and new congregational strategies, the ministry is becoming less clergy-dependent. The barriers of education and social class remain. Presbyterians need to bring this third challenge out of the closet and deal with it—either by targeting retirees, community college graduates, and business people; or by intentional efforts to develop more socioeconomically inclusive congregations.

Presbyterians bring to Appalachia a strong theological witness to the powerful sovereignty of a loving and gracious God. This has been conveyed in word and deeds for over two hundred years. That theology leads to a strong mission identity which compels Presbyterians to minister beyond their own membership to entire communities and regions. Because of their connectional government, Presbyterians "network" naturally to work cooperatively with ecumenical partners. Much of the Presbyterian legacy in the mountains was a feminine enterprise, "like leaven which a woman took and hid in three measures of meal, till it was all leavened" (Matt. 13:33 RSV). Perhaps the Presbyterian gift to Appalachia will continue to be leaven that causes the whole loaf to rise—to the glory of God.

Notes

1. Much of the history included here was first published in H. Davis Yeuell, *Moving Mountains* (Knoxville, Tenn.: Coalition for Appalachian Ministry, 1985).

2. Frederick Jackson Turner, *The Frontier in American History* (New York: Henry Holt & Co., 1920), 4.

3. Glenn T. Miller, "God's Light and Men's Enlightenment: Evangelical Theology of Colonial Presbyterianism," *Journal of Presbyterian History* 51, no. 2 (Summer 1973): 108.

4. Dorsey D. Ellis, *Look Unto the Rock* (Parsons, W.Va.: McClain Printing, 1982), 95.

5. Taken from the title of Robert F. Campbell, "Mission Work Among the Mountain Whites in Asheville Presbytery," pamphlet (Asheville, N.C.: Citizen Co., 1899), copy in Union Theological Seminary Library.

6. S. H. Doyle, *Presbyterian Home Missions* (Philadelphia: Presbyterian Board of Publications and Sabbath School Work, 1902), 196.

7. Marcia Clark Myers, "Presbyterian Home Missions in Appalachia: A Feminine Enterprise," Master of Divinity thesis, Princeton Theological Seminary, 1979.

8. Samuel Tyndale Wilson, *The Southern Mountaineers* (New York: Literature Department, Presbyterian Home Missions, 1914).

9. At this time, Presbyterian-Reformed churches, with the exception of the Cumberlands, did not ordain women to the office of minister, elder, or deacon.

10. See John Lankford, "The Impact of the Religious Depression upon Protestant Benevolence, 1925–1935," *Journal of Presbyterian History* 42, no. 2 (June 1964): 104–23.

11. Ernest Trice Thompson, *Presbyterians in the South*, vol. 3: *1890–1972* (Richmond, Va.: John Knox Press, 1973), 107.

12. Richard C. Smoot, "Medical History Notes from Appalachia," *Appalachian Heritage* 23 (Fall 1995): 22.

13. Thomas R. Ford, ed., *The Southern Appalachian Region: A Survey* (Lexington: Univ. of Kentucky Press, 1962).

14. *Mission Strategy in Appalachia* (Knoxville, Tenn.: Coalition for Appalachian Ministry, January 1985).

15. See the description in James Cushman, *Beyond Survival* (Parsons, W.Va.: McClain Printing, 1981).

16. Presbyteries chosen were: West Virginia, Shenandoah, Transylvania, East Tennessee, Holston, Abingdon, Peaks, and Western North Carolina. Average annual per-member contribution was $550.31; the national average, $553. The average annual per-member gift to mission was $66.61; the national average $47.84.

17. George Aichel, associate executive of the Presbytery of Transylvania, interview, Jan. 23, 1996.

18. Examples include Davis-Stuart, near Lewisburg, W.Va.; Buckhorn in eastern Kentucky; and the Grandfather Home for Children in Banner Elk, N.C.

19. James Cushman, executive presbyter, Presbytery of Middle Tennessee, interview, Jan. 31, 1996.

20. Ibid.

21. Aichel interview.

22. Paul Rader, director, Coalition for Appalachian Ministry, interview, Jan. 30, 1996.

23. Ibid.

Chapter 14

"Mountaineers Are Always Free":
The Stone-Campbell Traditions

ANTHONY DUNNAVANT

This essay sketches the broad features of the Stone-Campbell traditions in the light of Appalachian mountain religion.[1] Following Alasdair McIntyre, Dorothy Bass has written that "at the heart of a tradition is a pursuit, not a final attainment. Every tradition pursues certain 'goods,' which give to that tradition 'its particular point and purpose.'"[2]

The Stone-Campbell traditions often are characterized simply as a "Restoration Movement." But their common point and purpose may be described more fully as follows: Grateful for, and challenged by, the providential gift of American political and religious *freedom*, the shapers of the Stone-Campbell traditions sought to *unify* the church, on the basis of the *apostles' teachings*, for the sake of *evangelization*, which they understood to be participation in the salvific *mission* of the *coming Lord*, Jesus Christ.

While the foregoing is scarcely as convenient a shorthand as "restorationism," such a statement of the "goods" of the Stone-Campbell traditions does help to set the stage for a discussion of these traditions' relationship to Appalachian mountain Christianity.[3] A recognition of the importance of *freedom* (in many forms) in the constellation of Stone-Campbell values is especially important. To the Stone-Campbell traditions, "the Glorious Liberty of the Children of God" has meant "freedom to respond to the gospel," "freedom from creedalism," "deliverance from ignorance and superstition," "redemption from sin and death," as well as "liberation from oppression." Evangelism was, in part, understood as offering "the gift of freedom."[4]

The place of freedom among the "goods" of the Stone-Campbell traditions is highly relevant to the Appalachian setting. It is at the juncture of persons' *liberating* experience of apprehending the Christian *gospel of divine grace* ("gospel liberty") that the Stone-Campbell traditions and Appalachian mountain religion intersect most powerfully. "Mountaineers are always free," says the motto of the state of West Virginia, the only state in the union that falls entirely within the Appalachian region. By the grace of God, Christians are always free, too—so the heirs of Stone and the Campbells have insisted.

The Stone-Campbell traditions *were,* at least at the outset, Appalachian.[5] Extreme western Pennsylvania and what is now the northern panhandle of West Virginia form one of the sites where the Stone-Campbell traditions were born. This site is in the heart of northern Appalachia, as defined by the Appalachian Regional Commission (ARC).[6] Bethany, [now West] Virginia, was the long-time home of Alexander Campbell, the headquarters of his influential publishing activities, and the site of his formative Bethany College—which shaped much of the core of the Stone-Campbell traditions' early leadership.

During the middle third of the nineteenth century, especially, the most powerful leadership of the Stone-Campbell churches, in geographical terms, was Appalachian. This seldom has been stated. The leaders themselves (Alexander Campbell, for example) more likely would have thought of themselves as "westerners." Later historians, and the popular imagination, sometimes have cast them in the role of "pioneers" or "frontier"[7] folk. By current geographical definitions, however, the Campbells and their Bethany associates were Appalachians.

Similarly, the earlier root of these traditions, led by Barton W. Stone, was centered in north-central Kentucky (especially Bourbon County), near the western edge of the ARC-defined Appalachian region. Furthermore, much of the confluence of the Campbell-led and Stone-led roots of the Stone-Campbell traditions occurred in north-central Kentucky.[8] The growth of these churches in the years surrounding the "union" of the two roots of these traditions was especially significant in northeastern Ohio (the Western Reserve). This latter fact helps explain the conventional elevation of the Ohio evangelist Walter Scott to the status of "fourth founder" of these traditions.[9]

The Rise of the Stone-Campbell Traditions

The internal history of the Stone-Campbell traditions emerges in a context. Two related dimensions of that broad context which especially have been emphasized in recent studies are: (1) the significance of the Scots-Irish sacramental piety that underlay "American" revivalism; and (2) the growing influence of the laity in the late colonial and early national periods of United States history.[10] The second of these two dimensions is closely related to, if not synonymous with, what has been called the "growth of egalitarian ideals" and "democratization."[11]

Because the Stone-Campbell traditions regard the Cane Ridge revival (Bourbon County, Kentucky, 1801) as a founding event, relating this generative event to these contextual factors may begin to place these traditions themselves in a broader perspective. Although a number of recent works could contribute to this effort, *Cane Ridge: America's Pentecost*, by Paul K. Conkin, may be the one most pertinent to it.[12]

Informed to some degree by the recent work of Leigh Eric Schmidt and Marilyn J. Westerkamp, Conkin shows the long taproot of the 1801 Cane Ridge revival to have been in the Scottish Presbyterianism that was transplanted to Ulster and later brought to the United States.[13] Of particular relevance for Cane Ridge was the popular Scots-Irish approach to the communion service. During the first quarter of the seventeenth century, these communions were celebrated with preparatory fasts, prayers, and sermons, accompanied by careful examination of would-be participants, the use of lead tokens for admission to the table, and thanksgiving services on the Mondays after communion.[14]

These communions brought together many parishes and, with noncommunicants in attendance far outnumbering the communicants, manifested many social dimensions alongside the more formally sacramental ones. In Ulster, in the 1620s, "wild" communion services even included what later would be called the "falling exercise"—persons fainting into unconsciousness. About a century later, at Cambuslang, Scotland, communions took place that bore "an almost eerie resemblance to the one at Cane Ridge."[15]

Conkin finds the American roots of Cane Ridge to be especially entangled with those of an American Presbyterianism that developed in close relation to Scots-Irish immigration. The Cane Ridge revival emerged from a "great communion"—itself within a communion season that stretched from May to December and involved some fifty Kentucky congregations.

The religious excitement of that season came to center in Bourbon County, where Barton Stone, an "almost accidental Presbyterian" who was destined to become one founder of another tradition, was thrust by circumstances into the role of host and publicist.[16]

For the Stone-Campbell traditions, an especially significant consequence of recovering the "long view" with respect to Cane Ridge is to reemphasize the meeting's sacramental character.[17] As Samuel Hill has written, the "Stone-Campbell heritage, especially Stoneites, once wed sacrament and enthusiastic experience."[18]

Alongside the eucharistic/sacramental heritage of Scots-Irish popular piety in the late colonial and early national periods must be placed the contextual factor of "democratization." This process, recently described most notably by Nathan O. Hatch, "yoked strenuous demands for revivals" with "calls for the expansion of popular sovereignty." In various versions, each of the hallmarks of "democratizing" American Protestantism in the early national period—intellectual anticlericalism, Christian primitivism, anti-Calvinism, biblicism, and America-centered millennialism—was evident in the emerging Stone-Campbell traditions.[19]

"Democratization" has been advanced explicitly as an interpretive matrix for that generative Stone-Campbell event, Cane Ridge. The "revolt at Cane Ridge" was "the unsettled frontier, the post-revolutionary generation flexing its muscles. It was disappointed heirs of the American Revolution calling once more for freedom, and denying the legitimacy of any authority which questioned their way of exercising the freedom they claimed."[20]

Ellen Eslinger's research on Cane Ridge's local context (Bourbon County, Kentucky) has yielded the finding that the "neighborhood consistently elected representatives" to the state legislature "who were strong advocates of a more democratic and responsive state government." Further, Bourbon County recorded a number of "deeds of manumission" by which slaveholders living near Cane Ridge had freed their slaves in the decade and a half around the great revival. These facts, together with the conduct of the congregation's *lay* leaders in disciplining an alcohol-abusing minister, illustrate an "egalitarianism" at Cane Ridge prior to the famous revival.[21]

Recent historical studies, then, have sketched both larger and longer contextual elements for the rise of the Stone-Campbell traditions—Scots-Irish sacramental revivalism and democratization—and explicitly placed one founding event of those traditions, the Cane Ridge revival, within that context.

The "Goods" of the Traditions, as Articulated by Four Founders

The Stone-Campbell traditions look to four early-nineteenth-century leaders as their primary founders: Barton W. Stone, the host pastor of the Cane Ridge revival (1801), a co-author or at least a signer of the "Last Will and Testament of the Springfield Presbytery" (1804); Thomas Campbell, the principal author of "The Declaration and Address of the Christian Association of Washington, Pennsylvania" (1809); Alexander Campbell, Thomas's son and the editor of the periodicals, the *Christian Baptist* (1823–30) and the *Millennial Harbinger* (1830–66); and Walter Scott, the itinerant evangelist for the Mahoning (Ohio) Association (especially in 1827–28).

By 1796, Barton W. Stone was preaching for the Cane Ridge and Concord Presbyterian churches in Bourbon County, Kentucky. Although Stone recalled having "stumbled" upon the doctrine of the Trinity and having hedged in his affirmation of the Westminster Confession of Faith, accepting it only "as far as I see it consistent with the Word of God," he was ordained by the Transylvania Presbytery in 1798.[22] In early 1801, Stone visited Logan County, where McGready was giving leadership to the communion/revivals that prefigured the larger one at Cane Ridge.

Following the Cane Ridge revival, Stone and his associates became increasingly alienated from the Presbyterian judicatories in Kentucky. The alienated pro-revivalists, nicknamed "New Lights," briefly experimented with having their own presbytery. By the late spring of 1804, they issued "The Last Will and Testament of the Springfield Presbytery," accompanied by a "witness address," which pleaded to remove oppressive, divisive "human creeds and forms of government" from churches, so that "gospel liberty," "the universal spread of the gospel[,]" and the unity of the church" would result.[23]

Stone's commitment to Christian unity and his missionary concern were closely linked. It was significant to Stone that Baptist, Methodist, and Presbyterian preachers had worked side by side during the revival—a unified Christian effort made to confront an especially urgent missionary situation.[24] Part of Stone's interpretation of the Cane Ridge experience and the urgency of its context was an apocalyptic and premillennialist form of eschatology.[25]

Barton W. Stone's commitment to Christian unity was destined to become the best remembered of his ideals.[26] This commitment ultimately was acted out in Stone's giving leadership to the union of many of his followers, the New Lights (also called "Christians in the West" or "Stoneites"), with those of Thomas and Alexander Campbell (called Reformed Baptists, Reformers, Disciples, or "Campbellites"). This union was enacted at a number of sites in southern Indiana and central Kentucky in the late 1820s and early 1830s—most publicly, at Lexington in 1832.[27]

Although Stone sought union with the "Campbellites" because of his commitment to Christian unity and because of common theological ground, he also had been disturbed by the inroads that the United Society of Believers in Christ's Second Appearing (the "Shakers") had made among his associates. These inroads, and the "theological vacuity and disorganization" that had led some of the New Lights back to the Presbyterians, led Stone and many of his followers toward the Campbells.[28] Stone, however, retained his revivalist outlook, which saw the church as constituted for the worship of God and the salvation of sinners. It saw mission as belonging to such a church and regarded the early-nineteenth-century Missionary movement of the eastern denominations as "worldly." "Worldly things" were regarded by the revivalists as "'snares' that could divert one from relationship with God." Since, in relationship with God, God was the bringer of salvation to sinners, the revivalists believed that "the mark of a spiritually healthy self was humility."[29]

Barton W. Stone's revivalist point of view informed his sense of the "goods" that would become associated with the Stone-Campbell traditions. The normative form of those "goods" was articulated by two Campbells and popularized by their evangelist coworker, Walter Scott.

Thomas Campbell was born in 1763 in the Ulster section of Ireland. He studied at the University of Glasgow, where he was exposed to Common Sense philosophy, a form of Lockean philosophy which was congenial to a broad Christian outlook. After university, Thomas was trained theologically by the Anti-burgher, Seceder Presbyterians and took up pastoral duties in Ulster.[30]

By the late 1790s, Thomas Campbell was involved in the Evangelical Society of Ulster, a multidenominational voluntary association formed to promote the "spread of the gospel." The Anti-burgher Seceders' condemnation of the Evangelical Society in 1799 as "latitudinarian" (too broad) and Thomas's unsuccessful attempt to heal the burgher/Anti-burgher schism in Ireland in 1805 form the backdrop of his emigration to America in 1807.[31]

Although the American Seceder Synod happily received Thomas's credentials and assigned him to the Chartiers Presbytery in western (Appalachian) Pennsylvania, by 1808 Thomas was in trouble. Significantly, the "sacred story" of Campbell's "irregularities" that has been repeated in the

Stone-Campbell traditions is that Thomas offered the Lord's Supper to members of "various branches of the Presbyterian family . . . without reference to denominational differences."[32] The religiocultural context, in which Thomas Campbell gave leadership to a broad ("latitudinarian"), multidenominational (though Presbyterian!) communion, may well have been influenced by the transplanted tradition of Scots-Irish "Holy Fairs," described as the context for Cane Ridge.

By 1809, Thomas's troubles with the Seceder Presbyterians led to the creation of a Christian Association in Washington, Pennsylvania. "The Declaration and Address of the Christian Association of Washington, Pennsylvania" stands alongside "The Last Will and Testament of the Springfield Presbytery" as the other "founding" statement of the Stone-Campbell traditions.

Thomas Campbell viewed the religious liberty of the United States as a unique, providentially given, missional opportunity for the church and gave it great significance.[33] The commitment to Christian union is present in "The Declaration and Address," which states that "the Church of Christ upon earth is essentially, intentionally, and constitutionally one."[34]

Similarly, an emphasis on the Bible and primitivism are present in "The Declaration and Address." But, unlike Stone's approach, Campbell's emphases on the Bible and primitivism take the form of a more "constructive" restorationism. The inspired text of the New Testament, rather than the direct operation of the Spirit, is seen as constitutive of the church.[35]

"The Declaration and Address" articulates most, if not all, of the major elements that the Stone-Campbell traditions would come to pursue as their "goods," their self-conscious "Plea"—in this free land, for the unity of the church, on the basis of the Apostles' teaching, "that the world might believe."

In Alexander Campbell, Thomas's son, were combined a commitment to the notion of restoration and the confidence to specify the content of "the ancient gospel and ancient order." Alexander Campbell had been born in Ulster in 1788. He had been left in charge of his father's own academy when the elder Campbell emigrated in 1807. In 1808, Alexander, his mother, and his siblings set sail to join Thomas in the New World. Shipwreck led to a year's delay in their emigration and gave Alexander an opportunity to study at the University of Glasgow.

At Glasgow, Alexander Campbell came under the influence of an "evangelical" circle led by Greville Ewing, who was associated with the movement of James and Robert Haldane. Within this circle of association (and with the background of his father's "latitudinarianism"), Alexander began to question his Seceder Presbyterian allegiance. Again, the "sacred story" of Alexander Campbell's break with Presbyterianism has a sacramental setting. It was on the occasion of Seceder communion that Alexander symbolically broke with this denomination by "tossing" his lead token (his admission to the table) and declining to commune.[36]

When the elder and younger Campbells were reunited in America in 1809, they discovered the parallelism of their respective religious pilgrimages. Alexander is said to have read "The Declaration and Address" eagerly and endorsed its contents heartily. Alexander Campbell, however, was destined to approach this task with: (1) the assumption that the Bible may be interpreted with clarity and certainty; (2) a commitment to the union of all Christians (not all churches) in one body; and (3) a commitment to the restoration of an explicitly described primitive gospel and church order. All other "goods," in Alexander Campbell's mind, were to be "pursued" in order to fulfill the mission of the church—converting the world to Christ.

Alexander Campbell, too, was committed to liberty. First, he was committed to a liberty of opinion which would extend up to the point of "self-evident" Scripture. Second, Campbell condemned the existence of ecclesiastical establishments. Liberation from "human creeds" and "worldly establishments" was part of the restoration which would bring about Christian union and fulfill Christ's saving mission. From 1812 until his death in 1866, it was Alexander Campbell's leadership that most shaped the Campbell side of the Stone-Campbell traditions.

It was in 1812 that Alexander was brought to the forefront of the fledgling Christian Association–cum–church, through his insistence that the normative biblical form of baptism was the immersion of believers. This position led the Campbellites into a half-generation (circa 1815–30) of identity as Reformed Baptists (or Reformers) and into relation with Baptist associations. Again, a sacramental issue was determinative.

Specifically, the highly rationalistic and optimistic outlook of the younger Campbell, his triumphalistic New Testament dispensationalism, and his non-Calvinistic interpretation of baptism drove a wedge between him and the Baptists. His stance on baptism led to his being accused of "water regenerationism."

This controversy is important for positioning the Campbellite movement in relation to other religious traditions and for foreshadowing the discussion of the ministry of Walter Scott. The key concept for Alexander Campbell's understanding of baptism was "the gospel." This, "the testimony of the Apostles, which narrates the deeds of God in Jesus Christ," is what "discloses the proposition that God is love, which alone has the power to overcome the alienation of the sinner's heart." Campbell's position was that the belief in this gospel came as the result of evidence. Having received the gospel in faith, one could be baptized as an act of obedience and, through baptism, receive assurance of one's salvation.

The role of the Holy Spirit, in Campbell's understanding, was not to regenerate the sinner by its direct operation, but to work in and through the gospel in conversion and sanctification.[37] Campbell's view was a move toward a more "visible church" understanding of the sacrament of baptism than that which prevailed among the denominations of Calvinist/Reformed heritage. Campbell's view stood in contrast to understandings of conversion that stressed a "dramatic" regeneration wrought in the sinner by the Spirit and necessary *before* one could be baptized. Campbell's view had a "dramatic" effect on eastern Ohio and central Kentucky in the 1820s.

The Alexander Campbell who increasingly was coming to the public's attention in the 1820s was a "westerner." This was made manifest in his participation in Virginia's 1829 constitutional convention, in which he argued against using property as part of the basis for representation, for extending suffrage, and for judiciary reform. During that convention, he also worked with others toward the gradual emancipation of slaves and for public education. In each instance, these stands and efforts aligned Campbell *against* elements of Virginia's Tidewater and Piedmont aristocracies and *with* the interests and values of Virginia's western mountains—the region that was to become, in another generation, West Virginia.[38]

Walter Scott became the itinerant evangelist for the Mahoning (Ohio) Association in 1827. This nominally Baptist association was dominated by Campbellite Reformers. Scott's approach to evangelism was consistent with Campbell's understanding of the gospel and conversion and called for faith in the "Golden Oracle" (the messiahship and divine sonship of Jesus Christ), repentance, and submission to immersion baptism. God could be trusted to grant remission of sins, the gifts of the Spirit, and eternal life. Scott's rational, "orderly" arrangement of the gospel, or plan of salvation, sometimes was presented as a "five-finger exercise" by arranging the elements (faith, repentance, baptism, remission, gifts of the spirit, and eternal life) on the fingers (combining the gifts of the Spirit and eternal life). Many thousands were brought into the Stone-Campbell traditions by the preaching of Scott and his imitators.[39]

In the Stone-Campbell traditions, the memory of the sacramental-revival roots of Cane Ridge and of the revivalist world view of Barton W. Stone has been relatively weak. Different versions of the more rationalist, progressive, and optimistic (triumphalistic) outlook of the Campbells and Scott have held greater sway over the memory of these churches.

In sum, the four founders of the Stone-Campbell traditions articulated a vision of a New World Christianity that, by God's providence, might be more free, more faithfully biblical, more unified, and more evangelistically effective than the corrupted faith of the Old World. In Appalachia and to the west, this New World faith seemed to be taking hold; it seemed to have a real chance. The two root groups, the followers of Stone and of the Campbells, had much in common. Not the least of their commonalities was that each had a distinctive heritage of *popular* sacramentality: sacramental revivalism on the Stone side and "democratized" baptism on the Campbell side.

Appalachian Religion and the Traditions

There have been many attempts to depict a distinctively Appalachian approach to Christian faith.[40] A composite portrait of Appalachian mountain religion would have certain dominant "shades" in its world view, its theology, and its understanding of salvation and the nature of the church.

The Stone-Campbell traditions were born, in part, in northern Appalachia and on the Cumberland Plateau. It is not surprising, then, to find, among the "goods" that the Stone-Campbell traditions have pursued, "goods" of Appalachian mountain religious tradition as well. Three broad areas of common commitment are especially clear: the theocentric/providential world view, the passion for freedom in several forms, and a deep and immediate devotion to the Bible. Commitment to Christian unity for the sake of evangelism is a feature of the Stone-Campbell traditions that typically has *not* been identified as an Appalachian mountain religious value.

Beyond these areas of common commitment there is, in both the Stone-Campbell traditions and in Appalachian mountain religion, a heritage of combining a vigorous sacramental life with egalitarianism. This is noteworthy because, for much of Christian history in the United States and elsewhere, sacramental emphasis often has been linked to more hierarchically "ordered" forms of church life. The sacramental-and-egalitarian theme in the Stone-Campbell traditions has had, as its most enduring expressions, the weekly celebration of the Lord's Supper, the affirmation that "nonclergy" elders are authorized to pray and preside at the Lord's table, and the perception that the immersion of penitent adult believers is the scriptural form of baptism. There has been a tendency toward an "open Table" ("*we* neither invite nor debar, the Table is the Lord's") in the Stone-Campbell traditions. This, and the invitation for "whosoever will" to confess her or his faith and receive baptism, have epitomized the Stone-Campbell traditions' sacramental-and-egalitarian character.

One factor exerting powerful influence upon the self-understandings of the Stone-Campbell traditions has been the divisions among them. It has been noted that the Stoneites were pessimistic and premillennial in their outlook and that the Campbellites were optimistic and postmillennial in theirs.[41] The identification of this difference in outlook, bolstered by the geographical research of R. L. Roberts, suggests that, in the Stone-Campbell traditions, from the beginning, fissures were present along the lines of its two main communities of origin.[42]

As early as the 1840s, in the Stone-Campbell traditions two different "mind-sets" were perceptible on the issue of the legitimacy of missionary societies. Between the Civil War and 1906, opposition to missionary societies and opposition to the use of instrumental music in worship emerged as the two main hallmarks of the Churches of Christ. They have been predominantly a communion of the American South. Anti-Rebellion "loyalty resolutions," adopted by northern-sectional "rump" versions of the (Stone-Campbell) American Christian Missionary Society during the Civil War, were remembered with bitterness by southerners as the nineteenth century approached its conclusion. The divergent experiences of North and South during the Civil War and Reconstruction, combined with the pessimistic/progressive fissures of the prewar period, had the effect of producing a schism.[43]

David Lipscomb, Nashville church leader and long-time editor of the *Gospel Advocate*, became a spokesperson for the Churches of Christ. It was at his urging in 1906 that the Churches of Christ were listed as a separate religious body in the U.S. Census Bureau. On the northern side, the Christian Churches (the remainder of the Stone-Campbell traditions) were being reborn as a progressive denomination. With the (largely) southern conservatives gone from their midst, these churches proceeded to create most of the "bones and tissue" of what is now the Christian Church (Disciples of Christ).

Between 1874 and 1917, the Christian Churches (Disciples of Christ) created two new missionary societies, a council on Christian Union, and boards for benevolence, church extension, ministerial relief (pensions), publications, and higher education.[44] This period entailed organizational, geographical, and ideological change for this branch of the Stone-Campbell traditions. Organizationally, it embraced cooperative bodies beyond the congregational level—not only the aforementioned "national"-level agencies, but also multipurpose state missionary societies.[45]

Geographically, the population center of the Christian Churches (Disciples) was moving to the Midwest. By 1890, Missouri had supplanted the birthplace, Kentucky, as the most populous state for Disciples.[46] Furthermore, the generative sites and eventually the headquarters of the new organizations were located mainly in the Midwest, especially in Indianapolis and St. Louis. These would later become the "General Administrative Units" of the Christian Church (Disciples of Christ). Greater Kansas City alone eventually would become a "region" of the denomination and have three times more members within it than the entire state of West Virginia.[47] The influential urban centers in nineteenth-century Stone-Campbell circles had been Bethany (West Virginia), Cincinnati (Ohio), and Lexington (Kentucky), all much nearer to these traditions' Appalachian places of origin than were the new midwestern centers.[48]

Two different trajectories, then, led two different branches of the Stone-Campbell traditions away from their Appalachian geographical roots and, to a degree, their "Appalachian" theological inheritance. This theological inheritance has much in common with the revivalist theology and ecclesiology of Barton W. Stone. Churches of Christ, geographically, became more southern than Appalachian. Theologically, Allen writes, they eschewed Stone's revivalist apocalypticism for "a rigid and garrulous form of Campbell's biblical patternism and an exclusivism easily identifying Churches of Christ as the one true restored kingdom of God."[49] On the other hand, the Christian Churches (Disciples) became more midwestern than Appalachian. Theologically, they exchanged much of their sacramental-egalitarian and "enthusiastic" heritage for a theologically progressive, ecumenically cooperative, and formally institutionalized denominationalism (including a multidimensional ministry in Appalachia).[50]

A third branch of the Stone-Campbell traditions is the undenominational fellowship of Christian Churches and Churches of Christ, known informally as "independent" Christian Churches. This branch of the traditions gradually became distinct from the Christian Churches (Disciples) during the first two-thirds of the twentieth century. The decade 1917–27 was especially crucial. During these years, the Christian Churches (Disciples) developed a newly structured International Convention and a multipurpose United Christian Missionary Society, which the emergent "independents" regarded with growing concern. Further, the College of the Bible (in Lexington, Kentucky) abandoned its "restorationist" pedagogy in favor of progressive, historical-critical, "mainline" presuppositions. Most consequentially, the perception was growing that Disciples' "foreign" missionaries were practicing "open membership" (that is, accepting into congregational fellowship persons who had not been immersed as adult believers).[51]

Alarmed by each of these developments among the Christian Churches (Disciples), the "independent" group began to support "Congresses" and, by the end of the 1920s, a North American Christian Convention alongside, and eventually rather than, the International Convention of the Disciples of Christ. Soon the "independents" had developed a network for "directly" supporting missionaries who would continue to evangelize on the "restorationist" platform of immersion-only and who would be free from entanglement with the "ecclesiasticism" of the Disciples missionary societies. Finally, after the "fall" of the College of the Bible, the "independents" increasingly supported an alternative network of Bible colleges.

The schism between the "independent" Christian Churches and the Christian Churches (Disciples) was finally and formally completed when the latter, in 1968, adopted "The Design for the Christian Church (Disciples of Christ)" and constituted themselves the Christian Church (Disciples of Christ).

"Independent" Christian Churches and Churches of Christ, arguably, have remained somewhat closer to their Appalachian roots than either of the other branches of the movement. The contrast with the Christian Church (Disciples of Christ) can be drawn on the basis of the distribution of membership. The *proportion* of the "independent" Christian Churches' "total adherents" (United States) in the ARC-defined region (14 percent) is double that of the Christian Church (Disciples of Christ) (7 percent).

Although the proportion of the Churches of Christ's "total adherents" within Appalachia (15 percent)[52] is comparable to that of the "independent" Christians, the heavily southern character of the remainder of their members reinforces the association of the total group with *that* region. Furthermore, most of the prominent institutions (e.g., colleges and universities) of the Churches of Christ are situated to the south and west of Appalachia, in Middle Tennessee and Texas, especially.

In contrast to this, the "independent" Christian Churches and Churches of Christ continue to support a number of Bible colleges, seminaries, and a liberal arts college in or near Appalachia. East Tennessee is an especially important area for these institutions, containing a representative of each kind of school: Johnson Bible College (Kimberlin Heights), Emmanuel School of Religion (Johnson City), and Milligan College. Acting to a significant degree in and through these institutions, the "independent" Christian Churches have remained an important part of the religious culture of East Tennessee, located within Appalachia.[53]

Theologically, it has been among the "independent" Christian Churches and Churches of Christ that one sacramentally oriented version of the Stone-Campbell heritage has been continued. Identified by one scholar as a "high-church sacramentalist" group within these churches, this element would understand itself as representing a more "Campbellite" than "Stoneite-revivalist" understanding of sacraments. Nonetheless, it is notable that this group appears in the "relatively more Appalachian" branch of the Stone-Campbell traditions and is represented, in part, by an East Tennessee school—Emmanuel School of Religion.[54]

Toward the Future

The Stone-Campbell traditions, the Christian Church (Disciples of Christ), the Churches of Christ, and the undenominational fellowship of Christian Churches and Churches of Christ—all these have clear, strong historical roots in the Appalachian region. Further, significant contextual factors, especially the heritage of sacramental revivalism and of early national period "democratization," are common to the Stone-Campbell traditions and to Appalachian mountain religion. In part because of this shared history, some of the most cherished ideals of the Stone-Campbell traditions lie close to the heart of Appalachian mountain religion as well. A theocentric world view, a deep devotion to the Bible, and, especially, a fierce commitment to freedom characterize both Stone-Campbell and Appalachian religious traditions. It was in their understandings of mission that these traditions most diverged.

Two of the branches of the Stone-Campbell traditions, the Christian Church (Disciples of Christ) and the Churches of Christ, came to center outside Appalachia, in both the distribution of their membership and the operations of their major formal organizations or institutions. The Christian Church (Disciples of Christ) became a "denomination" of the Midwest and the Churches of Christ a "fellowship" of the American South. The third branch of these traditions, the undenominational fellowship of Christian Churches and Churches of Christ ("independent"), maintained a relatively larger share of its strength in Appalachia (defined as membership distribution *and* institutions).

It is consistent with this that the "independent" Christian Churches and Churches of Christ also have maintained what might be termed a more "Appalachian" theological character. Their emphatic sacramentality has continued to live as at least a minority strand within this branch of the Stone-Campbell traditions. And these churches are fiercely congregational.

Recently, the sacramental-revival roots of the Stone-Campbell traditions have been "rediscovered" and their exploration has begun. These traditions have much to gain from that process. Perhaps further investigation will grow from the recognition that these roots first grew in Appalachian mountain soil—soil that is rich and deep, fertilized by the humble conviction that God is the author of salvation, of religious experience, and of freedom.

Notes

1. See Deborah Vansau McCauley, *Appalachian Mountain Religion: A History* (Urbana: Univ. of Illinois Press, 1995). McCauley's understanding of Appalachian mountain religion and its central elements helps to shape the discussion to come.

2. I am using the term *goods* here and elsewhere in this essay in this sense. See Dorothy Bass, "Congregations and the Bearing of Traditions," in *American Congregations,* ed. James P. Wind and James W. Lewis (Chicago: Univ. of Chicago Press, 1994), 171. Bass adapts the term in this connection from Alasdair McIntyre, *After Virtue: A Study in Moral Theology,* 2d ed. (Notre Dame, Ind.: Univ. of Notre Dame Press, 1984).

3. For a brief account of the historiography of "goods" in the interpretation of the Stone-Campbell traditions, see Anthony L. Dunnavant, "Evangelization and Eschatology: Lost Link in the Disciples Tradition?" *Lexington Theological Quarterly* 28, no. 1 (Spring 1993): 43–54.

4. Ronald E. Osborn, *Experiment in Liberty: The Ideal of Freedom in the Experience of the Disciples of Christ,* Forrest F. Reed Lectures for 1976 (St. Louis, Mo.: Bethany Press, 1978), 51–64.

5. McCauley, *Appalachian Mountain Religion,* 64.

6. See, e.g., map 2 in ibid., 5.

7. Consider, e.g., the subtitle of Perry Gresham, ed., *The Sage of Bethany: A Pioneer in Broadcloth* (St. Louis, Mo.: Bethany Press, 1960), a book about Alexander Campbell; or the title of W. E. Garrison, *Religion Follows the Frontier: A History of the Disciples of Christ* (New York: Harper and Row, 1931).

8. Richard L. Harrison Jr., *From Camp Meeting to Church: A History of the Christian Church (Disciples of Christ) in Kentucky* (St. Louis, Mo.: Published for the Christian Church [Disciples of Christ] in Kentucky by the Christian Board of Publication, 1992), 53–71.

9. Lester G. McAllister and William E. Tucker, *Journey in Faith: A History of the Christian Church (Disciples of Christ)* (St. Louis, Mo.: Bethany Press, 1975), 22, 132–35.

10. Leigh Eric Schmidt, *Holy Fairs: Scottish Communions and American Revivals in the Early Modern Period* (Princeton, N.J.: Princeton Univ. Press, 1989), details the Scots-Irish eucharistic tradition. Marilyn J. Westerkamp, *Triumph of the Laity: Scots-Irish Piety and the Great Awakening, 1625–1760* (New York: Oxford Univ. Press, 1988), provides a case study of the influence of the laity, in this instance in support of the "awakening" in the Middle Colonies.

11. Ellen Eslinger, "Some Notes on the History of Cane Ridge Prior to the Great Revival," *Register of the Kentucky Historical Society* 91, no. 1 (Winter 1993): 22; Nathan O. Hatch, *The Democratization of American Christianity* (New Haven, Conn.: Yale Univ. Press, 1989).

12. Newton B. Fowler Jr. places some of the pertinent recent literature in perspective in "Cambuslang: The Scottish Predecessor to Cane Ridge," in *Cane Ridge in Context: Perspectives on Barton W. Stone and the Revival,* ed. Anthony L. Dunnavant (Nashville, Tenn.: Disciples of Christ Historical Society, 1992), 111–16; and in Fowler's review of Paul Conkin, *Cane Ridge: America's Pentecost* (Madison: Univ. of Wisconsin Press, 1990); of Schmidt, *Holy Fairs;* and of Westerkamp, *Triumph of the Laity,* in *Lexington Theological Quarterly* 29, no. 3 (Fall 1994): 193–95.

13. Westerkamp, *Triumph of the Laity,* focuses on the Great Awakening and its precedents within Presbyterianism in the Middle Colonies in the century and a third before 1760.

14. Schmidt, *Holy Fairs,* details the long history of this eucharistic tradition and, like Conkin, places Cane Ridge within and near the end of it.

15. Conkin, *Cane Ridge,* 19, 20.

16. Ibid., 26–31, 73 ff.

17. Keith Watkins, "The Sacramental Character of the Camp Meeting," *Discipliana: Quarterly Journal of the Disciples of Christ Historical Society* 54, no. 1 (Spring 1994): 2–19.

18. Samuel S. Hill, "Cane Ridge Had a Context: Let's See What They Were," in Dunnavant, *Cane Ridge in Context,* 121.

19. Hatch, *Democratization,* 7–9, 162–89.

20. Ronald P. Byars, "Cane Ridge from a Presbyterian Point of View," in Dunnavant, *Cane Ridge in Context,* 99–100.

21. Eslinger, "Some Notes on the History," 4–22.

22. McAllister and Tucker, *Journey in Faith,* 68.

23. "Witnesses' Address," in *Declaration and Address, by Thomas Campbell; Last Will and Testament of the Springfield Presbytery, by Barton W. Stone and Others,* with an introduction by F. D. Kershner (St. Louis, Mo.: Bethany Press, 1960), 20–22.

24. Barton Warren Stone, "A Short History of the Life of Barton W. Stone," in *The Cane Ridge Meeting House,* by James R. Rogers (Cincinnati, Ohio: Standard Publishing, 1910), 167.

25. Richard T. Hughes, "The Apocalyptic Origins of Churches of Christ," *Religion*

and American Life: A Journal of Interpretation 2, no. 2 (Summer 1992): 189–91; see also C. Leonard Allen, "'The Stone That the Builders Rejected': Barton W. Stone in the Memory of Churches of Christ," in Dunnavant, *Cane Ridge in Context,* 46–50.

26. Anthony L. Dunnavant, "From Precursor of the Movement to Icon of Christian Unity: Barton W. Stone in the Memory of the Christian Church (Disciples of Christ)," in Dunnavant, *Cane Ridge in Context,* 1–19.

27. Harrison, *From Camp Meeting to Church,* 51–72.

28. For a good treatment of this journey of the New Light Christians "From Freedom to Constraint," see Richard T. Hughes and C. Leonard Allen, *Illusions of Innocence: Protestant Primitivism in America, 1630–1875* (Chicago: Univ. Press of Chicago, 1988), 102–32.

29. D. Newell Williams, "The Social and Ecclesiastical Impact of Barton W. Stone's Theology," in *Explorations in the Stone-Campbell Traditions: Essays in Honor of Herman A. Norton,* ed. Anthony L. Dunnavant and Richard L. Harrison Jr. (Nashville, Tenn.: Published for the Disciples Divinity House at Vanderbilt University by the Disciples of Christ Historical Society, 1995), 11–42. On "Appalachian mountain religion," see McCauley, *Appalachian Mountain Religion,* 22, 26, 47, 16, 89.

30. The standard modern biography of Thomas Campbell is Lester G. McAllister, *Thomas Campbell: Man of the Book* (St. Louis, Mo.: Bethany Press, 1954).

31. David M. Thompson, "The Irish Background to Thomas Campbell's *Declaration and Address,*" *Discipliana: Quarterly Journal of the Disciples of Christ Historical Society* 46, no. 2 (Summer 1986): 23–27.

32. B. B. Tyler, *A History of the Disciples of Christ* (New York: Christian Literature Co., 1894), 44.

33. *Declaration and Address, by Thomas Campbell,* 30. The founders of the Stone-Campbell traditions were uniform in their commitment to civil disestablishment.

34. Ibid., 44.

35. Ibid., 45.

36. See, e.g., McAllister and Tucker, *Journey in Faith,* 115. This famous "scene" even has made it onto celluloid, as the opening sequence of the film *Wrestling with God.*

37. D. Newell Williams, "The Gospel as the Power of God to Salvation: Alexander Campbell and Experimental Religion," in *Lectures in Honor of the Alexander Campbell Bicentennial, 1788–1988,* ed. Lester G. McAllister, with an introduction by James M. Seale (Nashville, Tenn.: Disciples of Christ Historical Society, 1988), 138–44.

38. Eva Jean Wrather, "Campbell: Marx to Jackson," in McAllister, *Lectures in Honor of Campbell Bicentennial,* 154–62.

39. William A. Gerrard, III, *A Biographical Study of Walter Scott: American Frontier Evangelist* (Joplin, Mo.: College Press, 1992).

40. Catherine Albanese, in *America: Religions and Religion,* ed. Robert S. Michaelson,

221–43 (Belmont, Calif.: Wadsworth Publishing Co., 1981); Newton B. Fowler Jr., "The Religious Culture of Southern Appalachia," *Lexington Theological Quarterly* 30, no. 2 (Summer 1995); and McCauley, *Appalachian Mountain Religion,* were sources for the "composite portrait" of Appalachian mountain religion summarized here.

41. Allen, "Stone That the Builders Rejected"; Hughes, "Apocalyptic Origins."

42. R. L. Roberts and J. W. Roberts, "Like Fire in Dry Stubble: The Stone Movement, 1804–1832," pt. 1, *Restoration Quarterly* 7 (1963): 148–58; and pt. 2, *Restoration Quarterly* 9 (1965): 26–40.

43. On the sectional factor in the emergence of the Churches of Christ, see David Edwin Harrell Jr., *A Social History of the Disciples of Christ,* vol. 1: *Quest for a Christian America: The Disciples of Christ and American Society to 1866* (Nashville, Tenn.: Disciples of Christ Historical Society, 1966); and vol. 2: *The Social Sources of Division in the Disciples of Christ, 1865 to 1900* (Atlanta, Ga.: Publishing Systems, 1973), 325.

44. McAllister and Tucker, *Journey in Faith,* 16–17.

45. Anthony L. Dunnavant, *Restructure: Four Historical Ideals in the Campbell-Stone Movement and the Development of the Polity of the Christian Church (Disciples of Christ),* American University Studies, series 7: Theology and Religion, vol. 85 (New York: Peter Lang, 1993), 121–81.

46. Ibid., 132.

47. *Year Book and Directory, 1995, of the Christian Church (Disciples of Christ)* (Indianapolis, Ind.: Office of the General Minister and President, 1995), 570.

48. Ibid.

49. Allen, "Stone That the Builders Rejected," 56.

50. The Christian Church (Disciples of Christ) now has the Kentucky Appalachian Ministry as part of the mission of the region, the Christian Church (Disciples of Christ) in Kentucky and the general church's Division of Homeland Ministries. It also participates in the Appalachian Ministries Educational Resources Consortium through seminaries related to its Division of Higher Education.

51. Dunnavant, *Restructure,* 61–91; Mark G. Toulouse, "Practical Concern and Theological Neglect: The UCMS and the Open Membership Controversy," in *A Case Study of Mainstream Protestantism: The Disciples' Relation to American Culture, 1880–1989,* ed. D. Newell Williams (St. Louis, Mo., and Grand Rapids, Mich.: Chalice Press and Wm. B. Eerdmans Publishing Co., 1991), 194–235.

52. These proportions were arrived at from statistics in Bernard Quinn et al., *Churches and Church Membership in the United States, 1980* (Atlanta, Ga.: Glenmary Research Center); and "Appalachian Regional Commission: Religious Bodies Ranked According to Number of Total Adherents," photocopied computer printout provided to the writer by the Appalachian Ministries Educational Resources Consortium.

53. See Henry Webb, *In Search of Christian Unity: A History of the Restoration Movement* (Cincinnati, Ohio: Standard Publishing, 1990), 463–66. Also Henry Webb, "The Contributions of the Stone-Campbell Movement to the Religious Culture of East Tennessee," *Lexington Theological Quarterly* 29, no. 2 (Summer 1994): 123–34.

54. [George] Richard Phillips, "From Modern Theology to a Post-Modern World: Christian Churches and Churches of Christ," *Discipliana: Quarterly Journal of the Disciples of Christ Historical Society* 54, no. 3 (Fall 1994): 88.

Chapter 15

Wesleyan/Holiness Churches

Melvin E. Dieter

A discussion of the history and place of the Wesleyan/Holiness churches in Appalachian religious life faces two significant challenges. The first is methodological, rising from the large number and diverse sizes of the well-established groups that make up the movement. Even the larger Wesleyan/Holiness churches might not merit individual inclusion in studies such as this. However, to neglect the collective presence in American religion of the movement's five or six moderately-sized churches, together with the score or more of the smaller groups and agencies which constitute the larger family grouping, would be to ignore an important participant in the story.[1]

This discussion must navigate between the Scylla of doing justice to the movement as a whole and the Charybdis of failing to do justice to the five or six larger denominations that play the dominant role in shaping the movement's story. The brevity of this paper dictates the use of a very generalized *movement* approach to the historical explication of the *churches'* expansion and mission in Appalachia. However, because common threads make up the fabric of the ethos of the individual churches and because of the continuing association of all of the larger bodies in the Christian Holiness Association, this broad review in fair measure represents them all, large and small. Intermittent inclusion of specific anecdotal evidence of the contributions of the individual communions is a further effort to grapple with the dilemma.

The somewhat extended historical review in the first part of this chapter attempts to respond to a second and more complex challenge—a continuing confusion of *category* and *identity* when one attempts to talk about "Holiness churches" in either popular or scholarly circles. This murkiness exists at both ends of the developmental spectrum, where the larger part of the Wesleyan/Holiness revival's constituency moved out of Holiness evangelistic associations into institutionalized Holiness churches by the close of the nineteenth century. For its first fifty years, the movement was so deeply rooted in traditional Methodism that its early story is essentially lost within the larger history of that church. On the other hand, since the beginning of the century, the movement's identity commonly has been confused with a closely related, but paradigmatically distinct, Pentecostal/Holiness tradition. The Holiness movement took shape within the Methodist movement, and the Pentecostal movement developed from the Holiness communities.

The identity question became especially difficult as both Wesleyan/Holiness and Pentecostal/Holiness groups began their missions in the villages and mountains of Appalachia. There the similarities of worship and lifestyle have tended to meld popular, and even scholarly, perceptions of the two movements; and this confusion must be addressed before one can properly locate either of them in the religious culture of the area. Even a cursory survey of books and articles on religion in Appalachia will indicate that the use of the term "Holiness church" refers almost exclusively to churches of the Pentecostal/Holiness movement.[2] Exploring the historical background of the two groups should provide a fuller resolution of the identity problem and allow us to understand more readily the story of the Wesleyan/Holiness churches' expansion into Appalachia.

The Methodist Movement

The Wesleyan/Holiness churches commonly identify themselves with a historical tradition of Christian perfection which had come down from the fathers of eastern spirituality, through John Wesley, American Methodism, and the nineteenth-century Holiness/higher-life movement. The declared mission of American Methodists always had been "to reform the nation and to spread Christian holiness over these lands." The new Wesleyan/Holiness churches believed that they were—if not in polity, certainly in doctrine—faithful trustees of the heritage of pioneer Methodism. The names of two of the larger Wesleyan/Holiness bodies, the Wesleyan Methodist Church and the Free Methodist Church, testify to their self-understanding as Methodist denominations. Subsequent studies have verified the essential integrity of the Wesleyanism of these, as well as other, Holiness churches, such as the Church of the Nazarene Church, which did not retain Methodism in their church names.[3]

The Holiness Movement

This strong Wesleyan character resulted from the fact that, in pre–Civil War America, as Methodism was becoming the largest church in America, it also was becoming the main locus for the rise of a renewal of the preaching of Christian holiness within the American churches. The focus of the new revival movement was the Wesleyan doctrine of Christian perfection. Methodism's founder had taught that, just as the unbeliever had been justified by faith through grace, so, by a similar consequent act of faith and grace, believers could be cleansed from their inbred "bent to sinning." This "entire sanctification" would free individuals from a "bent to sinning" and empower them to love God and neighbor, as they continue to grow in grace and "walk in the light" of God's will for them.

By the time of the Layman's Revival of 1858, Holiness Methodists, Oberlin's revivalistic Calvinists, and significant representations of Protestants of every other kind, made up a loosely organized Holiness movement with its own life within the prevailing denominational structures. In 1867, a group of Methodist ministers organized the National Campmeeting Association for the Promotion of Holiness. Through the successes of its well-publicized and well-attended national camp meetings, it led the movement to further expansion and diversification. Within fifteen years, hundreds of city, county, and state Holiness associations, supporting scores of Holiness evangelists sponsoring hundreds of summer camp meetings, blanketed the nation.[4]

By that time as well, the pastors who made up the Methodist- oriented National Committee found it more and more difficult to discipline the multiplying local associations. The revival now had reached far beyond Methodism; by 1875, through the prevailing evangelical revival network, it had spread to England, the Continent, and around the world.

Soon, however, it was no longer simply a Methodist matter. By 1880, a substrata of leadership and power arose which represented a more populist, antiestablishment, radical Holiness evangelism. These groups increasingly chafed under any discipline which seemed to restrict "the work of the Spirit." Issues such as divine or faith healing and Darbyite premillennialism, then being agitated in contemporary revivalism, became fixed features of Holiness religion. The National Committee declared these new issues to be "side issues" to its central focus on the promotion of Christian Holiness and prohibited their discussion from its national camp platforms. Such strictures were unsuccessful in the movement in general, however, and the revival became a significant bearer of each of these developments in the evangelical churches of the time.

As the end of the century approached, tensions within the movement and between the associations and the established denominations became exacerbated. More and more of the Holiness leaders called for the organization of Holiness churches to provide church homes for the thousands of converts of the revival. Consequently an initial period of institutionalization in the early 1880s saw the organization of the first Holiness churches out of this competing phase of the movement. The Church of God (Anderson, Indiana), the Independent Holiness Churches in Kansas and Missouri, the Holiness Church of Southern California and Arizona, and the Holiness Christian Church in Pennsylvania set the pattern for future institutionalization within the movement. The Salvation Army, rooted in the Wesleyan Holiness tradition in England, brought its "blood and fire" gospel to the United States in 1880, reinforcing the institutional strength of the Holiness revivalists.

At first, many Holiness leaders joined the established denominations in denouncing these Holiness "comeouters." By the end of the century, however, many Holiness "critics" themselves became part of a second and much larger exodus of revival forces from the established churches. Within a decade, they created the largest number of new churches organized in so short a period in American religious history. The Pentecostal Church of the Nazarene (later Church of the Nazarene), the Apostolic Holiness Union (later Pilgrim Holiness Church), the Churches of Christ in Christian Union, and a dozen or more smaller new Holiness bodies joined the churches of the first exodus. Together with other churches which had identified themselves clearly as Holiness churches, such as the Wesleyan Methodists, the Free Methodists, the Holiness yearly meetings of the Society of Friends (now the Evangelical Friends), the Mennonite Brethren in Christ, and the River Brethren, these groups make up what is commonly known as the Wesleyan/Holiness family of churches.

The Holiness exodus was not total, however. Many other Holiness adherents chose to continue to worship within their traditional churches, but also continued their support of the movement by retaining their membership in the interdenominational Holiness associations. From that point to the present, this intricate network of action has constituted the Holiness movement. This network facilitated the revival's rapid expansion into Appalachia and the rest of the South following the turn of the century.

The Pentecostal Movement

About ten years after the larger part of the Wesleyan/Holiness forces began to organize their own churches, some evangelists within the extensive and pluralistic network of Holiness associations moved toward a more eschatological understanding of the movement's mission. They were responding to expectations of a more dynamic witness to the baptism of the Holy Spirit than that accepted by those in the traditional movement who held to Wesley's inner assurance of the Spirit.[5] When the phenomenon of "speaking in tongues" was proclaimed as the only biblical "witness" to Spirit baptism, a new paradigm for understanding the Holiness revival led to the rise of a younger sibling of the Wesleyan/Holiness movement, one which ultimately coalesced as the Pentecostal movement.[6]

Holiness teaching always had allowed for the possibility of the miraculous gift of being able, for the evangelistic declaration of the gospel, to speak in a known language which one had not learned—but not in an unknown tongue as proof of a spiritual experience. Therefore, when the Pentecostal revivalists at Azusa Street Mission in Los Angeles began to claim that the gift of speaking in such a tongue constituted the only true witness to one's having been baptized with the Holy Spirit, most of the movement brought charges of deception, delusion, or heresy against them.

The common historical roots of both movements in the Holiness revival, and the retention by the pioneer Pentecostal revival of much of the older Holiness movement's ethos and many of its teachings, have contributed to a popular confusion of the two. In the South, Pentecostal adherents continued to teach the Wesleyan's emphasis on entire sanctification as the experience of heart purity, but they insisted that the baptism of the Holy Spirit, with power for mission and miracles, was a "third blessing." The worship style, the preaching, the hymns and gospel songs, the lifestyle, and the general ethos of the newer movement, too, closely paralleled those of the Holiness revival, in which many of its earliest leaders had been initiated.[7]

In the northern United States, where the older Holiness movement had been most strongly Wesleyanized, and where former Methodists dominated the membership of most of the Holiness churches, direct defections to the new Pentecostal revival were individual and few. But in the southern region, where the Holiness movement never had been as strong and was not supported as warmly by southern Episcopal Methodism, the defections, though small, were significant. Three budding new Wesleyan/Holiness churches, which already had formed out of the Holiness exoduses from the churches—the Pentecostal Holiness Church, the Church of God (Cleveland, Tennessee), and the Church of God in Christ, the largest of the newly organized black Holiness churches—explicitly moved from the Wesleyan/Holiness movement into the new Pentecostal movement.

The Holiness Revival

The evidence of any pre–Civil War Appalachian work explicitly related to the Holiness movement is very limited. Certainly Bishop Asbury and many of his early circuit riders who pioneered and maintained Methodism's ministry in the area were supporters of the church's central commitment to Wesleyan perfectionism. Asbury crossed the mountains more than fifty times as he shepherded pioneer Methodism. Until the end of the century, with its formation of numerous new Wesleyan/Holiness denominations, however, the Holiness story is part of the story of the Methodist Episcopal Church and later also that of the Methodist Episcopal Church South in Appalachia.[8]

The establishment of the educational work at Berea, Kentucky, by John G. Fee, a lifelong adherent of the Holiness movement,[9] and the missions of the Wesleyan Methodists in North Carolina were the only exceptions. The abolitionist perfectionism of the Wesleyans in the Piedmont of North Carolina, however, did not play any better than Fee's did in the knobs of Kentucky. Their ministers were mobbed, jailed, and finally driven out.[10]

The Post–Civil War Years

Twenty years before the general expansion of the newer Holiness churches into Appalachia at the beginning of the twentieth century, the Wesleyan Methodist Connection made its first post–Civil War appointments in North Carolina in 1871. Only two remnant abolitionist congregations had survived from its prewar work there. In 1879, a struggling North Carolina Conference was organized. Its bounds included the western mountains, but expansion beyond the foothills of the mountains was slow. The insistence of the northern conferences that blacks and whites organize in one conference limited the enthusiasm for the church among many southerners.[11]

It was not until 1893 that the Wesleyans' work in South Carolina, begun by the North Carolina Conference, was organized into an annual conference. Its churches centered in the northwestern corner of the state, beyond Greenville, including fledgling Wesleyan Methodist mountain missions just across the border in North Carolina, in Oconee, Buncombe, Henderson, and Jackson counties.

The earliest efforts were not formally planned or organized, but were the work of individuals, the first of them women, who were personally concerned for the people of the area. Some of the work was done by Wesleyans from the North who had moved into the Southern Mountains for health or family reasons. They labeled their ministry "fireside ministry," as they worked mainly in the homes of the region.[12]

Other than the Wesleyan Methodists, the Salvation Army was the only other Holiness organization to perform significant work in Appalachia before the turn of the century. Like those of the Wesleyans, the Army's first initiatives after 1885 were unsuccessful because of the attention they gave to the black population and the affront which the Army's female officers offered to widespread southern beliefs concerning the place of women.[13] The Salvation Army's traditional urban orientation also slowed its expansion into the Southern Highlands. It was not until 1886, when the Army began its "village warfare" and Salvationists began to work in the smaller mountain towns of western Maryland and across the border in West Virginia, that the Army became part of Wesleyan/Holiness work in Appalachia.[14]

The fortunes of the Holiness revival in the Methodist Episcopal Church South further hindered the expansion of the Wesleyans and the Salvationists, and later the newer Holiness churches as well. Acceptance of the Holiness revival had been much more limited in the southern church than in its Methodist Episcopal home in the North, as already has been indicated. In 1894, the southern church's general conference codified the long-simmering antagonism of some of its members toward the movement. The conference passed legislation which denied Holiness evangelists, appointed by the church, access to Methodist church buildings for Holiness meetings without pastoral approval. Moreover, it denied their right to hold meetings anywhere within parish bounds without such approval.[15]

1900 and After

Despite their earlier presence in Appalachia prior to 1900, the Wesleyan Methodists and the Salvation Army did not really begin their general expansion into Appalachia much before the expansion of the newer Holiness denominations into the area. In 1900, the still-struggling North Carolina Conference of the Wesleyan Methodists established a foothold in Asheville, when it received a congregation formed from converts responding to Holiness evangelism carried on by Holiness associations in the area. That mountain city had become a strong center of the revival. Other Wesleyan work in the area spread out of North Carolina to the valleys and mountains of southwestern Virginia and eastern Tennessee. The Wesleyans established a mission at Knoxville, in East Tennessee, in 1909, and another in Roanoke, Virginia, in 1914, the same year that the first church was organized from the early mountain work of the South Carolina Conference at Glenville, Jackson County, North Carolina. As the number of self-supporting congregations grew in each of these areas, new annual conferences were organized.

As for the Salvation Army, William Booth's extensive and well-publicized tour of the South in 1903 did little to spur the faltering prior efforts of the organization in the area. The Army never was able to fulfill his announcement, in Nashville, Tennessee, that a farm colony was to be established there. The Army's much-publicized Kentucky Mountain Brigade's mounted sweep into Breathitt County, Kentucky, at the height of that area's feuds, was only a little more successful. Although a local judge allowed that the feuding sides got closer to each other at the Army's open-air meeting than they ever had been before, the brigade's leader, Colonel Holz, decided that the area was too rural to support an Army corps, and no permanent work developed.[16] It was not until after 1920 that the work began to flourish in places like Roanoke, Salem, and Radford, Virginia, and not until 1935 that it moved deeper into the Great Smoky Mountains. In 1948, the Army moved into the mountains of North Georgia.[17]

The story of the newer Holiness denominations, which were just starting to shape their organizations and beginning their expansion across the Southeast and its Appalachian regions, was very similar to that of the churches described above, which had represented the movement there for more than twenty years. Around 1900, the older and the newer Holiness churches both gathered many of their new members from the ranks of the thousands of Holiness association members—Methodists, Baptists, Cumberland Presbyterians, Christians—who had become disenchanted with the established churches.

This movement from association to denominational affiliation is best illustrated in the history of the Pentecostal Mission at Nashville, Tennessee, and its eventual merger with the Pentecostal Church of the Nazarene. The Pentecostal Mission, a nondenominational Holiness association founded in 1897, was one of the most influential Holiness promotional centers throughout Tennessee, Western North Carolina, and South Carolina. By 1903, the association already had established twenty-seven missions, including several in the Cumberland Mountains.

J. O. McClurkan, a Cumberland Presbyterian Holiness evangelist, led the nondenominational movement with the constant support of John T. Benson, a Methodist lay leader. Benson, later noted for his southern gospel music publications, headed the publishing interests of the mission. A Bible institute, later known as Trevecca College; *Living Water,* a Holiness periodical; and social services for the area's poor were parts of its ministry. One of its affiliates established the Elhanan Training and Industrial Institute for the children and youth of the Marion, North Carolina, area.

In 1915, after a decade of vacillation as to whether to continue as a nondenominational associational mission or to become part of one of the newly developing Holiness denominations, the Pentecostal Mission finally merged with the Pentecostal Church of the Nazarene, the largest and strongest of the new "competing" churches. McClurkan's Trevecca College and other mission organizations became the basis for much of the Nazarene expansion in the Southeast and in Southern Appalachia.[18]

Much of the Holiness associational network in central and western North Carolina, on the other hand, became part of the Apostolic Holiness Union (later the Pilgrim Holiness Church), founded at God's Bible School in Cincinnati, Ohio, in 1897. Lucius B. Compton, a member of that union, was known as the "Mountain Evangelist." He had been born in the mountains of western North Carolina and had carried on pioneer Holiness evangelism in the mountains of Kentucky and North Carolina. In 1903, supported by the union's network of Holiness camp meetings, which spanned the states along the eastern coast from Maine to Florida, Compton established "Faith Cottage" for unwed mothers and later the Elida Orphanage in the mountains outside of Asheville, North Carolina. Asheville quickly became one of the region's main social work centers. Compton's vision of combining Christian evangelism with concern for the poor was inspired by one of the founders of the union, Quaker Holiness evangelist Seth Cook Rees, who organized inner-city missions and homes for unwed mothers in the same period.[19]

By the beginning of World War I, this "gathering up" of the sympathetic constituencies of the revival network was largely complete. Most of the ministers and laypeople in the associational network had become members of one or another of the Wesleyan/Holiness denominations, or of one of the Pentecostal/Holiness churches. The rest had decided to stay with their old mainline church homes.

From that period on, expansion of the movement was fueled by the stream of new Christian converts won to the new churches by its persistent evangelism. The experiential, individualistic, somewhat antiestablishment stance of many of the movement's evangelists suited the religious inclinations of many of their Appalachian listeners well. This posture gave a more favorable flavor to the novelty of their main theme of Wesleyan Holiness.[20]

At the same time, many in the region, with its characteristically rich "hard-shell Baptist" religious culture, reacted violently against the Holiness movement's Arminianism, its synergism, and the seemingly unrealistic demands of its strict evangelical Christian lifestyle. Most of the Holiness churches prohibited the use of alcoholic beverages, sometimes even the use of soft drinks. Dancing was forbidden, as were cards, games of chance, and membership in secret orders. Even so, the strongly moralistic, ethical, and optimistic Wesleyan message, proclaiming the possibility of "full salvation" by the cleansing and baptism of the Holy Spirit, won its way in the mountains. The advance of the movement across Appalachia and the wider South was steady, if not dramatic.[21]

Another factor, more important in the advance of these Holiness churches historically rooted in the northern Holiness tradition, was the strong competition generated by the rise of the equally, if not more, vigorous evangelism of the new Pentecostal revivalists. Among the mountains of South Carolina and North Georgia, the barely established Wesleyan/ Holiness movement and the pioneer elements of the Pentecostal/Holiness movement engaged in an intense battle for the loyalties of both the people of the area who were disenchanted with their established local churches, and thousands of unchurched individuals, to whom evangelists and pastors regularly preached.

Although the movement's direct losses to the newly organizing Pentecostal bodies were modest numerically, those early converts from the Holiness to the Pentecostal cause provided a strong leadership base for the eventual expansion of the new Pentecostal churches, which subsequently enjoyed unusual success in the South, particularly in Appalachia.[22]

Despite the ongoing competition between the two movements,[23] the membership of the Holiness churches swelled with new recruits. Arguably the most famous of these early converts was the World War I hero, Tennessee mountaineer Sgt. Alvin C. York, who became a member of the Churches of Christ in Christian Union.[24] The spiritual fervor, the experiential focus, the revivalistic preaching, and the freedom and informality of worship which characterized both traditions—all were attractive to many in Appalachia. New congregations organized by Nazarenes, Pilgrims, Wesleyan and Free Methodists, Salvationists, and Church of God evangelists, as well as by many smaller Holiness bodies, began to spring up everywhere. By 1930, Wesleyan/Holiness churches dotted the towns and villages of West Virginia, eastern Kentucky, western Virginia, East Tennessee, western North Carolina, western

South Carolina, and North Georgia. In the evangelical spectrum, the movement had positioned itself somewhere between the fundamentalists on one side and the Pentecostals on the other.[25]

The Interdenominational Network

We have noted the evangelistic efforts of the Holiness denominations which scattered their churches throughout Southern Appalachia, but nondenominational Wesleyan/Holiness agencies were at work in the Highlands as well. In 1940, Mae Perry DesJardins, a Holiness minister in eastern Kentucky, wrote, "To get to my home from Mount Carmel, you go through War Creek, Bloody Creek, then to Devil's Creek; beyond that is Hell Creek and still farther on is Hell-Fer-Sartin Creek, but it was on Devil's Creek that Jesus found me."[26]

DesJardins was a convert of the Kentucky Mountain Holiness Association, a group similar to those earlier associations which already were spreading the movement's perfectionist message through an extensive network within the established churches before the formal organization of the Holiness churches. After the new denominations formed, continuing cooperation between new Holiness denominations and the older Holiness associations created extensive revival networks which expanded the Holiness work in Appalachia. These networks were especially strong in southern Ohio and central Kentucky, areas surrounding two independent Holiness schools and publishing centers at Cincinnati, Ohio, and Wilmore, Kentucky.

Northern Methodist Martin Wells Knapp's God's Bible School in Ohio, and the extensive support for its interdenominational network generated by his popular *God's Revivalist,* supplied and supported evangelists of both the older associations and the newly forming Holiness denominations. In the early decades of the twentieth century, graduates of the school, supported by the same interdenominational network, established many of the first Wesleyan Methodist, Nazarene, and Pilgrim Holiness churches in Appalachian West Virginia, eastern Kentucky, and mountain Virginia.[27]

In 1890, John Wesley Hughes, a member of the Kentucky Conference of the Methodist Episcopal Church South, established Asbury College in Kentucky. Known briefly as Kentucky Holiness University, Asbury quickly became a national interdenominational center for Holiness education and evangelism. There Methodist minister Henry Clay Morrison and his Wilmore evangelists rallied a national Holiness constituency which remained active within the older churches. The influence of Morrison's widely read *Pentecostal Herald* and the Holiness literature produced by his

Pentecostal Publishing Company, helped to preserve a strong mainline Methodist ambiance in the revival. This center served as an informal but effective bridge of communication and cooperation between new and mainline Methodism and the new Holiness churches.[28]

This kind of continuing cooperation and interaction is illustrated most readily by the history of a group of Holiness mountain missions established in eastern Kentucky in the 1920s. Asbury College, with its geographical proximity to the area and its strong but unofficial attachment to the Methodist Episcopal Church South, as well as to the new Holiness churches, led to the eventual establishment of three Kentucky mountain Holiness mission and settlement centers.[29] All of these operated within the context of the changing religious and social work developing in the Appalachian region in the first decades of the twentieth century.[30]

The first product of this network was the Free Methodist mission and school at Oakdale, in Breathitt County, Kentucky. Elizabeth E. O'Conner, a Free Methodist missionary from Pennsylvania, taught children in her Oakdale home in 1919 and founded a grade school in 1920. Ten years later, a high school, with a strong vocational education department, was added.[31]

The second Holiness movement center in eastern Kentucky was the Mount Carmel community at Lawson, Kentucky. It was founded by Lela G. McConnell, an Asbury student from Pennsylvania and later an ordained deaconess in the Kentucky Conference of the Methodist Episcopal Church South. In 1924, she began missionary work at Lawson, outside of Jackson, the county seat of Breathitt County. Her work quickly developed into a full-time, independent "faith ministry" there. With support from the strongly Methodist Holiness constituency of Asbury College, as well as interested members of the Wesleyan/Holiness Churches, this eventually became the strongest of the movement's Appalachian ministries. It established the Carmel High School in 1925, the Kentucky Mountain Bible Institute in 1931, and numerous churches, Sunday schools, and preaching points throughout Breathitt and the surrounding counties. These eventually organized as the Kentucky Mountain Holiness Association.[32]

Only four years after the founding Mount Carmel, a similar mission center was begun at Taulbee, Kentucky, in neighboring Wolfe County. Initial mission work in the area had been started by Mount Carmel missionaries—women students from Asbury. Male students from the college joined them, erecting the first building at the Taulbee site in 1928. Charles and Gwendolyn Blanchard, students from Asbury College and Seminary, had committed themselves to Holiness evangelism and educational and social services.

As the work grew, the decades-old Holiness quandary—whether to work within interdenominational associations or within agencies of organized denominations—was played out at Zion's Hill. In 1929, as personnel and financial needs increased, the missionaries there decided to ask the Wesleyan Methodists to administer and support the center, rather than moving ahead in association with the Mount Carmel work. A graded school opened in 1930, and satellite Sunday schools in the surrounding communities became centers of evangelism and social services. One of these was a sizable Sunday school among the black population of nearby Negro Creek. As the need for private education and social services declined after World War II, the centers which had survived became part of the regular appointments of the Kentucky Wesleyan Methodist Conference.[33]

Toward the Future

The three-decade expansion of the Holiness denominations, agencies, and associations throughout Appalachia after 1900, briefly outlined above, unspectacular as it commonly was, constitutes the most important part of the Holiness churches' Appalachian story. Many of the special Appalachian missions which also had a social mission finally yielded their functions to various governmental social agencies. The strong continuing social ministries of the Salvation Army, the Kentucky Mountain Holiness Association centers in that state, and newer centers such as the Hope Hill Orphanage, established by the Church of God (Anderson, Indiana) at Hope, Kentucky, in 1962,[34] still are supported by the movement's constituencies.

The current active constituency of the Wesleyan/Holiness churches in Southern Appalachia numbers about two hundred thousand persons, and in all of Appalachia about twice that number.[35] These Appalachian districts of the Holiness denominations struggle with the general malaise which afflicts many rural churches in America. The Church of the Nazarene, which accounts for the largest number of Holiness constituents in the area, has suffered a very slight loss there since 1980. The Church of God (Anderson, Indiana) has seen much greater attrition, particularly in West Virginia, where its greatest concentration of churches in Southern Appalachia lies.[36] Although the Holiness churches within the United States and Canada continue to grow at a modest rate, about 1 to 2 percent annually, it seems unlikely that their rural Appalachian churches will play any part in such modest expansion. The current concentration of most growth of the Holiness movement within U.S. suburban areas, combined with the realities of the social and demographic changes taking place in Appalachia, give little promise that there will be significant future Holiness church growth in that region.

Notes

1. David B. Barrett, *World Christian Encyclopedia: A Comparative Study of Churches and Religions in the Modern World, 1900–1920* (New York: Oxford Univ. Press, 1982), 14. Barrett's listing of the Holiness tradition separates Salvation Army statistics from the Holiness Church category. J. Gordon Melton, *The Encyclopedia of American Religions* (Wilmington, Del.: McGrath Publishing Co., 1978), 1:199–242. Arthur C. Piepkorn, *Profiles in Belief: The Religious Bodies of the United States and Canada* (San Francisco: Harper and Row, 1979), 4:v–vii, 4:1–85, lists more than 60.

2. For example, see Berthold E. Schwarz, "A Study in Some Provocative Psychosomatic Phenomena," in *Appalachian Images in Folk and Popular Cultures*, ed. W. K. McNeil, 285–305 (Knoxville: Univ. of Tennessee Press, 1995), reprinted from *Psychiatric Quarterly* 34 (July 1960): 405–29. Schwarz regularly uses "Holiness" to refer to Pentecostals. Also note Shelby Lee Adams and Lee Smith, *Appalachian Portraits* (Jackson: Univ. Press of Mississippi, 1993). No mention is made either of Wesleyan/Holiness churches which distinctively identify themselves as "Holiness" churches, or of the larger Pentecostal/Holiness denominations which also differentiate their traditions from those of the two more radical groups represented by Adams and Smith.

3. Thomas C. Oden, *Doctrinal Standards in the Wesleyan Tradition* (Grand Rapids, Mich.: Zondervan Publishing Corp., 1988), 128, provides a succinct listing of the Wesleyan/Holiness churches and their place within pan-Methodism.

4. Fuller historical accounts and analysis of the Holiness revival and movement may be found in Melvin E. Dieter, *The Holiness Revival of the Nineteenth Century* (Lanham, Md.: Scarecrow Press, 1996); Charles E. Jones, *Perfectionist Persuasion: The Holiness Movement and American Methodism, 1867–1936* (Metuchen, N.J.: Scarecrow Press, 1974); and John Leland Peters, *Christian Perfection and American Methodism* (New York: Abingdon, 1956).

5. See Melvin E. Dieter, "Primitivism in the American Holiness Tradition," *Wesleyan Theological Journal* 30, no. 1 (Spring 1995): 55–77.

6. See Donald W. Dayton, *Theological Roots of Pentecostalism* (Grand Rapids, Mich.: Francis Asbury Press, 1987); and Vinson Synan, *The Holiness-Pentecostal Movement in the United States* (Grand Rapids, Mich.: William B. Eerdmans Publishing Co., 1971).

7. Melvin E. Dieter, "Wesleyan-Holiness Aspects of Pentecostal Origins: As Mediated Through the Nineteenth-Century Holiness Revival," in *Aspects of Pentecostal-Charismatic Origins*, ed. Vinson Synan, 55–80 (Plainfield, N.J.: Logos International, 1975).

8. Elmer T. Clark and Dorothy McConnell, eds., *The Methodist Church in the Appalachian Highlands*, Homeland Series (New York: Joint Division of Education and Cultivation, Board of Missions and Church Extension, Methodist Church, n.d.), 11–12.

9. Fee endorsed the call to convene an ecumenical General Holiness Assembly, held in Chicago in 1901, just before his death; S. B. Shaw, ed., *Echoes of the General Holiness Assembly Held in Chicago, May 3–13, 1901* (Chicago: S. B. Shaw, Publisher, [1901]), 12. See also Henry D. Shapiro, *Appalachia on Our Mind: The Southern Mountains and Mountaineers in the American Consciousness, 1870–1920* (Chapel Hill: Univ. of North Carolina, Press, 1978).

10. Roy S. Nicholson, *Wesleyan Methodism in the South: Being the History of Eighty-Six Years of Reform and Religious Activities in the South, as Conducted by the American Wesleyans* (Syracuse, N.Y.: Wesleyan Methodist Publishing House, 1933), 25–104.

11. Ira Ford McLeister and Roy Stephen Nicholson, *History of the Wesleyan Methodist Church in America* (Marion, Ind.: Wesley Press, 1959), 456–57, Nicholson, *Wesleyan Methodism in the South,* 121–26.

12. James Benjamin Hilson, *History of the South Carolina Conference of the Wesleyan Methodist Church of America: Fifty-five Years of Wesleyan Methodism in South Carolina* (Winona Lake, Ind.: Light and Life Press, 1950), esp. chap. 13, "Work in the Blue Ridge Mountains," 219–27. Also see Nicholson, *Wesleyan Methodism in the South,* 181–62; and Ina Gaines, *Wesleyan Methodism in the Blue Ridge Mountains* (Syracuse, N.Y.: Department of Home Missions of the Wesleyan Church of America, 1950), 3–19.

13. Allen Satterlee, *Sweeping Through the Land: A History of the Salvation Army in the United States* (Atlanta, Ga.: Salvation Army Supplies, 1989), 32–35, 38, 40, 59–60, 139–40.

14. Ibid., 36–38.

15. See Timothy L. Smith, *Called unto Holiness: The Story of the Nazarenes, the Formative Years* (Kansas City, Mo.: Nazarene Publishing House, 1962), 180–81, for the experience of B. F. Haynes, once editor of the *Tennessee Methodist* and later Holiness advocate and Nazarene minister.

16. Satterlee, *Sweeping through the Land,* 71–73.

17. Ibid., 137–40, 170–71.

18. For details of these developments, see Timothy L. Smith, *Called unto Holiness,* 180–99; and John T. Benson Jr., *Holiness, Organized or Unorganized: A History, 1898–1915, of the Pentecostal Mission, Inc., Nashville, Tennessee* (Nashville, Tenn.: Trevecca Press, 1977), 13–27.

19. For Compton's biography and the early history of these institutions, see John G. Patty, *Life of Lucius Bunyan Compton: The Mountain Evangelist* (Cincinnati, Ohio: Revivalist Press, 1914).

20. E.g., T. P. Roberts, *Highlights of My Life and Ministry* (Wilmore, Ky.: N.p., 1952); C. L. Wireman, *Kentucky Mountain Outlaw Transformed* (Apollo, Pa.: West Publishing Co., n.d.); John Clement, *The Experiences of a Blue Ridge Mountain Evangelist* (High Point, N.C.: N.p., 1936).

21. Nicholson, *Wesleyan Methodism in the South,* 174–75.

22. Ibid., 178–81; Satterlee, *Sweeping through the Land*, 106–7; Synan, *Pentecostal-Holiness Movement*, 75–80.

23. Charles L. Blanchard, *The Wesleyan Work in Kentucky* (Syracuse, N.Y.: Department of Home Missions of the Wesleyan Methodist Church, 1950), 7.

24. York headed the Alvin York Agricultural Institute, begun in his honor in Fentress County, Tenn. See Sam K. Cowan, *Sergeant York and His People* (New York: Funk & Wagnalls, 1922), 204–9, for a description of a typical service in York's congregation.

25. See an excellent summary in Satterlee, *Sweeping through the Land*, 105–7.

26. Mae Perry DesJardins, "Saved to Serve," in *Called of God in the Kentucky Hills* (Lawson, Ky.: Kentucky Mountain Holiness Association, 1940), 8.

27. Patty, *Life of Compton*, 63–91.

28. Roberts, *Highlights of My Life*, 3–18; Wireman, *Kentucky Mountain Outlaw*, 12.

29. Fred J. Hood, "Kentucky," in *Religion in the Southern States: A Historical Study*, ed. Samuel S. Hill (Macon, Ga.: Mercer Univ. Press, 1983), 118–19.

30. Shapiro, *Appalachia on Our Mind*, 143–56.

31. *In the Land of Breathitt: A Guide to the Feud Country*, comp. Workers of the Writer's Program of the Works Project Administration in the State of Kentucky, American Guide Series (Northport, N.Y.: Bacon Percy and Daggett, 1941), 122–23, 140–41.

32. *In the Land of Breathitt*, 123, 138–40. Lela G. McConnell, *Faith Victorious in the Kentucky Mountains: The Story of 22 Years of Spirit-Filled Ministry* (Berne, Ind.: Economy Printing Concern, 1960); and *The Power of Prayer Plus Faith* (N.p: N.p., 1952).

33. For summary histories of the work, see Blanchard, *Wesleyan Work*, 3–26; and *Wesleyan Missionary*, April 1930 and subsequent issues.

34. "Being Built on Hope," *Bath County Outlook*, rpt. in *Hope Hill Messenger* 1, no. 3 (Dec. 1962): 1.

35. Clifford A. Grammich Jr., *Appalachian Atlas: Maps of the Churches and People of the Appalachian Region* (Knoxville, Tenn.: Commission on Religion in Appalachia, 1994), 70–73. While Grammich uses official membership statistics to provide a total of 217,630 Holiness adherents in all of Appalachia, the 200,000 figure used in the text is a more realistic estimate for Southern Appalachia alone. The total presence of Holiness adherents in all of Appalachia probably approaches 500,000 members.

36. Ibid., 41–43.

Chapter 16

Holiness in the Highlands: A Profile of the Church of God

Donald N. Bowdle

Pentecostalism is a coat of many colors.[1] No one person ever should presume to speak for the movement, nor any single denomination pretend fully to represent it, so diverse is it in both thought and practice. International in its range, Pentecostalism wears many faces, speaks a variety of languages, and exhibits a multiplicity of styles of expression. Perhaps for these reasons, no adequate *Kulturgeschichte* of the movement is likely to be written.[2]

Notwithstanding this diversity, Pentecostalism, wherever and however it is practiced, does evince certain commonalities. These shared distinctives transcend a panorama of differences that are doctrinal, devotional, and denominational in nature, defining the movement more clearly within the parameters of mission and motivation. Dynamic and pragmatic at its core, Pentecostalism addresses the daily existential concerns of the disenfranchised, offering hope and purpose to those who attend to its message.

The Church of God is the oldest continuing Pentecostal denomination in the United States. Indigenous to Appalachia, and maintaining its numerical and material strength in that region, the Church of God represents a dominant strain of religion in the mountains and provides a laboratory for populist religious expression. Focusing upon the Appalachian experience, this essay inquires into the denomination's heritage; profiles its history, thought, and worship; and projects an agenda for a church reluctantly but obviously in transition.

The Heritage

The Church of God emerged from the religious milieu of the 1880s. This period of ferment in the churches, no less than in the nation, lacked to a significant degree the spiritual and theological foundations that would have been provided by an aggressive and self-confident *antebellum* evangelical consensus. Tenuous and fragile, without a fundamental cohesion, the times were rife with conflicts, secessions, and new church formations.

How does one account for the holiness-separatist phenomenon during the waning years of the nineteenth century? A number of explanations have been posited, each with some justification, by a variety of scholars.[3] No single reason suffices, however, because complex issues defy easy resolution. The most plausible—but relatively unexplored—scenario is (1) a *reaction* against naturalism, socialism, "Romanism," and Protestant theological liberalism, as represented by the Social Gospel movement; (2) a *reaffirmation* of the devotional life vis-à-vis the perceived spiritual impoverishment of those bodies from which the defections occurred and their attendant resistance to revivalism; and (3) a *reconstruction* within some segments of conservative-evangelical scholarship to accommodate a premillennial eschatology.

Reaction, reaffirmation, and reconstruction—a complex of reasons for the Holiness schisms—became, incrementally, a procedural method for an effort that resonated with an ever wider cross-section of American denominational life. But no monolithic model emerged, for not all quarters, whether of Wesleyan or Keswick persuasions, responded proportionally.[4] Generalizations must be tentative at best, but the pattern developing was that, while the former prioritized according to things of the spirit, the latter proceeded from matters of the mind. Even so, two concerns in tandem became defining points of the Holiness enterprise at large: premillennial eschatology as a message and revivalism as its medium. Not even Appalachia, for all its remoteness, was beyond the reach of the Holiness mission.

Indeed, Appalachia already had proved fertile soil for revivals of religion.[5] The most celebrated of those, perhaps, was the outbreak of "enthusiasm" at Cane Ridge, Kentucky, at the turn of the nineteenth century. Many historians regard that revival as a "frontier phase" of the Second Great Awakening. One can only imagine that the Kentucky ex-

perience represented a plethora of similar transdenominational awakenings—localized, unheralded, and largely undocumented—throughout the Southern Highlands.

The Holiness revivals occurring later in the century, then, stood,
dispositionally, in the tradition of those phenomena. Although by no
means peculiar to Appalachia, "Holiness" both affected, and was itself
affected by, mountain mores. Such were the antecedents of the schism
out of which the Church of God was born.

History

In 1884 Richard G. Spurling, dissatisfied with the current trend away
from the Bible and with the formalities of public worship, committed
himself to prayer and to a renewed study of the Scriptures and church
history. He was joined by his son, Richard G. Spurling Jr., and several
other like-minded believers interested in revitalizing the worship experience and restoring an emphasis on holy living. Two years later, discouraged, in turn, by the apathy, resistance, and eventual hostility encountered from local denominations, the Spurlings led a group of six to
form a Christian Union at Barney Creek in Monroe County, Tennessee. As one historian has put it, a vague discontent had crystallized into
specific objections, and then a bold course of action had been pursued.[6]

The name "Christian Union" well identified the intent and scope
of the fledgling body, whose adherents considered themselves more an
association than a new denomination. They had deemed separation the
only viable alternative to the continuing accommodations made by the
existing churches to their culture. Now Spurling, himself a Baptist, regarded the union as "a reformation movement" designed "to restore
primitive Christianity and bring about the union of all denominations."[7]

During the first decade of its existence, the Christian Union made
only negligible gains. But in 1896, three persons,[8] a Methodist and two
Baptists with a Wesleyan understanding of holiness,[9] impacted the
mountain region by their fervent preaching and clarion calls to an experience of sanctification. Through their indirect mediation, a merger
of the Christian Union with a comparable seeking group at Camp
Creek in Cherokee County, North Carolina, was effected. With this
amalgamation, the center of the Christian Union became Camp Creek,
and the younger Spurling (the elder having died) shared leadership responsibilities of the growing body with W. F. Bryant, yet another layman pressed into ministerial service.

The revival of 1896 was marked by unusual demonstrations of the

Holy Spirit, reminiscent of frontier days. For the first time within the Christian Union, and issuing from long seasons of fervent prayer, about one hundred persons spoke in other tongues. The experience had not been sought, nor was it understood until the Scriptures were consulted and the experience discovered to be of divine authenticity. Two important observations are instructive here: (1) the Christian Union was a Holiness body (1886) ten years before it became a Pentecostal body (1896); and (2) those instances of glossolalia occurred a full decade prior to the Azusa Street Revival in Los Angeles (1906), popularly regarded as the beginning of the modern Pentecostal movement.[10]

Gains accruing from the revival of 1896 and subsequent evangelistic efforts soon were neutralized from within by fanaticism and false teaching, and from without by continuing hostility. In May 1902, the body was reorganized according to a simple plan of protective government and thereupon renamed the Holiness Church. By 1906, it would convene its first General Assembly near Camp Creek and launch an order of centralized government, judicial rather than legislative in nature, and a democratic polity to serve the growing network of congregations; in 1907, it would adopt the biblical name "Church of God," while maintaining the intentions of earlier nomenclature: the ideal of Christian union and the proclamation of holiness.

A new era began in 1903, when the body accepted into membership, and eventually into executive leadership, a colporteur (that is, a peddler of religious books) of the American Bible Society and the American Tract Society named A. J. Tomlinson, a Quaker from Indiana. Tomlinson moved from Camp Creek to Cleveland, Tennessee, the following year, uniting with the Christian Union a congregation which he pastored near there. Gradually, the focus of the group shifted to the more populous Cleveland, where its headquarters have remained[11] and from which center the movement has permeated the mountain culture.

Thus the roots of Pentecostal belief were planted and nurtured in Appalachian soil, during the Holiness revivals of the latter half of the nineteenth century. "In reality, the Pentecostal emphasis is simply an extension of the earlier holiness concepts. Many of its adherents stoutly maintain that Pentecostal and holiness precepts are inseparable, and regard themselves different among holiness believers only in the further spiritual experience they have received."[12] This is not to imply that the Church of God and Pentecostalism are coextensive, but rather to assert the denomination's historical priority in the field.[13]

Theology

It has been suggested, pejoratively, that Pentecostalism is an experience in search of a theology. The earliest constituents of the Church of God did, indeed, take their faith seriously, as evidenced by commitment to the Scriptures as the very Word of God. Evangelism, however, was quite the top priority, given limited means and an urgent message. An examination and codification of the faith were forthcoming, nevertheless, sometimes deliberately and at other times defensively, often in an *ad hoc* fashion but always painfully slowly. Regrettably, evangelism and biblical and theological scholarship frequently were perceived as being opposed.

From the time of the first General Assembly (1906), the Church of God has affirmed the authority of the Bible. Although it did not immediately set forth a roster of teachings, that General Assembly stated that "our articles of faith are inspired and given us by the Holy Ghost and written in the New Testament which is our rule of faith and practice."[14] The twenty-fifth General Assembly (1930) reflected and enlarged upon that commitment: "The Church of God stands now *as it has always stood,* for the whole Bible, rightly divided, and for the New Testament as the only rule for government and discipline . . . , our only rule of faith and practice."[15] The forty-second General Assembly (1948) offered a further word on Scripture, that time in the context of a fourteen-point Declaration of Faith. The initial article read: "We believe in the verbal inspiration of the Bible."[16] It was clear that the Church of God had overcome its antipathy to "man-made creeds."

At no time did Church of God constituents regard themselves as other than simple orthodox Christian believers, quite comfortable in affirming the "five fundamentals": the inerrancy of Scripture; the deity and virgin birth of Christ; the vicarious atonement of Christ; the bodily resurrection of Christ; and the literal return of Christ.[17] No "distinctive" superseded or supplanted the gospel and Lordship of Christ, for Christ remained the absolute center of divine revelation. Those commitments, then, rendered the Church of God thoroughly Protestant and unwaveringly conservative and evangelical, very much in tune with Appalachian religion at large.

But there was a discordant note, a distinctive which, to Church of God people, enhanced one's vision of Christ rather than diverting one's attention. Sought by some as a "second blessing" and by others as a "third,"[18] baptism in the Holy Spirit (or Spirit baptism) was regarded as the dynamic whereby the gospel of Christ could be proclaimed more effectively. The teaching of premillennial eschatology,[19] specifically, injected an urgency into Christian witness, and baptism in the Holy Spirit accommodated its dissemination. Premillennialism, intensely appealing to the depressed and disinherited, and the doctrine of subsequence,[20] although of more recent vintage, were, in themselves, hardly offensive to many mainline and most Holiness believers, but the stigmatizing "tongues" attending the experience were challenged by both groups, from a variety of vantage points. Some of the tension still remains.

The best evidence of the maturing of the Church of God is its acceptance of an invitation to charter membership in the National Association of Evangelicals, an effort at evangelical cooperation launched in 1942. While some Church of God ministers questioned the propriety of such close association with non-Pentecostals, a vast majority realized immediately the merits of such a relationship. Applauding the decision, Charles W. Conn writes:

> There is but a hair's breadth between the current of conviction and the shoals of bigotry. Many a church has begun with the simple faith that its organization is divinely ordained, only to end behind walls of its own ecclesiolatry. An aggressively evangelistic church is in danger of such absorption with its own affairs that it loses its outside perspective and looks askance at all others than itself. Sometimes this is done to the point of doubting the sincerity, fitness, or divine acceptance of others. The proposed association was a great step toward breaking down such barriers of distrust and misunderstanding.[21]

A fourteen-article Declaration of Faith was produced in 1948, as the denomination further tested the principle of "cooperation without compromise" in the spirit of the National Association of Evangelicals. Then in its sixty-second year, the Church of God was too old and too diverse to reach unanimity on details, so the document was intended to be brief and imprecise, but consensual—and remains so.[22]

Biblical and theological scholarship has developed belatedly and unevenly in the Church of God, covering the spectrum from suspicion to toleration to cultivation. Notwithstanding periods of passivity and "pockets" of resistance, generally there has been a positive predisposition toward learning. During the decade of the 1970s, four significant efforts combined both to preserve the heritage and to enlarge the vision of the church: the founding of a Society for Pentecostal Studies,[23] the establishment of a Pentecostal Research Center,[24] expansion of programs at Lee University,[25] and the founding of a theological seminary.[26]

Both continuity and discontinuity with the past characterize the posture of modern Pentecostalism. The Church of God maintains a continuity with the Reformation tradition of the sixteenth century and is not complimented by any designation as a "third force"[27]—alongside Roman Catholicism and Protestantism—that would suggest it is an alternative form of Christianity. It does, however, proclaim a fundamental discontinuity with the Holiness tradition specifically, for, while the denomination reaffirmed "holiness to be God's standard of living for His people," it insisted on "the baptism with the Holy Ghost subsequent to a clean heart" and "speaking with other tongues as the Spirit gives utterance and that it is the initial evidence of the baptism of the Holy Ghost."[28] In reality, the Pentecostal emphasis is but an extension of the earlier Holiness concepts. Church of God believers recognize that Pentecostalism and Holiness are inseparable and regard themselves as different from other Holiness believers only in the further spiritual experience they graciously have received.

Worship

Commitment to Scripture generated a burden to receive whatever it promised and a passion to avoid whatever it forewarned. For that reason, the Church of God offered, in 1911, a roster of "prominent teachings."[29] Doctrinal commitments therein would not be altered, while practical commitments would receive occasional modification, addition, and restatement. The Church of God worship experience was designed to affirm and impress those commitments through proof-text preaching, by a "feeling theology," and in the call to a holy life.

Who are the congregants? The Church of God is a denomination predominantly of small congregations.[30] Certain common and predictable characteristics, therefore, identify the corporate life of these small bodies, in addition to the aforementioned appeal to uniformity of thought and practice. In a typical Church of God worship service one would find, for example, a disarming pluralism.[31] Classes and races mingle comfortably, wherever such diversity is reflected in the life of the community at large, and especially so where the exigencies of daily living are uniformly hard and unrelenting. A familial spirit prevails, furthermore, as brothers and sisters in the Lord not only worship together but continue to care for one another long after their dismissal into the wider world. The unsaved and unaffiliated are welcomed to their company, too, becoming objects of prayer and targets of evangelism in the continuing life of the congregation.

What characterizes the worship? With few significant exceptions, Church of God congregational worship is uniform and predictable. Appalachian origins and nurture have been impressed indelibly upon the movement, and the mountain style prevails at large. Indeed, the Church of God has, with apparent intentionality, exported around the world an "Appalachianization" of the worship experience, often mistaking style for spirituality.

The typical worship service in the Church of God is simple, informal, and not always conducted with the dignity appropriate thereto. Few pastors would project an order of worship in a printed bulletin, lest they presume to "quench the Spirit." Noncreedal and nonliturgical, the worship is marked by spontaneity of hand-clapping during the singing of gospel songs and choruses, and by impassioned preaching, punctuated by verbal feedback and interrupted by the demonstration of spiritual gifts, notably speaking in tongues and interpretation of tongues. Concert prayer, prayer for the sick, and altar invitations to the unsaved and "backslidden" among the number are routine fare in these meetings.

Like Pentecostals generally, adherents of the Church of God insist that worship should influence the believer's lifestyle. A positive correlation is attempted, then, between worship and walk, for one's worship experience creates a mind-set that informs her or his practical expression. Democratization and participation in the church service are translated into a strict personal ethic, separatist in nature, when one leaves the sanctuary to live in "the world." Traditionally this ethic has been interpreted as forbidding use of alcohol, tobacco, and narcotics; wearing excessive jewelry and cosmetics; and indulging in such "worldly amusements" as gambling, dancing, and movie attendance.

While personal piety vis-à-vis a premillennial eschatology is a prominent theme in Church of God preaching, one should not conclude that a "fortress mentality" prevails. Individual introspection in light of Christ's imminent return has both primary and secondary ends. The primary end is one's own salvation; the secondary end, related to baptism in the Holy Spirit, is a gift of grace pursuant to the devotional life, as an enhancement of one's witness so that others will be drawn to Christ.

An Agenda

Well into its second century now, and reaping an increase in human and material resources, the Church of God has a promising future in "kingdom work." A collage of traditions and aspirations, the denomination must commit to transcending its own inhibiting conventions if it would respond responsibility and decisively to global opportunities in ministry. Even with so enlarged a vision, however, the Church of God remains no less accountable to the Appalachian Highlands which bore and nurtured it than it was in any yesteryear. Appreciative of its past, yet avoiding any narcissism of heritage, the church cannot but reaffirm what is best in that regional culture while manifesting sensitivity and discrimination respecting changes which it would propose or with which it would identify.

Approximately one-third of the members of the Church of God in the U.S. and Canada live in Southern Appalachia.[32] What initiatives might the denomination consider to enrich and enhance its ministry to the region? With few significant exceptions, the Church of God in Appalachia well represents the Church of God at large; therefore, an agenda offered for that part would apply generally to the whole.

An initiative deserving high priority relates to the informal educational enterprise. The general church well could launch a vigorous program directed at educating laypeople theologically. That there should be such an urgent need is contradictory to the denomination's high view of Scripture. The church's ministry in this regard would be to assist laypeople in discerning the theological meaning of what they are doing. The benefits for discipleship and Christian formation would be enormous; and, having been instructed in his or her faith, the layperson then would be prepared to relate that faith to the wider dimensions of life and mission in fresh, authentic, and relevant terms. An initiative of this nature would, furthermore, contribute to preparing laypeople, including women and ethic minorities, for general and local administrative services, which the denomination has been extremely loath to open up to other than its white male constituency. The Church of God has been conspicuously delinquent in such educational and service responsibilities, although the biblical mandate is sufficiently clear.

Another related concern involves a potential reassessment of the glossocentrism that continues to define the Church of God—and other Pentecostal denominations, for that matter. Speaking in tongues has too often been regarded as the consummatory salvific activity, rather than as a dynamic facilitating a fuller expression of Christian witness. In fact, the church well might consider a program whereby to reorient its constituency to what amounts to a more biblical perspective on the whole of pneumatology. This is not to suggest any less commitment to a Pentecostal posture; it is, instead, a more deliberate focusing upon the wider range of what the Holy Spirit has promised to effect, both in and through the believer. Baptism in the Holy Spirit remains the divine power whereby to discharge the Great Commission, but glossocentrism diverts one's attention from both the balanced spiritual life and the urgent responsibilities of Christian service.[33]

A secularization of holiness has become the spiritual "Achilles' heel" of the current Pentecostal denominationalism. The compromise with culture which it represents ultimately will prove a liability to those who fail to discern it and lack the will to address it. This condition is manifested by all those who, substituting style for substance, measure effectiveness in kingdom work in terms of numbers, finances, buildings, and programs. Far from an appeal to "the good old days" when legalism prevailed, this is a call to a maturity in worship that denies the "glitz" of much media Pentecostalism, a responsibility in stewardship of resources that is indicative of social concern, and a commitment truly to seek and to save the lost. The urgency of the times, the enormity of the task, and the terror of final accountability require no less.

Theological education of laity, discipleship formation, inclusion of women and ethnic minorities in administrative services, stewardship of social concern, pursuit of a balanced spirituality, denial of a distracting glossocentrism, repentance of any debilitating secularization of holiness—such are the matters which the Church of God must address with great intentionality. To do so can only enhance holistic and relevant ministry; not to do so well could render it, as a Pentecostal denomination, merely a curious footnote in the history of religion in America.

Pentecost means *harvest*—there is no mistaking the symbolism. For more than a century now, the Church of God has been reaping a spiritual harvest in Appalachia, investing in its people, its culture, and its institutions. Respectful of its Highlands heritage, the denomination is poised for even greater service to the region as each successive generation engages the distinctive language of Appalachia, the parlance of the gospel, and the art of translation.

Notes

1. J. S. Whale employed the expression "coat of many colors" in reference to the diversity of modern Protestantism. Here it applies to Pentecostalism.
2. See Walter J. Hollenweger, *The Pentecostals* (London: SCM Press, 1972).
3. Sydney E. Ahlstrom, *A Religious History of the American People* (New Haven, Conn.: Yale Univ. Press, 1972), offers "staid and predictable church ways" that replaced the "more earnest and old-time fervor," as well as a "tide of 'apostasy'"

(824). Martin E. Marty, *Righteous Empire: The Protestant Experience in America* (New York: Dial Press, 1970), projects "premillennialism" as the doctrine at issue (216). H. Shelton Smith, Robert T. Handy, and Lefferts A. Loetscher, *American Christianity; An Historical Interpretation with Documents* (New York: Charles Scribner's Sons, 1963), refer to "pietism" and "apocalypticism" as sources of discontent (2:314, 2:315). William Warren Sweet, *The Story of Religion in America* (New York: Harper and Row, 1950), assigns "economic cleavage" as virtually the sole motivation for the separations in question (352). Richard Hofstadter, *Anti-Intellectualism in American Life* (New York: Vintage Books, 1962), is quick to identify "anti-intellectualism" as the paramount precipitating principle (81 ff.).

Most sympathetic to the Holiness enterprise, Vinson Synan notes that "representing as it did a conservative movement to preserve a religious way of life of an earlier era, the holiness break constituted the religious counterpart of the political and economic revolt of the populists." Synan, *The Holiness-Pentecostal Movement in the United States* (Grand Rapids, Mich.: Wm. B. Eerdmans Publishing Co., 1971), 219; and Mickey Crews, *The Church of God; A Social History* (Knoxville: Univ. of Tennessee Press, 1990).

4. Keswick influence was stamped indelibly upon an emerging fundamentalism in America. See Vinson Synan, ed., *Aspects of Pentecostal-Charismatic Origins* (Plainfield, N.J.: Logos International, 1975).

5. See Bernard A. Weisberger, *They Gathered at the River* (Chicago: Quadrangle Books, 1966); and William Warren Sweet, *Revivalism in America* (New York: Abingdon Press, 1944).

6. Charles W. Conn, *Like a Mighty Army: A History of the Church of God, 1886–1995,* definitive ed. (Cleveland, Tenn.: Pathway Press, 1996), 11.

7. Ibid., 12 (note), citing Elmer T. Clark, *The Small Sects in America,* rev. ed. (Nashville, Tenn.: Abingdon-Cokesbury, 1949), 100.

8. These laypeople were William Martin, a Methodist, and Joe M. Tipton and Milton McNabb, Baptists. See Conn, *Like a Mighty Army,* 22.

9. Conn's comment that "the doctrine of sanctification is distinctly Arminian, and Arminianism rather than Calvinism has produced the greatest revival movements in this nation, especially in the South" (26) is arguable on both counts.

10. Robert Mapes Anderson, *Vision of the Disinherited: The Making of American Pentecostalism* (New York: Oxford Univ. Press, 1979), p. 250, n. 29, dismisses claims of glossolalia before the Azusa Street phenomenon as "suspect because they post-date that revival."

11. For the contribution of G. B. Cashwell, fresh from the Azusa Street Revival, to Tomlinson's own baptism in the Holy Spirit, see Conn, *Like a Mighty Army,* 83, 84; for events culminating in the establishing of the Tomlinson Church of God, later known as the Church of God of Prophecy, see 197–220.

12. Conn, *Like a Mighty Army,* xxv.

13. See also L. Howard Juillerat, comp. and ed., "A Brief History of the Church of God," introduction to *Book of Minutes* (Cleveland, Tenn.: Church of God Publishing House, 1922); and E. L. Simmons, *History of the Church of God* (Cleveland, Tenn.: Church of God Publishing House, 1938).

14. *Book of Minutes* (Cleveland, Tenn.: Church of God Publishing House, 1906), 1.

15. *Book of Minutes* (Cleveland, Tenn.: Church of God Publishing House, 1930), 23.

16. *Book of Minutes* (Cleveland, Tenn.: Church of God Publishing House, 1948), 188.

17. These tenets issued from the 1895 Niagara Bible Conference, a convocation that was to define the fundamentalist movement.

18. Pentecostal churches have sustained significant debate on the doctrine of sanctification. Those in the Keswick tradition have regarded sanctification as a progressive work, an extension of salvation, rendering the "second blessing" a baptism in the Holy Spirit in terms of empowerment, whereas those in the Wesleyan orientation have considered sanctification an instantaneous act, an experience separate from salvation, a "second blessing" in terms of purity, and baptism in the Holy Spirit a "third blessing," an empowerment. It is noteworthy that, before the emergence of tongues-speaking, the term "Pentecostal" was employed widely by Holiness people to mean sanctification. See Donald W. Dayton, *Theological Roots of Pentecostalism* (Grand Rapids, Mich.: Zondervan Publishing House, 1987); Melvin E. Dieter et al., *Five Views on Sanctification* (Grand Rapids, Mich.: Zondervan Publishing House, 1987); and John A. Sims, *Our Pentecostal Heritage* (Cleveland, Tenn.: Pathway Press, 1995).

19. Premillennial eschatology, the legacy of J. Nelson Darby, was imported from Keswick, England, in 1875 by Dwight L. Moody and popularized via publication of the *Scofield Reference Bible* in 1909.

20. The doctrine of subsequence relates to the Pentecostal interpretation of such passages as John 7:37–39 and Acts 1:8, 2:4. While Pentecostals acknowledge that the believer is indwelt by the Holy Spirit, they insist that a further experience in the Holy Spirit, a Spirit baptism subsequent to regeneration, is taught in the New Testament. Regeneration relates to salvation, Spirit baptism to service.

21. Conn, *Like a Mighty Army*, 312.

22. The Church of God Declaration of Faith reads, in full:

We believe:
1.   In the verbal inspiration of the Bible.
2.   In one God, eternally existing in three persons; namely, the Father, Son, and Holy Ghost.
3.   That Jesus Christ is the only begotten Son of the Father, conceived of the Holy Ghost and born of the Virgin Mary. That Jesus was crucified, buried and raised from the dead. That he ascended into heaven and is today at the right hand of the Father as the intercessor.

4. That all have sinned and come short of the glory of God, and that repentance is commanded of God for all and [is] necessary for forgiveness of sins.

5. That justification, regeneration, and the new birth are wrought by faith in the blood of Jesus Christ.

6. In sanctification subsequent to the new birth, through faith in the blood of Christ, through the Word, and by the Holy Ghost.

7. Holiness to be God's standard of living for His people.

8. In the baptism of the Holy Ghost subsequent to a clean heart.

9. In speaking with other tongues as the Spirit gives utterance, and that it is the initial evidence of the baptism of the Holy Ghost.

10. In water baptism by immersion, and all who repent should be baptized in the name of the Father, and of the Son, and of the Holy Ghost.

11. Divine healing is provided for all in the atonement.

12. In the Lord's Supper; and washing of the saints' feet.

13. In the premillennial second coming of Jesus. First, to resurrect the righteous dead and to catch away the living saints to Him in the air. Second, to reign on the earth a thousand years.

14. In the bodily resurrection; eternal life for the righteous and eternal punishment for the wicked.

Conn, *Like a Mighty Army*, 337. For explication, see, e.g., French L. Arrington, *Christian Doctrine: A Pentecostal Perspective*, 3 vols. (Cleveland, Tenn.: Pathway Press, 1992–94), and Donald N. Bowdle, *Redemption Accomplished and Applied* (Cleveland, Tenn.: Pathway Press, 1972).

23. The Society for Pentecostal Studies originated in 1971. A cooperative effort, it was founded to provide a forum for scholars in the Pentecostal and charismatic traditions.

24. The Pentecostal Research Center was founded by Lee University and its Alumni Association in 1971.

25. Lee University, established in 1918, currently enrolls approximately 3,000 students from around the world.

26. Launched in 1975, the Church of God Theological Seminary, autonomous and housed separately from but adjacent to Lee University, enjoys a mutually supportive relationship with the university. The seminary is a member of the Appalachian Ministries Educational Resource Center.

27. "Third Force" was first assigned by Henry P. Van Dusen in "Caribbean Holiday," *Christian Century* 72 (Aug. 17, 1955): 946–48.

28. Declaration of Faith, Art. 7–9.

29. *Book of Minutes* (Cleveland, Tenn.: Church of God Publishing House, 1911).

30. By January 1996, there were 6,175 Churches of God in the U.S. and Canada. Of that number, 1,662 reported membership of 50 or less, and 2,454 reported an average of 50 or less in morning worship service (from Department of Business and Records, Church of God International Offices, Cleveland, Tenn.).

31. By January 1996, there were 515 black Churches of God in the U.S. and Canada, with a combined membership of 44,800; and 453 Hispanic churches, with membership of 29,247 (from Department of Business and Records, Church of God International Offices, Cleveland, Tenn.). A few other ethnic congregations exist as well.

32. By January 1996, the worldwide membership of the Church of God was approximately 4,060,000. Some 752,000 resided in the U.S. and Canada, with approximately 265,000 in Southern Appalachia. (From Department of Business and Records, Church of God International Offices, Cleveland, Tenn.).

     Steven J. Land suggests that, at this point in the history of the Church of God, "one of her most promising features is the majority of members who are outside the United States. They can best lift up the needs of the poor and oppressed," becoming, in effect, "the salvation of the Church in North America from the idols of affluence." ("A Stewardship Manifesto for a Discipling Church," in *The Promise and the Power: Essays on the Motivations, Developments, and Prospects of the Ministries of the Church of God,* ed. Donald N. Bowdle [Cleveland, Tenn.: Pathway Press, 1980], 313.)

33. Pentecostals would do well to listen to the wise and responsible counsel of friends in the wider evangelical community. Richard Lovelace, "Baptism in the Holy Spirit and the Evangelical Tradition," in *Faces of Renewal,* ed. Paul Elbert (Peabody, Mass.: Hendrickson Publishers, 1988), 210, for example, correctly reminds us that the main criterion for Pentecostal activity is the presence of the Holy Spirit in renewing power, not the single gift of tongues. Indeed, seizing upon every individual or group that has legitimized speaking in tongues as their honorable precursor has put contemporary Pentecostals in some rather strange company. According to Lovelace, Pentecostalism is rooted in "the tradition of renewing activism which runs from patristic spirituality up through the Reformers." He suggests, furthermore, that "Pentecostals and Charismatics find their strongest ancestry not only in John Wesley but in the other great leaders of the Evangelical awakenings, whether or not these leaders promoted glossolalia." ("Baptism in the Holy Spirit and the Evangelical Tradition," in *Faces of Renewal,* ed. Paul Elbert [Peabody, Mass.: Hendrickson Publishers, 1988], 210.) Cf. James H. Smylie, "Testing the Spirits in the American Context: Great Awakenings, Pentecostalism, and the Charismatic Movement," *Interpretation* 33 (Jan. 1979): 32–46.

Chapter 17

Catholic Mission and Evangelization

Lou F. McNeil

When one's thinking begins with the parish and its members, rather than the gospel itself, it is likely that ministry and planning will not get beyond the parish and its membership. This has been the problem frequently confronting Catholicism: to free itself of the restrictions it has placed upon the availability of full ministry to its potential and actual constituencies. This myopia concerning the larger possibilities of ministry has severely hampered Catholicism's ministry and presence in Appalachia.

The first part of this chapter examines the early period of Catholicism in the United States and the influence of pre-Emancipation (i.e., Catholic emancipation in England and Ireland) attitudes upon the leadership of Catholicism in the U.S. In addition, the impact of social class is noted as a factor in the Catholic Church's failure to provide any significant ministry to Catholic immigrants in the South prior to 1840. We then look at early efforts that began to extend ministry to areas on the margins of Appalachia. The final portion of the chapter considers the impact of established American religious communities and immigrant Catholics who arrived in Appalachia in the late nineteenth and early twentieth centuries and largely have determined the current expression of Catholicism in Appalachia.

The thesis of this chapter is that, in addition to Catholicism's struggle with a more inclusive understanding and gospel imperative for ministry, there have been additional circumstances peculiar to the U.S. which account for its failure to be present more effectively in Appalachia. The first of these is the ethnocentrism that marked initial Catholic foundations in the U.S. The second is an elitism characteristic among its seminary-trained clergy, who preferred urban (and more established Catholic communities) to smaller, rural, or more isolated ones. The third is the identification, much later in time, of Catholicism in Appalachia with a distinctly non-Appalachian cultural expression.[1] The fourth and final point is Catholicism's propensity to focus ministry upon sacraments to such an extent that the church struggled with great difficulty to move beyond the pastoral nurture of its own members to address the larger local communities in which it was situated. The sacramental focus of Catholicism, while in many ways its strength, also was its shortcoming. It has proven difficult, once the sacramental system has been integrated into the symbol system of a people, to separate the former from the specific cultural context into which it was inserted.

The Maryland Context

Cecilius Calvert, the second Lord Baltimore, was given a charter to found the colony of Maryland. Along with a number of other Catholic families, his settlers constituted a significant portion of the founding population of the colony in 1634. As in England, however, the Catholics were careful to draw as little attention as possible to their faith. Discretion was the norm. In England the Catholic aristocracy had learned through hardship to be quite circumspect. Alienation of the Protestant majority of the colony could not be risked, lest whatever leverage Catholicism may have had be lost. The situation of Catholicism in England, therefore, set the context for, and shaped the behavior of, Catholics in Maryland.

Problematical Attitudes

American Catholicism became visible with the establishment of the first Catholic diocese in Baltimore in 1789. This event was possible because of the colonies' recent independence from England, where Catholicism remained under strict control and was denied public establishment. A handful of priests represented the official leadership of the U.S. Catholic Church in 1789. They gathered in Bowie, Maryland, to nominate Father John Carroll, a former Jesuit,[2] as the first U.S. Catholic bishop. Prior to this, they had opposed such an appointment, because the aristocratic overtones of an episcopacy and appointment by "a foreign tribunal" were believed offensive to Americans.[3] Carroll's acceptance of any such appointment had been conditioned upon a democratic selection by the priests. Both Carroll and the clergy argued that this would make the appointment, and the Catholic Church itself, more palatable to American tastes. The Maryland Catholic community was sensitive to and respectful of the democratic-egalitarian context in which they lived.[4] The consequence, however, was a process of assimilation with both positive and negative effects. Important for our consideration was the propensity among the Catholics of English extraction to hesitate, if not to run from, efforts to evangelize. They concentrated, instead, on nurturing their own flock. This timidity dictated an almost singular priority on the establishment of parishes where Catholics were settled most densely. It also encouraged a failure of imagination, resulting in the inability to note the arrival of Catholic immigrants beyond the range of the large cities of the East Coast.

The contributions of early Maryland Catholics were largely positive. This group bequeathed a tradition to American Catholicism which demonstrated that the church could adapt to and thrive in a democratic, pluralistic society. Furthermore, civil authority could be conceived of as deriving from the people and not understood simply as emanating from God and proceeding downward through hierarchical monarchies to local authorities. The Maryland experience also demonstrated to Catholics in Europe that the separation of church and state was not inimical to religion and, of course, that religious liberty could find a biblical foundation in the Synoptics.

The political and social contributions of early Maryland Catholicism, then, were very useful. However, the shortcomings—and they were major—were of tragic proportions. These were the consequences of social class elitism and ethnocentrism.[5] Both marked the leadership among Maryland Catholicism. These leaders were cautious, apologetic, and excessively deferential to their environment, yet they overlooked what the American context might have learned from, as well as taught, Catholicism. This shortsightedness, even in ecclesiastical matters, manifested itself quickly. Social class prevailed over ideals, as Jay Dolan observes, when Bishop John Carroll began to deal with a disparate clergy and people.[6]

The Catholic leadership could be decidedly myopic. This can be seen in the observations of Patrick Smyth, a priest who worked briefly in Maryland before returning to Ireland. In 1788 Smyth published a scathing attack upon Bishop John Carroll and his priests.[7] He charged that the "Jesuits"— i.e., the Maryland priests—had been forbidden by their superior to venture beyond Hagerstown, Maryland. Why would Carroll issue such an order? In a telling observation, Smyth quotes Bishop Carroll as asking, "Why do not the Catholics come and settle near us? Why should they be going into the backwoods?" Smyth suggests plausibly that such questions reflected Carroll's attitude—an attitude characteristic of Carroll's social peers in the Anglican, Presbyterian, and Lutheran traditions as well. They stayed largely in or near established urban centers of the East Coast, where they found more congenial social and educational circumstances. Early Catholic patterns in ministry indicate that the church likely lost countless members to Methodist and Baptists frontier preachers, because its ministers remained concentrated in the urban coastal areas.

Compounding the difficulty for Catholicism was its dependence upon a clerical system that restricted the membership to seminary-trained, celibate males. Both requirements severely restricted the numbers of those who might have been interested in moving beyond the urban centers along the coast.[8] As time passed, several additional factors helped impede the development of Catholic parochial life in the Appalachian Mountains. Among these were an elitism that reflected a decidedly urban bias and a lack of enthusiasm by the Maryland English Catholics for contact with uneducated and unruly Irish, Scottish Highlanders, and German Catholics.

Causes of Parochialism

John England, an Irishman, became the bishop of Charleston, South Carolina, in 1822. After becoming familiar with his diocese, which covered the present states of Georgia, North Carolina, and South Carolina, he estimated that over 3,750,000 Catholics had been lost to Catholicism by 1836 because of the lack of missionary evangelizing among Catholic immigrants in the rural South and in the Southern Mountains.[9] A century later, Bishop O'Shaughnessy, in his own fever to defend the "reputation of American Catholicism," refuted the figures of John England.[10] There is no question about the exaggeration in Bishop England's figures. Yet American Catholic historiographers have avoided dealing with the accuracy of Bishop England's first-hand observations. They have been too quick to accept a mix of assumptions and both statistical and qualitative evidence. Little attention has been given to the truth at the heart of the question addressed by critical analyses.

Bishop O'Shaughnessy estimates that the Irish population of the U.S. in 1790 was 550,000. He assumes that between 100,000 to 150,000 were Catholic—i.e., about 20 percent. The remainder, he assumes, were Ulster Irish and Protestant, since Irish Catholics would choose not to come to the U.S. because of its Protestant majority and the reputation the American colonies had for being inhospitable to Catholics. As regards the people who settled the southern U.S, this logic was, and has remained, commonplace in American historiography. It presupposes that uneducated and untraveled immigrants standing on the docks in Ireland and western Scotland booked passage on the basis of where they thought they would be most welcome. Only the U.S. South seems to have experienced this remarkable lack of Catholic Irish and Scottish Highlander immigration.[11]

Bishop England's observations gain credibility on two scores. First, many of the Catholic Celts arrived before the time covered by the census records upon which Bishop O'Shaughnessy relies—i.e., before 1790. This raises questions about the presuppositions regarding proportions of Catholics in the earlier period. Second, loyalist Catholic veterans of the American Revolution well may have immigrated to the land they had seen and served in, but kept their religious affiliation quite private. In Canada, after the Battle on the Plains of Abraham (1754), such immigration occurred, but, since immigrants had fought on the side of the victors, the need to conceal affiliation on official records was less imperative. This explanation would account, too, for the anomalous situation in the Carolinas, where the story of loyalist Celts often has been poorly explained. As Bishop England observed, these included a fair proportion of Catholics.[12]

A fair proportion of the German, Scottish, and Irish migrants into Appalachia were Catholics—certainly not as many as Bishop England claimed but still a significant share. Two cautious conclusions are that (1) the absence of Catholic parish life in the Appalachian Mountains well may have had much to do with the lack of ministry offered Catholic immigrants into the mountains in the years of its settlement; and (2) the ethnic antipathies between the Catholic Celts and the English Marylander Catholic tradition may have been too great to overcome.[13]

The ethnocentrism can be seen from the beginning. Smyth charged that Bishop Carroll refused to recruit priests or seek assistance from bishops and dioceses in Europe to provide ministry in the newly founded American Church.[14] It was surmised by Smyth that Bishop Carroll and his advisors wished to maintain control over the ministry in the U.S. Catholic Church. While Smyth's accusation is couched in inflammatory language, some evidence seems to support the substance of the claim. As early as 1785, Bishop Carroll, in his first report to the *Propaganda Fidei*, insists that there are problems with "incautious and imprudent priests."[15] He is careful not to say "bad" priests. John Carroll's successor, Archbishop Maréchal, in 1818 no longer complains of "imprudent and incautious priests," but of Irish priests "given to drunkenness or ambition." These and similar complaints about "European" priests were recurrent until at least 1829. The results, of course, were a severe restriction in the number of priests and the maintenance of control in episcopal hands.[16]

While the English Catholics and the Sulpicians (a French society of priests) themselves may have held quite diverse views on the issues of equality, fraternity, and liberty, they were similar socially. The social class typical of popular Catholicism and the Celtic immigrants, however, stood in stark contrast to the class status of both the Sulpicians and the Maryland Catholic elite.

In summary, we can suggest several important consequences for the Catholic parochial presence in Appalachia. Because of the "Americanist" and social-class commitments of the early Catholic leadership in Maryland, no attempts were made to provide or secure the resources for ministry among the significant numbers of Catholics who migrated into Appalachia between 1750 and 1840. The reasons were fourfold. (1) A bias existed against the traditional Catholicism (non-Enlightenment Catholicism) of the immigrants. (2) The restricted number of priests, even had the bias not been present, prevented the U.S. church from moving beyond parishes in the more densely settled areas. (3) Most ministries in Catholic settlements away from the larger cities of the East Coast did not appeal to a well-educated diocesan (as opposed to religious or missionary) clergy. The Catholic experience in Appalachia paralleled that of Anglicans and Presbyterians in this regard. Baptists and Methodists were much better equipped to provide local and indigenous leadership in the development of congregations to meet the needs of the frontier. (4) The earliest Catholic dynamics, outlined above, became paradigmatic for the entire Catholic church until the middle of the twentieth century.

Criteria for Establishing Churches

As valuable as the role of women religious in Catholicism in this country was and continues to be, prior to 1965 women religious would have been severely restricted by church codes and traditions, as regards the ministries and activities in which they could engage. Their presence in Appalachia prior to 1965 was limited to either hospitals or schools. Seldom would they have engaged the neighborhood beyond their convents.

Furthermore, in the earlier period of American Catholicism under diocesan leadership, the sense of the ministry much beyond nurture was not an abiding or shaping influence. The ethos of the diocese was pastoral nurture. Moreover, the diocese was oriented toward the "see" (the bishop's) city—that is, it was urban in orientation. The clergy gathered around the bishop and gauged themselves individually in relation to the appointments received from the bishop. The measure of "success" frequently came to be appointment to, and proximity to, the larger parishes or cities of the diocese. The more remote the parish, the less prestigious the appointment. For his part, the bishop's norm for the establishment of a parish was its ability to be self-supporting. The density of the Catholic population would be the major consideration. Thus urban parishes predominated, followed by parishes in middle-sized cities interspersed through the diocese. In this way, it was felt, Catholics were allowed the best possible access to churches, given the circumstances.

In the earlier period, Appalachia afforded virtually no locale in which, given these criteria, Catholic parishes would be established. This situation continued well into the twentieth century. Exceptions, of course, occurred, due mostly to the personalities and vigor of individual bishops and/or clergy. The exceptions would be found in the dioceses of Wheeling and Covington. Such exceptions demonstrate the significance of the absence of religious order clergy. If the latter had been welcomed and had become more numerous, their communal structure and their commitment to evangelize might have changed the character of the Catholic presence in Appalachia.

John England, bishop of Charleston, South Carolina, addressed his thirteenth annual diocesan convention in this way: "My brothers, I consider it to be one of the mistakes which has been hitherto greatly detrimental to our missions, to imagine that a diocese was sufficiently supplied with priests when one was located in every place where a congregation existed sufficiently numerous and sufficiently able to maintain a regular church and to give a competency to its pastor. How many of those desirous to hear the word of God are scattered widely from such places?"[17]

John England's vision did not prevail, and Catholicism in Appalachia, in the form of parish life, remained marginal at best. Most Catholics who migrated into the mountains found homes for the soul elsewhere. Certain efforts were successful, however, and eventually these came to constitute the base from which an effective presence would be launched.

Catholics in Appalachia Before 1850

Saint Peter's, Harpers Ferry

The first parish that may be classified fairly as Appalachian probably is Saint Peter's in Harpers Ferry, West Virginia. As early as 1790, Father Dubois began visiting the community. Harpers Ferry lies marginally west and south of Hagerstown. Today it would be a half-hour drive west from Frederick, Maryland, and more than a hour and a half from Baltimore. The town sits at the confluence of the Shenandoah and Potomac rivers and grew because of foundries that developed there. Its proximity to Baltimore clearly had an effect upon its development and upon the presence of immigrant Irish Catholics who entered the country through Baltimore. Harpers Ferry is relatively unique for Appalachia, because of its accessibility to the more developed Northeast. The first permanent church building was constructed in Harpers Ferry in 1823. It was replaced in 1833. Not long afterward, a mission church was established at Charles Town, a few miles away.

By the time of the Civil War, the population of Harpers Ferry had grown to three thousand. The church there was pastored by an Irish priest educated in Ireland at All Hallows College. In the East, Catholic leadership, dominated after 1840 by Irish immigrants, sought and received from overseas, particularly Ireland, numerous priests to staff parishes. The southeastern U.S., however, in 1850 still had very few parishes.[18]

Saint Joseph's, Somerset

While there is no evidence that Catholic parishes were established elsewhere in the Appalachian Mountains prior to 1840, this is not to say that the clergy failed entirely to follow or search out Catholics who might have migrated beyond the coastal cities. In fact, during the early decades of the nineteenth century, missionary priests penetrated the countryside and ministered to the needs of the people. They came from the west. The priests who migrated to this continent and moved beyond the influence of the Maryland Catholicism and diocesan life—i.e., French-Canadian missioners to the north and west, and some religious men from Bardstown, Kentucky—were among the most energetic pastors. Prior to 1840, these pioneers usually were Jesuits, with a sprinkling of Sulpicians. They worked under the auspices of the church at Quebec and its archbishop. Their influence and contributions, unfortunately, stayed far to the west and north of Appalachia.

Much later, however, other pastoral outreach occurred. While missionary outreach and evangelizing seemingly had died in Maryland for the reasons mentioned above, it came alive within a line of religious clergy who were independent of the Maryland diocesan tradition. These Dominicans and, to a lesser extent, Redemptorists were not diocesan priests. The Dominicans had settled around Bardstown in Kentucky. They established a parish and eventually a college at Somerset, Ohio.[19] The earliest of these efforts were confined to accessible river valleys and plains. Somerset functioned as an outpost from which Catholic settlers along the Ohio River could be served by occasional visits. As early as 1794, priests from Somerset visited Gallipolis, Ohio, to administer the sacraments.

The outpost at Somerset had been established at the urging of John Dittoe, an Alsatian of German extraction who had moved there in the 1790s from Frederick, Maryland. Over the years, he had sought the ministry of a priest from Baltimore, to no avail. In 1808 (or 1810; the exact date is uncertain) the Bardstown Dominicans settled there.

Scattered Catholics in the Mountains

There are reports of Catholics in Sumter and Fentress counties, Tennessee, from 1747 through 1791.[20] These Catholics had migrated from the Carolinas. Such early migrations to the mountains lend strength to the belief that Catholics were not too few and certainly were known to be among the early migrants to the southern colonies. There are records indicating that John Sevier, in 1799, sought from the bishop of Baltimore a priest to serve the needs of the Catholics gathered in the area around Knoxville. He estimated that there were about a hundred Catholic families in the vicinity.[21] No priest, of course, became available to meet the parochial needs of the Knoxville area that early. Catholics were to be found in settlements throughout Middle and East Tennessee in the eighteenth century. Carthage in Smith County also was recorded as being the home of Catholics as early as 1800.

If the one hundred families in the area around Knoxville in 1799 (and even later, in 1821) did not get a priest, we do know that in 1824 there was enough "Catholic activity" in the area of Pulaski (in Giles County, Middle Tennessee), Winchester (in Franklin County, on the cusp of the Cumberland Mountains and Middle Tennessee), and Knoxville that Bishop England's Catholic newspaper, the *U.S. Catholic Miscellany*, had Andrew Fay, John Brannigan, and James Dardus, respectively, as agents in these towns.[22]

In 1809, there was a German Catholic settlement in Burrville, Morgan County, Tennessee, about twenty-two miles from Knoxville. By 1846, this county's German community was centered in neighboring Wartburg and had petitioned for a regular Mass. Ironically, just a "stone's throw" from Burrville is the small community of Glenmary, whose name a century later is associated with the Catholic Home Missioners of America.

The history of Catholicism and its parish ministry in the Appalachian Mountains prior to 1850 is told in the annals of small communities and individual families. With the exception, as noted of a parishes begun in Harpers Ferry and Martinsburg, ministry among the Celts and German Catholics of the mountains was neglected.

Missionary Activities

Earlier leadership had tried to lead the U.S. Catholic Church in the direction of meaningful accommodation with the American experience by maintaining a low profile and accepting local traditions and mores as much as possible. By 1850, however, waves of Catholic immigrants had wrought a sea-change in the Catholic Church, giving it visibility and voice in the young nation, as well as new attitudes and energy.

During the 1850s, the Redemptorists were doing what they had done in Europe. In an attempt to revive and reestablish a Catholicism shaken by the modern world, "parish missions" (as Catholics called their "revivals") were being offered. The Redemptorists provided one of these "revivals" in 1852 at the diocesan cathedral in Wheeling, West Virginia. From there they went on to Lexington, Kentucky. This new ministry offered a more aggressive Catholic presence than ever before had existed in the U.S.[23]

In 1880, some of these Redemptorists continued and developed this tradition of preaching "missions" as members of a new religious community, the Missionaries of Saint Paul. Founded by Isaac Hecker, the Paulists, as they came to be known, were interested specifically in bringing the Catholic tradition into the mainstream of U.S. life. Their perspective was similar to that of John Carroll and early Maryland Catholicism in that regard, but the Paulists were more forceful and energetic in its pursuit. They criticized American culture, even as they called Catholicism to adapt to it.[24] Following their vision, the Paulists offered their "missions" everywhere; of particular note, they did not neglect smaller cities located away from the East Coast and its nearby foothills.

In 1880, Fathers Elliott and Robinson preached at a mission at Staunton, Virginia. This foothill parish was at least thirty years old when they arrived. From there they continued on to give missions at Harrisonburg, Greenville, and Lexington. All of these Shenandoah Valley towns had thriving, if small, Catholic parishes. The Paulist team reported that the local Harrisonburg pastor ministered to over five hundred Catholic families in these small valley communities! From there, the Paulists went on to Winchester, also in the Shenandoah Valley, where the previous summer a resident pastor had been assigned for the first time.[25]

Anti-Catholicism, characteristically virulent in the English dissenter tradition and Know-Nothingism, here seems to have been mild if not absent. Fairly consistently, one encounters remarks about the "ecumenical" openness found in foothill and mountain towns. Several factors may account for this. First, Know-Nothing hatred may have flourished more in the passing passions of political rhetoric than in the face of a "practical" ecumenism that develops among neighbors in face-to-face relationships. Second, anti-Catholicism may not have been as formative among these English Protestant settlers, because, to some extent, they, along with their Catholic neighbors, had migrated prior to, and as a consequence of, the Jacobite uprisings—that is, more because of punitive Tory commercial in-

terests than for religious freedom. Third, a Catholic cultural remnant may
have been present in larger proportion than usually is recognized, and this
may account for a very practical ecumenism that baffled both these Paulists
missioners and later researchers. In any case, the frontier, as we may term
the nineteenth-century American hill country, would not have been without a certain centrifugal push toward neighborliness, both because of community scale and the remoteness of European and Old World hatreds. Finally, economics may explain better than ideology the larger part of
migration to North America.

The Paulists regularly held missions throughout the Shenandoah Valley in the latter half of the nineteenth century. They also sent Father Bradley alone to a small outpost parish in Keyser, West Virginia, in 1873. Located in Mineral County, Keyser is eighteen miles from Cumberland and
quite distant from the Shenandoah Valley. A few weeks earlier, the Paulists
had preached a mission at Lynchburg, Virginia, and had written in their
report that "it was not a poor parish." At Staunton a few days later, Father
Bradley reported that, "as usual in Virginia, this mission attracted considerable attention among non-Catholics."

Reports of area residents' views of Catholics changed in tone in the
1880s. In Harrisonburg in February 1883, the Paulist team recorded that the
Catholic parish was home to the liquor sellers. As a result, "the Methodists got up a revival so as to keep their people away from our church."[26] The
neighborliness of a decade or so earlier apparently had disappeared. A strain
of anti-Catholicism described by Ray Allen Billington in *The Protestant
Crusade*[27] had begun to take hold. Catholic cultural presence and its
memory among formerly practicing Catholic families waned, even as the
church became more organized in the region.

After the conclusion of the Civil War, the national mood was set
more by northern antipathy toward "new immigrants" (often Catholics)
than by wartime southern sympathy toward Catholicism. Thus Catholicism, which at one point had been solidly "southern," emerged in both
the southern and the national consciousness as solidly immigrant and
"foreign." The national crusade against foreign encroachment began to
make inroads into the rural regions of the nation. On the other hand,
perhaps the ecumenical spirit of the earlier period simply reflected a reaction against outside "Yankee" pressure, one that enhanced solidarity
among the people in the valley and foothills.

In 1883, the Paulist team visited Martinsburg and noted that the parish had declined considerably since an earlier mission in 1879. In the course
of four years, twenty-five Catholic families had left the town. On the other
hand, the Daughters of Charity, after a forty-year absence, had returned to

run a parish school. While staying in Martinsburg, the Paulists took a day trip out to see Catholics at Berkeley Springs, West Virginia.

In 1887 the Paulists arrived for a mission at Leading Creek, West Virginia, about ten miles from Weston, in central West Virginia. Father John Tracy was pastor. While there, the Paulists, Fathers Deshon and Nevins, heard the confessions of 164 people. They noted that parishioners arrived for the sessions on horseback.[28] A few days later, at the larger town, Weston, they recorded that they heard 253 confessions. The Paulists also recalled that one pastor in town kept his people away. I can interpret that remark only as a comment on Paulist expectations. The team now usually expected to see a numerous crowd of Protestants at their missions in some towns, although not necessarily in all, as they recorded at other places in the Paulist chronicles.[29] The impact of Know-Nothing nativism varied in the mountain regions. The gauge probably is lost in the annals of various communities, each with its own peculiarities and sets of internal relationships.

In 1895, the Paulist mission band ventured as far south as Chattanooga. There they found an extremely hospitable community. The Chattanooga parish had existed for some time but had fallen upon difficult times because of indebtedness.[30] The Paulists recorded that their November 1895 mission was well received in this "New South" city. They recalled "the liberal and kindly feeling prevalent in the south towards the Church; at every service . . . we had numbers of non-Catholics present."[31] The openness of the Protestant community, however, created ambivalence in the local Catholic clergy: "But this spirit acts both ways, it leads Catholics to contract mixed marriages, weans them from their faith."[32] Two years later the same Paulist team reported that the mission at Roanoke in January 1897 met with "very little prejudice existing among the Protestants."[33]

The bright and hopeful notations of the 1890s changed abruptly, however, as the Paulist team of Fathers Youman, Clark, and Burke wrote in the chronicles that, upon return to Chattanooga in 1902, the Catholics attending the mission had dropped from 230 people to 20 at Saints Peter and Paul Parish.[34]

The Paulists conducted a mission at Cumberland, Maryland, during a two-week period in late March and early April 1900. They reported 1,885 confessions. It is difficult to know what to make of this extremely large figure other than that the number of Catholics in the Cumberland area must have been significant. Five years later, however, the Paulist mission team reported a very different picture. Then the number of confessions fell to 458![35] The drop was only temporary, though, since in 1909 confessions at

Cumberland during the mission numbered 1,560. The most striking piece of information recorded is that over 450 Protestants attended the mission. The following year, 1910, in Frostburg, Maryland, there were 2,180 confessions during the mission.[36]

New Immigrant Catholics

During this period, the Appalachian mining industry began to attract a sizable influx of Catholics from eastern and southern Europe and the Middle East. The character of Catholic parishes began to change again, as Lebanese, Hungarians, Italians, and others began arriving in the coal towns of Central Appalachia. Perhaps more than their Celtic and Germanic Catholic predecessors, these new migrants felt marginalized and often found in their Catholicism firm ground for personal and cultural identity in an alien and sometimes hostile environment.

Being, in their cultural diversity, more readily identifiable than the dominant groups, these later Catholic arrivals in Appalachia actually provided a stronger identity, a steadier presence, and greater support for the Catholic tradition as it moved into our own times. Appalachian Catholicism thereby came to reflect a stronger Mediterranean influence. This influence has contributed a distinctive quality to the Catholic parishes in Central Appalachia even today. The parishes are family-centered and informal in their activities and structures. Conservative and strict as Catholics, they nonetheless eschew legalisms and ideology which are irrelevant to their non-Enlightenment, popular Catholicism. Perhaps the clearest example of this has been the manner in which Appalachian Catholicism prefers to place itself firmly in the public square, rather than retreat into the sacred sphere.[37] Retreat may have marked immigrant Catholicism in the urban North (and, in a different manner, English Maryland Catholicism's nonevangelizing, privatizing style or presence). In the North, immigrants created large enclaves, separate worlds from which they could sally forth successfully, without suffering the usual bitter consequences of total economic or social isolation. In Appalachia, to the contrary, these Catholics and their parishes, eager to create niches in the communities in which they were small minorities, formed part of the woof and warp of town life.

Many Lebanese and Italian migrants into Appalachia were miners. Others, however, soon became shopkeepers. With these latter people and their concerns, a "bourgeois shopkeeper" mentality came to characterize local parishes, in ways unknown in most other areas of the country. This mentality introduced a civic and social conservatism into the life of the Appalachian Catholic parish, which was not as characteristic of Catholicism in the urban North or agrarian Midwest. The cultural alienation of Appalachian Catholicism tended to be that of shopkeepers vis-à-vis rural natives, miners, or industrial blue-collar workers. Catholicism, for both cultural and socioeconomic reasons, then, resisted inculturation within the Appalachian scene as a whole.

As a small minority, the Catholics of Appalachia in the twentieth century never stood much chance to influence public attitudes about religion and religious experience, but when the parish could be associated with a numerically small social class, they became even less able to do so. While sharing small-town professionals' social class and values, these Catholics, as cultural outsiders, were unable to influence the social and political establishment. At the same time, their roles and public image often foreclosed any effective influence on the very people with whom, economically and educationally, they did not identify. The original European settlers of Appalachia had absorbed the early Catholic immigrants, and now the residents circumscribed later Catholic arrivals as "outside" insiders—i.e., as members of the county-seat commercial establishment, but with such tenuous status within it that they held little, if any, social influence within that establishment.

In any case, the early twentieth century saw an Appalachian Catholicism whose numbers had been severely reduced through lack of Catholic ministry among, and assimilation of, the Scots and Irish (and some German) Catholics. The Catholics still to be found were few in number and reflected, depending on the community, a mixture of ethnic identities and social classes. These later immigrants largely supported and carried the Catholic parishes through the first half of this century.

Reaching Out

In light of this situation, William Howard Bishop, a priest of the Archdiocese of Baltimore-Washington, in 1936 published in the *American Ecclesiastical Review*,[38] a publication for Catholic priests, a plan for a rural mission society. By 1941, Howard Bishop's community of priests and brothers had established a Catholic parish with a full-time resident pastor in Sunfish, Kentucky. In rapid succession during the decade, more parishes were founded at West Portsmouth and Otway, Ohio; Saint Paul, Big Stone Gap/Appalachia, and Norton, Virginia; and Murphy, Sylva, and Bryson City, North Carolina. From such outposts, the newly founded Glenmary Missioners reached out into the byways of Appalachia in ways Catholics had not done before.[39]

The efforts of Howard Bishop reflected a mood that engulfed American Catholicism during the first part of the century. About the same time, similar efforts were begun in the Deep South by Father Thomas Judge, CM, who founded "cenacles" (after the room where Jesus held the Last Supper) of lay people to work among the scattered Catholics of the South. Eventually this group turned to work among those who often were ignored by the more established (and white) churches: black sharecroppers and mountaineers. As the lay people in the cenacles became increasingly dedicated, they evolved two religious communities, the Missionary Servants of the Blessed Trinity (women) and the Missionary Servants of the Most Holy Trinity (men). These two organizations continue to work in small parishes in both the Deep South and Appalachia.

The ministries of both Glenmary and the Missionary Servants filled a void that began to develop as the Paulists started withdrawing from their missionary commitment to the smaller towns and rural areas of the nation. The preaching mission teams that had been frequent visitors in the Shenandoah Valley and elsewhere in the South soon spent most, and eventually all, their time in the larger cities of the North, where the Catholic immigrant population demanded their attention.

While the mission teams eventually disappeared in the smaller and more remote areas, for a time the Paulists continued to pour great energy into the South. In 1900, the Paulists purchased a large mansion, Hundred Oaks, located at Winchester, Tennessee, southeast of Nashville (about sixty miles west of Chattanooga). From here they began mission outreach into the surrounding area. By 1926 they had established mission parishes throughout the region. A small parish in Eastland, Tennessee, consisted of forty Scottish Catholics. This Catholic community of miners (Bon Air mines) built its first church in 1950.[40] This community and others in Middle Tennessee initially were evangelized using a mobile trailer, the Saint Lucy Chapel. By means of this trailer, the Paulists, much like the mission preaching teams before them, visited various communities. The Saint Lucy mobile unit made forays into Tracy City, Mount Eagle, Shelbyville, and Cowan. The *Tennessee Register,* for example, reported on July 21, 1946, that trailer missions had begun eight years earlier. A report from Tracy City read: "Evidences of a once flourishing Catholic community of 35 years ago are noted in the many Irish Catholic family names. Younger generations of the Conry, McGovern, Flynn, and Gallagher clans still get their mail at the post office, but their names are not inscribed on the baptismal register of the Catholic Church. Leakage, mixed marriages, lack of priests and church, along with universal indifference to spiritual values are the causes of the present weak condition of the Church today."[41]

Notwithstanding the occasional forays into the hinterland that constituted the more traditional approach of the Paulists, whether the mission teams or the Winchester experiment, Fathers Bishop and Judge were determined that their missioners would move in and live among the people as an important and effective pastoral force. This approach had a major impact on Catholic presence in Appalachia as the century wore on.

The mood of American Catholicism changed during the first half of this century. That mood was reflected in the development of more ministries among religious men and women in parishes in Appalachia—including, in addition to Glenmary and the Missionary Servants, Benedictine men and women from Cullman, Alabama, and Belmont, North Carolina. Moreover, a striking missionary spirit arose within the dioceses of Wheeling and Covington. Both dioceses represented themselves well in the mountains. In the years between 1910 and 1929, both had established numerous parishes among the immigrants described above. The spirit of service was exceptional; other dioceses which also extended into the mountains did not approach the same expenditure of energy for the mountain constituency. These two dioceses, of course, were very largely mountain in composition. Wheeling, in particular, had a strong but very contained Catholic stronghold in the panhandle around the see city. From this base, vocations were plentiful enough to extend into the mountain counties to the south. Covington was somewhat similar, with its Catholic constituency located just across the river from Cincinnati. This Catholic enclave in northern Kentucky was large and prosperous enough to absorb diocesan energies more than Wheeling's did. Even so, Covington established nine parishes in the mountains by 1933 (included were Ashland, Corbin, Cumberland, Hazard, Jenkins, Middlesboro, Paintsville, and VanLear). The diocese itself, in 1933, described three of its mountain parishes (Paintsville, Jenkins, and Hazard) as "missions" in the strict sense, designating the pastors as diocesan missioners. Wheeling, on the other hand, had over seventy local churches, if mission stations are included.

Two other Catholic dioceses also were responsible, prior to 1960, for parts of Central and Southern Appalachia. The diocese of Raleigh had by 1933 established parishes in Asheville, Hendersonville, Hot Springs (staffed by Jesuits), Spruce Pine, Statesville, and Waynesville. These largely reflected a socioeconomic reality atypical of Appalachia. The parishes were in cities of some size where resorts were located, although Spruce Pine was something of an anomaly.

The other diocese was Nashville. By 1933, the diocese had established parishes in the more sizable towns for which it was responsible.

These included Chattanooga, Cleveland, Elizabethton, Gatlinburg, Harriman, Johnson City, and Knoxville. Changed circumstances had energized the Catholics of these areas. One factor was a heightened sense of religious identity, which created a stronger impetus to share the faith. A second factor that had developed after World War I was a sense of mission among the poor and marginalized. These ministries, from clothing stores to health care, flourished among the two established American missionary communities of Fathers Bishop and Judge. As the Paulists increasingly took a "pastoral turn" in their ministry to immigrants and their descendants in urban areas, these two younger religious communities or families took a more typical American "ecumenical turn." Focusing on conversion not so much of church members as of hearts, these groups fostered involvement in the civic community as a means of "uplifting" the moral vision of the communities where they labored in the name of Jesus.

After World War II

After World War II, the pace of Catholic development in the mountains accelerated. The growth of Catholic religious communities increased the number of ministerial personnel available for mountain ministries. After Vatican II, this was particularly true of women religious (treated elsewhere in this volume), but the dioceses of Covington and Wheeling had introduced the Sisters of Notre Dame and the Sisters of Divine Providence to the region much earlier. Bishop Watters of Raleigh also had encouraged lay volunteers and developed a program of lay mission leadership in his diocese in the 1950s.

A name that cannot be forgotten when dealing with the Catholic parish in the mountains is that of Father Ralph Beiting. He worked out of a number of parishes in the eastern mountains of Kentucky. His reputation as a missioner extended nationwide, and, whatever assessment one may make of specific projects, his presence in the mountains of eastern Kentucky for over forty years is unsurpassed in Catholic circles. Not only did he establish numerous parishes and keep the vision of mountain ministry clearly in view for the diocese of Covington through the years; but also he introduced to Appalachia many of the techniques traditionally associated, in the view of American Catholicism at the time, with overseas missionary activity. A strong provider of social and economic assistance to the needy, he pushed the parish to move beyond the boundaries of its own membership in service to the surrounding community.

Conclusion

We have attempted here to provide an overview of the role and place of the Catholic parish in Appalachia. Because of a complex of circumstances prior to 1840, the Catholic hierarchy was late in providing adequate ministry to its Catholic constituency in Appalachia. After 1840, the arrival of new immigrants and a new sense of identity, emerging among American Catholics, released some energy into Catholic life in Appalachia. Initially the Dominicans and Redemptorists, working at the region's geographical edges in the middle of the nineteenth century, and eventually the Paulists and diocesan priests, following upon that period, took on the challenge with a greater sense of adventure and mission through the end of the nineteenth and into the early twentieth centuries. There followed rapid growth in the numbers of both Catholics and the clergy in the middle decades of the twentieth century, with the consequence that an increasing number of personnel became available for mission work in the mountains, where Catholics were few. Finally, there has been a surge (1950s through the 1970s) and an ebbing (1980s) in Catholic activity since World War II.

The period from the middle to the late twentieth century has been remarkable. Catholic parishes that formerly focused largely on pastoral nurture emerged, only after World War II, to increased involvement by members in the civic community and in social service ministries.

Notes

1. By "Appalachian," I mean, of course, the cultural context established by the region's European settlers during the 18th and 19th centuries. This culture was distinctly English, dissenter, and clannish.
2. The Jesuits had been suppressed by the Holy See in 1773.
3. Jay Dolan, *The American Catholic Experience* (New York: Doubleday, 1985), 71, 106–7.
4. Ibid., 105–6, recalls U.S. Catholics' and John Carroll's enthusiasm for independence from intrusive domination by (in different manners, of course) England and Rome.
5. Ibid., 71.
6. Ibid., 117.
7. Patrick Smyth, *The Present State of the Catholic Mission in America* (Dublin, Ireland: P. Byrne, 1788), 9 and 28.

8. It is important to make some distinctions. The requirement of celibacy was likely to make diocesan priests wish to remain in regions where there were more Catholics, since social support for the priests was greater there. Religious priests, on the other hand, were more likely to missionize beyond the normal circles of Catholic strength, because such support was available from their religious communities.

9. John England, *The Works of the Rt. Reverend John England,* ed. Sebastian G. Messmer, 7 vols. (Cleveland, Ohio: Arthur H. Clark Co., 1908), vol. 3:337; and Lou McNeil, "Some Ecclesiological Dimensions of Bishop John England's Thought" (master's thesis, Univ. of St. Michael's College, Toronto, Ont., Canada, 1978), 133 ff.

10. Bishop Gerald O'Shaughnessy, *Has the Immigrant Kept the Faith?* (New York: Arno Press, 1969), represents a minority stand on evangelizing efforts during the earlier period of U.S. Catholicism. A more institutionally positive interpretation can be found in William Portier, "Catholic Evangelization in the United States from the Republic to Vatican II," in *The New Catholic Evangelization,* ed. Kenneth Boyak, 27–42 (Mahwah, N.J.: Paulist Press, 1992).

11. Evidence in migration records, not official census records, raises questions about the suppositions of later historians. St. Barra's Catholic Church, Christmas Island, Cape Breton, Nova Scotia, provides anecdotal evidence in support of Bishop England's observation, if not his figures. The founding families of the parish were immigrants from the highlands of Scotland. Other family members, at the same time, had boarded other ships headed for North Carolina. The remarkable thing, of course, is that these settlers were Catholic highlanders "on the run"; in both Nova Scotia and North Carolina, while Protestants constituted a majority among the earliest settlers, the majority was not huge. *History of St. Barra's Parish, Christmas Island,* photostatic copy available in Robards Library, Univ. of Toronto, Toronto, Ont., Canada. See Stephen Dunn, *Highland Settler* (Toronto, Ont., Canada: Univ. of Toronto Press, 1953).

12. See also Richard C. Madden, "Catholics in Colonial South Carolina," *Records of the American Catholic Historical Society of Philadelphia* 73, nos. 1–2 (1962): 10–44.

13. Mary de Lourdes Gohmann, *Political Nativism in Tennessee to 1860* (Washington, D.C.: Catholic Univ. Press, 1938), 33.

14. Smyth, *Present State,* 28–29.

15. Mar. 3, 1785, in John Tracy Ellis, *Documents of American Catholic History* (Wilmington, Del.: Michael Glazier Press, 1987), 1:149.

16. These priests are not termed "bad," but "imprudent and incautious." One may suppose that actually they were viewed as "un-American" in their commitments and beliefs.

17. England, *Works of John England,* 4:359.

18. According to figures reproduced by Michael McNally, "The Parish in the South-

east," in *The American Catholic Parish: A History from 1859 to the Present*, ed. Jay Dolan (Mahwah, N.J.: Paulist Press, 1987), 1:226 ff., in 1850 there were no Catholic parishes with resident pastors in the mountain areas of Georgia, North Carolina, South Carolina, Virginia, or West Virginia, except for Harpers Ferry/ Charles Town.

19. Walter H. Maloney, *Our Catholic Roots: Old Churches East of the Mississippi* (Huntington, Ind.: Our Sunday Visitor Press, 1992), 433 ff.

20. Gohmann, *Political Nativism*, 34.

21. Ibid., 35.

22. Ibid., 33–36.

23. An interesting series of six articles is Andrew Sheabeck, CSsR, "The Most Rev. William Gross: Missionary of the South," *Records of the American Catholic Historical Society of Philadelphia* 65–66 (1954–55).

24. Recently a Catholic historian friend suggested that such a formulation implies a dichotomy, not merely a tension. The difficulty with this contention, of course, is that it classifies the groups outside normal alignments. For example, where does Avery Dulles fit in, if not in both camps? The only logic, it seems, is a common attack on the "liberal" political spectrum as strategy, not genuine theoretical analysis. It tends to reduce the issue of inculturation to assimilation, and gospel critique to biblical or magisterial infalliblism (a Catholic expression of fundamentalism). The Paulists and the American Catholic tradition have struggled with being both American culturally and believers in the gospel as transformative, not simply supportive of institutional, bureaucratic, and traditional commitments. Unlike Dorothy Day's position, however, the anarchist dimension is replaced with a commitment to the American pragmatist tradition. In this sense, my friend and many other historians fail to locate the sympathies of the Catholic leadership of an earlier era. They stray. They make these leaders either too radical (Dorothy Day) or too conservative (Michael Novak or David Schindler). The immigrants were neither.

25. Paulist *Mission Chronicles*, vol. 1 (1851–62), passim; and vol. 2 (1862–82), 366; in Paulist Archives, St. Paul's College, Washington, D.C.

26. Ibid., vol. 3 (1882–89), 92.

27. Ray Allen Billington, *The Protestant Crusade* (New York: Rhinehart, 1952).

28. Paulist *Mission Chronicles* 3:258.

29. See, e.g., Paulist *Mission Chronicles* 2:366, 3:92, 4:174.

30. See *The Columban* 8 (1926): 5, 3–4, for an interesting account from this ministry and the eventual founding of the Catholic parish at Chattanooga or Ross's Landing in 1839, to the first liturgy and settled pastor in 1850.

31. Paulist *Mission Chronicles* 5:148.

32. Ibid.

33. Ibid., 5:205.

34. Paulist *Mission Chronicles* 6:119.

35. Ibid., 6:205.

36. Paulist *Mission Chronicles* 6:119.

37. I take exception here to a recent series of essays and anthropological studies of southern Catholicism: Jon W. Anderson and William B. Friend, eds., *The Culture of Bible Belt Catholics* (Mahwah, N.J.: Paulist Press, 1995). One of the essays proposes a theme of "sacred space" as one of the significant tasks of Catholicism in the South—i.e., withdrawal into the parochial and sacramental.

38. William Howard Bishop, "A Plan for an American Society of Catholic Home Missions to Operate in the Rural Sections of the United States," *American Ecclesiastical Review* 88 (Apr. 1936): 3–13.

39. Christopher J. Kauffman, *Mission to Rural America* (Mahwah, N.J.: Paulist Press, 1991); and Lou F. McNeil, *Moving Beyond Confined Circles: The Home Mission Writings of William Howard Bishop* (Atlanta: Glenmary Research Center, 1990).

40. Winchester, Box 001, in Paulist Archives, St. Paul's College, Washington, D.C.

41. Statistical information on Catholicism, including founding years of parishes, is readily available in *Official Catholic Directory,* published annually by P. J. Kennedy & Sons/Bowker Co., Chicago. The annual directory first became available over a century ago.

Chapter 18

A Baptism by Immersion in Big Stone
Gap: From South Side Chicago to
Southern Appalachia

Monica Kelly Appleby

Introduction

Helen Lewis

During the 1950s, a small group of Catholic women created the
Home Mission Sisters of America to work in the rural South.
Known as the Glenmary Sisters, they were different from most orders of Sisters of the time because they did not run Catholic schools
or hospitals. Their constitution stated that they were "non-institu-
tional." They worked throughout Central Appalachia and in the
urban ghettoes to which Appalachians had migrated in the 1950s
and 1960s. When they came to Appalachia, they had no idea that
their destinies would be entwined with the vast changes sweeping
the region or that they would become pioneers in a new form of
missionary work.

Big Stone Gap, Virginia, was a center to which many of the
young Sisters came in beginning their service. Little did they know
what they were getting into or, really, what they were doing when

they visited homes in the coal camps and hollers of southwestern Virginia. In places with names like Straight Hollow, Bear Wallow, and Sawmill Hollow; around the towns of Dante, Derby, Big Stone Gap, Inman, and Appalachia; in Artesian Well Hollow, Bonnie Blue, and Keokee—here they became involved in people's lives. Beginning with summer Bible schools with children, they learned about family and community situations. Home visits and conversation led them to begin a thrift store in the backyard of their Big Stone Gap home. Then came connections with families, as they moved to Dayton, Ohio, and other northern cities; then the War on Poverty and changes in the regional Council of Southern Mountains; then the Appalachian Volunteers and the formation of all kinds of local community groups. These involvements set up reverberations that ultimately changed the individual Sisters and their friends, their religious community, other orders of Sisters, the institutional church, and the people of Appalachia.

Les Schmidt, a Glenmary priest, said, "The Glenmary Sisters were one of the most prophetic elements in the church during the 1960s. They were a moment of threat for many bishops." Catherine Rumschlag, the Sisters' first mother general, beginning in 1953, and a community leader until 1967, explained that changes made by the young community in response to the Second Vatican Council (1962–65), which had called for renewal of religious life, "angered Cincinnati Archbishop Karl Alter who claimed the Glenmary Sisters were a 'secular institute'." After a year of trying to negotiate with the bishop and other members of the Roman Catholic Church hierarchy, the Sisters were dismissed by the hierarchy, who appointed a priest to serve as their superior, replacing the women they had elected as their leaders.

In 1967, in response to the church's lack of support, eighty Catholic Sisters left the Glenmary order because they felt Rome's rules impeded their work. Forty-four of the Sisters left the order as an organized group and founded the Federation of Communities in Service (FOCIS) as a vehicle to carry on their work. In an article titled "The Revolutionary Mary" in the *Washington Post,* Coleman McCarthy writes: "In the 1960s, both the Immaculate Heart of Mary Sisters of Los Angeles and the Glenmary Sisters of Cincinnati came up against the male-centered conservatism of local bishops. Empowered by the renewals of the Second Vatican Council, large numbers of Sisters in both these orders left to form their own communities and serve those of low degree."

For twenty-five years, women of FOCIS have started health clinics, worker cooperatives, factories, homeless shelters, and hundreds of grassroots organizations throughout Appalachia and have created a model for community development that puts power in the hands of rural people. Instead of handing out funds, as other charities did, FOCIS gave people skills so that they could create their own community projects. Their beliefs about helping people were so strong that they were willing to give up their role as Sisters to accomplish their social agenda. FOCIS continues as an ecumenical community with sixty women, men, and children. Members live throughout the region and work in many different types of service. Husbands and some non-Catholic friends have joined the group.

The account below is written by one of these Sisters and FOCIS members, Monica Kelly Appleby. Monica tells her story of growing up in Chicago, joining Glenmary Sisters soon after high school, coming to Big Stone Gap, and being changed by her experiences there. She was baptized—immersed—in the mountains.

A Baptism by Immersion in Big Stone Gap

Growing up Catholic on the South Side of Chicago, joining the Glenmary Sisters to work in the rural South, and living for more than thirty years in southwestern Virginia, I must have a propensity for the South. Or perhaps my internal compass simply points southward. Or— and this is what I believe—I have found a home in the Southern Mountains, where I can make sense out of life.

On the South Side of Chicago, I grew up, as my parents did, in the ethnic neighborhoods around the Chicago Stockyards. My mother's parents were immigrants from Poland, and my father's mother was born in Czechoslovakia. His father's people were from Ireland—County Sligo and the Isle of Guernsey. The neighborhood where I lived, from the seventh grade through high school, was an Irish neighborhood. There I was Irish. My name was Pat Kelly, so I could pass.

When someone asked about my neighborhood, my response was, "Little Flower." We were known in the community through our parish churches—Saint Nicholas of Tolentine, Saint Joseph, Visitation, Saint Basil, or Saints Cyril and Methodius. Each parish was identified with an ethnic group. In the Catholic schools during the 1920s and 1930s, children were taught English and helped to assimilate into American society. My parents, especially my mother, wanted my three brothers and me to assimilate.

Although my parents went to public schools, they were determined to send their children to Catholic schools. Little did they know that it would be the culture of the Catholic schools and the Archdiocese of Chicago that would capture my imagination and eventually take me away from home.

I was always fascinated by the Sisters who taught us. They were strict and mysterious. I would stay after school and help wash the blackboards and pound the erasers for my classroom Sister. Later I graduated to cleaning the convent chapel; and, as I grew older and more experienced, I was permitted to answer the doorbell of the convent. I preferred to work for the Sisters than at my family home.

I spent my quiet time reading *Lives of the Saints*, fascinated by the missionary-saints, especially those sent to China. I also learned about women's and girls' places in the church and in society. As I walked home from high school, very often I would stop at the parish church, make a visit to the Blessed Virgin Mary's altar, and pray that I could become a priest someday. I think that instinctively I knew I did not want to spend my life as a Sister's helper or subsequently as a priest's helper. I was the first patrol *girl* at Little Flower grammar school.

Our family was not particularly religious. We did not say prayers before meals, pray the rosary, or have any other prayers together. On Sundays, however, we went to Mass every Sunday as a family, followed by Sunday dinner together.

Sports were a mainstay of our family togetherness. Both my parents were members of their ethnic cultural, social, and athletic clubs, the Polish Falcons and the SOKOL. Family, sports, work, church, and school were intertwined in an intricate web of meaning.

In Catholic school, we were taught the social pronouncements of the Catholic Church through the Papal Encyclicals. We also were given the chance to practice "Catholic Action," an important concern of the times. I began high school in 1950, joining the school Sodality, in which we would recite certain prayers and do good works. I attended the monthly meetings of the Chicago Inter-Student Catholic Action (CISCA) and joined students from all the Catholic high schools in common projects. I stuffed envelopes for mailings and volunteered at Friendship House, an interracial inner-city settlement house, where I helped serve meals to "street people." I read about its founder, Baroness Catherine von Hueck, and her partner, the newspaper writer Eddie Doherty. They were like the saints I had read about in my books. I volunteered at the CYO (Catholic Youth Organization) Summer Day Camps, spending time in neighborhoods different from my own—those that were considered less well off. I also participated in track and field events sponsored by the CYO, in which our team, O'Halloren Playground, competed against mostly "Negro" teams.

Now I can see that the overriding social problem of that time was racial prejudice and separation. The very close-knit community that formed my parish neighborhood kept other people out and isolated us from others. In a subtle way, we were taught to be fearful of "colored" people.

As a youth, I participated in the "Catholic Revival," as it came to be known. In the period from the mid-1930s to the mid-1960s, several movements were emerging which made significant changes in the Roman Catholic Church. These movements were influenced by European founders and embodied two major characteristics: (1) the lay apostolate, or "Catholic Action"; and (2) an awareness of the social problems of urban life, accompanied by an effort to create ties to rural values and places. The Archdiocese of Chicago, through the work of Bishop Sheil, was the place where many of these movements found a home. I was involved in this revival movement, through groups such as Friendship House, CISCA, the CYO, and later the Young Christian Students (YCS). Other groups were the Catholic Workers, the National Catholic Rural Life Conference, and the Grail.

This Catholic Action was slowly separating me from my family; they did not understand why I was spending so much time away from home. They worried about the places in the city where I worked. The ideas that were beginning to form through these experiences were beginning to alienate me from my parents' experiences and their aspirations for me.

All through Catholic schooling, we were urged to consider our vocation. The most important vocation was to be a priest or a "religious" sister or brother. We were encouraged to listen for the call to a religious vocation.

During high school, the Sisters of Mercy arranged for us to visit their novitiate. When two of the best volleyball players on our city championship team entered the convent after graduation, I visited them. I also made inquiries to two missionary orders, the Society of the Divine Word, based near Chicago; and Maryknoll. One of the curates at Little Flower parish told me about the Glenmary Home Missioners, an order of priests, Brothers, and Sisters who worked in rural America. The images in my mind of a Glenmary Sister were of a young woman riding a tractor, wearing a simple gray habit, working in the rural South where there were few Catholics. It sounded patriotic and adventurous.

Glenmary, the Home Missioners of America, was based in Glendale, Ohio, near Cincinnati; and I convinced my parents to let me visit there during my senior year. I remember the farmhouse convent, so different from the parish convent I helped clean. The food was good, especially the homemade brown bread. The Sisters were friendly and had lots of energy. I decided I wanted to join them, to become a Glenmary Sister. My parents reacted negatively. They did not want me to join the convent. I prayed fervently, talked with my close girlfriends, and went to a lot of convent "good-bye parties" for my high-school crowd. During the mid-1950s, joining the convent was an alternative choice to early marriage and was reinforced as the highest female vocation in the Catholic culture. As a nun, you could join your girlfriends and help the less fortunate.

After graduation, to comply with my parent's wishes, I went on to Marquette University. In the spring of my freshman year, I convinced two of my friends from high school, who also were attending Marquette, to take a weekend off to visit the Glenmary Sisters. After that visit, two of us decided to join Glenmary. The adventure, the uniqueness, and the rebellion all were part of the motivation to join Glenmary. I wanted to change the world, and I did not have to go as far as China. The people of the rural South needed Catholic Action, and, of course, the true faith.

My parents made the best of my decision. I shopped for my convent things. I made my own postulant dress. I gave away my clothes and my favorite possessions to my girlfriends. I said farewell to Bill, my boyfriend and chief romantic crush. I said a grand good-bye to Chicago. In September 1955, I was off to save the world and my immortal soul, to become a missionary to my own country.

During the years 1955–59, I was trained as Glenmary Sister Mary Monica. In what seemed to be a spiritual boot camp, I relinquished my past—family, friends, name, identity, belief in my ability, sexuality, and more. Luckily, while I was at it, I found my life in Big Stone Gap.

Big Stone Gap, Wise County, Virginia, was one of the first full-time missions of the Glenmary Sisters. For two summers before I was permanently "missioned" there, I was "stationed" in Saint Paul, on the edge of Wise and Russell counties, to do summer Bible schools and visit families in the coal camps. Two of us new missioners lived in a small trailer behind Saint Theresa Catholic Church in the town of Saint Paul. When I heard the news that I was going to be "missioned" full-time at the Holy Cross Center in Big Stone, I was delighted. I loved the mountains and the people I was learning to know.

The Glenmary Fathers had been assigned the territory of the coal counties of southwestern Virginia by the bishop of the Wheeling (West Virginia) diocese. They in turn invited the Sisters to come to Virginia each summer during the late 1940s. A permanent mission had been set up in the parish of Appalachia, which included Big Stone Gap, the town where the company people lived and where Westmoreland Coal Company was located. From the town of Appalachia, five coal camps radiated. It was here that the Southern Railroad had a coal tipple yard called "the Southern."

The parish church in Appalachia was located right next to the railroad tracks. It was built with the contributions of immigrant miners, foreigners—Poles, Italians, Hungarians—who came into the coalfields. In Appalachia and other towns, several of the stores were run by people with Lebanese roots. They had come to the coalfields and walked the camps with trading packs on their backs. It was a major change to move from Chicago and Cincinnati, where the Catholic Church was a recognized and powerful force in society, to Big Stone, where it was a minority church, often suspected by the majority of the population. The parishioners were happy to have the Sisters to take care of their children's religious education and perhaps to serve as a reminder of what church life had been for them in the past.

By the late 1950s, the immigrant mining families were better off than most other families in the camps. The men had become foremen or leading union organizers. Two of the company mining engineers were Catholics. Many of the clothing stores were run by Catholics. Several of the Catholic women had married servicemen after the war and had settled in the mountains. The accents in the voices of the Catholics were strange indeed—evoking Poland, Lebanon, the Bronx, Quebec, or southeastern Pennsylvania. The children talked like mountain people. There were a few "converts" from the area, but they tended to be from the margins of society, definitely not from the influential class.

The mission in Big Stone Gap began in 1955, and it had put down roots and established routines by the time I arrived in September 1959. Four Sisters were stationed there. Sister Mary Joseph was the first superior. She was an Irish Catholic (very Catholic, as only the Irish can be) from New York City. Sister Mary Joseph set the standard for the way we would be present in the community. She was totally available to the people whom we visited and who knocked on our door. It was all connected to our purpose for being there. This purpose was to help the poor and to serve the Catholic parish. Since there were so few Catholics and a great many people who were experiencing hard times, we spent much of our time interacting with non-Catholics.

From the beginning, our house was called Holy Cross Center, not a convent. We were a "stand-alone"—not attached to a school or parish church. We had a little chapel where Mass was said once a week. On other days, we drove to the town of Appalachia, reciting a portion of our prayers on the way. The house was big, with two floors and ten rooms. The bottom floor we used for classes for our Bible schools. The kitchen, dining room, living room, and recreation room became classrooms on Bible school days. During the school year, the kids from the Bland Colored School came over after school on Tuesday. These were still the days of segregated schools, and the African American children all went to one school located in Big Stone. After class, which consisted of prayers, singing, and some active teaching, we would drive the children home back up to Derby, a coal camp on the southern edge of Appalachia. During the summer, we had Bible school for the children in Artesian Well Holler, Cadet, Appalachia, and the coal camps.

On a regular day, during the morning we made home visits with the families whose children we knew or who requested emergency food and clothing. These were friendly visits and rarely, if ever, did we talk about Catholic faith or church attendance. I always was impressed by the difficulty of their lives and by the religious language they used. Bible verses were spoken within everyday conversation as a way to make sense out of their situations. Most people belonged to a church, but they did not regularly go to church on Sunday. My family experience had been the opposite. We always went to church on Sunday but did not use religious language.

People were friendly and always invited us into their homes. We talked about gardens, canning vegetables, flowers, family concerns, and how they were going to get by. When we would get ready to leave their homes, they would say, "Don't go 'way. Stay with us." In the beginning of my visiting days, I would sit down and stay longer. It was only later that I realized that this was a polite "turn of phrase" through which people said good-bye.

Very often clothing was requested by the people we were getting to know. Soon after I arrived in Big Stone, a garage-like building was constructed in the back of our house to store used clothing that was sent from Catholic contacts "up North." Once a month, we had a clothing sale in our backyard, and people would arrive very early to be first in line.

The increase in desperation in our area was related to the coal mining economy, always a boom-and-bust kind of situation. This time, however, when the layoffs came, there were very few hire-backs. In the late 1950s, coal mine operations were becoming more mechanized. The "continuous miner" machine more and more was incorporated in the local operations of Westmoreland. In one of the camps where at one time two thousand men had worked, now only two hundred men were hired. (In less than two years, there would be none. The Derby mine was closed.) The mining camp homes, at that time all rentals, were in disrepair; and all the central buildings—store, movie house, school, and even the church building—were either closed or torn down. The coal camps were beginning to look like ghost towns. The roads were not repaired. The road in the Derby "Colored" camp at the tail end of the line of houses which had never been paved was full of holes repaired with cinders. It was very easy for the children to be dirty from ordinary play games. It was also easy for people to come in from the outside, take photographs, and make judgments about the sorry parents who could not even keep their children clean. Some of the time our own Sisters, new to the region or passing through, would make similar judgments; but all of us who lived there for very long and got to visit people in their homes for an extended time knew different. These were people doing the best they could in very difficult situations.

Looking back, I can see that we were beginning to make a social analysis of the situation based on our close relationships with people. What a different view from that of the school classroom or hospital sickbed. The "Irish" Sisters who ran Saint Mary's hospital in Norton, the big town in Wise County, were loved by people for their kindness. But when we joined them for "Sister days," we had little in common regarding our work and our views. They were more traditional in their piety and practice. We were unschooled and available, young and energetic, and we were making it up as we went along.

In the 1960s, while John Kennedy campaigned for the presidency, we began to experience the problem of government policy as applied to the poor. We often took people to welfare and public health offices, only to find that services were refused them. We Sisters were even told that the clients had to come on their own and that we could not accompany them to the offices.

As we became more involved in public life, we learned about what agency services were available to people. One of the things we learned was that agency people who wanted to reach poor people often were unable to interest them in coming to their projects. For example, the Virginia Extension Service home demonstration agent was not able to attract women to attend food preservation classes or anything else she was offering. So we got this idea of asking the agent to come to our house to do the class, and we would invite the people. Now it sounds simple, but it was a breakthrough at the time. With the classes at our

house, we were able to hear what went on and then listen to the comments of the people as we drove them home. We realized then that
classes were not what very poor people wanted—they needed money,
and they wanted to work.

Another thing we noticed after visiting people in their homes was
that the women and men liked to make things with their hands. Hand-
made quilts, of course, were used not for decoration but for covering
and warmth. The people also made cloth dolls for their children. We
encouraged the women to make dolls and other sewn objects which we
would sell to visitors who came to our house and to the donors on our
mailing list. We would provide the fabric, usually donated by various
supporters. When we visited in the camps and "holler" communities, we
would collect items made by the "craft women." We sold them and returned the profits to the women. It was all very informal, but the
women certainly appreciated the small amounts of money they earned.
Later we suggested that the women use their stitching skills to make
banners with popular sayings on them. One of the designs was "War Is
Not Healthy for Children and Other Living Things." It was a popular
saying during the turbulent 1960s.

One of the "craft women," Edith Toney, was known as "the Banner Lady." She loved flowers and made up original designs using her
favorites. Many families had a knack for making things out of available
materials. They needed money and wanted to work.

I also tried to introduce the Catholic children to Catholic Action.
It began with a Young Christian Student group. Meetings began with
a gospel study, followed by a discussion of problems the students could
"observe, judge, act," or otherwise identify in their work, school, or
neighborhood situation. The YCS was called a "cell movement" and was
founded by a Belgian priest, Canon Cardijn. Soon the group included
several non-Catholic students. We attended several Young Christian
Student meetings at Notre Dame University and at the Benedictine
Center in Cullman, Alabama, experiencing the spirit of a large gathering of active young people. Looking back, it seems that this, too, was
part of the Catholic Revival experience.

Not all the work we did with Catholics involved social concerns. In
fact, most of it was traditional parish work. Church services were still
in Latin, and we sang the Gregorian chant almost every morning of the
week. We sang and prayed in Latin in the Church of the Sacred Heart
next to the railroad tracks in Appalachia. We prepared the children for
the sacraments of Holy Eucharist and Confirmation. We washed and
ironed altar linens and prepared the church and the altar for Mass.

The relationship between the priests and the Sisters was definitely one of masters and servants. We were the priests' helpers. The priests were friendly, and we had a warm, "kidding" relationship with most of them, but it was never a relationship between equals. Although quite subtly, our thought patterns and attitudes very much were shaped by the priests' words. It was the practice to serve the priest cookies and a drink after Confession. One of us was assigned this task so that we could have a very brief conversation. Talking with the priest, especially alone, was very rare and was viewed as a special privilege.

The third year I was in Big Stone, both a new superior and a new priest were assigned to the order and the parish. Sister Juliana, the superior, was a very dynamic person with lots of convictions and ideas. She and the pastor, who was cautious, did not get along. It was a real battle—or, rather, guerrilla warfare, because, as a Sister, one never could be directly confrontational. There were no resources for participation in decision making in ministry. I attempted to act as a kind of mediator, seeking to establish trust on the part of both the Sister Superior and the pastor. I got an ulcer in the process. Living under the conditions of the Sister code was extremely debilitating in the area of adult development. I survived, but it took some effort years later actually to grow up and develop a genuine self.

There was a movement in our Glenmary community, and among religious communities of women, to send Sisters for a college degree before they went on mission. A branch of the University of Virginia, Clinch Valley College, was located in Wise, the county seat, about forty-five minutes away. I was the first Sister in our community to go to college "on mission," and I am sure I was the first Catholic Sister who ever attended classes at Clinch Valley College. I took sociology and European history. The sociology class was "Social Problems," and we read novels and discussed the experiences of the people involved. We listened to popular music. I was touched to the depths by the music of the Civil Rights movement. My world view was broadening.

I was twenty-five years old, and I drove to Wise by myself! This was a breakthrough, because, before this, even on home visits we had to travel in pairs. By rule we were not allowed to go out by ourselves. Sometimes such rules were ridiculous, and we did not comply. For instance, when we drove the children home from Bible School classes and then picked up the crafts that women made, we would go by ourselves. Little by little, we started questioning the practicality of this rule of traveling in pairs in the 1960s. It just did not make sense.

We questioned other rules as well. We were not allowed to eat or drink with "secular" people, so when someone offered us a cup of coffee or a Coca-Cola on a home visit, we were not supposed to take it. It was, however, impolite and totally against the cultural habits of the people to refuse. Gradually, we started drinking and eating with people in their homes. Many were curious about our dress, wondering why we wore long gray wool dresses with black veils and starched headbands that covered our hair when we were walking around coal camps in mountain towns or studying at the local college.

This style of dress was perfectly impractical and culturally insensitive, but the tradition went so deep that it took quite awhile for the issue to arise in our Glenmary community. When it did, even the thought of changing our dress caused an outcry in the larger Catholic hierarchical world. At the time we did not realize the impact of what we were doing. Changing habits—changing what we wore as a uniform in the church "militant"—was a pivotal question which opened the door to other questions and consequences.

In 1963, I was appointed Sister Superior at the Big Stone Gap Mission. My only "subject" was the woman who had been my novice mistress. She was appointed to a mission so she could get some experience before she finished college at Marquette University, which had become the location of our House of Studies. This was the period when the decision was made to educate our Sisters before they went out on mission. There was a real shortage of Sisters to do mission work. There were only two of us in the ten-room house. That year, all we could do was keep our head above water. We realized that we needed help from lay volunteers.

In 1963, when there were just two of us Sisters assigned to Big Stone, we came up with the idea that volunteers could live with us during the year and assist in the work. The practices of prayers, grand silence, bells ringing to announce various movements of the day, and permissions from the superior to have toothpaste and other personal items—none of this made sense when there were only two Sisters and young women volunteers living with us. The practices seemed contradictory and strange. The work always was more demanding, and the religious schedule had to be adapted to the mission work.

During this time, the mission experience in Big Stone began pushing us toward the need for changes. It was also the time of Vatican II (1962–68). Our experience "on mission" and the "open windows" of the Second Vatican Council were powerful forces for innovation. The winds were blowing and the earth shaking beneath our feet. The foundations upon which the religious life of Sisters was built were crumbling.

In a sense, the War on Poverty originated in Appalachia when John

Kennedy campaigned in West Virginia. Local Community Action committees formed to enable federal money to be funneled into the area. The VISTAS (Volunteers in Service to America) came to town. From the beginning they found us and our house, came to visit and to learn about our experience. The local leadership never appreciated the young outsiders who came with their new ideas. Many of them lived with people in the hollers and were isolated from the towns. They would come to our place sometimes just to take a shower, have some company, and talk about what they were experiencing. These programs were unique in that they were not controlled completely on the local level. We had found an opening.

I served on the local committee which planned the first Community Action program in the county. There was a request for proposals for funding projects. The Glenmary Sisters submitted one for a traveling health van. While our proposal seemed the most innovative, it was not approved. The local elites were consolidating their power, and those of us who actually were concerned about ending poverty were excluded from decision-making positions. I began to learn at first hand about power elites. It hurt to be excluded, because I had done so much of the groundwork for the committee.

Many of the regional "anti-poverty" workers used our house as an information center. All of us were naïve about how coal company interests would react to the idea that local people should have a voice in determining the conditions of their own lives. This experience pushed us into developing a social analysis of why things were the way they were and investigating "Who Owns Appalachia?" But all that came later.

During the early 1960s, we started getting involved with the Council of Southern Mountains, a regional group based in Berea, Kentucky. Every year an annual conference brought together the teachers, missionaries, and social workers who lived and worked in the region. Glenmary Sisters from the Motherhouse in Cincinnati started attending the meetings. We were tolerated and then befriended by a few of the leaders of the group when we participated with enthusiasm and reported genuine experience with the people. Characteristically for the times, we often spoke of the Appalachian people as objects of benevolence, and probably we told too many stories using quaint sayings and traditional music. But we were learning to think of Appalachia as a region, for us a real breakthrough in awareness.

The Council of Southern Mountains was the only regional organization in Appalachia at the time of the War on Poverty programs. It became the vehicle through which federal dollars flowed into the region. One of the programs sponsored by the council was the Appalachia Volunteers. The idea was to train VISTA volunteers specifically for Appalachian communities and to administer the program from within the region.

The Glenmary Sisters reflected changes going on in the church and in society. As part of the effort to educate our Sisters, some of the older and most respected members of the community were sent to college. Loyola University of Chicago was the choice of Sister Marie (Cirillo), who was a member of our community's elected decision-making body. Marie had started the mission in Pond Creek near Portsmouth, Ohio, and rebuilt the major building complex for our training center in Fayetteville, Ohio. In Chicago, she decided to study sociology, but she was no ordinary college student. She sought out Appalachian migrants in the city and moved to a typical parish convent located in an Appalachian ethnic neighborhood known as Uptown. She and the others started the Appalachian Field Study Center, which became our training program in community development. It was in Uptown that we became aware of the continuity of Appalachian culture, and it was through the connection between Uptown and Big Stone that the Glenmary Sisters became known to the larger world. Our work in Chicago brought us to the attention of the media.

In 1964, Sister Philip (Anne Leibig) was assigned to Big Stone. She was an innovative thinker, and on her first day in Big Stone she suggested that, instead of working as catechists (our new name for ourselves) only within our parish, we start a program in the three Glenmary parishes in southwestern Virginia. We called all the pastors together to propose the idea. From that time forward, we looked beyond the parish framework. Until that time, we were owned by the parish where we were based. It was another breakthrough in awareness and action.

In 1965, I began working for the diocese as a community development coordinator. I represented the diocese in various meetings, one of which involved initial planning for the Commission on Religion in Appalachia (CORA). During that year, we also started wearing the experimental habit— a gray short skirt and overblouse, with a short veil. Big Stone was the place where experiments could be implemented. In Big Stone, we had good relationships with the local pastor, the Glenmary priests, and the diocese, which allowed our "experimental" way of living and working.

During the same period, I was invited to serve as the youth representative on the board of the Council of Southern Mountains. Through these meetings, I met many of the key people who were working for change in the mountains. Among them were Sue Ella Easterling and her parents, Myles Horton of the Highlander Research Center, Phil

Young and Dick Austin of the Presbyterian Church, the Episcopalian priest B. Loyd, and many other church people. On most of these regional boards, I was one of only a handful of women.

In 1966, Glenmary Sisters were able to start a new mission in McDowell County, West Virginia. McDowell was the most productive coal county in all of West Virginia. Part of my job as the coordinator of community development was to establish this new mission and give support to the Sisters assigned there. This was a chance to start implementing the fresh ideas that were in experimental stages in Big Stone and Chicago.

The biggest changes that had taken place involved our conception of what it meant to be a missionary. At this point, we could not turn back. We not only looked different in our new habits, but we were acting differently from the way we had acted in the late 1950s. Our experience with a broad range of people in the mountains had taught us a new way of thinking, working, living, and praying.

At the center of my Glenmary experience was the constant effort to foster creativity. Since we were noninstitutional, we, unlike most religious orders, did not run schools or hospitals. We had no enclosures. We had to get out there and make it up as we went along. We had to be creative.

Creativity was fostered by our way of life. Many of the people who joined Glenmary were artistic in a practical way. They were musicians, artists, writers. Music was important. We sang together, both in church and in our prayers. We sang when we traveled in the car or during recreation. We made our own fun, which involved telling stories from home or everyday life. We wrote poems for special events, or we read the words of poets aloud. When Sister Eileen (Maureen Linneman) became an Appalachian Volunteer in 1966, one her responses to her experience in Artesian Well Holler and other communities was to write the song "This Land Is Home to Me." It later became the title and the main theme of the first Appalachian Pastoral of the Catholic Bishops. As a community, we expressed ourselves more easily through art than through intellectual theories. We wanted to express this creativity in the place where we lived and worked. Somehow, in the process, we got too far ahead of the institutional church, and that is where things went wrong.

We justified this new current of our "missionary" work as "pre-evangelization" work. As part of the Sister Formation movement, some of our Sisters had studied both theology and catechetics in Europe and were able to help us identify the theological categories for what we were doing. "Pre-evangelization" was the word for what we were doing, as it was the "word" for creating a fertile and receptive "soil" in which to plant the seed of the Catholic faith. This was a way to explain the path we were taking away from the traditional Sister roles (as helpers of priest and parish), the uniform we wore, and the context in which we worked.

In the winter of 1966, I went to "the Chicago program," by now named the Appalachian Field Study Center. That fall, a larger group of Sisters was stationed in Big Stone, including Sister Ruth (Margaret Gregg), one of our community artists. She made a small, speckled, textured paper hanging for me with the words "Woman You Have Great Faith." I believed there was an important connection to be made in the Uptown neighborhood of Chicago—my hometown and a very big city. I was moving in reverse, going back to my roots after eleven years.

This was the time when I learned the importance of in-depth interviewing and multidisciplinary, self-directed learning. My experience involved connecting the inward and the outward, the personal and the social. At the Appalachian Field Study Center, the process was named something like "Living, Learning, and Working in Community." We spent most mornings in small groups discussing the books we read, which included sociology, psychology, anthropology, philosophy, and drama. Each class concentrated on one of the social institutions. Our group's focus was "family." Subsequent "classes" talked with people about education, recreation, and religion. I realized that home visiting was a powerful environment in which relationships could be developed that would lead to organized events and personal, educational reflection and growth.

During the time when I was in Chicago, Michael Novak was commissioned to write an article on the "New Nuns" for the *Saturday Evening Post*. The Glenmary Sisters were featured, and I was photographed in the short habit, walking down a Chicago alley with a suitcase and playing with children. To us it was normal, but to the outside world it was a dramatic image. As a community we began receiving extensive media attention, and that focused the scrutiny of the institutional church upon us. Before this, we had been a small community of 125 members at our largest. We had permission from the bishop of Cincinnati, our "protector" bishop, to experiment with our mission work and religious practices. "Experimental" had been our way for quite a long time, so what we were doing in Chicago did not seem that unusual.

In 1966, a request came to all religious orders to have a special chapter to reform religious life in keeping with the vision of the founder of the order and the demands of the modern world. Within six months, in December 1966, we had the Chapter and made our recommendations to the Sacred Congregation for Religious in Rome through our "protector," the archbishop of Cincinnati.

We were well prepared for the request. We had conducted a Chapter in August 1965, at the regularly scheduled interval, in which a lot of controversial topics had been addressed. The decision to change our habit to the experimental design used in Big Stone, Chicago, and later in other places was critical; it symbolized other decisions about our religious life and mission work. A key area of discussion had been how decisions would be made. We voted on decentralizing our organizational structure, based on the principle of "subsidiary" articulated by Vatican II.

In the meantime, I was able, through the Office of Appalachian Ministry within the Diocese of Wheeling, to obtain funding for a "religious research" project, in which we would interview people in Virginia and West Virginia about their religious values and practices. Similar research already had been done in the Uptown neighborhood in Chicago, in the training "class" that Sister Anne (Leibig) participated in. Her special interest was the role religion played in the life of Appalachian people.

This was our first "formal" project. We did in-depth interviews, beginning with the question, "How do you view the good life?" And people went from there. One of the big things we learned in Chicago was how to do unstructured interviews. The main concern was to learn from Appalachian people. By this time we had realized that our views were different from theirs and we had to learn to listen. We also believed that the interviews themselves would help both interviewer and interviewee learn something they did not know about what each thought and felt.

Another project in the works at this time eventually was named "An ARTS Approach to Community Development: Discovery, Expression, Communication." In our first proposals to the local Virginia Community Action Program, we named what we wanted to do "Cultural Caravans." We could not just float into a community and say we were there to listen. In a sense, we expanded on the summer Bible school work we had done for so long, but now we included whole families and did not have any "Bible" teaching at all. In one community, for instance, we gathered stories from the older people, put on improvised puppet shows with the children based on the stories, and then did a show for the parents at a community event at the end of the week. Music always formed part of the event, and local adults always were willing to perform. Always the music was religious. We learned to sing new songs: "I Come to the Garden Alone," "When the Roll Is Called Up Yonder," and "Jesus Loves Me." These were part of the religious context of the mountain churches.

Another current that was developing, one that flowered later, was that college programs in the East and North, such as the Friends World Institute, began sending their students to Appalachia to do field work. We were one of the few contacts in the region. We placed the students with families we knew and organized "rap" sessions about their experiences. Of course, they "hung out" at our house. After awhile we got the idea that the people who were acting as their "field teachers" ought to be able to get the same kind of college credit that the students were getting. Helen Lewis started the Appalachian Studies Program at Clinch Valley College. She had been involved in field-study learning for a long time, and we became partners in this effort.

The strains in our lives as Roman Catholic Sisters in southwestern Virginia now became apparent. We were doing what made sense in relation to developments "on mission." At the same time, the Roman Catholic Church hierarchy had other priorities. We had been juggling these two pulls for a long time. Now the time had come to make a choice.

The letter arrived in March 1967. It was signed by Cardinal Antoniutti, prefect of the Sacred Congregation for Religious in Rome, and was issued as a decree. A Franciscan priest based in Cincinnati was appointed to "direct the government of the Congregation, especially in the accurate formation of its members, in the observance of religious discipline. . . . All things contrary notwithstanding." Everything that had taken place up to that time did not count. Our experience "on mission," our work in the context of a changing Appalachia and a changing church, the fact that all this had been done with permission through the appropriate structures within the church—none of this made any difference. Our lives and our work were being carried out in a manner contrary to the wishes of the church hierarchy. We were not consulted.

The process which began with that letter culminated just six months later with the breakup of the Glenmary Sisters. This is a story in itself. The upshot was that forty-four members left Glenmary to form a new organization unconnected to the church, within which we could continue our "mission" work. It was called the Federation of Communities in Service (FOCIS). Another twelve women stayed as Glenmary Sisters, and the rest chose to continue their lives of service without an organization. Those of us who created FOCIS negotiated a settlement of the property and territory with the Glenmary Sisters. Mother Catherine and most of the members of the General Council joined the new group. It was like a divorce.

In Big Stone, we continued to live in the same house and do the same work. The bishop of Wheeling, Bishop Joseph Hodges, supported the changes. I remained as the field coordinator of the Office of Appalachian Ministry and, because of my mission experience, was elected president of the new FOCIS. The time of convergence, the time when things came together, became the time when things fell apart only to come together in a new way. But that, too, is another story.

Even thirty years later, I still miss those high-energy days. I loved being a Glenmary Sister in Big Stone Gap. I loved the house and the places where so many lives and movements converged. I had a name, a voice, and a recognized role. I was part of a group of women who did significant things. Lifelong friendships were forged during this time.

I did not like the games we had to play to stay afloat as a community of women within the church. We followed the rules, but we lost in the end. The destruction of our community was an act of institutional violence toward women. I believe such acts still continue in the Roman Catholic Church. I am on the periphery of such struggles now. Yet my memories remain. I was part of a southward movement of community women who had significant work to do.

Here is the first entry, in June 1955, in the *Annals of the Glenmary Sisters in Big Stone Gap*: "Sister Mary Joseph, Pius, Martin, and Clifford began their trip to Virginia this morning about 9:30 A.M. After a blow-out, a flat, a stop in Pond Creek to leave four Sisters there, and a stop in Portsmouth to have a tire fixed, we arrived in Big Stone about 12:30 A.M. on the 16th. On the 18th, Bible School classes began in St. Charles."

It may have been the work of pre-evangelization, of preparing the ground and planting the seed, but I do not think so. That is too active an image for what we were experiencing and what actually happened within me personally. For me, it was more like I jumped into the water feet first; I touched bottom, felt it, came up; I took a breath, floated with the current, swam upstream; and then I dove in again, deeply, with my eyes opened. I came up singing a new song, never to be the same again. It was a baptism by immersion in Big Stone Gap.

Chapter 19

The Virtue of Hope

SAMUEL S. HILL

Because the study of religion in the Central Appalachian culture is a subject complex and dauntingly difficult to grasp, and therefore susceptible to multiple interpretations, attempts to carry it out regularly have displayed innumerable biases. Doubtless this one, too, will. Its aim, even so, is to continue others' efforts to be accurate, discriminating, and perceptive, partly through standing on their shoulders.

Compounding the difficulty of our task is the fact that some comparing must be done among forms of this religion which exist in the region. That is, there are several quite diverse forms. Such an effort is evident in the many chapters of this volume. That is also one part of the program here, but the principal interest of this essay is in a different kind of comparing—viewing the Southern Highlands alongside the rest of the South, the "broader South." This is possible because an impressive commonality of beliefs and practices characterizes Appalachian religious life. Often the folk of the Highlands cultures acknowledge that condition with their feet, comfortably attending services and enjoying fellowship in congregations other than their own.

Essays in this book examine selected aspects of Christianity in Central Appalachia. They describe mountain churches and denominationally connected congregations, evangelical, mainline, and Pentecostal ones, Protestants and Catholics. We acknowledge that this is a collection of *profiles*, offering glimpses into religious groups—especially more traditional ones—occupying the landscape of a specific region. While this concluding chapter makes no attempt to summarize others, it does suggest that one more profile may be important—distinguishing Appalachian Christianity from that of a broader region, the American South.

Christianity in the South has been the subject of innumerable studies. Religious Appalachians exist within that geographical region but occupy a distinct subregion within the broader southern context. This chapter surveys similarities and differences between those two important areas. Study and reflection have brought me around to Catherine Albanese's contention of twenty years ago that the religious culture of the Southern Appalachian region qualifies it as a unique American religious region, although, in my view, it qualifies more accurately as a subregion.[1] An arresting datum that is, inasmuch as all the other such regions reflect the prominence of received traditions which, while modified, are recognizably intact. Is it possible that there is more originality, more true distinctiveness, in this (sub)regional religious culture than in any other in the country?

As the other essays in this volume illustrate, the names of the religious bodies are much the same in Appalachia as elsewhere. "Baptist" is not anything else, "Holiness" and "Pentecostal" in this application bear resemblance to movements going by those names in other places. Just the same, as we rather readily know, denominational family titles turn out to be temptingly close to homonymous.[2] Chapters presented here suggest basic ways in which Appalachian Baptists differ from Southern Baptists or American Baptists or National Baptists, and the case is similar for branches of the Holiness and Pentecostal families. Further comparisons, no doubt, are needed. It suffices here to say that the distinctions are not neatly unifactored. Polity, theology, congregational life, concept of mission, and other aspects—all figure in the equation. It does seem to this observer that polity scales highest. A fiercely localist self-government animates much of traditional Appalachian church life; hence many churches—even those in more connectional denominations—exhibit little, or at least limited, interest in elaborate affiliation with regional or national organizations. Others, of course, maintain closer connections.

Whence comes this fondness for we'll-govern-ourselves, and this aversion to affiliating with church people who are, in many instances, likeminded? For some traditionally Appalachian congregations (mountain churches, for instance), it may stem from a sense of cultural separateness, really distinctiveness, that in turn grows out of a heritage of relative isolation and attendant unfamiliarity with others' modes of operation. Historically it has attitudinal connection with an old and quite general American suspicion of centralized authority. The American religious yearning for freedom has applied to "federalism" in denominational organization life, as well as in First Amendment legal and legislative rights. We may affirm the insistence of several authors cited here that Appalachian religion assuredly is not "frozen in time," without proceeding to deny that a high degree of separateness, even isolation, long has prevailed. It has shown creative, dynamic qualities in the context of having its own integrity and going its own unique way. At the same time, Central Appalachia exists within yet another broader region, the American South, itself a much-studied subregion of the United States.

Again, as indicated in previous chapters, church traditions of Central Appalachia, then, are not reactive, much less reactionary; instead they reflect the culture's history and its capacity for making particular faith forms its own. Yet we need to note that many have resisted the blandishments of cooperative efforts for "positive" reasons. Many traditions in the (sub)region have practiced the belief that the congregation of a community is where worship and fellowshiping occur most authentically. Moreover, certain Baptist and evangelical Scots-Irish heritages have inclined the (sub)region to localist polity. Beyond that, its meager sense of participation in a larger (general American) society has reinforced its left-wing Protestant tendency to concentrate on personal ministries rather than on social ministries. Finally, a strain of the Calvinist influence that affects many Appalachian forms often has forbidden or restrained mission outreach undertakings, a mentality that easily carries over into the way churches design their polity.

One of the most arresting descriptions of one segment of Appalachian Christianity that I have run across appears in the Peacock and Tyson study of the Primitive Baptists, *Pilgrims of Paradox*.[3] The work offers insights which help summarize the theology and practice of many of the traditions surveyed in this volume. Their interviews pried loose the conviction that "hope is the chief theological virtue." In addition to carrying a ring of biblical authenticity, that dictum significantly demarcates the traditional religion found among many Central Appalachian people, a large portion of them, from the popular religion of the broader South. Within the latter evangelical heritage, hope is, revealingly, displaced by fruition and accomplishment. Theological accomplishment, if I may so refer to it, is personal salvation consciously realized and essentially "wrapped up." More of that later. Here let us mark the contrast by describing the process by which so many Appalachian Christians place so much stock in hope.

To suggest that "hope is the chief theological virtue" is to make quite a statement. While all Christians talk about hope and surely live with it, it is a quality that seems abstract, or at least not very existential.

Intense personal religion and active piety typically desire more—in fact, demand more. Especially in American society does hope seem far away, a mark of laziness or inattention or settling for too little. American institutions, not least among them the churches, desire to see results; and hope is not exactly a result.

When you combine piety's craving for directness and the institution's insistence on results, you are not likely to develop a love affair with hope. Wherever in the American South you encounter conversionist evangelistic forms of Evangelicalism, you detect urgency or impatience to realize an achievable goal. The revivalistic styles of church life that are so influential in Baptist and Baptist-like circles regard delay in attaining success as failure.

Institutionally that is true. Indeed, one passion that links congregations to each other and to organized denominations mirrors this determination to succeed. We can almost hear them say: "There is much to do; many of us joining our resources and efforts have a far better chance of reaching those goals." My impression is that the local-polity Baptist tradition among many southern and Appalachian white people is modulated, and in some sense compromised, for functional reasons—a huge task requires organized cooperative efforts—rather than because of some substratum of connectionalism buried within the body's mind and heart.

We do well, too, to recall the emergence of Primitive Baptists in the non-Appalachian South in the first half of the nineteenth century. In eastern North Carolina and Kentucky, especially, only a minority of churches shared their leadership's enthusiasm for the society's new fascination with large-scale organizing, notably local and state governments and the transregional Triennial Convention (Baptist missionary society—1814). Recent studies are showing that these Primitive Baptists—or Hard Shells or Black Rockers—were not the disfranchised or alienated classes of society, but rather were a sector of deep-dish Baptists who had convictions about how to evangelize. They stood four-square against treating faith or salvation as a commodity, as if it were a product to market. That is the sense in which they were localists and anti-institutionalists. Traditional Baptist polity, in other words, retained for them the power of unswerving conviction at a time when organizing and mobilizing were becoming a social premium. A roughly comparable response occurred within Southern Baptist Convention life a bit later and farther west, in the Landmark movement. Its animating goal was to arrest a creeping "boardism" that was on its way to bureaucratic and near-sacred magnitude by the 1850s. The earlier Primitive formation had less to rebel against; instead, it was noting an insidious trend. The antimission Baptists, and the later Landmarkists, show much the same pigmentation, a point that, when seen, helps prevent us from regarding the Old Regular and Primitive folk of the mountain culture as, in effect, a new strain of Baptists. Such polity allies have been around in the South for a long time. To my knowing, however, the nature of their connection is theological—historic Baptist—rather than strictly lineal.

Just as fundamentally, the command to be saved requires immediate action and certain knowledge—misleadingly referred to as assurance—in the direct experience of the person standing in desperate personal need. "Misleadingly" does not impugn the integrity of the evangelistic Southern Baptists. What has happened over time, as if to confirm the anxiety of the early Primitive Baptists, is that "assurance" has become the imperative of certainty resting on its genuine possibility. "Assurance" is the term used in all their witnessing exercises, and the full intention is to speak of the convert's certainty that he or she has been saved. Integrity and intention notwithstanding, assurance gradually has shifted from the general category of hope to the claim of virtual certainty. The concept begins with the warning, you must be saved; continues with the clarification, if you are, you must and will know it; to the conclusion that you are justified in counting yourself among those who have passed from death to life. Hope is hardly absent from this configuration, and it is acknowledged as a New Testament teaching. In practice, the fruition to which hope points has effectively taken place. Hope is still "hanging around," so to say. Of this much we may be confident: wherever there is genuine piety, hope is present, and where hope lives, trust has power; where trust characterizes, certainty has more to do with God's reliability than with the believer's condition.

Complexity is amply evident in the case of the Appalachian theology where "hope is the chief theological virtue"—and where it is common for Christians to refer to each other as "brothers and sisters in hope." Hope as a quality entails complexity—indeed, hope is inherently open-ended, not even subject to definition. It belongs to a category we often reserve for poets and artists, pilgrims and adventurers. Probably not many have thought of Calvinist Baptists as poets and pilgrims. At any rate, scholars Peacock and Tyson have given their study of Primitives the title *Pilgrims of Paradox*; one wonders if they knew what they were getting into when they launched their inquiry. Perhaps some such inchoate rumbling helped impel their work. (Of course hope can also be a category in use by rationalists, though perhaps never without at least a dash of the poetic.)

Students of Calvinism know that, in theological terms, hope, or certainty, is what this discursus is about. How much of God's way with the world can be known? How complete is our knowledge of God, how reliable what we claim to know? How comprehensively informed are we capable of being? What is the nature of mystery; how substantive or ethereal, alternatively, is it? What should be the human posture toward comprehending God's ways and his revelation? Is there correspondence between what and whom we rely on and the appropriation made by the ones relying? How deep is the human Fall with respect to capacity for discernment and understanding? Those are questions all Christians must contend with, but they are defining issues for the Calvinist theological program.

Historically, we are bound to take Calvinism into account in any treatment of Appalachian religion. The inner logic of Calvinist thought sets many of the questions and perspectives that animate mountain religion, in the process distinguishing it from the popular forms on the slopes and in the lowlands extending out therefrom. Calvinism, of course, had been a major way of viewing the Christian faith early in the South's history, through both Presbyterian and Baptist presences. But the former failed to capture the central ground, and the latter incrementally exchanged that heritage for a more "down-to-earth," experience-based understanding of Christian theology. Those developments carried many implications, among which an unusually weighty one had to do with *mystery*. A mysterious and even mystifying concept, mystery paradoxically has a specifiable identity; that is true theologically but more directly in its import for a believer's mode of entering the life of faith and therefore for the constituency of a congregation.

We have been noting that the South's popular theology, especially as articulated through the large denominations, largely has dismantled mystery and developed ways of regularizing the ways of God with people, especially as regards personal salvation. The faith articulated by many Appalachian Christian communions has retained the Calvinist perspective and its affirmation of mystery; that is the necessary context for hope being "the chief theological virtue." If you do not know for certain, but believe the Bible to be totally reliable and God to be altogether just and gracious, you are affirming the substantial reality of mystery. Elaborated, mystery is not a vagueness or an ultimate plasticity. Instead it reflects a solid conviction that everything is under control, in the control of God who is animated by purpose, not overtaken by randomness. The fact of mystery is affirmed, but the contours and details of mystery are mysterious.

In the context of our study of Christianity in Appalachia, a religious (sub)region that seemingly is an intrusion into the South as a religious region, the single point of sharpest differentiation lies in the issue of personal salvation. All around them, if not prominently in their mountain towns, coves, hollows, and valleys, the upland Calvinists know about the evangelistic Evangelicals who yearn to convert, to effect a conversion experience that is accompanied by a testimony that borders on a claim of certainty. For representatives of Appalachian mountain religion, for example, one source of their knowing this is the extensive efforts made by their lowlander neighbors, from near and far, to set right their theology, especially with respect to the evangelistic message. As certain essays included here indicate, many of the home missionaries who come to their neighborhoods to minister to them are not condescending and do not deprecate their worth. Even so, they have come, and keep coming. For these "outsiders," elements of the relative poverty, low educational standards, and inferior health services often characteristic of mountain communities make up part of the impelling forces behind the domestic mission enterprises. At the same time, the evangelists come, too, because they are obligated to approach those who do not grasp that they must declare their personal salvation known assuredly in the conversion experience.

Those more typical southern conversionists, Baptists and others, have constructed a large and complex "culture of conversion," or system for evangelizing the world. Viewing that system, which has modulated up and up to the status of a culture, provides an illuminating device for comparing segments of popular southern conversionist Evangelicalism (SCE) with Appalachian Calvinism, moderate and strict. The device referred to is the technique of revivalism. These subgroups reflect the search for hope within certain communities of faith.

The theological predicates upon which SCE rests are: every person must be saved; every person can be saved; if you are saved, you will know it. Those three steps spell divine judgment, human capacity, and the reliability of conversion consciousness. Arising from the first as urgency, from the second as confidence of success, and from the third as the seal of fruition, revivalism was appearing on these shores by the first decade of the nineteenth century. Its roots reached back to eighteenth-century Britain; its full development as a culture occurred over many decades. But public means or "measures" were beginning to implement these theological rudiments nearly two centuries ago.

Juxtaposing the southern culture of conversion with the mystery-based Appalachian Calvinism shows how fully the Calvinist heritage, despite being not far in the background of Baptists, has been extirpated. Mystery, so important to one, is all but inoperative in the other. Faith-based but mystifying responses to the major questions concerning God's ways with the world have been dispelled by common-sense, experience-based, cause-and-effect courses of action among the southern conversionists. Over time, these created formulaic conventions. Sharper contrasts among nominally

Protestant kinspeople are hard to conceive. Acknowledgment that only God knows for sure (both questions and answers), and that his sovereignty preempts the use of that trope, stands over against a full-scale rationalization of those divine-human issues.

Max Weber (who makes a fascinating cameo appearance in *Pilgrims of Paradox*) provided us with categories of interpretation a long time ago. He wrote of disenchantment (*Entzauberung*), of de-mystification, his terms capturing those results that modernity has wrought on Western civilization.[4] A world—really a universe and an attendant cosmology—that once withheld its secrets from us, to our spiritual benefit, confounds us modern people no more. It teases us, it challenges us to unlock its mathematical language; and we have rushed to accept the challenge. Our massive dedication to science and technology proceeds therefrom, with a host of brilliant results. But it has done so at a high cost, bifurcating reality into nature and spirit, as Immanuel Kant, a century before Weber, postulated that it was essential for us moderns to do. The spiritual dimensions of humanity and cosmology—for which, also read the poetic, the dramatic, the imaginative, the musical—have been relegated to secondary rank.

When demystification and disenchantment are applied to the Appalachian Calvinists and the SCE, some startling conclusions emerge. The former, in their remote habitats, are proving to be carriers of an ancient sense of wholeness, a sense of reality in which spiritual and natural are unified. Sometimes dismissed as reactionary, typically denigrated as provincial, they testify that reality is in fact unified in this way. In contrast, the conversionists embrace modernity's schemes for organizing and being effective. Moreover, they play to optimal advantage the instruments of communication that the mathematization of modern sensibilities has composed.

Is being "old-fashioned" an unmitigated liability? Is modernity an unalloyed asset? It is at least reasonable to judge that those who bear an older, time-tested tradition—who are set in those ways—are worth honoring. While I myself have no calling to defend selected segments of traditional Appalachian Christianity or to hold the line against all critical assessments, I submit that the tenacity of many small, often-overlooked communions, for maintaining mystification and enchantment, serves us all well.

Returning to the SCE "culture of conversion," we note that a successful mode of operation has been functioning for most of this century. Each person's life is divided into two parts, a sort of personal B.C. and A.D. Up to the point of one's conversion experience, he or she is without Christ and his salvation. That is the fundamental condition of the person's existence from birth until the Blessed Event, and there are no exceptions to its reality. Conversion eradicates the prior condition and replaces it with the new one of being saved or born again.

In logic appropriate to SCE understanding, a conception of schedule appeared. Before the Turning Point, the person has one identity; after it, he or she has another. Thus the Turning Point is all-important; moreover, it is locatable, specifiable. The notion of schedule is fundamental to the SCE culture of conversion; clearly, mystery is uncharacteristic in such thinking and planning. There the diagnosis of a person's sickness-unto-death is readily available, the cure equally so. Most important, the means to effect the transition are available, time-tested, and guaranteed to accomplish God's ends when the recipient so testifies. Accordingly, the stages, phases, and conditions are universal, just as the transition and subsequent new identity are exact and certifiable.

The culture of conversion rests upon this methodology for identifying what is wrong and what to do about it. It is a highly rationalized system, held to be universally effective and binding. In fact, actualizing it has become the principal and dominant mission of the churches subscribing to it. I believe that it is fair to say that, for many millions of southern white people from the Chesapeake Bay to the Rio Grande, this is the operative view of what religion is and what the churches do.

The culture of conversion is thoughtfully arranged. It begins by identifying the problem, it proclaims the solution, then it correlates problem and solution by providing means for the latter to dissipate the former, typically through the Sunday school for children and the revival meeting for people of all ages. We conclude that it lives with a theology largely devoid of mystery, upon which it then appropriately capitalizes by devising a rationalized, efficiency-driven list of means and measures for carrying out its mission. This culture of conversion grew from the native soil of nineteenth-century America and over time has acquired a special profile in the region.

In highlighting the contrast between mystery as context and conversionist Evangelicalism, we might seem to imply that the Appalachian churches make no effort to evangelize. That is indeed true in the strictest Calvinist circles, where the doctrine of election (predestination) is taught and believed uncompromisingly. There one finds some men and women who have been a part of a church's life for many years but who have not yet received the calling to salvation. In most other church settings, however, the mission to convert the lost is a specifiable and central activity. The most common pattern is a distinctively Appalachian one, according to much scholarly opinion, and is referred to as the "episodic conversion experience."[5]

While this way of understanding the divine salvific action in a person's life prevails in most kinds of Baptist services, it is also representative of Holiness church life. As other essays suggest, that fact by itself, in view of the prominence of Holiness in the mountains, enlarges the episodic conversion experience to major proportions. Indeed, Deborah McCauley regards that community of churches together, with the various Baptist ones, as standing at the center of the representative form, the independent nondenominational church. The Holiness people speak most explicitly of "getting a blessing" and being "slain in the Spirit." As McCauley learned from Brother Coy Miser (to whom her book is dedicated), the Holiness folk know the Spirit's coming in two stages, conversion and the Baptism of the Holy Ghost.[6] Note that these stages may occur more than once during a person's life journey.

An incoherent concept, surely, to the culture of conversion, the episodic conversion experience is mountain religiosity's formulation of conversion as something one knows as much more than a single event within the human consciousness. In McCauley's words, episodic conversion is a "religious experience renewed time and time again."[7] Tellingly, this understanding of how conversion takes place reveals how rooted in history the Appalachian religious tradition is—Scots-Irish history, that is. McCauley's summary aids our investigation of mountain evangelism, and of episodic conversion in particular: "Revivalism has not always been a tool of aggressive evangelization or rooted in the assumption that salvation is a rational, free-will decision. Revivalism has gone through many transmutations over the centuries, reflecting different types of religiosity."[8]

Appalachian revivalism always has made much of the New Testament imagery of the new birth. As with popular southern religion, the individual is not born saved, on his way to heaven, with a natural love for God in her heart that needs only to be watered to flower. Total depravity incarcerates upland mountain souls as it does others. Nevertheless, there are distinctions between the general revival tradition of the surrounding region and that practiced in Appalachia. The major reason is the Scots-Irish heritage that gave initial shape to the region's religious culture and has shown staying power. Appearing earliest in Scotland of the 1740s, that revival tradition was associated with observance of the sacrament of communion in the Church of Scotland. Such gatherings were called "sacramental meetings" and emphasized the communal nature of evangelism.[9]

Revivals of this heritage issue in participation—you are not a bystander at a Christian gathering where you receive the elements of the Lord's Supper. In addition, they create a sense of group unity, of being "tied to the community-building emphasis of Scots-Irish religiosity."[10] Those outside the fold of believers were invited to, and often did, "come to grace." Even so, those Calvinists were reluctant to mark out the unconverted, unless they were notoriously wicked sinners. Thus all who came to the sacramental meeting were part of the community of invisible saints. The effect this conception had was to unite the assembly, more and less devout individuals, into an event of worship and dedication that included everyone. No "singling out" occurred, no division into camps of the saved and the lost; all were equally standing in the need of God.

The drama of a "communal conversion" service, where "communal" implies Communion, is very different from what occurs in American revivalism. in the former, staging takes place "up front," in a kind of neutral zone between pulpit and pew. In the Scottish Calvinist heritage, there is no altar, only a pulpit. There is no priest; instead there is a minister of Word and Sacrament. Yet there is a table at which a minister presides; that table occupies a space of its own, being neither the minister's pulpit nor the congregation's pews. "Neutral" thus does not really fit, since the table belongs to the transcendent, though present, God. In a sense the same may be said of pulpit and pew, but when the minister and the people receive the table's bounty, they do so only on God's terms. In that venue there is no sermon or commentary; there is no overt expectation from communers beyond that they participate. The service at the Lord's table is out of control—or, more properly, out from under the control of speaker or listener, server or consumer.

Few practices and patterns distinguish more keenly the broader southern and the Appalachian religious practices. The conventional revival of the former presents parallels with the communal conversion services of the latter. What each points to tells a great deal about its history and its driving theological convictions. The South inherited a mostly English disposition, through Wesleyanism, toward the "intensely personal," where the gift of the grace of forgiveness and new life is specifically the individual's. The others around participate in bringing the rescue to pass, but they do not share in the benefits received. Appalachia's history is closer to Scotland's, where Presbyterianism fostered the "vibrantly communal."[11] There each should submit to inventory his or her own spiritual condition (more "condition" than "standing") before God, but no person is more called to table and self-examination than any other. The standard response on such an occasion is to receive the bounty thoughtfully but casually, for oneself without any sense of being an isolate or even a free-standing unit. Communion is by its nature a communal event.

Darting in and out of our reflections has been the subject of sacraments. Were this a study of SCE by itself, an extended treatment of the subject would not be pertinent—certainly not by that name. Those churches talk about and practice "ordinances," baptism and the Lord's Supper, intentionally never calling them "sacraments." Of the two non-verbal/symbolic practices, baptism is the more celebrated, since great emphasis is placed on the fact and the moment of entry into the Christian life. The American South qualifies as the only place in Christendom where the symbolic rite for entry receives higher priority than the symbolic rite for ongoing nurturance—a fascinating datum. Also, an "ordinance" is a more specified action than a "sacrament" is—that is, the latter is susceptible to general applicability within human experience, whereas the term "ordinances," referring to regulations or required observances, limits the number and scope. One cannot conceive of an "ordinantal" perspective on the world, but a "sacramental" view of the universe is a widely held commitment. To reiterate: when you say "ordinances," you refer to specific church practices that are required; when you say "sacraments," you are declaring that mundane matter somehow reveals God in or through itself, and you are formulating a cosmic theology.

Throughout the broader South, the majority practice is "ordinances." To those Baptists, Pentecostals, Holiness people, and other ecclesiastically "low church" traditions, "sacrament" suggests something they do not believe. Not far distant from many of them are the mountain churches where the theology of "the ordinary disclosing the extraordinary" is standard—whether the term "sacrament" is used much or not.

The corporate worship life of the people across a wide denominational sweep regularly includes three material-cum-spiritual practices. The Lord's Supper and baptism, of course, are elemental. The washing of feet is very nearly as common. Baptism uses the material world's water—quite a draught of it, since immersion is the accepted mode. Communion involves the ingestion of bread and the liquid fruit of the vine, still quite commonly the fermented wine of New Testament custom.

Baptism and foot washing are more celebrated than communion, even though baptism occurs only as there are candidates. Foot washing regularly accompanies communion. But the list of sacramental practices extends farther. Anointing children with oil is reasonably common, as is anointing the sick when a preacher is present to utter words from Scripture and pray spontaneous prayers. The sacramental nature of all these events is clear: some kind of synergic relation exists between spiritual and physical. Other instances of this conviction include love feasts, the "holy kiss," the laying on of hands, and the right hand of fellowship.

The ceremonial washing of feet is the most legendary of Appalachian religious practices. Descriptions of such occasions by Howard Dorgan, Peacock and Tyson, and others disclose how lively and powerful they are, and how far they diverge from sermons that reach high-decibel levels and employ rapid and repetitive speech patterns.[12] This ceremony is soft and gentle, emotionally moving to male and female participant alike.

The washing of feet, in accordance with Christ's example recorded in John 13, seems to embody two values that mountain religion treasures: humility and community. Concerning understanding life before God as more communal than individualist, we have noted the Scots-Irish heritage of communal revivalism, with the observance of the Lord's Supper as the high point of the gathering. Humility, absolutely elementary to the drama of a person's bending to wash another's feet, is a hallmark of the churches' practice. All students of this religious tradition are struck by the sacrificial humility of church leaders, there being multiple reports of how really good these people are, not self-serving, deeply devoted to living out the ethic of Jesus. An "empire-building" impetus is impressively absent from mountain religious culture. The preacher's calling is not to be successful in institutional terms, but rather to be faithful and personally holy.

Necessarily we must make some reference to snake handling; proportional to the degree of the churches' practice, it will be brief. The handling of snakes is a sacramental part of those services in which it is carried out. Obviously, "matter" is a means to the experience of "spirit," material-cum-spiritual once again. Mary Lee Daugherty teaches us that another dimension of the worshipers' faith is exemplified by this sensational practice, namely "the deep longing for holiness." In her words, "the search for holiness is dramatized in their willingness to suffer terrible pain from snake bite, or even death itself, to get the feeling of God in their lives."[13] Thus, although this ritual is far from common even in independent Holiness churches, it represents an extension of the widespread mountain religious belief that God uses the physical world to penetrate deep into the hearts of those who earnestly seek him.

One wishes that Max Weber could have stayed a little longer in the Appalachian vicinity when he visited a kinsman of his wife's near Mount Airy, North Carolina, in 1904. If so, he might have had to modify his analysis that Calvinism managed to devalue radically any sacramental understanding of the divine revelation. Among Appalachian Calvinists, there remained (was revived?) some sense of God's sacramental dealings with his people. Thus, in an area where we find much quintessential Calvinism, forms of Protestant sacramentalism live.

A sacramental understanding, then, joins the affirmation of mystery and the practice of the episodic conversion experience as primary, and distinguishing, traits and practices of Appalachian mountain religion. When those and their counterparts in the Southern Conversionist Experience culture are placed side by side, a clear contrast looms. Their shared identity as Protestant Christians means that they hold much in common, of course. But their divergent historical experiences issue in significant differences that leave neither quite at home with the other.

In view of the distinctiveness of mountain religion, I see as paradoxical my efforts to depict the outlines of the religious practice south of Mason-Dixon as fitting the area's Appalachian subculture as well as they do the rest of the South as a religious region. Both are Protestant, both are left-wing Protestant, and, emphatically, Roman Catholic thinking is foreign to both. Thus, when the comparison focuses on the distinction between the whole and this one of its parts—stretching the truth a bit—and on nothing else, the difference is negligible.

But sharpened focus on Appalachian mountain religion discloses how the two do not coordinate equally, how they even are somewhat distinctive regions. Up to a point, we are entitled to say that Appalachian Christianity is a subset of popular southern religion. But we are driven to see that it stands as a distinctive religious culture—indeed, *cultures*—even if we insist that it is no more than a (sub)region.

The formulator of a list of traits that aim to characterize religious patterns in the broader South has been enlightened by comparing it with a pattern close to home—upstairs, so to speak. I now see that my formulation for the region at large was in the interest of comparing it with the nation at large, taking serious note of the old European churches, especially the Roman Catholic, that are strong to dominant in so many places.

To speak personally, then, I have profited from an assignment taking me into the Southern Highlands, especially its religious cultures. In summary, and while recognizing diversity, we might say of Appalachian Christianity, that it is there, it is distinctive, it exhibits an authenticity and richness that invite its preservation. In the course of comparative reflection, I found myself mumbling the words of a text and a hymn known to both highlanders and lowlanders: "So near and yet so far."

Notes

1. Catherine L. Albanese, *America: Religions and Religion* (Belmont, Calif.: Wadsworth Publishing Co., 1981), chap. 9. Albanese does not employ "regional" precisely as sev-

eral social scientists—Wilbur Zelinsky, James R. Shortridge, and Roger Stump, for example—do, dividing the nation into several "religious regions."

2. See Samuel S. Hill, *One Name but Several Faces: Varieties of Popular Denominations in Southern History* (Athens: Univ. of Georgia Press, 1996).

3. James L. Peacock and Ruel W. Tyson Jr., *Pilgrims of Paradox: Calvinism and Experience Among the Primitive Baptists of the Blueridge* (Washington, D.C.: Smithsonian Institution Press, 1989).

4. Max Weber, *The Protestant Ethic and the Spirit of Capitalism* (New York: Charles Scribner's Sons, 1958), 105 and 147.

5. Albanese, *America: Religions and Religion,* 230.

6. McCauley, *American Mountain Religion* (Urbana: Univ. of Illinois Press, 1995), 321.

7. Ibid., 170.

8. Ibid., 170–71.

9. Ibid., 176–79.

10. Ibid., 170.

11. Marilyn J. Westerkamp, *Triumph of the Laity* (New York: Oxford Univ. Press, 1988), 34.

12. See Howard Dorgan, *The Old Regular Baptists of Central Appalachia* (Knoxville: Univ. of Tennessee Press, 1989); and Howard Dorgan, *Giving Glory to God in Appalachia* (Knoxville: Univ. of Tennessee Press, 1987).

13. Mary Lee Daugherty, "Serpent-Handling as Sacrament," in *Religion in Appalachia,* ed. John D. Photiadis, 103–11 (Morgantown: West Virginia Univ., 1978).

Contributors

Monica Kelly Appelby is director of a micro-enterprise program in Montgomery County, Virginia. She is a member of the Federation of Communities in Service (FOCIS) and is an active Catholic.

Donald Bowdle is professor of history and religion at Lee University, Cleveland, Tennessee.

Mary Lee Daugherty is founder of the Appalachian Ministries Educational Resource Center, Berea, Kentucky.

Mel Dieter is emeritus professor of church history at Asbury Theological Seminary, Wilmore, Kentucky.

Howard Dorgan is professor of speech communications at Appalachian State University, Boone, North Carolina.

Anthony Dunnavant is associate professor of church history at Lexington Theological Seminary, Lexington, Kentucky.

GARY FARLEY is the bivocational director of missions for the Baptist Association in Pickens County, Georgia. For many years he was rural church consultant with the Home Mission Board of the Southern Baptist Convention.

SAMUEL S. HILL is professor of religion emeritus at the University of Florida, Gainesville, Florida.

LOYAL JONES is a nationally known writer and commentator on Appalachian folklore. He retired in 1995 as director of the Appalachian Center at Berea College, Berea, Kentucky, where he taught for many years.

BILL J. LEONARD is dean of the Wake Forest University Divinity School, Winston-Salem, North Carolina.

CHARLES LIPPY is Leroy A. Martin Professor of Religious Studies at the University of Tennessee, Chattanooga.

DEBORAH VANSAU MCCAULEY is an independent scholar and lecturer living and writing from her home in New Jersey.

LOU F. MCNEIL is professor of religion at Georgian Court College, Bay Head, New Jersey.

MARCIA CLARK MYERS is a Presbyterian minister, serving as transitional executive staff for the Presbytery of Transylvania in eastern Kentucky.

BENNETT POAGE is a minister in the Christian Church (Disciples of Christ) and director of the Disciples of Kentucky Appalachian Ministry.

IRA READ teaches history at Appalachian State University in Boone, North Carolina.

JAMES SESSIONS is on the staff of the Highlander Research Center, New Market, Tennessee. He is former director of the Commission on Religion in Appalachia.

BARBARA ELLEN SMITH is professor of women's studies at the Women's Studies Center, University of Memphis, Memphis, Tennessee.

JANET BOGGESS WELCH has had a varied career as an editor, public relations director, and tenured sociology professor. She is currently based at the University of Charleston in West Virginia.

H. DAVIS YEUELL is a retired presbytery executive, having served Presbyterian churches and presbyteries in Virginia and Missouri.

Index

Christianity in Appalachia was designed and typeset on a Macintosh computer system using PageMaker software. The text is set in Caslon, and the
titles in Light Helvetica. This book was designed by Kay Jursik, composed
by Kimberly Scarbrough, and manufactured by Thomson-Shore, Inc. The
recycled paper used in this book is designed for an effective life of at least
three hundred years.